WHO WAS WHO
IN THE
BIBLE

The Ultimate
A TO Z™
RESOURCE
FULLY ILLUSTRATED

MJF BOOKS
NEW YORK

Published by MJF Books
Fine Communications
322 Eighth Avenue
New York, NY 10001

Who Was Who in the Bible
LCCN 2003103203
ISBN-10: 1-56731-624-7
ISBN-13: 978-1-56731-624-7

Published by arrangement with Thomas Nelson Publishers.

Manufactured in the United States of America.
MJF Books and the MJF colophon are trademarks of Fine Creative Media, Inc.

VB 12   11   10   9   8   7   6   5   4   3   2

By agreeing with David that Nabal had acted with great disrespect, she stemmed David's anger. To Abigail's credit, she did not leave her godless husband. When Nabal died, apparently from shock at discovering his near brush with death, David married Abigail and she later bore him a son, Chileab.

2. A sister or half-sister of David and mother of Amasa, whom Absalom made captain of the army instead of Joab (2 Sam. 17:25; Abigal, NRSV, REB; 1 Chr. 2:16–17). She may be the same person as No. 1.

ABIGAL

A form of ABIGAIL.

ABIHAIL [AB ih hail] (father of strength)

The name of three men and two women in the Old Testament:

1. A Levite and the father of Zuriel in the time of Moses (Num. 3:35).

2. The wife of Abishur, a descendant of Hezron of the tribe of Judah (1 Chr. 2:29).

3. The head of a family in the tribe of Gad who lived in Gilead of Bashan (1 Chr. 5:14).

4. A daughter of Eliab (David's brother) and the wife of King Rehoboam (2 Chr. 11:18).

5. The father of Queen Esther, who became the wife of Ahasuerus (Xerxes I, 485–464 B.C.), king of Persia, in the place of Vashti. Abihail was therefore also an uncle of Mordecai (Esth. 2:15; 9:29).

ABIHU [a BIH hoo] (he is my father)

Second son of Aaron and Elisheba (Ex. 6:23). Abihu was destroyed, along with his brother NADAB, in the Wilderness of Sinai for offering "profane fire" (Lev. 10:1) before the Lord. Exactly why the fire was "profane" is not certain; perhaps Abihu and Nadab rebelled against the au-

thority of Moses and Aaron by presuming to bring an unauthorized offering before the Lord. If so, their action implies pride and arrogance, which the Lord despises.

ABIHUD [a BIH hud] (father of honor)

A son of Bela, who was the oldest son of Benjamin (1 Chr. 8:3).

ABIJAH [a BUY jah] (the Lord is my Father)

The name of eight people in the Old Testament:

1. A son of Jeroboam who died in youth, in fulfillment of the prophecy of Abijah (1 Kin. 14:1–18).

2. The wife of Hezron, a man of the tribe of Judah (1 Chr. 2:24).

3. A descendant of Benjamin (or perhaps of Zebulun) through Becher (1 Chr. 7:8).

4. A descendant of Aaron, who was a priest in the time of David (1 Chr. 24:10).

5. A king of Judah and son of Rehoboam and Maacah, the granddaughter of Absalom (2 Chr. 11:20, 22). Also see ABIJAM.

6. The mother of Hezekiah, king of Judah (2 Chr. 29:1). Abijah is also called Abi (2 Kin. 18:2).

7. A priest who signed Nehemiah's covenant (Neh. 10:7).

8. A priest who returned to Jerusalem from Babylon with Zerubbabel (Neh. 12:1–4, 12–17).

ABIJAM [a BUY jam] (the sea is my father)

A king of Judah and son of Rehoboam and Maacah the daughter of Absalom. When King Rehoboam died, Abijam succeeded to Judah's throne. He had 14 wives, 22 sons, and 16 daughters. When he died, after reigning for three years, his son ASA became king (1 Kin. 14:31).

He is also called Abijah (2 Chr. 11:20, 22). The KJV has Abia (Matt. 1:7), listing him as an ancestor of Jesus.

ABIMAEL [ah BIM uh ell] (my Father is God)

The ninth of the 13 sons of Joktan, a descendant of Shem (Gen. 10:28; 1 Chr. 1:22).

ABIMELECH [uh BIM eh leck] (my father is king)

The name of five men in the Old Testament:

1. The king of Gerar in the time of Abraham (Gen. 20:1–18; 21:22–34). Fearing for his own safety, Abraham introduced Sarah, his wife, as his sister when he entered Abimelech's territory. Abimelech claimed Sarah for his harem, only to be warned in a dream that he had taken the wife of another man. Then Abimelech returned Sarah to Abraham. The two men made a covenant with each other, and Abraham asked God to reward the king by giving him many children. Many scholars believe that the word Abimelech is not a proper name but a royal title of the Philistine kings, just as Pharaoh was a title for Egyptian kings.

2. The king of Gerar in the time of Isaac (Gen. 26:1–31).

3. The ruler of the city of Shechem during the period of the judges (Judg. 8:30—10:1; 2 Sam. 11:21). Abimelech was a son of Gideon by a concubine from Shechem. Abimelech tried to become king, and he did reign over Israel for three years (Judg. 9:22). In order to eliminate all who might challenge his authority, he killed all the other sons of Gideon—his brothers and half-brothers—who were potential successors of his father (Judg. 9:5).

Abimelech was killed in a battle at Thebez, a city northeast of Shechem, which he surrounded with his army. When Abimelech ventured too close to the city tower, a woman dropped a millstone on his head, crushing his skull. Abimelech commanded his armorbearer to kill him so it could not be said that he died at the hands of a woman (Judg. 9:50–54; 2 Sam. 11:21).

4. A priest in the time of David (1 Chr. 18:16).

5. A Philistine king whom David met while fleeing from King Saul (Psalm 34, title). Abimelech is apparently the royal title of ACHISH the king of Gath (1 Sam. 21:10–15).

ABINADAB [uh BIN a dab]

The name of four Old Testament men:

1. An Israelite of the tribe of Judah in whose house the Ark of the Covenant was placed after being returned by the Philistines (1 Sam. 7:1; 1 Chr. 13:7).

2. The second son of Jesse; a brother of David (1 Sam. 17:13; 1 Chr. 2:13).

3. A son of King Saul slain at Mount Gilboa by the Philistines (1 Sam. 31:2; 1 Chr. 10:2).

4. The father of one of Solomon's officers, who was set over Dor in the territory of Issachar (1 Kin. 4:11).

ABINOAM [ah BIN oh am] (father of pleasantness)

The father of Barak of the tribe of Naphtali (Judg. 4:6; 5:1).

ABIRAM [ah BY ram] (my father is exalted)

The name of two people in the Old Testament:

1. A son of Eliab, a Reubenite, who joined in the rebellion of KORAH and conspired against Moses and Aaron in the wilderness. He died in an earthquake, which served as a fitting judgment for his sin (Num. 16:1–33).

A

2. The firstborn of Hiel, who rebuilt the city of Jericho (1 Kin. 16:34).

ABISHAG [AB ih shag]

A young woman from Shunem employed by David's physicians to care for him in his old age (1 Kin. 1:1–4, 15). The treatment implies that through physical contact Abishag's youth could revive a dying David. The treatment failed. After David's death, one of his sons, Adonijah, asked permission to marry Abishag (1 Kin. 2:17). Solomon saw Adonijah's request as an attempt to seize the throne. He had Adonijah killed (1 Kin. 2:13–25).

ABISHAI [ah BISH a eye]

The oldest son of Zeruiah, David's half-sister, and brother of Joab and Asahel (2 Sam. 2:18). He was one of David's mighty men (2 Sam. 23:18; 1 Chr. 11:20). He helped David in the fight with Ishbi-Benob the giant (2 Sam. 21:16–17). A headstrong and impulsive man, he nevertheless maintained an unswerving loyalty to David through such crises as the rebellions of Absalom and Sheba (2 Sam. 16:9; 18–20).

ABISHALOM [ah BISH ah lom]

A form of ABSALOM (see 1 Kin. 15:2, 10).

ABISHUA [ah BISH you ah] (father of salvation)

The name of two men in the Old Testament:

1. The son of Phinehas and the fourth high priest of Israel (1 Chr. 6:4–5).

2. The fourth son of Bela, who was a son of Benjamin (1 Chr. 8:4).

ABISHUR [ah BY shur] (my father is a wall)

The second son of Shammai, of the tribe of Judah (1 Chr. 2:28–29).

ABITAL [ah BY tuhl] (father of dew)

A wife of King David and the mother of Shephatiah, the fifth son born to David while he was at Hebron (2 Sam. 3:4; 1 Chr. 3:3).

ABITUB [ah BY tub] (my father is good)

A descendant of Benjamin listed in the family tree of King Saul (1 Chr. 8:11).

ABIUD [ah BY ud]

An ancestor of Jesus, listed in the Gospel of Matthew (Matt. 1:13).

ABNER [AB nar] (the father is a lamp)

The commander-in-chief of the army of Saul, first king of the nation of Israel (1 Sam. 14:50–51; 17:55).

As Saul's highest military official, Abner occupied a seat of honor in the king's court (1 Sam. 20:25). He was the person who inquired about David after his battle with the giant, Goliath, and who introduced David to King Saul (1 Sam. 17:55–58). Abner also was the commander of the guard that was supposedly protecting Saul when David entered the camp of the king while everyone was asleep (1 Sam. 26:5–7).

After the death of Saul and his three sons in a battle with the Philistines (1 Sam. 31:1–6), Abner established Saul's son Ishbosheth as king. His capital was at Mahanaim on the east side of the Jordan River. Only the tribe of Judah, of the 12 tribes of the nation, followed the leadership of David (2 Sam. 2:8–11). In the warfare that broke out between the forces of David and Ishbosheth, Abner killed a brother of Joab—one of David's military officers—in self-defense (2 Sam. 2:12—3:1).

Still later, a crisis developed between Abner and Ishbosheth when Abner took one of Saul's concubines. Ishbosheth accused Abner of plotting to take over the kingship. The rift between them became so pronounced that Abner eventually shifted his loyalties to David. This move by Abner was significant, because Abner was able to persuade the elders of all the tribes of Israel to follow David's leadership (2 Sam. 3:6–21).

Soon after this turning point in David's political career, Abner was killed by David's commander Joab in an act of vengeance over the death of his brother (2 Sam. 3:22–30). This presented David with a troublesome situation. Abner's death looked like the execution of an opponent who had delivered the tribal loyalties the king needed to establish control over the entire nation. To counter any backlash, David reprimanded Joab publicly and had Abner buried with full honors (2 Sam. 3:27–39).

ABRAHAM [AY bruh ham] (*father of a multitude*); originally Abram (*exalted father*)

The first great patriarch of ancient Israel and a primary model of faithfulness for Christianity. The accounts about Abraham are found in Genesis 11:26—25:11, with the biblical writer focusing on four important aspects of his life.

The Migration

Abraham's story begins with his migration with the rest of his family from Ur of the Chaldeans in ancient southern Babylonia (Gen. 11:31). He and his family moved north along the trade routes of the ancient world and settled in the flourishing trade center of Haran, several hundred miles to the northwest.

While living in Haran, at the age of 75 Abraham received a call from God to go to a strange, unknown land that God would show him. The Lord promised Abraham that He would make him and

his descendants a great nation (Gen. 12:1–3). The promise must have seemed unbelievable to Abraham because his wife Sarah (called Sarai in the early part of the story) was childless (Gen. 11:30–31; 17:15). But Abraham obeyed God with no hint of doubt or disbelief. He took his wife and his nephew, Lot, and went to the land that God would show him.

Abraham moved south along the trade routes from Haran, through Shechem and Bethel in the land of Canaan. Canaan was a populated area at the time, inhabited by the warlike Canaanites; so Abraham's belief that God would ultimately give this land to him and his descendants was an act of faith. The circumstances seemed quite difficult, but Abraham's faith in God's promises allowed him to trust in the Lord.

The Famine and the Separation from Lot

Because of a severe famine in the land of Canaan, Abraham moved to Egypt for a short time (Gen. 12:10–20). During this trip, Abraham introduced Sarah to the Egyptians as his sister rather than as his wife in order to avoid trouble. Pharaoh, the Egyptian ruler, then took Sarah as his wife. It was only because "the Lord plagued Pharaoh and his house with great plagues because of Sarai, Abram's wife" (Gen. 12:17), that Sarah was returned to Abraham.

Upon his return from Egypt, Abraham and his nephew, Lot, quarreled over pasturelands and went separate ways (Gen. 13:8–9). Lot settled in the Jordan River Valley, while Abraham moved into Canaan. After this split, God reaffirmed His promise to Abraham: "And I will make your descendants as the dust of the earth; so that if a man could number the

ACSAH [ACK sah]

A form of Achsah.

ADAH [A duh] (*adornment*)

The name of two women of the Old Testament:

1. One of the two wives of Lamech and the mother of Jabal and Jubal (Gen. 4:19–21, 23).

2. One of Esau's wives and the daughter of Elon the Hittite (Gen. 36:1–4). She was the mother of Esau's firstborn, Eliphaz, and the ancestress of the Edomites.

ADAIAH [a DYE yuh] (*the Lord has adorned*)

The name of eight or nine men in the Old Testament:

1. A man of Bozcath whose daughter Jedidah was the mother of King Josiah of Israel (2 Kin. 22:1).

2. An ancestor of Asaph (1 Chr. 6:41–43).

3. A son of Shimei of the tribe of Benjamin (1 Chr. 8:1, 21).

4. A descendant of Aaron who returned to Jerusalem following the Captivity (1 Chr. 9:10–12).

5. The father of Maaseiah (2 Chr. 23:1).

6, 7. Two different men, one of the family of Bani and one of the family of Binnui (NRSV), who divorced their pagan wives after the Captivity (Ezra 10:29, 39).

8. A son of Joiarib and a descendant of Judah by Perez—and thus a member of the royal line of David (Neh. 11:5).

9. A Levite of the family of Aaron, probably the same as No. 4 (Neh. 11:12).

ADALIA [uh DAY lyuh]

One of the ten sons of Haman who were hanged like their father (Esth. 9:8–10).

ADAM [ADD um] (*red, ground*)

The first man, created by God on the sixth day of creation, and placed in the Garden of Eden (Gen. 2:19–23; 3:8–9, 17,

ADAM

20–21; 4:1, 25; 5:1–5). He and his wife
EVE, created by God from one of Adam's
ribs (Gen. 2:21–22), became the ancestors of all people now living on the earth.
Adam was unique and distinct from the
animals in several ways. His creation is
described separately from that of the animals and the rest of God's creative acts
(Gen. 1:3–25; 1:26–27; 2:7).

God breathed into Adam's body of
"dust" the divine "breath of life; and man
became a living being" (Gen. 2:7). God
also made man in his own image and
likeness. The exact words are, "Let Us
make man in Our image, according to
Our likeness" (Gen. 1:26). The apostle
Paul interprets this to mean that God created man with spiritual, rational, emotional, and moral qualities (Eph. 4:24–32;
Col. 3:8–10).

God placed Adam in the Garden of
Eden where he was to work the ground
(Gen. 2:5, 15) and take care of the animals
(Gen. 1:26–28; 2:19–20). God made Eve
as a "helper comparable to" Adam (Gen.
2:20), creating her out of one of Adam's
ribs so they were "one flesh" (Gen. 2:24).

God told the human pair, "Be fruitful
and multiply; fill the earth" (Gen. 1:28).
As a consequence, they had a number of
children: Cain, Abel, Seth, and a number
of other sons and daughters (Gen. 4:1–2;
5:3–4). Created in innocence, they did
not know sin (Gen. 2:25).

Genesis 3 tells how Adam failed to
keep God's command not to eat of the
tree of the knowledge of good and evil.
The consequence of this disobedience
was death (Gen. 2:17), both physical (Gen.
5:5) and spiritual (Eph. 2:1). Eve disobeyed first, lured by pride and the
desire for pleasure (Gen. 3:5–6; 1 Tim.
2:14). Then Adam, with full knowledge
of the consequences, joined Eve in rebellion against God (Gen. 3:6).

The consequences of disobedience
were: (1) loss of innocence (Gen. 3:7);
(2) continued enmity between the seed
of the woman [Christ] (Gen. 3:15; Gal.
3:16) and the seed of the serpent [SATAN
and his followers] (John 8:44); (3) the
cursing of the ground and the resultant
hard labor for man (Gen. 3:17–19); (4) the
hard labor of childbirth (Gen. 3:16);
(5) the submission of woman to her husband (Gen. 3:16; Eph. 5:22–23); and
(6) separation from God (Gen. 3:23–24;
2 Thess. 1:9). Adam lived 930 years (Gen.
5:5).

The New Testament emphasizes the
oneness of Adam and Eve (Matt. 19:3–9),
showing that Adam represented man in
bringing the human race into sin and
death (Rom. 5:12–19; 1 Cor. 15:22). In
contrast, Christ, the "last Adam," represented His redeemed people in bringing
justification and eternal life to them
(Rom. 5:15–21).

ADBEEL [AD bee el]

The third of the 12 sons of Ishmael
(Gen. 25:13). Adbeel is also believed by
scholars to be the name of an Arabian
tribe located in northwest Arabia.

ADDAR [ad DAR] (*cloudy*)

A son of Bela and the grandson of Benjamin (1 Chr. 8:3), also called ARD (Num.
26:40).

ADDI [AD ee]

An ancestor of Joseph listed in the genealogy of Jesus Christ (Luke 3:28). Addi
is the Greek form of IDDO.

ADER [A duhr]

A form of EDER.

ADIEL [A dih el] (*ornament of God*)

The name of three men in the Old
Testament:

1. One of the family heads of the tribe of Simeon in the time of Hezekiah (1 Chr. 4:36).

2. The father of Maasai, who helped rebuild the Temple after the Captivity (1 Chr. 9:12).

3. The father of Azmaveth (1 Chr. 27:25).

ADIN [A dun]

The father and ancestor of a family known as "the people of Adin" (Ezra 2:15), "the sons of Adin" (Ezra 8:6), or "the children of Adin" (Neh. 7:20). This family returned from captivity in Babylonia to Jerusalem with Zerubbabel and Ezra (Neh. 10:16).

ADINA [AD uh nah] (ornament)

The son of Shiza the Reubenite and one of David's mighty men (1 Chr. 11:42).

ADINO [AD ih noe]

The name given to JOSHEB–BASSHE-BETH the Tachmonite, chief captain of David's mighty men. He was given the name Adino the Eznite "because he had killed 800 men at one time" (2 Sam. 23:8).

ADLAI [AD lay]

The father of Shaphat, a chief herdsman (1 Chr. 27:29) in the time of David.

ADMATHA [AD mah thah]

A high Persian official at Shushan, one of seven princes "who had access to the king's presence" (Esth. 1:14).

ADNA [AD nuh] (pleasure)

The name of two men in the Old Testament:

1. A son of Pahath–Moab who divorced his pagan wife (Ezra 10:30).

2. A priest who returned from the Captivity in the time of the high priest Joiakim (Neh. 12:12, 15).

ADNAH [AD nuh] (pleasure)

The name of two men in the Old Testament:

1. A warrior of the tribe of Manasseh who joined David's army at Ziklag (1 Chr. 12:20).

2. A man of high military rank in King Jehoshaphat's army (2 Chr. 17:14).

ADONI–BEZEK [a DAWN ih BEE zek] (lord of Bezek)

A king of Bezek, which was located in the territory allotted to Judah. After he was captured by the men of Judah and Simeon, his thumbs and big toes were cut off (Judg. 1:5–7). Adoni–Bezek reaped what he had sown, for he himself had previously cut off the thumbs and big toes of 70 kings (Judg. 1:7).

ADONI–ZEDEK [a DAWN ih ZEH deck] (my lord is righteousness)

One of the five kings of the Amorites who fought against Joshua at Gibeon (Josh. 10:1–27). When Adoni–Zedek and his four allies took refuge in a cave near Makkedah, Joshua had them sealed inside while he pursued their armies. Later, the Israelites returned to the cave, removed the five kings, and "put their feet on their necks" (Josh. 10:24) as a sign of triumph. After they were killed, their bodies were hung on five trees for public display. Then they were taken down and cast into the cave, which was sealed with stones.

ADONIJAH [add oh NYE juh] (the Lord is my Lord)

The name of three men in the Old Testament:

1. The fourth of the six sons born to David while he was at Hebron (2 Sam. 3:4). Adonijah's mother was Haggith. With the exception of Absalom, David

apparently favored Adonijah over his other five sons. When David was old, Adonijah attempted to seize the throne, although he probably knew that his father intended Solomon to succeed him (1 Kin. 1:13).

Adonijah won two important people to his cause—Joab, the captain of the army, and Abiathar, the priest. At an open-air feast at the stone of Zoheleth beside En Rogel, he had himself proclaimed king.

But Adonijah had not won over Zadok the priest, Benaiah the commander of the royal bodyguard, or Nathan the prophet. Bathsheba, Solomon's mother, and Nathan told David of Adonijah's activities; David immediately ordered Solomon, who had been divinely chosen as David's successor, to be proclaimed king. When Adonijah sought sanctuary at the altar (1 Kin. 1:5–50), Solomon forgave him.

Adonijah, however, foolishly made another attempt to become king—this time after David's death. He asked that the beautiful Abishag, who had taken care of David during his final days, be given to him in marriage. According to the custom of the day, claiming a king's wife or concubine amounted to the same thing as claiming his throne. This time Solomon ordered that Adonijah be killed (1 Kin. 2:13, 25).

2. One of the Levites sent by Jehoshaphat to instruct the people of Judah in the law (2 Chr. 17:8).

3. A chieftain who, with Nehemiah, sealed the covenant (Neh. 10:14–16); he is also called ADONIKAM (Ezra 2:13).

ADONIKAM [ad oh NYE kum] (*my lord has risen*)

An Israelite whose descendants returned to Palestine from Babylonia after the Captivity (Ezra 2:13; 8:13; Neh. 7:18).

Apparently he is the ADONIJAH of Nehemiah 10:16.

ADONIRAM [ad oh NYE rum] (*my Lord is exalted*)

The son of Abda and an officer under kings David, Solomon, and Rehoboam. David placed Adoniram "in charge of revenue" (2 Sam. 20:24), and Solomon appointed him "over the labor force" (1 Kin. 4:6; 5:14)—a group sent to work in his enforced labor crews in Lebanon.

When the northern tribes rebelled against Rehoboam, Rehoboam sent Adoniram to force the rebels to obey the king, but "all Israel stoned him . . . and he died" (1 Kin. 12:18; 2 Chr. 10:18). Adoniram also was called Adoram (2 Sam. 20:24; 1 Kin. 12:18) and Hadoram (2 Chr. 10:18).

ADORAM [a DOH rum]

A form of ADONIRAM.

ADRAMMELECH [a DRAM uh leck]

A son of the Assyrian king Sennacherib. He and his brother, Sharezer, killed their father (2 Kin. 19:37; Is. 37:38).

ADRIEL [A drih el] (*God is my help*)

A son of Barzillai the Meholathite, of the tribe of Issachar. Adriel was also the husband of Merab, the daughter of King Saul, who was given to Adriel in marriage (1 Sam. 18:19; 2 Sam. 21:8).

AENEAS [ee NEE us]

A paralyzed man at Lydda healed by Peter (Acts 9:34–35).

AGABUS [AG uh bus]

A Christian prophet of Jerusalem who went to Antioch of Syria while Paul and Barnabas were there, and "showed by the Spirit that there was going to be a

AHISAMACH [a HIS ah mack] (*my brother sustains*)

A man of the tribe of Dan and a craftsman who worked on the tabernacle (Ex. 31:6).

AHISHAHAR [a HISH ah har] (*brother of the dawn*)

According to 1 Chronicles 7:10, a son of Bilhan, a grandson of Jediael, and a great-grandson of Benjamin.

AHISHAR [a HIGH shar] (*brother of song*)

An official or servant of King Solomon (1 Kin. 4:6).

AHITHOPHEL [a HITH oh fell] (*brother of folly*)

One of David's counselors who assisted Absalom in his revolt. When Absalom rebelled against David, Ahithophel apparently believed his own popularity would bring success to Absalom's revolt. Possibly sensing a chance to rise to power himself, Ahithophel advised Absalom to take David's harem (2 Sam. 15:12; 16:21)—an act equivalent to claiming the throne.

Ahithophel also advised Absalom to pursue David, who had fled Jerusalem. But Absalom chose to listen to Hushai, who advised the prince not to pursue his father. Sensing that Absalom's rebellion was doomed, Ahithophel put his household in order and hanged himself (2 Sam. 17:23)—one of the few cases of suicide in the Bible.

AHITUB [a HIGH tuhb] (*my brother is goodness*)

The name of three men in the Old Testament:

1. A son of Phinehas and grandson of Eli. Ahitub probably became high priest upon his grandfather's death (1 Sam. 4:11).

2. A son of Amariah and father of Zadok, who later was made high priest by King Saul after Ahimelech's death (2 Sam. 8:17; 1 Chr. 6:7–8, 52; 18:16; Ezra 7:2). The Ahitub of 1 Chronicles 6:8, 11–12 is probably the Azariah of 2 Chronicles 31:10.

3. The father of Meraioth and "officer over the house of God" (1 Chr. 9:11).

AHLAI [A lih]

The name of two people in the Old Testament:

1. One of several daughters of Sheshan (1 Chr. 2:31) and a descendant of Perez, Judah's older son by TAMAR (Matt. 1:3).

2. The father of one of David's mighty men (1 Chr. 11:41).

AHOAH [a HOE uh]

A son of Bela in the genealogy of Benjamin (1 Chr. 8:4). Ahoah is called Ahijah in 1 Chronicles 8:7.

AHOLIAB [a HOE lih ab] (*tent of the father*)

A son of Ahisamach of the tribe of Dan. During the time of Moses, he was chosen to work with Bezaleel and other craftsmen in preparing the furniture of the tabernacle (Ex. 31:6; 35:34; 36:1–2; 38:23; Oholiab, NRSV, NIV).

AHOLIBAMAH [a HOE lih BAH muh] (*tent of the high place*)

The name of one man and one woman in the Old Testament:

1. A wife of Esau (Gen. 36:5, 14). In Genesis 26:34 she is called "Judith the daughter of Beeri the Hittite."

2. The chief of an Edomite clan (Gen. 36:41; 1 Chr. 1:52; Oholibamah, NRSV, NIV).

AHUMAI [a HUE mih]

A son of Jahath and a descendant of Judah (1 Chr. 4:2).

AHUZAM [a HUE zem]

A form of AHUZZAM.

AHUZZAM [a HUZ um] (*possessing*)

A son of Ashhur and Naarah in the genealogy of Judah (1 Chr. 4:6; Ahuzam, KJV).

AHUZZATH [a HUZZ ath]

A friend of Abimelech, who was "King of Gerar" (Gen. 20:2) or "King of the Philistines" (Gen. 26:1). Ahuzzath accompanied King Abimelech on a journey from Gerar to Beersheba in an effort to make a covenant with Isaac (Gen. 26:26).

AHZAI [A zih] (*the Lord has seized*)

A priest who lived in Jerusalem in Ezra's time (Neh. 11:13; Ahasai, KJV).

AIAH [a EYE ah] (*falcon*)

The father of Rizpah, a concubine of King Saul (2 Sam. 3:7). Two of his grandsons were hanged by King David to appease the Gibeonites (2 Sam. 21:8, 10–11).

AJAH [A jah] (*hawk*)

A son of Zibeon (Gen. 36:24; 1 Chr. 1:40).

AKAN [A ken]

A son of Ezer and grandson of Seir the Horite (Gen. 36:27). Akan is also called JAAKAN (1 Chr. 1:42).

AKKUB [ACK kub]

The name of four men in the Old Testament:

1. A son of Elioenai, a descendant of Zerubbabel and of King David (1 Chr. 3:24).
2. The head of a family of Levite gatekeepers in the Temple after the Captivity (Ezra 2:42; Neh. 7:45).
3. The head of a family of Temple servants (Nethinim) who returned to Jerusalem after the Captivity (Ezra 2:45).
4. A Levite who helped Ezra read and interpret the law (Neh. 8:7).

ALAMETH [AL ah meth]

A form of ALEMETH.

ALEMETH [AL eh meth]

The name of two men:
1. A son of Becher and the grandson of Benjamin (1 Chr. 7:8; Alameth, KJV).
2. A son of Jehoaddah (1 Chr. 8:36). Alemeth also was a descendant of Jonathan and King Saul.

ALEXANDER [EH leg zan dur] (*defender of men*)

The name of five or six men in the Bible:
1. Alexander III (the Great), son of Philip II (King of Macedon) and founder of the Hellenistic (Greek) Empire. He was born in 356 B.C. and ascended the Macedonian throne in 336 B.C. Advised by his teacher Aristotle that he could rule the world if he could make people adopt the Greek culture, Alexander extended his empire east from Greece, around the Mediterranean Sea to Egypt, and then to the borders of India. He died in Babylon in 323 B.C. at the age of 33. Because he did not leave an heir who could continue his reign, Alexander's three generals divided his kingdom, with Ptolemy taking Egypt, Seleucus the East, and Cassander Macedonia.

Although Alexander the Great is not mentioned directly in the Old or New

religious officials. By vocation, he claimed to be nothing but "a herdsman and a tender of sycamore fruit" (Amos 7:14), but he pointed out that his right to speak came from the highest authority of all: "The Lord took me as I followed the flock, and the Lord said to me, 'Go, prophesy to My people Israel'" (Amos 7:15).

Amos spoke because the Lord had called him to deliver His message of judgment. This is one of the clearest statements of the compulsion of the divine call to be found in the Bible.

The theme of Amos' message was that Israel had rejected the one true God in order to worship false gods. He also condemned the wealthy class of the nation for cheating the poor through oppressive taxes (Amos 5:11) and the use of false weights and measures (Amos 8:5). He urged the people to turn from their sinful ways, to acknowledge God as their Maker and Redeemer, and to restore justice and righteousness in their dealings with others.

Amaziah the priest, who served in the court of King Jeroboam, made a report to the king about Amos and his message (Amos 7:10–13). This probably indicates that the prophet's stern warning created quite a stir throughout the land. But there is no record that the nation changed its ways as a result of Amos' message. About 40 years after his prophecies, Israel collapsed when the Assyrians overran their capital city, Samaria, and carried away the leading citizens as captives.

After preaching in Israel, Amos probably returned to his home in Tekoa. No facts are known about his later life or death. He will always serve as an example of courage and faithfulness.

AMOZ [A mozz] (*strong*)

The father of the prophet Isaiah (Is. 1:1; 13:1; 38:1). According to a tradition of the rabbis, Amoz was a brother of King Amaziah of Judah (reigned about 796–767) and, like his son Isaiah, also a prophet.

AMPLIAS [AM plih ahs] (*large, enlarged*)

A Christian in Rome greeted by the apostle Paul as "my beloved in the Lord" (Rom. 16:8; Ampliatus, NASB, REB, NIV, NRSV).

AMPLIATUS [am plih AY tus]

A form of AMPLIAS.

AMRAM [AM ram] (*exalted kinsman*)

The name of three men in the Old Testament:

1. A son of Kohath and an ancestor of Moses, Aaron, and Miriam through Jochebed, Kohath's sister (Ex. 6:18, 20). Amram was the father of the Amramites, the Levitical family that served in the wilderness tabernacle and perhaps in the Temple in Jerusalem (Num. 3:27; 1 Chr. 26:23).

2. The KJV spelling of Hamran (1 Chr. 1:41). The name should probably be HEMDAN, as recorded in the Septuagint (Greek) version (Gen. 36:26).

3. A son of Bani who divorced his foreign wife after the Captivity (Ezra 10:34).

AMRAPHEL [Am rah fell]

A king of Shinar who invaded Canaan during Abraham's time (Gen. 14:1, 9). Amraphel is not to be identified with Hammurapi, founder of the first Babylonian dynasty.

AMZI [Am zih] (*my strength*)

The name of two men in the Old Testament:

1. A descendant of Merari, of the tribe of Levi (1 Chr. 6:46).

2. An ancestor of Adaiah (Neh. 11:12).

ANAH [A nah]

The name of one woman and two men in the Old Testament:

1. Zibeon's daughter and the mother of one of Esau's wives, Aholibamah (Gen. 36:2, 14, 18, 25).

2. A son of Seir and brother of the Horite chief Zibeon (Gen. 36:20, 29; 1 Chr. 1:38). This Anah may be a tribal name rather than a personal name.

3. A son of Zibeon who discovered hot springs in the wilderness (Gen. 36:24; 1 Chr. 1:40–41).

ANAIAH [a NIGH uh] (the Lord has answered)

The name of one or two men in the Old Testament:

1. A leader who helped Ezra read the law (Neh. 8:4).

2. An Israelite who sealed the covenant under Nehemiah (Neh. 10:22). He may be the same person as No. 1.

ANAK [A knack]

A son of Arba, who gave his name to Kirjath Arba, or Hebron (Josh. 15:13–14). Anak had three sons, whose descendants were giants, the Anakim.

ANAN [A nan] (a cloud)

A leader of the Israelites who sealed the covenant after returning from the Captivity (Neh. 10:26).

ANANI [a NAY nih]

A son of Elioenai, a descendant of Zerubbabel and King David (1 Chr. 3:24).

ANANIAH [an uh NYE uh]

An ancestor of Azariah (Neh. 3:23).

ANANIAS [an uh NYE us] (the Lord is gracious)

The name of three New Testament men:

1. A Christian in the early church at Jerusalem (Acts 5:1–11). With the knowledge of his wife, SAPPHIRA, Ananias sold a piece of property and brought only a portion of the proceeds from its sale to Peter, claiming this represented the total amount realized from the sale. When Peter rebuked him for lying about the amount, Ananias immediately fell down and died. Sapphira later repeated the same falsehood, and she also fell down and died. Apparently, their pretense to be something they were not caused God to strike Ananias and Sapphira dead.

2. A Christian disciple living in Damascus at the time of Paul's conversion (Acts 9:10–18; 22:12–16). In a vision the Lord told Ananias of Paul's conversion and directed him to go to Paul and welcome him into the church. Aware of Paul's reputation as a persecutor of Christians, Ananias reacted with alarm. When the Lord informed him that Paul was "a chosen vessel of Mine" (Acts 9:15), Ananias went to Paul and laid his hands upon him. Paul's sight was restored immediately, and he was baptized (Acts 9:18).

3. The Jewish high priest before whom Paul appeared after his arrest in Jerusalem following his third missionary journey, about A.D. 58 (Acts 23:2). Ananias was also one of those who spoke against Paul before the Roman governor Felix (Acts 24:1). Ananias was appointed high priest about A.D. 48 by Herod. In A.D. 52 the governor of Syria sent Ananias to Rome to be tried for the Jews' violent treatment of the Samaritans. Ananias was acquitted of the charges

through Agrippa's influence, and he was returned to his office in Jerusalem. About A.D. 59 Ananias was deposed by Agrippa. Known to the Jews as a Roman collaborator, Ananias was murdered by a Jewish mob at the beginning of the Jewish–Roman War of A.D. 66–73.

ANATH [A nath]

The father of SHAMGAR (Judg. 3:31; 5:6), the third judge of Israel. Some scholars believe Anath is a contraction of Beth Anath, an ancient fortified city of the Canaanites near the border of Naphtali and Asher. If this is correct, then Anath was the place from which Shamgar came, not his father.

ANATHOTH [AN uh thoth]

The name of two men in the Old Testament:

1. A son of Becher (1 Chr. 7:8).
2. A leader of the people who placed his seal on the covenant, along with Nehemiah (Neh. 10:19).

ANDREW [AN droo] (manly)

Brother of Simon Peter and one of Jesus' first disciples. Both Andrew and Peter were fishermen (Matt. 4:18; Mark 1:16–18) from Bethsaida (John 1:44), on the northwest coast of the Sea of Galilee. They also had a house at Capernaum in this vicinity (Mark 1:29).

According to the Gospel of John, Andrew and an unnamed friend were among the followers of John the Baptist (John 1:35–40). When John the Baptist identified Jesus as the Lamb of God, both he and Andrew followed Jesus (John 1:41). Andrew then brought his brother Simon to meet the Messiah (John 1:43–51)—an action that continues to be a model for all who bring others to Christ.

At the feeding of the 5,000, Andrew called Jesus' attention to the boy with five barley loaves and two fish (John 6:5–9). Later Philip and Andrew decided to bring to Jesus the request of certain Greeks for an audience with Him (John 12:20–22). Andrew is mentioned a final time in the gospels, when he asked Jesus a question concerning last things in the company of Peter, James, and John (Mark 13:3–4).

All lists of the disciples name Andrew among the first four (Matt. 10:2–4; Mark 3:16–19; Luke 6:14–16; Acts 1:13). According to tradition, Andrew was martyred at Patrae in Achaia by crucifixion on an X-shaped cross. According to Eusebius, Andrew's field of labor was Scythia, the region north of the Black Sea. For this reason he became the patron saint of Russia. He is also considered the patron saint of Scotland.

ANDRONICUS [an droe NYE kus]

A Christian in Rome to whom the apostle Paul sent greetings (Rom. 16:7). Andronicus had become a Christian before Paul. He may have been well known as a traveling evangelist or preacher.

ANER [A nare]

An Amorite chief who joined forces with Abraham in his battle with Chedorlaomer (Gen. 14:13, 24).

ANIAM [a NIGH am]

A son of Shemida of the tribe of Manasseh (1 Chr. 7:19).

ANNA [AN ah] (favor)

A widow, daughter of Phanuel of the tribe of Asher (Luke 2:36). She was at the Temple in Jerusalem when Mary and Joseph brought Jesus to be dedicated (Luke 2:27). Anna recognized Jesus as the long-awaited Messiah (Luke 2:37–38).

ANNAS [AN us] (*grace of the Lord*)

One of the high priests at Jerusalem, along with CAIAPHAS, when John the Baptist began his ministry, about A.D. 26 (Luke 3:2). Quirinius, governor of Syria, appointed Annas as high priest about A.D. 6 or 7. Although Annas was deposed by Valerius Gratus, the Procurator of Judea, about A.D. 15, he was still the most influential of the priests and continued to carry the title of high priest (Luke 3:2; Acts 4:6).

After his removal, Annas was officially succeeded by each of his five sons, one grandson, and his son-in-law CAIAPHAS, the high priest who presided at the trial of Jesus (Matt. 26:3, 57; John 18:13–14). During His trial, Jesus was first taken to Annas, who then sent Jesus to Caiaphas (John 18:13, 24). Both Annas and Caiaphas were among the principal examiners when Peter and John were arrested (Acts 4:6).

ANTHOTHIJAH [an thoe THIGH juh]

A form of ANTOTHIJAH.

ANTIOCHUS [an TIE oh kus] (*withstander*)

The Book of Daniel prophesies about the following three rulers, although it mentions none of them by name:

1. Antiochus II (261–246 B.C.), surnamed Theos ("god"). He was a drunken, immoral ruler easily swayed by favorites. The prophecy in Daniel 11:6 probably refers to him; for he divorced his wife Laodice, who was his half sister, to marry Berenice, the daughter of Ptolemy, the ruler of Egypt.

2. Antiochus III (223–187 B.C.), surnamed Megas ("the Great"). He was the second son of Seleucus II Callinicus and the successor of his older brother, Seleucus III Soter. The Seleucids of Syria and the Ptolemies of Egypt waged a continual struggle for control in Palestine. Antiochus III finally defeated the Egyptian general Scopas at Pani, or Panias (the New Testament Caesarea Philippi), in 198 B.C., giving the Seleucids complete control of Palestine. This victory eventually led to the worst persecution the Jews had yet endured. Some scholars see Daniel 11:10–19 as a reference to Antiochus III, but the allusion is vague.

3. Antiochus IV (175–164 B.C.), surnamed Epiphanes (God manifest) but called by his Jewish enemies Epimanes (madman). Antiochus IV was one of the cruelest rulers of all time. Like his father, Antiochus III the Great, he was enterprising and ambitious; however, he had a tendency to cruelty that bordered on madness. His primary aim—to unify his empire by spreading Greek civilization and culture—brought him into direct conflict with the Jews. This conflict broke into open rebellion in 167 B.C. Accounts of these conflicts are found in the apocryphal book of 2 Maccabees.

The revolt began with Antiochus' edict that sought to unite all the peoples of his kingdom in religion, law, and custom. The Jews were the only people who would not adhere to this edict. Antiochus issued regulations against observing the Sabbath, practicing circumcision, and keeping all food laws. These regulations were followed by the "Abomination of Desolation" (Dan. 11:31)—the desecration of the altar of the burnt offering in the Temple of Jerusalem. Jews were forced to participate in heathen activities and were put to death if they were caught with the Book of the Law in their possession.

As the revolt, led by the pious priest Mattathias and his sons, gained momentum, the Jews united to overthrow Seleu-

dealt the Ethiopians a humiliating blow (2 Chr. 14:11–12). But his second confrontation did not yield such glorious results. When Baasha, king of Israel, fortified Ramah in an attempt to blockade Asa and prevent anyone from traveling to or from Jerusalem, Asa hired Ben–Hadad, king of Syria, to thwart Baasha's plans (2 Chr. 16:1–6). Ben–Hadad invaded northern Israel and forced Baasha to withdraw from Ramah. When the prophet ("seer") Hanani rebuked him for relying on Ben–Hadad instead of the Lord, Asa was enraged and put Hanani into prison (2 Chr. 16:7–10).

When Asa contracted a disease in his feet in the 39th year of his reign, he did not seek the Lord, but he consulted physicians instead (2 Chr. 16:12). Shortly thereafter, he died and was buried in Jerusalem.

2. A son of Elkanah and a Levite who lived in one of the villages of the Netophathites (1 Chr. 9:16).

ASAHEL [AS ah hell] (God has made)

The name of four men in the Old Testament:

1. A son of Zeruiah, David's half-sister, and the brother of Joab and Abishai. Asahel was "as fleet of foot as a wild gazelle" (2 Sam. 2:18), but his ability to run swiftly was his downfall. When Asahel pursued Abner in battle, Abner killed him with his spear (2 Sam. 2:23).

2. One of the Levites sent by King Jehoshaphat to teach the Law to the people (2 Chr. 17:8).

3. A Levite appointed by King Hezekiah as an overseer of the Temple offerings (2 Chr. 31:13).

4. The father of Jonathan. Jonathan opposed Ezra (Ezra 10:15).

ASAHIAH [as ah HIGH ah]

A form of ASAIAH.

ASAIAH [as EYE ah] (the Lord has made)

The name of four men in the Old Testament:

1. An officer of King Josiah. Asaiah inquired of HULDAH the prophetess about the Book of the Law discovered in the Temple (2 Kin. 22:12, 14; Asahiah, KJV, NRSV).

2. A descendant of Simeon (1 Chr. 4:36).

3. A descendant of Merari. Asaiah helped move the Ark of the Covenant from the house of Obed–Edom to Jerusalem (1 Chr. 15:6, 11–12).

4. A Shilonite who lived in Jerusalem after the Captivity (1 Chr. 9:5). He was also called Maaseiah (Neh. 11:5).

ASAPH [AY saf] (God has gathered)

The name of five Old Testament men:

1. The father of Joah (2 Kin. 18:18, 37).

2. A Levite and the son of Berachiah the Gershonite (2 Chr. 20:14). Asaph sounded cymbals before the Ark of the Covenant when it was moved from the house of Obed–Edom to Jerusalem (1 Chr. 15:16–19). Asaph's family became one of the three families given responsibility for music and song in the Temple (1 Chr. 25:1–9). Following the Captivity, 128 singers from this family returned from Babylon and conducted the singing when the foundations of Zerubbabel's temple were laid (Ezra 2:41; 3:10). Twelve psalms (Psalms 50; 73–83) are attributed to the family of Asaph.

3. A Levite whose descendants lived in Jerusalem after the Captivity (1 Chr. 9:15).

4. A Levite descendant of Kohath (1 Chr. 26:1).

5. The keeper of the king's forest under the Persian king ARTAXERXES I Longimanus (Neh. 2:8).

ASAREEL [ah SAY reh el]

A form of ASAREL.

ASAREL [AS ah rel] (*God has joined*)

A son of Jehaleleel in the genealogy of Judah (1 Chr. 4:16, Asareel, KJV).

ASARELAH [as ah RAY lah]

A form of ASHARELAH.

ASENATH [AS ih nath]

The Egyptian wife of Joseph and the mother of Manasseh and Ephraim (Gen. 41:45, 50–52; 46:20). Asenath was the daughter of Poti–Pherah, priest of On. Pharaoh himself may have arranged the marriage between Joseph and Asenath to help Joseph adjust to life in Egypt.

ASER [AY zer]

Greek form of ASHER.

ASHARELAH [ash ah REE la]

A son of Asaph appointed by King David to be in charge of the Temple music (1 Chr. 25:2, 14; Asarelah, Jesharelah, KJV; Jesarelah, NIV).

ASHBEL [ASH bell] (*man of Baal*)

A son of Benjamin (1 Chr. 8:1) and the ancestor of a tribal family known as the Ashbelites (Num. 26:38).

ASHCHENAZ [ASH keh nazz]

A form of ASHKENAZ.

ASHER [ASH err] (*happy*)

The eighth son of Jacob, the second by Leah's maidservant, Zilpah (Gen. 30:13). On his deathbed Jacob blessed Asher: "Bread from Asher shall be rich,

and he shall yield royal dainties" (Gen. 49:20).

ASHHUR [ASH shure]

A son of Hezron and Abiah and the father of TEKOA (1 Chr. 2:24; 4:5; Ashur, KJV). Ashhur probably was the "father" of Tekoa, a city in Judah situated between Bethlehem and Hebron, in the sense of being its settler or founder.

ASHKENAZ [ASH keh nazz]

The oldest son of Gomer and a grandson of Japheth. Ashkenaz also became the name of a people that settled in the vicinity of Armenia. It is also spelled Ashchenaz (1 Chr. 1:6, KJV; Jer. 51:27, KJV, NKJV).

ASHPENAZ [ASH peh nazz]

The master of the eunuchs at Babylon during the reign of King Nebuchadnezzar. The king entrusted the people of Israel who had been taken captive to his care (Dan. 1:3).

ASHRIEL [ASH rih ell]

A form of ASRIEL.

ASHUR [ASH shure]

A form of ASHHUR.

ASHURBANIPAL [a shoor BAN ih pal] (*Asshur is creating an heir*)

The last of the great kings of Assyria (668–626 B.C.). He was the son and successor of the Assyrian king Esarhaddon. Most scholars now identify him with the "great and noble" OSNAPPER of Ezra 4:10. Apparently, Ashurbanipal was the monarch who made King Manasseh of Judah, along with 21 other kings, pay tribute to him and kiss his feet.

A large part of Ashurbanipal's reign was spent in a tug-of-war with his own brother, Shamash-shum-ukin, who was viceroy of Babylon. Outright rebellion against Ashurbanipal broke out in 652 B.C. and ended in 648 B.C. following a two-year siege of Babylon by the Assyrians that resulted in famine.

The mighty Assyrian Empire disintegrated under Ashurbanipal's son, Sinsharishkun (627[?]–612 B.C.). Upon his death Babylon fell immediately to Nabopolassar, founder of a new Babylonian Empire; and the Medes and Babylonians destroyed Nineveh, the capital city of Assyria.

ASHURNASIRPAL [ash er NAS ir pal]
(*Asshur is guarding an heir*)

A king of Assyria who reigned early in the ninth century B.C., when Assyria was at the height of its power (about 884–860 B.C.). King Jehoshaphat of Judah (873–848 B.C.) and King Ahab of Israel (874–853 B.C.) were his contemporaries.

ASHVATH [ASH vath]

A son of Japhlet, of the tribe of Asher (1 Chr. 7:33).

ASIEL [AY zih el] (*God is maker*)

A descendant of Simeon and an ancestor of Jehu (1 Chr. 4:35).

ASNAH [AS nah]

One of the Nethinim (Temple servants) whose descendants returned to Jerusalem after the Captivity in Babylonia (Ezra 2:50).

ASNAPPER [as NAP per]

A form of OSNAPPER, the biblical name for ASHURBANIPAL.

ASPATHA [as PAY thah]

A son of Haman who was hanged like his father (Esth. 9:7).

ASRIEL [AS rih ell]

A man of the tribe of Manasseh, of the house of Gilead, who was listed in the second census (Josh. 17:2; Ashriel, 1 Chr. 7:14, KJV).

ASSHUR [AS shoor]

A descendant of Shem (1 Chr. 1:17). He is regarded as the ancestor of the Assyrians.

ASSHURIM [a SHOO rim]

A son of Dedan or an obscure tribe that traced its family tree to him (Gen. 25:3).

ASSIR [AS err]

The name of three Old Testament men:

1. A son of Korah (Ex. 6:24; 1 Chr. 6:22).

2. A son of Jehoiachin, king of Judah (1 Chr. 3:17).

3. A son of Ebiasaph (1 Chr. 6:23, 37).

ASYNCRITUS [a SIN cry tus]
(*incomparable*)

A Christian in Rome to whom the apostle Paul sent greetings (Rom. 16:14).

ATARAH [AT a rah] (*crown*)

The second wife of Jerahmeel and mother of Onam (1 Chr. 2:26–28).

ATER [AY tehr]

The ancestor of a family that returned from Babylonia after the Captivity (Neh. 7:21).

ATHAIAH [a THAY yah]

A son of Uzziah and a member of the tribe of Judah in Nehemiah's time (Neh. 11:4). He may be the same person as Uthai (1 Chr. 9:4).

ATHALIAH [ath ah LIE ah] (*the Lord is strong*)

The name of one woman and two men in the Old Testament:

1. The queen of Judah for six years (2 Kin. 11:1–3). Athaliah was the daughter of King Ahab of Israel. Presumably, Jezebel was her mother.

Athaliah married Jehoram (or Joram), son of Jehoshaphat, king of Judah. Jehoram reigned only eight years and was succeeded by his son Ahaziah, who died after reigning only one year. Desiring the throne for herself, Athaliah ruthlessly killed all her grandsons—except the infant Joash, who was hidden by his aunt (2 Kin. 11:2).

Athaliah apparently inherited Jezebel's ruthlessness. She was a tyrant whose every whim had to be obeyed. As her mother had done in Israel, Athaliah introduced Baal worship in Judah and in so doing destroyed part of the Temple.

Joash was hidden in the house of the Lord for six years (2 Kin. 11:3), while Athaliah reigned over the land (841–835 B.C.). In the seventh year, the high priest Jehoiada declared Joash the lawful king of Judah. Guards removed Athaliah from the Temple before killing her, to avoid defiling the Temple with her blood (2 Kin. 11:13–16; 2 Chr. 23:12–15).

Athaliah reaped what she sowed. She gained the throne through murder and lost her life in the same way. She also failed to thwart God's promise, because she did not destroy the Davidic line, through which the Messiah was to be born.

2. A son of Jeroham, a Benjamite (1 Chr. 8:26).

3. The father of Jeshaiah (Ezra 8:7).

ATHLAI [ATH lay eye] (*the Lord is strong*)

A son of Bebai who divorced his pagan wife (Ezra 10:28).

ATTAI [AT ay eye]

The name of three Old Testament men:

1. A grandson of Sheshan the Jerahmeelite through Sheshan's daughter Ahlai and her husband Jarha (1 Chr. 2:35–36).

2. A Gadite soldier who joined David at Ziklag (1 Chr. 12:8).

3. The second son of King Rehoboam by his second wife, Maacah (2 Chr. 11:20).

AUGUSTUS [aw GUS tus] (*consecrated, holy, sacred*)

A title of honor bestowed upon Octavian, the first Roman emperor (27 B.C.–A.D. 14). Luke refers to him as "Caesar Augustus" (Luke 2:1). A nephew of Julius Caesar, Octavian was born in 63 B.C. In 43 B.C., Octavian, Lepidus, and Mark Antony were named as the Second Triumvirate, the three rulers who shared the office of emperor. Octavian eventually became the sole ruler of Rome and reigned as emperor for more than 44 years, until his death in A.D. 14. It was during his reign that Jesus was born (Luke 2:1).

Augustus reigned during a time of peace and extensive architectural achievements. After his death, the title "Augustus" was given to all Roman emperors. The "Augustus Caesar" mentioned in Acts 25:21, 25, for instance, is not Octavian but Nero.

Also see CAESAR.

AZALIAH [az ah LIE ah] (*the Lord is noble*)

A son of Meshullam and the father of Shaphan the scribe (2 Kin. 22:3).

AZANIAH [AZ ah NIE ah] (*the Lord has heard*)

A Levite who sealed the covenant under Nehemiah (Neh. 10:9).

AZRIEL [AZ rih el] (*God is helper*)

The name of three Old Testament men:

1. A chief of the tribe of Manasseh (1 Chr. 5:24).

2. An ancestor of Jerimoth (1 Chr. 27:19).

3. The father of Seraiah (Jer. 36:26).

AZRIKAM [AZ rih kam] (*my help has risen*)

The name of four men in the Old Testament:

1. A descendant of King David through Zerubbabel (1 Chr. 3:23).

2. The oldest son of Azel and a descendant of King Saul (1 Chr. 8:38; 9:44).

3. A Levite who lived in Jerusalem after the Captivity (1 Chr. 9:14; Neh. 11:15).

4. The governor of the house of Ahaz (2 Chr. 28:7).

AZUBAH [a ZOO buh] (*forsaken*)

The name of two women in the Old Testament:

1. The mother of Jehoshaphat, a king of Judah (1 Kin. 22:42).

2. Caleb's first wife and the mother of his three sons, Jesher, Shobab, and Ardon (1 Chr. 2:18–19).

AZUR [AY zer] (*helper*)

The father of Hananiah the false prophet (Jer. 28:1; Azzur, NRSV, NIV, REB).

AZZAN [AZ an]

The father of Paltiel, of the tribe of Issachar. Paltiel helped Eleazar and Joshua divide the land among the tribes (Num. 34:26).

AZZUR [AZ err] (*helper*)

The name of two men in the Old Testament:

1. An Israelite who sealed the covenant under Nehemiah (Neh. 10:17).

2. The father of Jaazaniah, a prince whom Ezekiel saw in a vision (Ezek. 11:1; Azur, KJV).

and the anger of the Lord was aroused against Israel" (Num. 25:1–3).

In condemning "the way of Balaam," the New Testament condemns the greed of all who are well paid to tempt God's people to compromise their moral standards.

BALADAN [BAL uh dan]

The father of MERODACH–BALADAN (2 Kin. 20:12; Is. 39:1), king of Babylon during the reign of HEZEKIAH, king of Judah.

BALAK [BAY lack]

The king of Moab near the end of the wilderness wanderings of the Israelites. Because Balak feared the Israelites, he hired BALAAM the soothsayer to curse Israel (Num. 22—24; Josh. 24:9). But Balaam blessed Israel instead.

BANI [BAY nee] (*built*)

The name of several Old Testament men:

1. A Gadite who was one of David's mighty men (2 Sam. 23:36).

2. A Levite of the Merari family and a son of Shamer (1 Chr. 6:46).

3. A descendant of Judah through Perez (1 Chr. 9:4).

4. The founder of a family that returned with Zerubbabel from Captivity in Babylonia (Ezra 2:10). Some members of his family had taken foreign wives (Ezra 10:29). A representative of this family sealed the covenant (Neh. 10:14). The family is also called Binnui (Neh. 7:15).

B

BALAAM

5. A descendant of No. 4 who married a foreign wife while in Captivity (Ezra 10:34, 38).

6. The father of Rehum, who was one of the Levites who helped repair part of Jerusalem's walls (Neh. 3:17; 8:7).

7. A Levite who sealed the covenant and regulated the people's devotions after Ezra explained the Law (Neh. 10:13). He may be the same person as No. 6.

8. A Levite of the sons of Asaph (Neh. 11:22). He may be the same person as No. 6 or No. 7.

BARABBAS [buh RAB bas]

A "robber" (John 18:40) and "notorious prisoner" (Matt. 27:16) who was chosen by the mob in Jerusalem to be released instead of Jesus. Barabbas had been imprisoned for insurrection and murder (Luke 23:19, 25; Mark 15:7). Pilate offered to give the crowd either Jesus or Barabbas. The mob demanded that he release Barabbas and crucify Jesus. Ironically, the name Barabbas probably means "son of the father." There is no further mention of Barabbas after he was released.

BARACHEL [BAR ah kell] (God has blessed)

The father of Elihu, who was one of Job's "friends" (Job 32:2, 6).

BARACHIAH [bar ah KIE uh]

A form of BERECHIAH.

BARACHIAS [bar ah KIE us]

A form of BERECHIAH.

BARAK [BAR ack] (lightning)

A son of Abinoam of the city of KEDESH. Barak was summoned by DEBORAH, a Prophetess who was judging Israel at that time. Deborah told Barak to raise a militia of 10,000 men to fight JABIN, king of Canaan, who had oppressed Israel for 20 years. The commander-in-chief of Jabin's army was SISERA.

Apparently during the battle, the Lord sent a great thunderstorm. The rain swelled the Kishon River and the plain surrounding the battle area, making Sisera's 900 iron chariots useless (Judg. 5:21). The Israelites routed the Canaanites. The victory is described twice: in prose (Judges 4) and in poetry, the beautiful "Song of Deborah" (Judges 5). Barak is listed in the New Testament among the heroes of faith (Heb. 11:32). Also see BEDAN.

BARIAH [buh RIE ah]

A son of Shemaiah, of the tribe of Judah (1 Chr. 3:22).

BAR–JESUS [bar GEE zus] (son of Jesus)

A false prophet who opposed Barnabas and Paul at Paphos, a town on the island of Cyprus (Acts 13:4–12). He is also called Elymas, which means "magician" or "sorcerer." Bar–Jesus was temporarily struck blind because of his opposition to the gospel.

BAR–JONAH [bar JO nuh] (son of Jonah)

The family name of the apostle PETER (Matt. 16:17; John 1:42; 21:15–17).

BARKOS [bar KOS]

An ancestor of a family of servants in the Temple who returned from the Captivity with Zerubbabel (Ezra 2:53; Neh. 7:55).

BARNABAS [BAR nuh bus] (son of encouragement)

An apostle in the early church (Acts 4:36–37; 11:19–26) and Paul's companion on his first missionary journey (Acts

13:1—15:41). A Levite from the island of Cyprus, Barnabas' given name was Joseph, or Joses (Acts 4:36). When he became a Christian, he sold his land and gave the money to the Jerusalem apostles (Acts 4:36–37).

Early in the history of the church, Barnabas went to Antioch to check on the growth of this early group of Christians. Then he journeyed to Tarsus and brought Saul (as PAUL was still called) back to minister with him to the Christians in Antioch (Acts 11:25). At this point Barnabas apparently was the leader of the church at Antioch, because his name is repeatedly mentioned before Paul's in the Book of Acts. But after Saul's name was changed to Paul, Barnabas' name is always mentioned after Paul's (Acts 13:43).

Because of his good reputation, Barnabas was able to calm the fear of Saul among the Christians in Jerusalem (Acts 9:27). He and Saul also brought money from Antioch to the Jerusalem church when it was suffering a great famine (Acts 11:27–30). Shortly thereafter, the Holy Spirit led the Antioch church to commission Barnabas and Paul, along with John Mark, Barnabas' cousin (Col. 4:10), to make a missionary journey (Acts 13:1–3) to Cyprus and the provinces of Asia Minor.

A rift eventually developed between Barnabas and Paul over John Mark (Col. 4:10). Barnabas wanted to take John Mark on their second missionary journey. Paul, however, felt John Mark should stay behind because he had left the first mission at Cyprus (Acts 13:13). Paul and Barnabas went their separate ways, and Barnabas took John Mark with him on a second mission to Cyprus (Acts 15:36–39). A pseudepigraphic epistle named after Barnabas is falsely attributed to him.

BARSABAS [BAR sah bus] (*son of the sabbath*)

The name of two men in the New Testament:

1. Joseph, surnamed Justus, one of the two disciples nominated to replace Judas Iscariot as an apostle (Acts 1:23; Barsabbas, NASB, REB).

2. A disciple who, along with Silas, was sent as a delegate to accompany Paul and Barnabas to Antioch of Syria (Acts 15:22, 27). These delegates carried a letter from the Jerusalem Council to the Gentile Christians in Antioch, Syria, and Cilicia, informing them of the council's action (Acts 15:23).

BARSABBAS [bar SAH bus]

A form of BARSABAS.

BARTHOLOMEW [bar THOL oh mew] (*son of Tolmai*)

One of the twelve apostles of Jesus, according to the four lists given in the New Testament (Matt. 10:3; Mark 3:18; Luke 6:14; Acts 1:13). Many scholars equate Bartholomew with NATHANAEL (John 1:45–49), but no proof of this identification exists, except by inference. According to church tradition, Bartholomew was a missionary to various countries, such as Armenia and India. He is reported to have preached the gospel along with Philip and Thomas. According to another tradition, he was crucified upside down after being flayed alive.

BARTIMAEUS [bar tih MEE us] (*son of Timaeus*)

A blind man of Jericho healed by Jesus (Mark 10:46–52). As he sat by the road begging, Bartimaeus cried out, "Jesus, Son of David, have mercy on me!" (v. 47). Jesus replied, "Go your way; your faith has made you well" (v. 52).

BARTIMEUS [bar tih MEE us]

A form of BARTIMAEUS.

BARUCH [bah RUKE] (*blessed*)

The name of three or four men in the Old Testament:

1. A son of Zabbai. Baruch helped Nehemiah repair the walls of Jerusalem (Neh. 3:20).

2. A man who sealed the covenant with Nehemiah (Neh. 10:6). He may be the same person as No. 1.

3. A son of Col–Hozeh and a returned captive of the tribe of Judah (Neh. 11:5).

4. The scribe or secretary of Jeremiah the prophet (Jer. 32:12–16; 36:1–32; 45:1–5). A son of Neriah, Baruch was a member of a prominent Jewish family. In the fourth year of the reign of Jehoiakim, king of Judah (605 B.C.), Baruch wrote Jeremiah's prophecies of destruction from the prophet's dictation (Jer. 36:1–8). Baruch read Jeremiah's words publicly on a day of fasting, then read them to the officials of the king's court. A clay seal inscribed "Baruch son of Neriah the scribe," dating from Jeremiah's time and clearly belonging to his secretary (see Jer. 36:32), was recently discovered in a burnt archive in Israel.

BARZILLAI [bar ZILL ay eye] (*made of iron*)

The name of three men in the Old Testament:

1. A Meholathite whose son was married to one of King Saul's daughters (1 Sam. 18:19; 2 Sam. 21:8).

2. A member of the tribe of Gilead from Rogelim who brought provisions to David and his army at Mahanaim, where they had fled from Absalom (2 Sam. 17:27–29). On his deathbed, David remembered Barzillai's kindness and re-

minded Solomon to care for his children (1 Kin. 2:7).

3. A priest whose genealogy was lost during the Captivity (Ezra 2:61; Neh. 7:63). Apparently he married a daughter of No. 2 and adopted his wife's family name.

BASEMATH [BASE math]

The name of three women in the Old Testament:

1. One of Esau's wives and the daughter of Elon the Hittite (Gen. 26:34; Bashemath, KJV). She is also called Adah (Gen. 36:2). Esau married her out of spite because Isaac, Esau's father, was displeased with Esau's other wives, who were Canaanites.

2. One of Esau's wives and the daughter of Ishmael (Gen. 36:3–4, 10, 13, 17; Bashemath, KJV). She is also called Mahalath (Gen. 28:9).

3. A daughter of Solomon and wife of Ahimaaz (1 Kin. 4:15; Basmath, KJV).

BASHEMATH [BASH eh math]

A form of BASEMATH.

BASMATH [BAHS math]

A form of BASEMATH.

BATHSHEBA [bath SHE buh] (*daughter of oath*)

A wife of Uriah the Hittite and of King David (2 Sam. 11; 12:24). Standing on the flat roof of his palace in Jerusalem one evening, David saw the beautiful Bathsheba bathing on the roof of a nearby house. With his passion aroused, David committed adultery with Bathsheba. Out of that union Bathsheba conceived a child.

When David discovered her pregnancy, he hurriedly sent for Uriah, who was in battle with the Ammonites. But Uriah refused to engage in marital rela-

B

BEN–HANAN [ben HAY nan] (*son of grace*)

A son of Shimon, of the tribe of Judah (1 Chr. 4:20).

BEN–HAYIL [ben HAY ill]

A form of BEN–HAIL.

BEN–HESED [ben HEE sid] (*son of faithfulness*)

One of Solomon's 12 supply officers, in charge of three cities in the Plain of Sharon: Arubboth, Sochoh, and Hepher (1 Kin. 4:10).

BEN–HUR [ben HER] (*son of Hur*)

One of Solomon's 12 supply officers responsible for providing food for the royal household (1 Kin. 4:8).

BEN–JAHAZIEL [ben juh HAY zih el] (*son of Jahaziel*)

A chief of the people who returned from the Captivity in Babylon (Ezra 8:5).

BEN JOSIPHIAH [ben joe zy FIE uh] (*son of Josiphiah*)

One of the sons of Bani who returned from the Captivity with Ezra (Ezra 8:10).

BEN–ONI [ben OWN ih] (*son of my pain*)

The name given by the dying Rachel to her son (Gen. 35:18). Jacob changed the name to BENJAMIN.

BEN–ZOHETH [ben ZOE heth] (*son of Zoheth*)

A son of Ishi, of the tribe of Judah (1 Chr. 4:20).

BENAIAH [beh NIE yuh] (*the Lord has built*)

The name of 12 men in the Old Testament:

1. One of David's mighty men (2 Sam. 23:30; 1 Chr. 27:14).

2. A loyal supporter of David and Solomon (1 Kin. 1:8; 4:4; 1 Chr. 27:5). Benaiah commanded the Cherethites and the Pelethites, David's bodyguard (2 Sam. 8:18; 20:23; 1 Chr. 18:17; 27:5–6). A Levite, Benaiah remained loyal to David when David's son Absalom rebelled. When another of David's sons, Adonijah, tried to seize the king's throne and prevent Solomon from becoming king, Benaiah escorted Solomon to Gihon, where he was anointed king (1 Kin. 1:32–45). Benaiah carried out Solomon's orders to execute Adonijah (1 Kin. 2:25) and Joab (1 Kin. 2:34). Solomon then made Benaiah commander in chief over the army (1 Kin. 2:35; 4:4). Benaiah was famous for three courageous deeds: (1) climbing down into a pit and killing a lion; (2) killing two lion-like warriors of Moab; and (3) killing an Egyptian giant with the giant's own weapon (2 Sam. 23:20–22; 1 Chr. 11:22–24).

3. The head of a family of the tribe of Simeon during Hezekiah's reign (1 Chr. 4:36).

4. A priest who played the harp before the Ark of the Covenant when it was being brought by David to Jerusalem (1 Chr. 15:18, 20, 24; 16:5–6).

5. The father of one of David's counselors (1 Chr. 27:34).

6. The grandfather of JAHAZIEL (2 Chr. 20:14).

7. A Levite overseer of offerings in the Temple during Hezekiah's reign (2 Chr. 31:13).

8, 9, 10, 11. Four men who had married pagan wives during the Captivity and who heeded Ezra's call to divorce them. They were sons of Parosh, Pahath-Moab, Bani, and Nebo respectively (Ezra 10:25, 30, 35, 43).

12. The father of PELATIAH (Ezek. 11:1, 13).

BENINU [beh NIE noo] (*our son*)

A Levite who sealed the covenant after returning from the Captivity (Neh. 10:13).

BENJAMIN [BEN juh mun] (*son of the right hand* or *son of the south*)

The name of three or four men in the Old Testament:

1. Jacob's youngest son, born to his favorite wife, RACHEL (Gen. 35:18, 24). After giving birth to Benjamin, the dying Rachel named him Ben–Oni (Gen. 35:18), which means "son of my pain." But Jacob renamed him Benjamin. When Jacob lost his beloved son JOSEPH, he became very attached to Benjamin because Benjamin was the only surviving son of Rachel. When his sons went to Egypt in search of food to relieve a famine, Jacob was reluctant to let Benjamin go with them (Gen. 43:1–17).

It is apparent that Joseph also loved Benjamin, his only full brother (Gen. 43:29–34). During this trip Joseph ordered that his silver cup be planted in Benjamin's sack. The reaction of Jacob and Benjamin's brothers shows the great love they had for Benjamin (Gen. 44). Benjamin had five sons and two grandsons, and he became the founder of the tribe that carried his name (Gen. 46:21; Num. 26:38–41; 1 Chr. 7:6–12; 8:1–40).

2. A son of Bilhan, a Benjamite (1 Chr. 7:10).

3. A son of Harim who lived in Jerusalem following the return from the Captivity. Benjamin divorced his pagan wife at Ezra's urging (Ezra 10:31–32).

4. A priest during the time of Nehemiah (Neh. 12:34) who helped repair and dedicate the wall of Jerusalem (Neh.

3:23). He may be the same person as No. 3.

BENO [BEE noe] (*his son*)

A descendant of the tribe of Levi through MERARI (1 Chr. 24:26–27).

BEOR [BEE or]

The name of two men in the Old Testament:

1. The father of Bela, king of Edom (Gen. 36:32; 1 Chr. 1:43).

2. The father of Balaam, the seer hired by Balak to curse the Israelites (Deut. 23:4; Josh. 24:9). Beor is also called Bosor (2 Pet. 2:15, KJV).

BERA [BEE rah]

A king of Sodom (Gen. 14:2). During the time of Abraham he was defeated by Chedorlaomer in the Valley of Siddim.

BERACAH [BEHR ah kah]

A form of BERACHAH.

BERACHAH [BEHR ah kah] (*blessing*)

A Benjamite who joined David's army at Ziklag (1 Chr. 12:3; Beracah, NASB, NIV, NRSV).

BERACHIAH [behr ah KIE uh]

A form of BERECHIAH.

BERAIAH [beh RIE uh] (*the Lord has created*)

A chief of the tribe of Benjamin (1 Chr. 8:21).

BERECHIAH [behr ah KIE uh] (*the Lord has blessed*)

The name of seven men in the Old Testament:

1. A son of Zerubbabel and a descendant of David (1 Chr. 3:20).

2. A Levite who lived in Jerusalem after the Captivity (1 Chr. 9:16).

3. A Levite, the father of Asaph the singer (1 Chr. 15:17), also called Bera-chiah (1 Chr. 6:39).

4. One of the "doorkeepers for the ark" (1 Chr. 15:23) in David's time.

5. A chief of the tribe of Ephraim (2 Chr. 28:12).

6. The father of Meshullam (Neh. 3:4, 30; 6:18).

7. A son of Iddo and the father of Zechariah (Zech. 1:1, 7; Matt. 23:35; Bar-achias, KJV; Barachiah, NRSV; also see Jeberechiah, Is. 8:2).

BERED [BEH rid] (hail)

A descendant of Ephraim (1 Chr. 7:20). Bered is also called Becher (Num. 26:35).

BERI [BEH rih]

A son of Zophah, of the tribe of Asher (1 Chr. 7:36).

BERIAH [beh RYE uh]

The name of four men in the Old Testament:

1. A descendant of Asher and the father of Heber and Malchiel (Gen. 46:17; Num. 26:44–45; 1 Chr. 7:30–31). Beriah was the head of the family of Beriites (Num. 26:44).

2. A descendant of Ephraim (1 Chr. 7:23), born after his brothers were killed by the Philistines.

3. A descendant of Benjamin (1 Chr. 8:13, 16).

4. A Levite, a son of Shimei the Ger-shonite (1 Chr. 23:10–11).

BERNICE [ber NIECE] (victorious)

The oldest daughter of Herod Agrippa I, who ruled Palestine A.D. 37–44 (Acts 25:13). According to the historian Josephus, she was first married to a man named Marcus and later to her uncle Herod, king of Chalcis, who soon after-ward died. She later married Polemo,

king of Cilicia, but deserted him shortly after their wedding. Then she made her way to Jerusalem, where she lived with Agrippa II. She was with Agrippa II when the apostle Paul made his defense before him (Acts 25:13, 23; 26:30).

Bernice eventually became a mistress of the Roman emperor Vespasian, then of his son Titus. Bernice and her sister Drusilla (Acts 24:24) were two of the most corrupt and shameless women of their time.

BERODACH–BALADAN [bih ROE dak BAL uh dan]

A form of Merodach–Baladan.

BESAI [BEE sigh]

A man whose descendants returned to Jerusalem with Zerubbabel after the Captivity (Ezra 2:49; Neh. 7:52).

BESODEIAH [bes oh DEE yuh] (in the intimate counsel of the Lord)

The father of Meshullam, who helped repair the Old Gate of Jerusalem (Neh. 3:6).

BETH–RAPHA [beth RAY fuh] (house of healing)

A man listed in the genealogy of Ju-dah. He was a son of Eshton (1 Chr. 4:12).

BETH ZUR [beth ZOOR] (house of rock)

The name of a person in the Old Testament. A son of Maon (1 Chr. 2:45).

BETHLEHEM [BETH luh hem] (house of bread or house of [the god] Lahmu)

A son of Salma, a descendant of Caleb (1 Chr. 2:51). As the "father" of Bethle-hem, Salma may have been the founder of Bethlehem rather than being the fa-ther of a son named "Bethlehem."

BETHUEL [beh THUE el] (*house of God*)

A son of Nahor and Milcah. Bethuel also was Abraham's nephew and the father of Laban and Rebekah (Gen. 22:22–23).

BETHUL [beh THOOL]

A form of BETHUEL.

BEZAI [BEE zay eye]

The founder of a family of Israelites who returned from the Captivity (Ezra 2:17; Neh. 7:23).

BEZALEEL [BEZ uh leel] (*in the shadow of God*)

The name of two Old Testament men:
1. The chief architect and designer of the tabernacle (Ex. 36:1–2; Bezalel, NASB, REB, NIV, NRSV). Along with Aholiab of the tribe of Dan, Bezaleel supervised the tabernacle's construction and the manufacture of its furniture.
2. A man who divorced his pagan wife after the Captivity (Ezra 10:30).

BEZALEL [BEZ uh lel]

A form of BEZALEEL.

BEZER [BEE zur]

A son of Zophah, one of the chiefs of Asher (1 Chr. 7:37).

BICHRI [BICK rih] (*firstborn*)

A Benjamite, the father of Sheba who rebelled against King David (2 Sam. 20:1–22; Bicri, NIV).

BIDKAR [BID car]

One of Jehu's captains. Bidkar threw the body of King JORAM (Jehoram) into the field of Naboth the Jezreelite after Jehu killed him (2 Kin. 9:25).

BIGTHA [BIG thuh] (*gift of God*)

One of the seven eunuchs, or chamberlains, who had charge of the harem of King Ahasuerus (Xerxes) of Persia (Esth. 1:10).

BIGTHAN [BIG than] (*gift of god*)

One of the two eunuchs or chamberlains who conspired to take the life of King Ahasuerus (Xerxes) of Persia. They were executed for their treachery when Mordecai discovered their conspiracy (Esth. 2:21; 6:2; Bigthana, NIV).

BIGVAI [BIG vah eye]

The head of one of the families who returned from Babylonia with Zerubbabel (Ezra 2:2).

BILDAD [BILL dad]

The second of the "friends" or "comforters" of Job. In his three speeches to Job (Job 8:1–22; 18:1–21; 25:1–6), Bildad expressed the belief that all suffering is the direct result of one's sin. He had little patience with the questionings and searchings of Job. He is called "Bildad the Shuhite" (Job. 2:11), which means he belonged to an Aramean nomadic tribe that lived in the Transjordan area southeast of Canaan. Also see ELIHU; ELIPHAZ; ZOPHAR.

BILGAH [BILL guh]

The name of two men in the Old Testament:
1. Chief of the 15th group of priests officiating in Temple service in King David's time (1 Chr. 24:14).
2. A chief of the priests who returned from the Captivity with Zerubbabel (Neh. 12:5, 18). He is also called BILGAI (Neh. 10:8).

BILGAI [BILL gay eye]

A priest who sealed the covenant after the Captivity (Neh. 10:8). He is also called Bilgah (Neh. 12:5, 18).

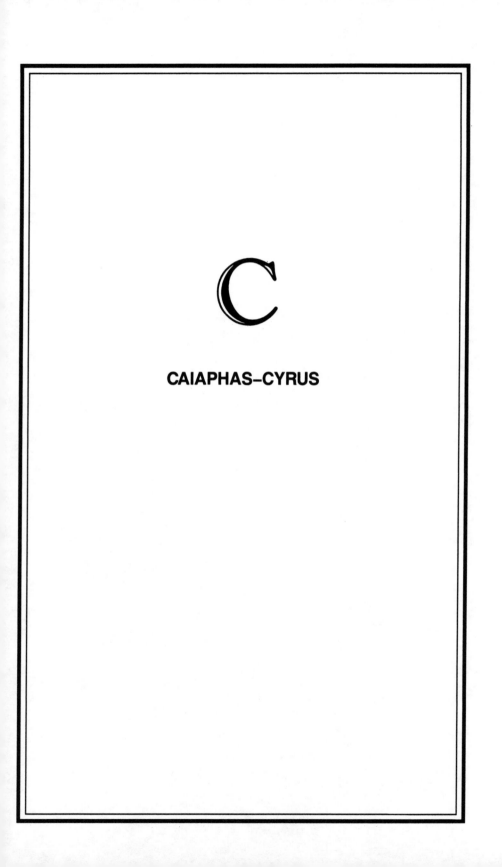

C

CAIAPHAS–CYRUS

CAIAPHAS [KY uh fuhs]

The high priest of Israel appointed about A.D. 18 by the Roman procurator, Valerius Gratus. Caiaphas and his father-in-law, Annas, were high priests when John the Baptist began his preaching (Matt. 26:3, 57; Luke 3:2). Caiaphas also was a member of the Sadducees.

After Jesus raised LAZARUS from the dead, the Jewish leaders became alarmed at Jesus' increasing popularity. The Sanhedrin quickly called a meeting, during which Caiaphas called for Jesus' death. As High Priest, Caiaphas' words carried great authority, and his counsel was followed (John 11:49–53). Subsequently, Caiaphas plotted the arrest of Jesus (Matt. 26:3–4) and was a participant in the illegal trial of Jesus (Matt. 26:57–68).

The final appearance of Caiaphas in the New Testament was at the trial of Peter and John. He was one of the leaders who questioned the two disciples about the miraculous healing of the lame man "at the gate of the temple which is called Beautiful" Acts 4:6–7). In 1990, an ornate ossuary bearing the name of Caiaphas and containing the bones of a 60-year-old man was found outside of Jerusalem. The bones may be those of Caiaphas himself.

CAIN [kane] (metalworker)

The oldest son of Adam and Eve and the brother of Abel (Gen. 4:1–25). Cain was the first murderer. A farmer by occupation, Cain brought fruits of the ground as a sacrifice to God. His brother Abel, a shepherd, sacrificed a lamb from his flock. The Lord accepted Abel's offering but rejected Cain's (Gen. 4:7). The proof of Cain's wrong standing before God is seen in his impulse to kill his own brother Abel when his own offering was rejected (Gen. 4:8). Cain was the ancestor of a clan of metalworkers (Gen. 4:18–19, 22).

The New Testament refers to Cain in three places. Abel's offering to God was "a more excellent sacrifice" than Cain's because Abel was "righteous." His heart was right with God, and Cain's was not (Heb. 11:4). John calls Cain "the wicked one" and asks why he murdered his brother; the answer was, "Because his works were evil, and his brother's righteous" (1 John 3:12). Jude warns his readers to beware of those who have "gone in the way of Cain" (Jude 11).

CAINAN [kay EYE nuhn]

The name of two men in the Bible:

1. A son of Enosh and an ancestor of Jesus (Gen. 5:9–14; Luke 3:37), also spelled Kenan (1 Chr. 1:2, KJV, NIV).

2. A son of Arphaxad and an ancestor of Jesus (Luke 3:36).

CALCOL [KAL kahl]

A descendant of Judah (1 Chr. 2:6), also spelled Chalcol (1 Kin. 4:31).

CALEB [KAY lubb] (dog)

The name of two men in the Old Testament:

1. One of the 12 spies sent by Moses to investigate the land of Canaan (Num. 13:6, 30; 14:6, 24, 30, 38). Ten of the 12 spies frightened the Israelites with reports of fortified cities and gigantic peoples. Compared to the giants in the land, they saw themselves as "grasshoppers" (Num. 13:33).

Joshua and Caleb also saw the fortified cities in the land, but they reacted in faith rather than fear. They advised Moses and Aaron and the Israelites to attack Canaan immediately (Num. 13:30). The Israelites listened to the spies rather than the two, and the Lord viewed their fear as a lack of faith and judged them for their spiritual timidity. Of all the adults alive at that time, only Caleb and Joshua would live to possess the land (Josh. 14:6–15).

Caleb was also part of the group selected by Moses to help divide the land among the tribes. He was 85 years old when Canaan was finally conquered. Hebron was given to Caleb as a divine inheritance.

2. A son of Hezron of the family of Perez of the tribe of Judah (1 Chr. 2:18–19, 42). Descended from this Caleb were Aaron's associate Hur and Hur's grandson Bezaleel, a skilled craftsman. An alternate spelling of the name is Chelubai (1 Chr. 2:9).

CANAAN [KANE un] (land of purple)

The fourth son of Ham and the grandson of Noah (Gen. 9:18–27; 10:6, 15). Ham's descendants were dispersed into several distinctive tribes, such as the Jebusites and the Zemarites. These people became known collectively in later years as the Canaanites, pagan inhabitants of the land that God promised to Abraham and his descendants. Under the leadership of Joshua, the people of Israel occupied the land of Canaan and divided it among the twelve tribes.

CANAANITE, SIMON THE [KANE un ite]

(See SIMON.)

CANANAEAN [kane uh NEE uhn]

(See SIMON.)

CANDACE [KAN duh see]

A queen of Ethiopia (Acts 8:27). Candace, a title, did not refer to a particular queen but to a line of queens. The eunuch of the Candace in Acts was converted to Christianity by Philip the evangelist (Acts 8:26–39).

CARCAS [KAHR cuss]

One of the seven eunuchs, or chamberlains, who had charge of the harem of King Ahasuerus (Xerxes) of Persia (Esth. 1:10; CARKAS, NRSV).

CAREAH [keh REE ah]

A form of KAREAH.

CARKAS [KAHR cuss]

A form of CARCAS.

CARMI [KAHR mye] (vineyard owner, vinedresser)

The name of two or three men in the Old Testament:

1. A son of Reuben who went to Egypt with Jacob (Gen. 46:1–9).

2. A descendant of Judah and the father of Achan (Josh. 7:1, 18), or Achar (1 Chr. 2:7).

3. A son of Judah (1 Chr. 4:1). He may be the same person as Carmi No. 2, although some scholars see this Carmi as an alternative form of Caleb.

CARPUS [KAHR puhs] (fruit)

A resident of Troas with whom the apostle Paul left his cloak. Paul later sent for the cloak (2 Tim. 4:13).

CARSHENA [kahr SHE nuh]

A high Persian official at Shushan (Susa). He was one of seven princes "who had access to the king's presence" (Esth. 1:14). The "king" was Ahasuerus, generally identified as Xerxes I (485–464 B.C.).

CEPHAS [SEE fuhs] (rock)

The Aramaic name of Simon the son of Jonah (John 1:42), given to him by Christ.

CAIN

C

CHEDORLAOMER [ked awr LAY oh muhr] (*servant of* [the Elamite god] *Lagamar*)

A king of Elam, a country east of Babylonia, in Abraham's day (Gen. 14:1, 4–5, 9, 17; Kedorlaomer, NIV). Allied with three other Mesopotamian kings—Amraphel of Shinar, Arioch of Ellasar, and Tidal of "nations"—Chedorlaomer led a campaign against southern Canaan and defeated the inhabitants in the Valley of Siddim near the Dead Sea. The conquered people served Chedorlaomer for 12 years, but in the 13th year they rebelled (Gen. 14:4).

Chedorlaomer came again with his allies and conquered the region east of the Jordan River from Bashan southward to the Red Sea as well as the plain around the Dead Sea, thus gaining control of the lucrative caravan routes from Arabia and Egypt through Canaan. In making this conquest, Chedorlaomer captured Lot, Abraham's nephew. Aided by his allies and numerous servants, Abraham launched a night attack on Chedorlaomer at Dan, defeating him and recovering Lot and the spoils. Although Chedorlaomer has not been identified in references outside the Old Testament, the elements of his name are typically Elamite.

CHELAL [KEE lal] (*completeness*)

An Israelite who divorced his pagan wife after the Captivity (Ezra 10:30; Kelal, NIV).

CHELLUH [KEL oo]

A form of CHELUH.

CHELUB [KEE luhb] (bird's cage)

The name of two men in the Old Testament:

1. A brother of Shuhah, a Judahite (1 Chr. 4:11).

2. The father of Ezri, a supervisor of those who tilled the soil during David's reign (1 Chr. 27:26; Kelub, NIV).

CHELUBAI [kih LOO bye]

A son of Hezron and grandfather of Caleb (1 Chr. 2:9). Chelubai is also spelled Caleb (1 Chr. 2:18–19, 42).

CHELUH [KEL oo] ([Jehovah is] perfect)

A Levite who divorced his pagan wife after the Captivity (Ezra 10:35; Chelluh, KJV; Cheluhi, NRSV, NASB; Keluhi, NIV, REB).

CHELUHI [keh LOU high]

A form of CHELUH.

CHENAANAH [kih NAY uh nuh]

The name of two men in the Old Testament:

1. The father or ancestor of Zedekiah (1 Kin. 22:11, 24; 2 Chr. 18:10, 23).

2. A son of Bilhan, listed in the family of Benjamin (1 Chr. 7:10; Kenaanah, NIV).

CHENANI [kih NAY nigh]

A Levite who assisted at Ezra's public reading of the Book of the Law (Neh. 9:4; Kenani, NIV).

CHENANIAH [ken uh NYE uh] (the Lord has established)

A chief Levite during the days when David brought the Ark of the Covenant to the Temple (1 Chr. 15:22, 27; Kenaniah, NIV).

CHERAN [KEE ruhn]

A son of Dishon (Gen. 36:26; 1 Chr. 1:41; Keran, NIV).

CHESED [KEE sed]

The fourth son of Nahor and a nephew of Abraham (Gen. 22:22; Kesed, NIV).

CHILEAB [KIL ih ab]

A son of David and Abigail (2 Sam. 3:3; Kileab, NIV); he also was called Daniel (1 Chr. 3:1).

CHILION [KIL ih ahn] (wasting away)

The younger son of Elimelech and Naomi and the husband of Orpah, Ruth's sister-in-law (Ruth 1:2, 5; 4:9–10; Kilion, NIV).

CHIMHAM [KIM ham]

A friend and political supporter of David, perhaps the son of Barzillai the Gileadite. After Absalom's defeat, he returned from beyond the Jordan River with David to Jerusalem (2 Sam. 19:37–40; Kimham, NIV). The "habitation [or lodging place] of Chimham" (Jer. 41:17; Geruth Kimham, NIV) may have been an inn given to Chimham by David as a reward for his loyalty.

CHISLON [KIZ lahn]

The father of ELIDAD (Num. 34:21; Kislon, NIV).

CHLOE [KLOH ee]

A woman, presumably a Christian, possibly from Corinth or Ephesus, who knew of the divisions and dissensions within the church at Corinth (1 Cor. 1:11).

CHRIST (anointed one)

A name for Jesus that showed that He was the long-awaited king and deliverer.

C

For centuries the Jewish people had looked for a prophesied Messiah, a deliverer who would usher in a kingdom of peace and prosperity (Ps. 110; Is. 32:1–8; 61:1–3; Amos 9:13). Jesus was clearly identified as this Messiah in Peter's great confession, "You are the Christ, the Son of the living God" (Matt. 16:16). Also see JESUS CHRIST; MESSIAH.

CHUZA [KOO zuh]

A steward (business manager) of Herod Antipas and evidently a man of position and wealth. His wife, Joanna, was one of the women who "provided for Him [Jesus] from their substance" (Luke 8:3; Cuza, NIV).

CLAUDIA [CLAW dih uh]

A Roman Christian who joined Paul in sending Timothy Christian greetings (2 Tim. 4:21). Some scholars suggest that Claudia was the wife of the Pudens mentioned in the same verse and that Linus, who would become a bishop of Rome, was their son.

CLAUDIUS [CLAW dih us]

The fourth emperor of the Roman Empire (A.D. 41–54), Tiberius Claudius Nero Germanicus, who suppressed the worship activities of the Jewish people in the city of Rome.

Early in his reign as emperor, Claudius was favorable toward the Jews and their practice of religion. But he later forbade their assembly and eventually "commanded all the Jews to depart from Rome" (Acts 18:2). This edict may have extended also to Christians, who were considered a sect of the Jews at that time.

Aquila and Priscilla, who became friends of the apostle Paul, were refugees from Italy because of this order of the Roman emperor (Acts 18:1–2). The Book of Acts also refers to a great famine that "happened in the days of Claudius Caesar" (Acts 11:28).

CLAUDIUS LYSIAS [CLAW dih us LISS ih us]

(See LYSIAS.)

CLEMENT [KLEM ent] (*merciful*)

A Christian who worked with the apostle Paul, apparently at Philippi (Phil. 4:3). Writers such as Origen, Eusebius, and Jerome supposed this Clement to be the apostolic father known as Clement of Rome. Modern scholars, however, believe this identification is highly unlikely.

CLEOPAS [KLEE uh pus]

One of the two disciples with whom Jesus talked on the Emmaus Road on the day of His resurrection (Luke 24:18). Cleopas is apparently not the same person as Cleophas—or Clopas (NRSV)—of John 19:25.

CLEOPHAS [KLEE uh fus]

A form of CLOPAS.

CLOPAS [KLOE puhs]

The husband of Mary, one of the women who was present at the crucifixion of Jesus (John 19:25; Cleophas, KJV). According to tradition, Clopas was the same person as Alphaeus, the father of James the Less and of Joses (Matt. 10:3; Mark 15:40). Most scholars agree that Clopas is not the same person as CLEOPAS (Luke 24:18).

COL-HOZEH [kole HOE zeh] (*wholly a seer*)

The name of one or two men in the Old Testament:

1. The father of Shallun, the man who repaired the Fountain Gate of Jerusalem after the Captivity (Neh. 3:15).

2. The father of Baruch of the tribe of Judah (Neh. 11:5). This is possibly the same person as Col–Hozeh No. 1.

CONANIAH [kone ah NYE ah] (*the Lord establishes*)

A chief of the Levites who assisted in the celebration of the Passover during the reign of King Josiah (2 Chr. 35:9). Also see CONONIAH.

CONIAH [koe NYE ah]

A form of JEHOIACHIN.

CONONIAH [kone oh NYE ah] (*the Lord establishes*)

A Levite appointed overseer of the tithes and offerings at the Temple during the reign of King Hezekiah (2 Chr. 31:12–13; Conaniah, NRSV, NIV).

CORNELIUS [kor NEEL yus]

A Roman soldier stationed in Caesarea who was the first recorded Gentile convert to Christianity (Acts 10:1–33).

Cornelius was a God-fearing man strongly attracted to the Jewish teaching of monotheism (the belief in one God), as opposed to pagan idolatry and immorality, and to the concern expressed in the law of Moses concerning helping the poor and needy (Acts 10:2). He is introduced in the Book of Acts as a representative of thousands in the Gentile world who were weary of paganism and who were hungry for the coming of the Messiah—the Christ who would deliver them from their sins and lead them into an abundant, Spirit-filled life.

God sent a heavenly vision both to Cornelius and to Simon Peter. Obeying his vision, Cornelius sent some of his men to Joppa, about 58 kilometers (36 miles) south of Caesarea, to find Peter. Peter, in turn, obeyed his own vision (which he interpreted to mean that Gentiles were to be included in Christ's message) and went to Cornelius. While Peter was still preaching to Cornelius and his household, "the Holy Spirit fell upon all those who heard the word" (Acts 10:44). And Peter commanded them to be baptized in the name of the Lord.

This incident marked the expansion of the early church to include Gentiles as well as Jews (Acts 10:34–35; 11:18). Peter alluded to Cornelius' conversion at the Jerusalem Council (Acts 15:7–11).

COSAM [KOE sam]

A descendant of David and an ancestor of Jesus (Luke 3:28).

COZBI [KOZ bih] (*lying, deceitful*)

A Midianite princess slain by Phinehas, the grandson of Aaron, because Zimri apparently took her to be his wife or concubine against the orders of Moses (Num. 25:15, 18).

CRESCENS [KRESS enz]

A Christian mentioned by Paul (2 Tim. 4:10). For some reason, Crescens left Paul and departed for Galatia.

CRIMINALS, TWO

Two men who were crucified at the same time as Jesus, one on His right hand and the other on His left (Luke 23:32–33, 39; malefactors, KJV). Apparently, these men not only broke the law but also were guilty of armed, violent rebellion against Roman rule.

CRISPUS [KRIS pus]

The ruler of the Jewish synagogue at Corinth who was converted to Christ (Acts 18:8) and personally baptized by the apostle Paul (1 Cor. 1:14).

DALAIAH [duh LAY ah]

A form of DELAIAH.

DALPHON [dal FON]

The second of the ten sons of Haman, who was the adviser to King Ahasuerus. All of Haman's sons were hanged like their father (Esth. 9:7).

DAMARIS [DAM uh riss]

A woman of Athens converted as a result of Paul's sermon on Mars' Hill (Acts 17:34). The fact that she was singled out along with Dionysius the Areopagite, one of the court judges, may indicate she was a woman of distinction.

DAN [dan] (*a judge*)

The fifth son of Jacob and the first born to Rachel's handmaid Bilhah (Gen. 30:1-6). Dan had one son—Hushim (Gen. 46:23), or Shuham (Num. 26:42). Jacob's blessing of Dan predicted:

Dan shall judge his people
As one of the tribes of Israel.
Dan shall be a serpent by the way,
A viper by the path,
That bites the horse's heels,
So that its rider shall fall backward
    (Gen. 49:16–17).

Nothing else is known of Dan himself.

DANIEL [DAN yuhl] (*God is my judge*)

The name of three or four men in the Bible:

1. A son of David and Abigail (1 Chr. 3:1). He is also called Chileab (2 Sam. 3:3).

2. A priest of the family of Ithamar who returned with Ezra from the Captivity (Ezra 8:2). Daniel sealed the covenant in the days of Nehemiah (Neh. 10:6).

3. A wise (Ezek. 28:3) and righteous man (perhaps non-Israelite), mentioned together with Noah and Job (Ezek. 14:14, 20), to be identified with an ancient Ca-naanite worthy named Daniel or equated with No. 4.

4. A prophet during the period of the Captivity of God's Covenant People in Babylon and Persia (Dan. 1:6—12:9; Matt. 24:15). Daniel also wrote the book in the Old Testament that bears his name.

Daniel was a teenager when he was taken from Jerusalem into captivity by the Babylonians in 605 B.C. He was in his 80s when he received the vision of the prophecy of the 70 weeks (Daniel 9). In more than 60 years of his life in Babylon, Daniel faced many challenges. But in all those years, he grew stronger in his commitment to God.

We know very little about Daniel's personal life. His family history is not mentioned, but he was probably from an upper-class family in Jerusalem. It seems unlikely that Nebuchadnezzar, the king of Babylon, would have selected a trainee for his court from the lower classes. Neither do we know whether Daniel married or had a family. As a servant in Nebuchadnezzar's court, he may have been castrated and made into a eunuch, as was common in those days. But the text does not specify that this happened. It does indicate that Daniel was a person of extraordinary abilities.

We tend to think of Daniel as a prophet because of the prophetic dimension of his book. But he also served as an advisor in the courts of foreign kings. Daniel remained in governmental service through the reigns of the kings of Babylon and into the reign of Cyrus of Persia after the Persians became the dominant world power (Dan. 1:21; 10:1).

Daniel was also a person of deep piety. His book is characterized not only by prophecies of the distant future but also by a sense of wonder at the presence of

God. From his youth Daniel was determined to live by God's law in a distant land (see Daniel 1). In moments of crisis, Daniel turned first to God in prayer before turning to the affairs of state (2:14–23). His enemies even used his regularity at prayer to trap him and turn the king against him. But the grace of God protected Daniel (chap. 6).

After one of his stunning prophecies (chap. 9), Daniel prayed a noble prayer of confession for his own sins and the sins of his people. This prayer was based on Daniel's study of the Book of Jeremiah (Dan. 9:2). He was a man of true devotion to God.

So the Book of Daniel is more than a treasure of prophetic literature. It also paints a beautiful picture of a man of God who lived out his commitment in very troubled times. We should never get so caught up in the meanings of horns and beasts that we forget the human dimension of the book—the intriguing person whose name means "God Is My Judge."

DARA [DARE uh]

A son of Zerah, of the tribe of Judah (1 Chr. 2:6). Also see DARDA.

DARDA [DAR duh] (*pearl of wisdom*)

A wise man with whom Solomon was compared (1 Kin. 4:31). He may have been the same as Dara (1 Chr. 2:6). As one of the "sons of MAHOL," Darda was a member of the musical guild.

DARIUS [duh RYE us]

The name of several rulers of ancient Persia:

1. Darius I, the Great, who reigned from about 522 to 485 B.C. He was one of the most able Persian kings, and is also known as Darius Hystaspis, or Darius, son of Hystaspis.

Darius spent the first three years of his reign putting down rebellions in the far-flung regions of his empire. After he had secured his power, he divided the empire into 29 satrapies, or provinces, each ruled by Persian or Median nobles. He made Shushan, or Susa, his new capital and created a code of laws similar to the Code of Hammurapi; this code of Darius was in effect throughout the Persian Empire.

An effective organizer and administrator, Darius developed trade, built a network of roads, established a postal system, standardized a system of coinage, weights, and measures, and initiated fabulous building projects at Persepolis, Ecbatana, and Babylon.

Darius continued Cyrus the Great's policy of restoring the Jewish people to their homeland. In 520 B.C., Darius' second year as king (Hag. 1:1; Zech. 1:1), the Jews resumed work on the still unfinished Temple in Jerusalem. Darius assisted with the project by ordering it to continue and even sending a generous subsidy to help restore worship in the Temple (Ezra 6:1–12). The Temple was completed in 516–515 B.C., in the sixth year of Darius' reign (Ezra 6:15).

The final years of Darius' reign were marked by clashes with the rising Greek Empire in the western part of his domain. He led two major military campaigns against the Greeks, both of which were unsuccessful.

2. Darius II Ochus, the son of Artaxerxes I, who ruled over Persia from about 424 to 405 B.C. He was not popular or successful, and he spent much time putting down revolts among his subjects. His rule was marked by incompetence and misgovernment. Darius II may be the ruler referred to as "Darius the Persian" (Neh. 12:22).

D

3. Darius III Codomannus, the king of Persia from 336 to 330 B.C. This Darius is probably the "fourth" king of Persia mentioned by the prophet Daniel (Dan. 11:2). Darius III underestimated the strength of the army of ALEXANDER the Great when the Macedonians invaded Persia. He was defeated by Alexander in several major battles. He attempted to rally the eastern provinces of his empire, but he was hunted down in 330 B.C. and assassinated by his own followers. For all practical purposes, these events brought the Persian Empire to an end and marked the beginning of the period of Greek dominance in the ancient world.

4. Darius the Mede, successor of Belshazzar to the throne of Babylon (Dan. 5:31). He is called the "son of Ahasuerus, of the lineage of the Medes" (Dan. 9:1). Darius the Mede has not been identified with certainty; he is not mentioned by Greek historians or in any Persian literature.

Darius the Mede was the Persian king who made Daniel a governor, or ruler, of several provincial leaders (Dan. 6:1–2). Daniel's popularity with his subjects caused the other governors and the satraps under them to become jealous of Daniel and to plot against him. It was Darius the Mede who had Daniel thrown into the den of lions (Dan. 6:6–9), but who ultimately issued a decree that all in his kingdom "must tremble and fear before the God of Daniel" (Dan. 6:26).

Much confusion and mystery have clouded the identity of Darius the Mede. Some scholars have denied the existence of such a ruler, concluding that the writer of the Book of Daniel was historically inaccurate in saying that Darius the Mede was the person who "received the kingdom" (Dan. 5:31) when Belshazzar, king of Babylonia, was slain. Persian cuneiform inscriptions show that Cyrus II ("the Great") was the successor of Belshazzar.

One possible answer to this problem is that "Darius the Mede" was the army general sent by Cyrus to conquer Babylon. It is also possible that "Darius the Mede" was an alternative name or title used by the writer of the Book of Daniel for Cyrus the Persian himself. Indeed, in Daniel 11:1, the Septuagint—the Greek translation of the Old Testament—has Cyrus instead of Darius. Thus, a quite legitimate translation of Daniel 6:28 might read: "Daniel prospered during the reign of Darius, that is, the reign of Cyrus the Persian" (NIV, margin). Such a logical and reasonable interpretation silences the skepticism about this passage in the Book of Daniel.

DARKON [DAR kahn]

A servant of Solomon whose descendants returned to the land of Israel after the Captivity (Ezra 2:56; Neh. 7:58).

DATHAN [DAY thun]

A chief of the tribe of Reuben who, along with Korah and others, tried to overthrow Moses and Aaron (Num. 16; Deut. 11:6; Ps. 106:17). He and his conspirators and their households were swallowed up by the earth (Num. 16:31–33).

DAVID [DAY vid] (beloved)

Second king of the United Kingdom of Israel, ancestor of Jesus Christ, and writer of numerous psalms. The record of David's life is found in 1 Samuel 16—31; 2 Samuel 1—24; 1 Kings 1—2; and 1 Chronicles 10—29. An Aramaic inscription including the words "house [dynasty] of David" was found in 1993 in the ruins of the city of Dan. It dates to the 9th century B.C. and is the only known mention of David in ancient contemporary writings outside of the Old Testament itself.

David as a Youth.

David's youth was spent in Bethlehem. The youngest of eight brothers (1 Sam. 16:10–11; 17:12–14), he was the son of Jesse, a respected citizen of the city. His mother was tenderly remembered for her godliness (Ps. 86:16). As the youngest son, David was the keeper of his father's sheep. In this job he showed courage and faithfulness by killing both a lion and a bear that attacked the flock.

As a lad, he displayed outstanding musical talent with the harp, a fact that figured prominently in his life. When Saul was rejected by God as king, the prophet Samuel went to Bethlehem to anoint David as the future king of Israel. Apparently, there was no public announcement of this event, although David and his father surely must have been aware of it.

David's Service Under Saul.

King Saul, forsaken by God and troubled by an evil spirit, was subject to moods of depression and insanity. His attendants advised him to secure a harpist, whose music might soothe his spirit. David was recommended for this task. As harpist for Saul, David was exposed to governmental affairs, a situation that prepared him for his later service as king of Israel. Apparently, David did not remain with Saul all the time, since the Bible indicates he returned to Bethlehem to continue caring for his father's sheep.

During one of these visits to his home, the Philistines invaded the country and camped 24 kilometers (15 miles) west of Bethlehem. Saul led the army of Israel to meet the enemy. Three of David's brothers were in Saul's army, and Jesse sent David to the battle area to inquire about their welfare. While on this expedition, David encountered the Philistine giant, GOLIATH.

David as Warrior.

Goliath's challenge for an Israelite to do battle with him stirred David's spirit. Weighted with heavy armor, Goliath was equipped to engage in close-range combat. David's strategy was to fight him at a distance. Taking five smooth stones from a brook, David faced Goliath with only a sling and his unflinching faith in God. Goliath fell, struck by a stone from David's sling. For this feat, he became a hero in the eyes of the nation. But it aroused jealousy and animosity in the heart of Saul. Saul's son, Jonathan, however, admired David because of his bravery, and they soon became good friends. This friendship lasted until Jonathan's death, in spite of Saul's hostility toward David.

Saul had promised to make the victor in the battle with Goliath his son-in-law, presenting one of his daughters as his wife. He also promised to free the victor's family from taxation. But after the battle, David was no longer allowed to return occasionally to his father's house. He remained at Saul's palace continually. Perhaps Saul realized that Samuel's prediction that the kingdom would be taken from him could reach fulfillment in David. On two occasions, he tried to kill David with a spear; he also gave his daughter, whom he had promised as David's wife, to another man. As David's popularity grew, Saul's fear increased until he could no longer hide his desire to kill him. David was forced to flee with Saul in pursuit.

David as Fugitive Hero.

David gathered a handful of fugitives as his followers and fled from Saul. On at least two occasions, David could have killed Saul while the king slept, but he refused to do so. Perhaps David hesitated to kill Saul because he realized that he

would be king one day, and he wanted the office to be treated with respect. If he had killed Saul, David also would have entered the office of king through his own personal violence. Perhaps this was a situation he wanted to avoid.

When the Philistines battled Saul and his army at Gilboa, they were victorious, killing Saul and his son, Jonathan, whom David loved as a dear friend. When David heard this news, he mourned their fate (2 Samuel 1).

David as King of Judah.

At Saul's death the tribe of Judah, to whom David belonged, elected him as king of Judah and placed him on the throne in Hebron. The rest of the tribes of Israel set up ISHBOSHETH, Saul's son, as king at Mahanaim. For the next two years civil war raged between these two factions. It ended in the assassination of Ishbosheth, an event that saddened David.

David as King of All Israel.

On the death of Ishbosheth, David was elected king over all the people of Israel. He immediately began work to establish a United Kingdom. One of his first acts as king was to attack the fortified city of Jebus. Although the inhabitants thought it was safe from capture, David and his army took it. He then made it the capital city of his kingdom and erected his palace there. Also known as Jerusalem, the new capital stood on the border of the southern tribe of Judah and the other tribal territories to the north. This location tended to calm the jealousies between the north and the south, contributing greatly to the unity of the kingdom.

After establishing his new political capital, David proceeded to re-establish and strengthen the worship of God. He moved the Ark of the Covenant from Kir-jath Jearim (Josh. 15:9) and placed it within a tabernacle that he pitched in Jerusalem. Next, he organized worship on a magnificent scale and began plans to build a house of worship. But God brought a halt to his plans, informing David that the building of the Temple would be entrusted to his successor.

Although David was a righteous king, he was subject to sin, just like other human beings. On one occasion when his army went to battle, David stayed home. This led to his great sin with BATHSHEBA. While Uriah, the Hittite, Bathsheba's husband, was away in battle, David committed adultery with her. Then in an effort to cover his sin, he finally had Uriah killed in battle. David was confronted by the prophet NATHAN, who courageously exposed his wrongdoing. Faced with his sin, David repented and asked for God's forgiveness. His prayer for forgiveness is recorded in Psalm 51.

Although God forgave David of this act of adultery, the consequences of the sin continued to plague him. The child born to David and Bathsheba died. The example he set as a father was a bad influence on his sons. One son, Amnon, raped and humiliated his half-sister. Another son, ABSALOM, rebelled against David and tried to take away his kingdom by force.

One of David's deep desires was to build a temple in Jerusalem. But he was prevented from doing so. The prophet Nathan informed David that he would not build the temple because he had been a warrior. David did not build the temple, but he did gather material for the temple to be built later. It was Solomon, David's son and successor, who finally erected the first temple in Jerusalem.

David died when he was 71 years old, having been king for a total of over 40 years, including both his reign in Hebron and his kingship over the United Kingdom.

David as Psalmist.

Early in his life David distinguished himself as the "sweet psalmist of Israel" (2 Sam. 23:1). Many of the psalms in the Book of Psalms are attributed to him.

David's fondness for music is recorded in many places in the Bible. He played skillfully on the harp (1 Sam. 16:18–23). He arranged worship services in the sanctuary (1 Chr. 6:31). He composed psalms of lament over Saul and Jonathan (2 Sam. 1:17–27). His musical activity was referred to by Amos (Amos 6:5), Ezra (Ezra 3:10), and Nehemiah (Neh. 7:24, 46).

David as Ancestor to Jesus Christ.

Jesus was referred to as the Son of David. The genealogy of Jesus as recorded in the Gospels of Matthew and Luke traced Jesus back through the ancestry of David. God promised David a kingdom that would have no end. This prophecy was fulfilled in Jesus (Luke 1:31–33), who came to establish the Kingdom of God. Jesus was born in Bethlehem because this was the "city of David" (Luke 2:4), David's birthplace and boyhood home.

Although David committed deep sin, he still was known as a man who sought God's will. Certainly he was not perfect, but he was willing to repent of his wrongdoing and to follow God's leadership. His influence for good in the life of his nation was great, since every king of Judah after David was compared to the standard he established.

A capable musician, David unquestionably gave great encouragement to this fine art in the life of his people. As a warrior and military man, he was resourceful and courageous. As a king, he was without equal in the life of his nation. As a religious leader, he was exceptional. Many of his writings will continue to be the favorite devotional literature for honest souls who seek a closer walk with God.

The Jewish historian Josephus praised David by saying, "This man was of an excellent character, and was endowed with all the virtues that were desirable in a king." David was truly a man after God's own heart (1 Sam. 13:14; Acts 13:22).

DEBIR [duh BEER]

A king of Eglon (Josh. 10:3). He was one of five allied Amorite kings who unsuccessfully attempted to halt Joshua's invasion of the land of Canaan (Josh. 10:1–27). Joshua soundly defeated these forces at Gibeon in the famous battle at the time of "Joshua's long day" (Josh. 10:12–13). The five kings were killed and hanged on five separate trees until evening. Their bodies were then placed in the cave where they had hidden (Josh. 10:16–27).

DEBORAH [DEB uh rah] (bee)

The name of two women in the Old Testament:

1. A nurse to Rebekah, Isaac's wife (Gen. 24:59; 35:8). Deborah accompanied Rebekah when she left her home in Mesopotamia to become Isaac's wife and lived with Jacob and Rebekah. She probably spent her years caring for their sons, Jacob and Esau. Deborah died at an advanced age. She was buried below Bethel under a tree that Jacob called Allon Bachuth (literally "oak of weeping")— a fitting name for the burial place of one who had served so long and so faithfully (Gen. 35:8).

2. The fifth judge of Israel, a prophetess and the only female judge (Judg. 4—5). The Bible tells us nothing about her family except that she was the wife of Lapidoth. Deborah's home was in the hill country of Ephraim between Bethel and Ramah. The palm tree under which she sat and judged Israel was a landmark; it became known as "the palm tree of Deborah" (Judg. 4:5).

Deborah summoned Barak (Judg. 4; 5:1; Heb. 11:32) and told him it was God's will that he lead her forces against the mighty warrior, Sisera. Sisera was the

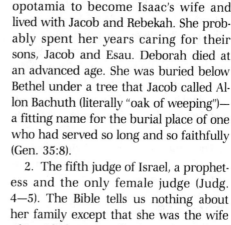

DAVID

commander of the army of Jabin, king of Canaan, who had terrorized Israel for 20 years. Barak accepted on one condition: Deborah must accompany him. Deborah and Barak's army consisted of only 10,000, while Sisera had a multitude of fighters and 900 chariots of iron.

God was on Israel's side, however. When the battle ended, not a single man of Sisera's army survived, except Sisera himself, who fled on foot. When Sisera took refuge in the tent of Heber the Kenite, Jael (the wife of Heber) drove a tent peg through his temple (Judg. 4:21), killing him.

The "Song of Deborah" (Judges 5) is one of the finest and earliest examples of Hebrew poetry.

DEDAN [DEE dun]

The name of two men in the Old Testament:

1. A descendant of Cush (Gen. 10:7; 1 Chr. 1:9).

2. A son of Jokshan and a grandson of Abraham and Keturah (Gen. 25:3; 1 Chr. 1:32).

DELAIAH [dih LAY yah]

The name of five men in the Old Testament:

1. The sixth son of Elioenai, a descendant of Zerubbabel and King David (1 Chr. 3:24; Dalaiah, KJV).

2. A descendant of Aaron and one of David's priests (1 Chr. 24:18).

3. One of the Nethinim (Temple servants) who returned from the Captivity with Zerubbabel (Ezra 2:60; Neh. 7:62).

4. The father of a contemporary of Nehemiah (Neh. 6:10).

5. A son of Shemaiah who pleaded with King Jehoiakim not to destroy the scroll containing Jeremiah's prophecies (Jer. 36:12, 25).

DELILAH [dih LIE lah]

The woman loved by Samson, the mightiest of Israel's judges. She was probably a Philistine. She betrayed Samson to the lords of the Philistines for 1,100 pieces of silver (Judg. 16:5). Deluding Samson into believing she loved him, Delilah persuaded him to tell her the secret of his strength—his long hair, which was the symbol of his Nazirite vow. While Samson slept at her home in the Valley of Sorek, the Philistines entered and cut his hair. With his strength gone, Samson was easily captured and imprisoned, then blinded.

No biblical evidence supports the popular belief that Delilah was deeply repentant over her actions. She even may have been one of the 3,000 Philistines buried beneath the temple of Dagon Samson destroyed when his God-given strength returned (Judg. 16:27–30).

DEMAS [DEE mus]

A friend and co-worker of the apostle Paul at Rome. Demas later deserted Paul, "having loved this present world" (2 Tim. 4:10; Col. 4:14; Philem. 24).

DEMETRIUS [dih ME tree us]

The name of two men in the New Testament:

1. A silversmith at Ephesus (Acts 19:24, 38) who made and sold silver models of the city's famed temple of the goddess Diana (Artemis). Alarmed at what the spread of the gospel would do to his business, Demetrius incited a riot against the apostle Paul. For two hours, the mob cried, "Great is Diana of the Ephesians!" (Acts 19:28, 34). The mob was quieted by the city clerk (Acts 19:35–40). Later, Paul left Ephesus for Macedonia (Acts 20:1).

2. A Christian commended by John because he had "a good testimony from all" (3 John 12).

DEUEL [DEW el] (knowledge of god)

The father of Eliasaph, who was leader of the tribe of Gad when the people of Israel were numbered at Sinai (Num. 1:14; 7:42; 10:20). He is also called Reuel (Num. 2:14).

DIBLAIM [dib LAY im] (double cakes of figs)

The father-in-law of Hosea the prophet (Hos. 1:3).

DIBRI [DIB rye]

A descendant of Dan whose daughter married an Egyptian. Her son was stoned to death for blaspheming the name of the Lord (Lev. 24:10–23).

DIDYMUS [DID ih mus] (twin)

The Greek name of THOMAS, one of the twelve disciples of Christ (John 11:16; 20:24; 21:2).

DIKLAH [DICK la]

A descendant of the family of Shem (Gen. 10:27; 1 Chr. 1:21).

DINAH [DIE nah] (one who judges)

Jacob's daughter by Leah (Gen. 30:21; 34:1). When she was raped by Shechem, the son of Hamor the Hivite, her brothers were enraged. Later, when Shechem wanted Dinah for his wife, he asked his father to make arrangements for him to marry her. Dinah's brothers consented on the condition that all the Hivites be circumcised.

The Hivites agreed; but after they had been circumcised, Simeon and Levi, two of Dinah's brothers, suddenly attacked them "on the third day, when they were in pain" (Gen. 34:25) and killed all the males. Jacob did not condone the deed; in fact, upon his deathbed he denounced it (Gen. 49:5–7).

DIONYSIUS THE AREOPAGITE [die oh NISS e us; air e OP uh ghyte]

A member of the Areopagus, the supreme court of Athens. Dionysius became a Christian after hearing the gospel preached by the apostle Paul (Acts 17:34). Nothing else is known about him except by tradition. One tradition says he was martyred in Athens during the reign of the Roman emperor Domitian.

DIOTROPHES [die OTT ruh fees] (nourished by Jupiter)

An unruly believer reprimanded by John (3 John 9–10). He appears to have been a strong personality or a prominent church leader who rejected both John and certain of his followers. Diotrophes stands in contrast to both Gaius (verse 1) and Demetrius (verse 12).

DIPHATH [DIE fath]

The second son of Gomer (1 Chr. 1:6). He is the same person as RIPHATH (Gen. 10:3).

DISHAN [DIE shan]

The seventh son of Seir the Horite, a clan chief in Edom (Gen. 36:21; 1 Chr. 1:38). Also see DISHON No. 2.

DISHON [DIE shahn]

The name given to two descendants of Seir the Horite:

1. The fifth son of Seir and a clan chief in Edom (Gen. 36:21, 26, 30; 1 Chr. 1:38).

2. A son of the Horite clan chief Anah and a grandson of Seir (Gen. 36:25; 1 Chr. 1:41). Also see DISHAN.

DODAI [DOE die]

A form of DODO No. 2.

DODANIM [DOE dah nim]

A son of Javan (Gen. 10:4), also called Rodanim (1 Chr. 1:7). The reference may be to the people who lived on the island of Rhodes, and on the neighboring islands in the Aegean Sea.

DODAVAH [DOE duh vah] (*beloved of the Lord*)

The father of Eliezer of Mareshah (2 Chr. 20:37; Dodavahu, NRSV, NIV, NASB, REB). Eliezer prophesied the destruction of Jehoshaphat's ships.

DODO [DOE doh] (*beloved*)

A name given to three Old Testament men:

1. The grandfather of Tola, a judge of the tribe of Issachar (Judg. 10:1).

2. The father of Eleazar, one of David's mighty men (2 Sam. 23:9; 1 Chr. 11:12). Also spelled Dodai (1 Chr. 27:4).

3. The father of Elhanan of Bethlehem, one of David's mighty men (2 Sam. 23:24; 1 Chr. 11:26).

DOEG [DOE egg]

An Edomite who was the chief of Saul's herdsmen. Doeg betrayed David and, on Saul's orders, killed 85 priests at Nob (1 Sam. 21:7; 22:9).

DORCAS [DOR cuss] (*gazelle*)

A Christian woman from Joppa known for befriending and helping the poor (Acts 9:36–43); Tabitha was her Aramaic name (it also means "gazelle"). She was raised from the dead by the apostle Peter. The Bible tells us little about her background, but it is possible that she was a woman of some wealth, or at least had connections with the wealthy. Dorcas may well have been one of the early converts of Philip the evangelist, who established a Christian church at Joppa.

DRUSILLA [droo SILL uh]

Youngest daughter of Herod Agrippa I by his wife Cypros. Drusilla was the wife of Felix, the governor of Judea. While he was a prisoner, the apostle Paul pleaded his case before Felix and Drusilla: "Now as he [Paul] reasoned about righteousness, self-control, and the judgment to come, Felix was afraid" (Acts 24:25). The Scriptures do not record Drusilla's reaction.

According to the Jewish historian, Josephus, Drusilla was a Jewess who married Azizus, king of Emesa, who then converted to Judaism. Because of Drusilla's great beauty, Felix desired her for his wife. Drusilla then left Azizus and married the Gentile Felix in defiance of Jewish law (Acts 24:24).

DUMAH [DEW mah]

A descendant of Ishmael and the ancestor of an Arabian tribe (Gen. 25:14; 1 Chr. 1:30).

DELILAH

sent as emissaries to Nebuchadnezzar and who carried Jeremiah's letter to the Babylonian captives (Jer. 29:3).

ELDAAH [el DAY ah]

The fifth of Midian's five sons. Midian was the son of Abraham and Keturah, Abraham's concubine (Gen. 25:4).

ELDAD [EL dad] (God has loved)

One of 70 elders chosen by Moses at the command of God to help "bear the burden of the people" (Num. 11:17). Eldad and MEDAD were absent from the tabernacle of meeting; nevertheless "the Spirit rested upon them [and] . . . they prophesied in the camp." When a young man told Moses, "Eldad and Medad are prophesying," Joshua was jealous. Moses refused to restrain them, however, answering, "Oh, that all the LORD's people were prophets and that the LORD would put His Spirit upon them!" (Num. 11:26–29).

ELEAD [EL e ad] (God is witness)

A son of Ephraim. Elead attempted to steal cattle near the Philistine city of Gath and was killed (1 Chr. 7:20–22).

ELEADAH [el ih AY duh]

A form of ELADAH.

ELEASAH [el ee A sah] (God has made)

The name of two men in the Old Testament:

1. A son of Helez, of the tribe of Judah (1 Chr. 2:39–40).

2. A son of Raphah, a descendant of King Saul (1 Chr. 8:37; Rephaiah, 1 Chr. 9:43).

ELEAZAR [el e A zur] (God is helper)

The name of seven men in the Bible:
1. Aaron's third son by his wife, Elisheba (Ex. 6:23). Eleazar was the father of

Phinehas (Ex. 6:25). Consecrated a priest, he was made chief of the Levites after his elder brothers, Nadab and Abihu, were killed for offering unholy fire (Lev. 10:1–7). Before Aaron died, Eleazar ascended Mount Hor with him and was invested with Aaron's high priestly garments (Num. 20:25–28). Eleazar served as high priest during the remainder of Moses' life and throughout Joshua's leadership. He helped in the allotment of Canaan among the twelve tribes of Israel (Josh. 14:1), and was buried "in a hill that belonged to Phinehas his son . . . in the mountains of Ephraim" (Josh. 24:33). Phinehas succeeded him as high priest (Judg. 20:28).

2. The son of Abinadab who was charged with keeping watch over the ark while it stayed in Abinadab's house in Kirjath Jearim (1 Sam. 7:1).

3. The son of Dodo the Ahohite (1 Chr. 11:12). He was one of David's three mighty men (2 Sam. 23:9).

4. A man from the tribe of Levi, the family of Merari, and the house of Mahli (1 Chr. 23:21–22).

5. The Levite son of Phinehas (Ezra 8:33). He assisted the high priest.

6. A priest who acted as a musician when the rebuilt walls of Jerusalem were dedicated (Neh. 12:27, 42).

7. Eliud's son and one of the ancestors of Jesus (Matt. 1:15).

Also see ELIEZER.

ELECT LADY

The person or church to which 2 John is addressed (2 John 1).

ELHANAN [el HAY nun] (God is gracious)

The name of one or two men in the Old Testament:

1. A son of Dodo the Bethlehemite

and one of David's mighty men (2 Sam. 23:24; 1 Chr. 11:26).

2. A warrior who killed a giant during the time of David (2 Sam. 21:19; 1 Chr. 20:5).

ELI [EE lie] *(the Lord is high)*

A judge and high priest with whom the prophet Samuel lived during his childhood (1 Sam. 1—4; 14:3).

The first mention of Eli occurs when the childless Hannah poured out to him her unhappiness over her barren condition. Later, her prayers for a son were answered when Samuel was born. True to her word, she brought her son to the tabernacle and dedicated him to God. There the future prophet lived with the high priest Eli.

Eli was a deeply pious man whose service to the Lord was unblemished. However, he was a lax father who had no control over his two sons. Phinehas and Hophni took meat from sacrificial animals before they were dedicated to God. They also "lay with the women that assembled at the door of the tabernacle" (1 Sam. 2:22). God pronounced judgment on Eli because of his failure to discipline his sons.

God's judgment was carried out through the Philistines. Hophni and Phinehas carried the Ark of the Covenant into battle to help the Israelites. Both were killed, and the ark was captured. When Eli, 98 years old and nearly blind, heard the news, he fell backward and broke his neck. God's final judgment against Eli and his descendants occurred when Solomon removed Abiathar, Eli's descendant, and put Zadok in his place as high priest of the nation (1 Kin. 2:35).

ELIAB [e LIE ab] *(God is my Father)*

The name of six men in the Old Testament:

1. A chieftain of the tribe of Zebulun during Israel's wandering in the wilderness (Num. 2:7; 7:24).

2. The father of Dathan and Abiram, Reubenites who rebelled against Moses.

3. David's oldest brother (1 Sam. 16:6–7; Elihu, 1 Chr. 27:18). Eliab's bearing was so striking that when Samuel saw him, he thought Eliab must surely be God's chosen one. Eliab's daughter' Abihail married one of David's sons (2 Chr. 11:18).

4. A Levite ancestor of Samuel (1 Chr. 6:27; Elihu, 1 Sam. 1:1; Eliel, 1 Chr. 6:34).

5. A Gadite warrior who joined David at Ziklag (1 Chr. 12:8–9).

6. A Levite who served in the tabernacle in David's time (1 Chr. 15:18; 16:5).

ELIADA [e LIE uh duh] *(God knows)*

The name of three men in the Old Testament:

1. A son of David born at Jerusalem (2 Sam. 5:16; Beeliada, 1 Chr. 14:7).

2. The father of Rezon of Zobah, the "captain over a band of raiders" who annoyed King Solomon (1 Kin. 11:23).

3. A Benjamite and one of Jehoshaphat's chief captains (1 Chr. 17:17).

ELIAHBA [e LIE a ba] *(God conceals)*

One of David's mighty men (2 Sam. 23:32; 1 Chr. 11:33).

ELIAKIM [e LIE uh kim] *(God is setting up)*

The name of five Old Testament men:

1. A son of Hilkiah and overseer of the household of King Hezekiah of Judah (2 Kin. 18:18; 19:2). When the invading Assyrian army approached Jerusalem (701 B.C.), Eliakim was one of three men sent by Hezekiah to confer with Sennacherib's forces. Hezekiah then sent these men to report the Assyrians' an-

swer to the prophet Isaiah, who praised Eliakim highly (Is. 22:20–23).

2. The original name of JEHOIAKIM, a son of King Josiah of Judah, who was made king of Judah by Pharaoh Necho (2 Chr. 36:4). Jehoahaz reigned only three months after Josiah's death before the Egyptian pharaoh carried him away captive. Necho then changed Eliakim's name to Jehoiakim to demonstrate his authority over him.

3. One of the priests who took part in the cleansing of the rebuilt walls of Jerusalem (Neh. 12:41).

4. An ancestor of Christ descended from Zerubbabel (Matt. 1:13).

5. An ancestor of Christ, descended from David, who lived before the Captivity (Luke 3:30).

ELIAM [e LIE um] (The God of my people)

The name of two Old Testament men:
1. The father of Bathsheba, who became the wife of Uriah the Hittite and later of King David (2 Sam. 11:3; Ammiel, 1 Chr. 3:5).
2. One of David's mighty men (2 Sam. 23:34).

ELIAS [e LIE us]

Greek form of ELIJAH.

ELIASAPH [e LIE uh saf] (God has added)

The name of two men in the Old Testament:
1. The head of the tribe of Gad during Israel's wilderness journey (Num. 1:14; 2:14). He was the son of Deuel (or Reuel; Num. 2:14).
2. The head of the Gershonites during Israel's wilderness journey (Num. 3:24).

ELIASHIB [e LIE uh shib] (God restores)

The name of six or seven men in the Old Testament:
1. A son of Elioenai, a Judahite and descendant of Zerubbabel (1 Chr. 3:24).
2. A priest in David's time (1 Chr. 24:12).
3. One who helped Ezra resolve the problem of pagan wives following the Captivity (Ezra 10:6; Neh. 12:22–23). Possibly the same as No. 7.
4. A Levite and singer who divorced his pagan wife after the Captivity (Ezra 10:27).
5. A son of Zattu who divorced his pagan wife after the Captivity (Ezra 10:36).
6. A son of Bani who divorced his pagan wife after the Captivity (Ezra 10:36).
7. The high priest in Nehemiah's time (Neh. 3:1; 13:4, 28). Possibly the same as No. 3.

ELIATHAH [e LIE uh thah] (God has come)

The head of a division of Temple musicians during David's reign (1 Chr. 25:4, 27).

ELIDAD [e LIE dad] (my God is a friend)

A chieftain of the tribe of Benjamin appointed to represent his tribe in the division of Canaan (Num. 34:21).

ELIEHOENAI [el ih oh EE nigh]

A form of ELIOENAI No. 4 and ELIHOENAI.

ELIEL [e LIE el] (My God is God)

The name of eight or nine Old Testament men:
1. A chief of the half-tribe of Manasseh (1 Chr. 5:24).
2. A Levite ancestor of the prophet

Samuel (1 Chr. 6:34; Elihu, 1 Samuel 1:1; Eliab, 1 Chr. 6:27).

3. A Benjamite son of Shimei (1 Chr. 8:20).

4. A Benjamite son of Shashak (1 Chr. 8:22).

5. One of David's captains and a Mahavite (1 Chr. 11:46).

6. One of David's mighty men (1 Chr. 11:47).

7. A Gadite who joined David at Ziklag when David was hiding from Saul (1 Chr. 12:11). Possibly the same as No. 5 or 6.

8. A Levite who helped bring the ark from the house of Obed–Edom during the reign of King David (1 Chr. 15:9).

9. A Levite overseer of the Temple tithes and offerings during the reign of King Hezekiah of Judah (2 Chr. 31:13).

ELIENAI [el ih EE nigh] (*my eyes are on my God*)

A son of Shimei, of the tribe of Benjamin (1 Chr. 8:20).

ELIEZER [el ih EE zur] (*My God is helper*)

The name of 11 men in the Bible:

1. Abraham's chief servant (Gen. 15:2). If Abraham had never had a son, Eliezer of Damascus would have been his heir.

2. Moses' second son by Zipporah (Ex. 18:4; 1 Chr. 23:15).

3. A son of Becher, of the tribe of Benjamin (1 Chr. 7:8).

4. A priest who blew the trumpet before the ark when it was moved from Kirjath Jearim to Jerusalem (1 Chr. 15:24).

5. A son of Zichri and the officer over the tribe of the Reubenites during David's reign (1 Chr. 27:16).

6. A prophet who predicted that the ships of King JEHOSHAPHAT of Judah would be wrecked because he had joined

forces with King AHAZIAH of Israel (2 Chr. 20:37).

7. A leader whom Ezra sent to bring Levites to Jerusalem (Ezra 8:16).

8, 9, 10. Three men who divorced their pagan wives after the Captivity. One was a priest (Ezra 10:18); one was a Levite (Ezra 10:23); and one was a son of Harim (Ezra 10:31).

11. An ancestor of Joseph, the husband of Mary (Luke 3:29).

Also see ELEAZAR.

ELIHOENAI [el ih oh EE nigh] (*my eyes are toward Jehovah*)

One of the sons of Pahath–Moab who returned with Ezra from the Captivity (Ezra 8:4; Eliehoenai, NRSV, NIV, NASB).

ELIHOREPH [el ih HO ref] (*God of harvest rain*)

A son of Shisha and one of King Solomon's scribes (1 Kin. 4:3).

ELIHU [eh LIE hew] (*He is my God*)

The name of five men in the Old Testament:

1. The great-grandfather of the prophet Samuel (1 Sam. 1:1; Eliab, 1 Chr. 6:27; Eliel, 1 Chr. 6:34).

2. A captain of Manasseh who joined David at Ziklag to hide from King Saul (1 Chr. 12:20).

3. A Levite of the family of Kohath who served as a tabernacle gatekeeper during David's reign (1 Chr. 26:7).

4. The oldest son of Jesse and a brother of David (1 Chr. 27:18; Eliab, 1 Sam. 16:6).

5. The youngest of Job's "comforters." Elihu spoke to Job after the three friends—BILDAD; ELIPHAZ, and ZOPHAR—failed to give convincing answers to Job's questions. Elihu is called "the son of Barachel the Buzite of the family of Ram" (Job 32:2). Like Job's other friends, Elihu was

time on earth was finished (1 Kin. 19:16). Elisha ministered for about 50 years in the northern kingdom of Israel, serving God during the reigns of Jehoram, Jehu, Jehoahaz, and Joash. The period of his ministry dates from about 850–800 B.C. Elisha's work consisted of presenting the Word of God through prophecy, advising kings, anointing kings, helping the needy, and performing several miracles.

Elisha was the son of Shaphat of Abel Meholah, a town on the western side of the Jordan River. Elijah found Elisha plowing with a team of oxen. As Elijah walked past Elisha, he threw his mantle over the younger man's shoulders.

Elisha "arose and followed Elijah, and became his servant" (1 Kin. 19:21), but Elisha is not mentioned again until 2 Kings 2:1, shortly before Elijah ascended to heaven in a chariot of fire. Before taking his leave, Elijah fulfilled the final request of Elisha by providing him with a double portion of his prophetic spirit (2 Kin. 2:9–10), making him his spiritual firstborn. Upon receiving Elijah's mantle, Elisha demonstrated this gift by parting the waters of the Jordan River, allowing him to cross on dry land (2 Kin. 2:14). In this way, Elisha demonstrated that he had received God's blessings on his ministry as Elijah's successor.

Elisha cultivated a different image from his predecessor. Instead of following Elijah's example as a loner and an outsider, Elisha chose to work within the established system. He assumed his rightful place as the head of the "official" prophetic order in Israel, where his counsel and advice were sought out by kings. In contrast to Elijah's strained relationship with the king and his officials, Elisha enjoyed the harmonious role of trusted advisor. This is not to say that Elisha never had a word of criticism for the government, as for example in the part he

played in the overthrow of Jezebel and the dynasty of Ahab (2 Kin. 9:1–3).

Elisha's appearance was much more typical and average than Elijah's. He was bald (2 Kin. 2:23), while Elijah had been an extremely hairy man (2 Kin. 1:8). Elisha did not wander as extensively as Elijah. Instead, he had a house in Samaria (2 Kin. 6:32). Much tension had existed between Elijah and his audience. Elisha's ministry provided a strong contrast as he was welcomed into virtually all levels of society.

In perhaps the most important part of his ministry, however, Elisha followed in Elijah's footsteps. This consisted of his performance of miracles, which answered a wide variety of needs in every level of society. He had a reputation for sympathizing with the poor and the oppressed. Elisha's activities and miracles as a prophet were often focused on those who were abused by officials in positions of power.

One of Elisha's "community service" miracles was his purification of an unhealthy spring near Jericho. After learning that the spring was bad, Elisha threw a bowl of salt into it, making it pure (2 Kin. 2:19–21). The Bible reports that "the water remains healed to this day" (2 Kin. 2:22).

In another miracle, Elisha helped the widow of one of the sons of the prophets. To help her pay off creditors who intended to take the widow's two sons, Elisha multiplied the amount of oil in one jar to fill all available containers. This brought in enough money to pay off the debts and provided a surplus on which the widow and her sons could live (2 Kin. 4:1–7).

Elisha became a friend of a wealthy family in Shunem. The Shunammite woman displayed hospitality toward the prophet by regularly feeding him and building a room onto her home where he could lodge. Elisha repaid the childless couple by promising them a son (2 Kin. 4:8–17). Later, when tragedy struck the child, Elisha raised him from the dead (2 Kin. 4:18–37). When Elisha learned that a famine would strike Israel, he warned the family to flee the land. When the family returned seven years later, the king restored their property because of their relationship with Elisha (2 Kin. 8:1–6).

Elisha also advised kings and performed miracles for them. He helped Jehoram, king of Israel, and Jehoshaphat, king of Judah. He also helped the king of Edom defeat Mesha, king of Moab (2 Kin. 3:1–19).

Elisha ministered to all people, regardless of their nationalities. He cured Naaman, the commander of the Syrian army (2 Kin. 5:1–14), of leprosy, but he also advised the king of Israel of the plans (2 Kin. 6:8–10) of their Assyrian enemies. Even the bones of the dead Elisha had miraculous powers. When a corpse was hidden in Elisha's tomb, it came back to life as it touched the prophet's bones (2 Kin. 13:21).

ELISHAH [eh LIE shah] (*God is Savior*)

The oldest son of Javan and a descendant of Noah (Gen. 10:1–4). The home of his descendants. is described as "the coasts of Elishah," which supplied the Phoenicians with dyes of royal "blue and purple" (Ezek. 27:7). The name may refer to the island of Cyprus, known in ancient times as Alashiya.

ELISHAMA [e LISH uh muh] (*God hears*)

The name of six Old Testament men:
1. Leader of the tribe of Ephraim at the beginning of the Israelites' journey (Num. 2:18). This son of Ammihud was

one of Joshua's ancestors (1 Chr. 7:26–27).
2. One of the sons born to David after he was crowned king at Jerusalem (2 Sam. 5:16; 1 Chr. 3:8; 14:7).
3. The father of Nethaniah and the grandfather of Ishmael (Jer. 41:1).
4. A Judahite, a son of Jekamiah (1 Chr. 2:41).
5. One of two priests sent by Jehoshaphat to teach the Law to the people in Judah (2 Chr. 17:8).
6. A scribe or secretary of King Jehoiakim (Jer. 36:12, 20–21).

ELISHAPHAT [e LISH uh fat] (*my God is judge*)

A son of Zichri and one who supported the revolt against Queen Athaliah in favor of seven-year-old Joash (2 Chr. 23:1).

ELISHEBA [ee LISH ih buh] (*my God is fullness*)

The wife of AARON and the mother of Nadab, Abihu, Eleazar, and Ithamar (Ex. 6:23). She was a daughter of Amminadab and a sister of Naashon.

ELISHUA [el ih SHOE uh] (*God is salvation*)

A son of David born at Jerusalem (2 Sam. 5:15; 1 Chr. 14:5; 1 Chr. 3:6, where another reading is Elishama).

ELIUD [e LIE ud] (*God is majestic*)

A son of Achim and the father of Eleazar in the genealogy of Jesus (Matt. 1:14–15).

ELIZABETH [ee LIZ uh buth] (*God is my oath*)

The mother of John the Baptist (Luke 1). Of the priestly line of Aaron, Elizabeth was the wife of the priest ZACHARIAS. Although both "were . . . righteous before God, they had no child, because Elizabeth was barren" (Luke 1:6–7). But God performed a miracle, and Elizabeth conceived the child who was to be the forerunner of the Messiah.

Elizabeth was privileged in another way. When her cousin Mary visited her, Elizabeth, six months pregnant, felt the child move as if to welcome the child whom Mary was carrying. Elizabeth recognized the significance of this action and acknowledged the Messiah before He had been born.

ELIZAPHAN [el ih ZAY fun] (*my God has concealed*)

The name of two Old Testament leaders:

1. A Levite of the family of Kohath, a chief during the wilderness journey and a son of Uzziel (Num. 3:30). He helped remove the bodies of Nadab and Abihu, who had led a revolt against Moses, from the Israelite camp (Lev. 10:4; Elzaphan, Ex. 6:22).

2. A leader of the tribe of Zebulun during the wilderness journey (Num. 34:25). He was the son of Parnach.

ELIZUR [eh LIE zur] (*My God is a rock*)

A chief of the tribe of Reuben who assisted Moses in taking a census of Israel during the wilderness journey (Num. 1:1–5; 2:10).

ELKANAH [el KAY na] (*God has possessed*)

The name of eight Old Testament men:

1. A grandson of Korah (Ex. 6:24).

2. The husband of Hannah and Peninnah and the father of the prophet Samuel (1 Sam. 1:1–23).

3. A Levite of the family of Kohath and a son of Joel (1 Chr. 6:25, 36).

4. A Levite of the family of Kohath and a son of Mahath (1 Chr. 6:26, 35).

5. A Levite who lived in a village of the Netophathites in Judah near Bethlehem (1 Chr. 9:16).

6. A Benjamite warrior who joined David at Ziklag (1 Chr. 12:6).

7. A doorkeeper of the Ark of the Covenant during the time of King David (1 Chr. 15:23).

8. A high-ranking court official of Ahaz king of Judah (2 Chr. 28:7).

ELMODAM [el MOE dam]

An ancestor of Jesus. He was a son of Er (Luke 3:28; Elmadam, NIV, NRSV).

ELNAAM [el NAY am] (*God is pleasantness*)

The father of Jeribai and Joshaviah, two of David's mighty men (1 Chr. 11:46).

ELNATHAN [el NAY thun] (*God has given*)

The name of four men in the Old Testament:

1. The leader of the party sent to Egypt to bring back the prophet Uriah, who had displeased Jehoiakim by his prophecy (Jer. 26:22).

2, 3, 4. Three men sent by Ezra to invite priests and Levites to come to Jerusalem when the Israelites were in captivity in Babylon (Ezra 8:16).

ELON [EE lahn] (*oak*)

The name of three men in the Old Testament:

1. A Hittite and the father of Basemath, who became one of Esau's wives (Gen. 26:34).

2. The second son of Zebulun and founder of a tribal family, the Elonites (Num. 26:26).

3. A Zebulunite who judged Israel for ten years (Judg. 12:11–12).

E

ELPAAL [el PAY al] (*God is working*)

A descendant of Benjamin (1 Chr. 8:11–12, 18).

ELPALET [el PAY let]

A form of ELPELET.

ELPELET [el PEA let] (*God is deliverance*)

A son of David (1 Chr. 14:5; Elpalet, KJV). Also spelled Eliphelet (1 Chr. 3:6).

ELUZAI [e LOO zuh i] (*God is my strength*)

A Benjamite warrior who left King Saul's forces to join David at Ziklag (1 Chr. 12:5).

ELYMAS [EL ih mas]

A false prophet who was temporarily struck blind for opposing Paul and Barnabas at Paphos on Cyprus (Acts 13:8). Described as "a Jew whose name was Bar–Jesus" (Acts 13:6), he apparently had some influence with Sergius Paulus, the Roman governor of the island. Elymas was jealous of the gospel that Paul preached and tried to turn the governor away from accepting the Christian faith.

ELZABAD [el ZAY bud] (*God has given*)

The name of two men in the Old Testament:
1. A Gadite warrior who joined David at Ziklag (1 Chr. 12:12).
2. A gatekeeper in the Temple (1 Chr. 26:7).

ELZAPHAN [el ZAY fun]

(See ELIZAPHAN.)

ENAN [E non]

The father of Ahira, leader of the tribe of Naphtali in the days of Moses. Ahira assisted in taking the first census of Israel during their years in the wilderness (Num. 1:15).

ENOCH [EE nuck] (*initiated* or *dedicated*)

The name of two men in the Bible:
1. The firstborn son of Cain (Gen. 4:17–18).
2. A son of Jared and the father of Methuselah (Gen. 5:18–24; Henoch; 1 Chr. 1:3, KJV). After living for 365 years, Enoch was "translated," or taken directly into God's presence without experiencing death (Gen. 5:24; Heb. 11:5–6).

ENOS [E nos]

A form of ENOSH.

ENOSH [EE nosh] (*man, humankind*)

A grandson of Adam, a son of Seth, and the father of Cainan (Gen. 5:6–11). He lived 905 years. Enosh is listed in Luke's genealogy of Jesus (Luke 3:38; Enos, KJV).

EPAENETUS [eh PEE nee tus] (*praiseworthy*)

A Christian, formerly from Asia, who later lived in Rome (Rom. 16:5; Epenetus, NIV). He was the first convert to Christ in the province of Asia.

EPAPHRAS [EP uh frus] (*charming*)

A Christian preacher who spread the gospel to his fellow Colossian citizens (Col. 1:7; 4:12). When Paul was a prisoner in Rome, Epaphras came to him with a favorable account of the church at Colossae. He remained with Paul in Rome and was, in a sense, his "fellow prisoner" (Philem. 23).

EPAPHRODITUS [ih paf ruh DIE tus] (*charming*)

A messenger sent by the church at Philippi with a gift for the apostle Paul, who was under house arrest in Rome (Phil. 2:25; 4:18). While in Rome Epaphroditus became ill and word of his sickness spread to Philippi. As soon as Epaphroditus was well enough, Paul sent him back home to relieve the church's anxiety and to deliver Paul's letter to the Philippians.

EPENETUS

A form of EPAENETUS.

EPHAH [E fa]

The name of two men and one woman in the Bible:

1. A son of Midian and a grandson of Abraham and Keturah, Abraham's concubine (Gen. 25:4).

2. A concubine of Caleb (1 Chr. 2:46).

3. A son of Jahdi (1 Chr. 2:47).

EPHAI [EE fie]

A resident of Netophah in Judah whose sons were among those who joined Gedaliah at Mizpah (Jer. 40:8-13). Ephai and his sons were promised protection and were subsequently murdered by Ishmael (Jer. 41:3).

EPHER [EE fur]

The name of three men in the Old Testament:

1. The second son of Midian and a grandson of Abraham and Keturah, Abraham's concubine (Gen. 25:4).

2. A descendant of Judah through Ezrah (1 Chr. 4:17).

3. A head of a family in the half-tribe of Manasseh east of the Jordan River (1 Chr. 5:24).

EPHLAL [EFF lal]

A descendant of Perez, of the tribe of Judah (1 Chr. 2:37).

EPHOD [EE fahd]

The father of Hanniel. Hanniel was a leader of the tribe of Manasseh and one of Moses' assistants in dividing the land of Canaan (Num. 34:23).

EPHRAIM [EE freh em] (doubly fruitful)

The second son of Joseph by Asenath. When Ephraim was born to Joseph in Egypt, he gave him his name meaning "fruitful" because "God has caused me to be fruitful in the land of my affliction" (Gen. 41:52). Even though Joseph was a foreigner (a Hebrew) in Egypt, he had been blessed by God as he rose to a high position in the Egyptian government and fathered two sons. Later this same theme of fruitfulness and blessing was echoed by Joseph's father, Jacob, as he accepted Ephraim as his grandson (Gen. 48:5). Eventually Ephraim's thousands of descendants settled in the land of Canaan as one of the most numerous of the tribes of Israel (Gen. 48:19; Num. 1:10).

EPHRATHAH [EF ray thah] (fertility)

A wife of Caleb, the son of Hezron (1 Chr. 2:19; Ephrath, NIV; 4:4). She was the mother of Hur and the grandmother of the Caleb who spied out the land of Canaan.

EPHRON [EE fron]

A Hittite from whom Abraham purchased a field containing the cave of Machpelah. It became the burial place of the patriarchs Abraham, Isaac, and Jacob (and also of their wives, Sarah, Rebekah, and Leah; Gen. 23:8-17; 25:9; 49:29-30; 50:13).

EPIPHANES [e PIFF uh knees] (a god revealed)

A shorter name for Antiochus IV, the king of Syria (reigned 175-163 B.C.). He defiled the Jewish Temple in Jerusalem by sacrificing swine on the altar and by setting himself up as a god to be worshiped. Also see ANTIOCHUS.

ER [ur]

The name of three men in the Bible:

1. A son of Judah (Gen. 38:3, 6–7).

2. A son of Shelah, the youngest son of Judah (1 Chr. 4:21).

3. An ancestor of Jesus who lived between the time of David and Zerubbabel (Luke 3:28).

ERAN [EE run]

A descendant of Ephraim through Shuthelah, Ephraim's oldest son and the founder of a tribal family, the Eranites (Num. 26:36).

ERASTUS [ih RAS tus] (beloved)

The name of one or more Christians in the early church:

1. A Christian sent with Timothy from Ephesus into Macedonia while the apostle Paul stayed in Asia (Acts 19:22).

2. The "treasurer of the city" (Rom. 16:23) in Corinth who sent greetings to Rome. If an inscription found in the pavement of the amphitheater at ancient Corinth and bearing the name "Erastus" refers to this man, Erastus is the earliest Christian name attested outside of the Bible.

3. One who remained at Corinth (2 Tim. 4:20).

Any two of the above—or perhaps all three—may be identical.

ERI [EE rye] (watchful)

The fifth son of Gad (Gen. 46:16) and leader of the Erites (Num. 26:16).

ESARHADDON [eh sar HAD un]

The favorite, though not the oldest, son of Sennacherib, who succeeded his father as king of Assyria. Sennacherib's favoritism toward Esarhaddon so enraged two other brothers, Adrammelech and Sharaezer, that they assassinated their father about 681 B.C., then escaped into Armenia (2 Kin. 19:36–37; 2 Chr. 32:21; Is. 37:37–38). At the time of the assassination, Esarhaddon was conducting a military campaign, probably in Armenia. He returned to Nineveh, the Assyrian capital, ended the civil strife, and assumed the Assyrian throne.

Esarhaddon was a wise ruler, both militarily and politically. He restored the city of Babylon, which his father had destroyed in an earlier campaign against Babylonia; and he successfully waged war against numerous groups that had been persistent in creating problems for the Assyrian Empire. Among his most notable military achievements was his conquest of Egypt, Assyria's competitor for world domination. In 677 B.C. Esarhaddon captured Memphis and then conquered the rest of Egypt. He then used native rulers and Assyrian advisers to rule the distant country.

Egypt rebelled in 669 B.C. On his way to Egypt to put down the rebellion, Esarhaddon became ill and died. As his father before him had done, Esarhaddon had provided for an orderly succession in the affairs of Assyria. His younger son, Ashurbanipal, ascended to the Assyrian throne.

Esarhaddon participated in the resettling of Samaria with foreigners long after this capital city of the northern kingdom of Israel fell to Assyrian forces in 722 B.C. (Ezra 4:2). This was an example of the Assyrian policy of intermingling cultures in the nations that they conquered to make them weak and compliant.

ESAU [EE saw]

A son of Isaac and Rebekah and the twin brother of Jacob. Also known as Edom, Esau was the ancestor of the Edomites (Gen. 25:24–28; Deut. 2:4–8).

Most of the biblical narratives about Esau draw a great contrast between him and his brother, Jacob. Esau was a hunter and outdoorsman who was favored by his father, while Jacob was not an outdoors type and was favored by Rebekah (Gen. 25:27–28).

Even though he was a twin, Esau was considered the oldest son because he was born first. By Old Testament custom, he would have inherited most of his father's property and the right to succeed him as family patriarch. But in a foolish, impulsive moment, he sold his birthright to Jacob in exchange for a meal (Gen. 25:29–34). This determined that Jacob would carry on the family name in a direct line of descent from Abraham and Isaac, his grandfather and father.

The loss of Esau's rights as firstborn is further revealed in Genesis 27. Jacob deceived his blind father by disguising himself as Esau in order to receive his father's highest blessing. Esau was therefore the recipient of a less blessing (Gen. 27:25–29, 38–40; Heb. 11:20). He was so enraged by Jacob's actions that he determined to kill him once his father died. But Jacob fled to his uncle Laban in Haran and remained there for 20 years. Upon Jacob's return to Canaan, Esau forgave him and set aside their old feuds (Gen. 32:1—33:17). Years later, the two brothers together buried their father in the cave at Machpelah without a trace of their old hostilities (Gen. 35:29).

Esau in many ways was more honest and dependable than his scheming brother Jacob. But he sinned greatly by treating his birthright so casually and selling it for a meal (Heb. 12:16–17). To the ancient Hebrews, one's birthright actually represented a high spiritual value. But Esau did not have the faith and farsightedness to accept his privileges and responsibilities. Thus, the right passed to his younger brother.

ESH–BAAL [esh BAY al] (man of Baal or Baal exists)

The original name of the son and successor of King Saul as king of Israel (1 Chr. 8:33; 9:39). He was also called Ishbosheth ("man of shame") because Baal was a shameful deity (2 Sam. 2:8–15; Jer. 11:13).

ESHBAN [ESH bun]

A son of Dishon (Gen. 36:26).

ESHCOL [ESH cuhl] (cluster of grapes)

A brother of Mamre and Aner. All three brothers helped Abram defeat CHEDORLAOMER (Gen. 14:13, 24).

ESHEK [EE sheck]

A Benjamite; descendant of King Saul through Jonathan (1 Chr. 8:39).

ESHTEMOA [esh teh MOH uh] (listening post)

1. A descendant of Caleb, of the tribe of Judah (1 Chr. 4:17).
2. A Maachathite of the tribe of Judah (1 Chr. 4:19).

ESHTEMOH [ESH teh moh]

A form of ESHTEMOA.

ESHTON [ESH ton]

A descendant of Judah through Caleb (1 Chr. 4:11–12).

ESLI [ES lie]

An ancestor of Jesus (Luke 3:25).

ESTHER [ESS ter] (star)

The Jewish queen of the Persian king AHASUERUS (Xerxes). Esther saved her people, the Jews, from a plot to eliminate them. A daughter of Abihail (Esth. 2:15; 9:29) and a cousin of Mordecai (Esth. 2:7, 15), Esther was raised by Mordecai as his own daughter after her mother and father died. Esther was a member of a family carried into captivity in Babylon that later chose to stay in Persia rather than return to Jerusalem. Her Jewish name was Hadassah, which means "myrtle" (Esth. 2:7).

The story of Esther's rise from an unknown Jewish girl to become the queen of a mighty empire illustrates how God used events and people as instruments to fulfill His promise to His Chosen People. Following several days of revelry, the drunken king Ahasuerus—identified with Xerxes I (reigned 486–465 B.C.)—asked his queen, Vashti, to display herself to his guests. When Vashti courageously refused, she was banished from the palace. Ahasuerus then had "all the beautiful young virgins" (Esth. 2:3) of his kingdom brought to his palace to choose Vashti's replacement.

Scripture records that "the young woman [Esther] was lovely and beautiful" (Esth. 2:7). The king loved Esther more than all the other women. He appointed her queen to replace Vashti (Esth. 2:17).

At the time, HAMAN was Ahasuerus' most trusted advisor. An egotistical and ambitious man, Haman demanded that people bow to him as he passed—something that Mordecai, a devout Jew, could not do in good conscience. In rage, Haman sought revenge not only on Mordecai but also on the entire Jewish population of the empire. He persuaded the king to issue an edict permitting him to kill all the Jews and seize their property.

With great tact and skill, Esther exposed Haman's plot and true character to the king. As a result, Ahasuerus granted the Jews the right to defend themselves and to destroy their enemies. With ironic justice, "they hanged Haman on the gallows that he had prepared for Mordecai" (Esth. 7:10).

Even today Jews celebrate their deliverance from Ahasuerus' edict at the Feast of Purim (Esth. 9:26–32), celebrated on the 14th and 15th days of the month of Adar.

ETHAN [EE thun] (long-lived)

The name of three or four Old Testament men:

1. A renowned wise man in the time of Solomon called "Ethan the Ezrahite" (1 Kin. 4:31).

2. A son of Zerah, Judah's son by Tamar, and the father of Azariah (1 Chr. 2:6, 8). He may be the same person as No. 1.

3. A descendant of Gershon and an ancestor of Asaph (1 Chr. 6:42; perhaps Joah, 1 Chr. 6:21).

4. A descendant of Merari, son of Levi (1 Chr. 15:17, 19).

ETHBAAL [eth BAY al] (with him is Baal)

A king of Sidon and the father of Jezebel, the idolatrous wife of King Ahab of Israel (1 Kin. 16:31). During his reign, a year-long drought occurred (1 Kings 17—18).

ETHIOPIAN EUNUCH [YOU nuck]

A person baptized by Philip who held a responsible position as the royal treasurer in the court of Candace, queen of Ethiopia (Acts 8:26–40). The word eunuch refers to an emasculated servant who could rise to positions of power and

F

FELIX–FORTUNATUS

FELIX [FEE lix] (happy)

Roman governor of Judea before whom the apostle Paul appeared.

Felix was an unscrupulous ruler. In addition to having three wives, he considered himself capable of committing any crime and avoiding punishment because of his influence with the courts. Because of Felix's tyranny, a group of Jewish revolutionaries, known as the Sicarii ("assassins"), flourished. Retaliation against the Sicarii by the Roman government eventually led to the downfall and destruction of Jerusalem.

Felix is best known for his encounter with the apostle Paul (Acts 23:23). Arrested in Jerusalem as a disturber of the peace, Paul was sent to Caesarea for judgment by Felix. After his initial appearance before Felix, Paul was confined to the judgment hall until his accusers arrived. After five days, they arrived under the leadership of Ananias, the Jewish high priest. The case against Paul was managed by Tertullus, who sought to win Felix over by expressing gratitude on the part of the Jews (Acts 24:1–2).

Tertullus then proceeded to accuse Paul of committing rebellion against the Romans, being the ringleader of a troublemaking religious sect, and profaning the Jewish Temple. The purpose of these accusations was to persuade Felix to surrender Paul to the Jewish courts, in which case he would have been assassinated.

When Felix gave Paul permission to speak, Paul refuted each of these charges; and Felix postponed his judgment. Several days later, Paul was brought before Felix a second time. On this occasion Paul gave his testimony as a Christian. Felix was visibly moved; and he dismissed Paul, indicating he would talk with him again on a more convenient day.

Felix kept Paul in suspense about his judgment because he hoped Paul would give him a bribe. He sent for Paul on several occasions. But his hopes for a bribe were unfulfilled, and he kept Paul a prisoner for two years.

Meanwhile, the atmosphere in Judea became more embarrassing, and Felix was finally removed as procurator by the Roman authorities. Because the Jews were making numerous accusations against Felix, Paul was left in prison in Caesarea for two years in an effort to appease the Jewish officials (Acts 24:27). Paul eventually appealed to Rome, which was his right as a Roman citizen, and finally was released from prison and taken to Rome.

FESTUS, PORCIUS [FESS tuss POUR shih us]

The successor of FELIX as Roman procurator, or governor, of Judea (Acts 24:27). After Festus arrived at Caesarea, he went to Jerusalem and met with the high priest and other Jewish leaders. They informed him of Paul's confinement in prison. Paul had been left in prison when Felix was removed as procurator by the Roman authorities.

The Jewish leaders requested that Paul be brought from Caesarea to Jerusalem so he could be tried before the Jewish Sanhedrin (Acts 25:3). Their real intent, however, was to have Paul killed along the way. Festus refused and told the Jewish leaders they must meet with Paul in Caesarea.

A few days later, Paul was summoned before Festus, who asked if he would be willing to go to Jerusalem. Paul, knowing that danger awaited him on such a trip, used his right as a Roman citizen to appeal to Rome for trial (Acts 25:11).

About this time, Herod Agrippa, with his sister, Bernice, came to Caesarea to visit Festus. The result was a meeting between the three and Paul in which Paul was declared innocent. But because Paul had appealed to Caesar, he had to be sent to Rome (Acts 26:32).

FORTUNATUS [for chuh NAY tus] (*fortunate*)

A Christian of Corinth who, along with Stephanas and Achaicus, encouraged and comforted the apostle Paul at Ephesus (1 Cor. 16:17). These three men possibly carried Paul's letter (1 Corinthians) with them when they returned to Corinth.

the Shunammite woman who had welcomed him into her home. Gehazi suggested that the childless woman and her husband might be given a child. A son was eventually born to the couple, but after a few years he died. The Shunammite woman sought Elisha's help. In an attempt to show Gehazi that faith healed, and not magic, Elisha sent him to lay the prophet's staff on the dead child's head. Nothing happened. But when Elisha himself went to the child, the child revived.

Gehazi's true character came out in the story of NAAMAN the Syrian, whom Elisha cured of a skin disease. Elisha refused any reward, but Gehazi ran after Naaman to claim something for himself. He told Naaman that Elisha wanted a talent of silver and two changes of clothing for the needy. Because of his greed, lying, and misuse of the prophetic office, Elisha

cursed Gehazi with the same disease from which Naaman had been cured.

GEMALLI [geh MAL ih] (*camel owner*)

The father of one of the spies who explored the land of Canaan (Num. 13:12).

GEMARIAH [ghem ah RYE ah] (*Jehovah has accomplished*)

The name of two men in the Old Testament:

1. A citizen of Judah who carried tribute money to Nebuchadnezzar of Babylon and took a letter from Jeremiah to the Jews in Captivity (Jer. 29:3).

2. A son of Shaphan who tried to stop Jehoiakim, king of Judah, from destroying Jeremiah's scroll (Jer. 36:10–12, 25).

GENUBATH [geh NOO bath]

A son of Hadad (a fugitive Edomite prince) and his wife, who was the sister

GABRIEL

of Queen Tahpenes of Egypt (1 Kin. 11:20).

GERA [GHEE rah]

The name of four men from the tribe of Benjamin:

1. A son of Bela (Gen. 46:21).
2. The father or ancestor of the judge Ehud (Judg. 3:15).
3. The father or ancestor of Shimei, who cursed David when David fled from Absalom (1 Kin. 2:8).
4. A son or descendant of Bela (1 Chr. 8:3, 5, 7).

GERSHOM [GUR shom] (a sojourner there)

The name of four men in the Old Testament:

1. The firstborn son of Moses and Zipporah (Ex. 2:22).
2. The father of Jonathan, a Levite who became a priest to the Danites at Laish during the time of the judges (Judg. 18:30).
3. The oldest son of Levi (1 Chr. 15:7), also called GERSHON.
4. A descendant of Phinehas and a family leader who returned with Ezra from the Babylonian Captivity (Ezra 8:2).

GERSHON [GUR shun]

The oldest of the three sons of LEVI; his brothers were Kohath and Merari (Gen. 46:11; Num. 3:17). He is also called Gershom (1 Chr. 15:7). Gershon was founder of the family called the Gershonites (Num. 26:57), one of three main divisions of the Levitical priesthood. Gershon was apparently born to Levi before Jacob's family moved to Egypt to escape a famine (Ex. 6:16). Although Gershon was the oldest of Levi's sons, it was through the line of Gershon's younger brother, Kohath, that the priestly line

of Aaron sprang years later after the Exodus of the Hebrew people from Egypt.

GESHEM [GEH shim] (rain)

An Arab who sought to hinder the building of the wall of Jerusalem by Nehemiah (Neh. 2:19; 6:6; Gashmu, KJV).

GETHER [GHEE thur]

The name of two men in the Old Testament:

1. A son of Aram (Gen. 10:23).
2. A son or descendant of Shem (1 Chr. 1:17).

GEUEL [geh YOU ell] (majesty of God)

One of the 12 men sent by Moses to spy out the land of Canaan (Num. 13:15).

GIBBAR [GIB bahr] (mighty man)

A man whose descendants returned from the Captivity with Zerubbabel (Ezra 2:20).

GIBEA [GIB ee ah] (hill)

A grandson of Caleb, of the tribe of Judah (1 Chr. 2:49).

GIDDALTI [gih DAL tih] (I have magnified [God])

A son of Heman and one of those in charge of the music services in the Temple in David's time (1 Chr. 25:4, 29).

GIDDEL [GID dell] (magnified)

The name of two men whose descendants returned from the Captivity to Jerusalem:

1. The ancestor of a family of Nethinim (Temple servants) who returned with Zerubbabel (Ezra 2:47).
2. The ancestor of a family of Solomon's servants (Neh. 7:58).

GOG [gog]

The name of two men in the Bible:

1. A descendant of Joel, of the tribe of Reuben (1 Chr. 5:4).

2. The leader of a confederacy of armies that attacked the land of Israel. Described as "the prince of Rosh, Meshech, and Tubal," Gog is also depicted as being "of the land of Magog" (Ezek. 38:2–3), a "place out of the far north" of Israel. Ezekiel prophetically describes Gog and his allies striking at Israel with a fierce and sudden invasion (Ezekiel 38—39). According to Ezekiel's prophecy, Gog will be crushed on the mountains of Israel in a slaughter so great it will take seven months to bury the dead (Ezek. 39:12).

In the Book of Revelation, Gog and Magog reappear as symbols of the nations of the world that will march against God's people in the end times (Rev. 20:7–8).

GOLIATH [goe LIE ahth]

A Philistine giant whom David felled with a stone from his sling (1 Sam. 17:4–

GOLIATH

G

51). Goliath, who lived in the Philistine city of Gath, was probably a descendant of a tribe of giants known as the Anakim, or descendants of Anak (Num. 13:33). These giants probably served in a capacity similar to that of a foreign mercenary or soldier of fortune.

Based on the figures in the Bible (1 Sam. 17:4), Goliath was over 9 feet tall. The magnificence of Goliath's armor and weapons—his bronze coat of mail, bronze greaves, bronze javelin, spear with an iron spearhead, and huge sword—must have made him appear invincible.

For 40 days this enormous man challenged Saul's army to find one man willing to engage in hand-to-hand combat. The winner of that one battle would determine the outcome of the war. The young David, chosen by God as Israel's next king, accepted the challenge, felling Goliath with a single stone to the fore-head from his sling. When David beheaded the fallen giant, the Philistines fled in panic.

GOMER [GOAM ur]

The name of a man and a woman:

1. The oldest son of Japheth (Gen. 10:2–3).

2. A prostitute who became the wife of the prophet HOSEA (Hos. 1:1–11). When Gomer left Hosea and became the slave of one of her lovers, Hosea bought her back at God's command for the price of a slave. Gomer's unfaithfulness and Hosea's forgiveness symbolized God's forgiving love for unfaithful Israel.

GUNI [GOO nih]

The name of two Old Testament men:

1. A son of Naphtali and founder of the Gunites (1 Chr. 7:13).

2. The father of Abdiel (1 Chr. 5:15).

HAAHASHTARI–HYMENAEUS

HAAHASHTARI [hay uh HASH tur eye]

A descendant of Judah through Ash-hur. His mother was Ashhur's second wife, Naarah (1 Chr. 4:6).

HABAIAH [huh BIGH yuh] (*The Lord has hidden*)

The ancestor of a Jewish family whose name could not be found in the genealogical records (Ezra 2:61–62; Neh. 7:63–64; Hobaiah, NRSV, NIV).

HABAKKUK [huh BAK uhk]

A courageous Old Testament prophet and author of the Book of Habakkuk. The Scriptures say nothing of his ancestry or place of birth. A man of deep emotional strength, Habakkuk was both a poet and a prophet. His hatred of sin compelled him to cry out to God for judgment (Hab. 1:2–4). His sense of justice also led him to challenge God's plan to judge the nation of Judah by the pagan Babylonians (Hab. 1:12—2:1). His deep faith led him to write a beautiful poem of praise in response to the mysterious ways of God (Habakkuk 3).

HABAZZINIAH [hab uh zih NIGH yuh]

The grandfather of Jaazaniah, leader of the Rechabites (Jer. 35:3; Habaziniah, KJV).

HACALIAH [hah kuh LIGH uh]

The father of Nehemiah, the governor of Israel after the Captivity (Neh. 1:1; Hachaliah, KJV; Neh. 10:1).

HACHMONI [hak MOE nigh] (*wise*)

The father of Jehiel (1 Chr. 27:32; Hacmoni, NIV).

HADAD [HAY dad] (*thunderer*)

A name of four men in the Old Testament:

1. A son of Bedada and king of Avith, a city of Edom. Hadad defeated Midian in the field of Moab (Gen. 36:35–39; Hadar, NASB, REB, NRSV).

2. A prince of the Edomites. As a young child, Hadad escaped from Edom to Egypt during the six-month period when Joab, the leader of Israel's army, was killing every male in Edom. The pharaoh gave Hadad a house, land, and food. He also gave the sister of Queen Tahpenes to Hadad for a wife. After David and Joab died, Hadad became an enemy of Solomon (1 Kin. 11:14–25).

3. The eighth of the 12 sons of Ishmael and the grandson of Abraham (1 Chr. 1:30), also called Hadar (Gen. 25:15, KJV).

4. A king of Edom who ruled from the city of Pai (1 Chr. 1:50–51).

HADADEZER [HAD uh DEE zur] (*Hadad is* [my] *helper*)

The son of Rehob and king of Zobah in Syria. Hadadezer's army was defeated by the forces of David and Joab (2 Sam. 8:3–12). He is also called Hadarezer (2 Sam. 10:16, 19, KJV).

HADAR [HAY dahr]

A form of HADAD Nos. 1 and 3.

HADAREZER [HAY duh REE zur]

A form of HADADEZER.

HADASSAH [hah DAH suh] (*myrtle*)

The original Hebrew name for ESTHER (Esth. 2:7).

HADLAI [HAD ligh]

The father of Amasa, a chief of the tribe of Ephraim (2 Chr. 28:12).

HADORAM [hah DOHR uhm] (*Hadad is exalted*)

The name of three Old Testament men:

1. A son of Joktan, who was descended from Shem and Noah (Gen. 10:27).

2. A son of Tou (or Toi), king of Hamath during David's reign (1 Chr. 18:10). Hadoram is also called Joram (2 Sam. 8:10).

3. The superintendent of forced labor under Rehoboam (2 Chr. 10:18). When the ten tribes revolted, Hadoram was sent to Israel as a messenger, but he was stoned to death (2 Chr. 10:18). He is also called Adoniram (1 Kin. 4:6; 5:14) and Adoram (1 Kin. 12:18).

HAGAB [HAY gab] (locust)

An ancestor of a family of Nethinim (Temple servants) who returned to Jerusalem after the Captivity (Ezra 2:46).

HAGABA, HAGABAH [HAG uh buh] (locust)

The ancestor of a family of Nethinim (Temple servants) who returned to Jerusalem after the Captivity (Ezra 2:45).

HAGAR [HAY gahr]

The Egyptian bondwoman of Sarah who bore a son, ISHMAEL, to Abraham (Gen. 16:1–16). After waiting ten years for God to fulfill his promise to give them a son, Sarah presented Hagar to Abraham so he could father a child by her, according to the custom of the day. Sarah's plan and Abraham's compliance demonstrated a lack of faith in God.

When Hagar became pregnant, she mocked Sarah, who dealt with her harshly. Hagar then fled into the wilderness, where, at a well on the way to Shur, she encountered an angel of the Lord. The angel revealed Ishmael's future to Hagar—that his descendants would be a great multitude. Tradition has it that Hagar is the ancestress of all the Arab peo-

ples and of the prophet Muhammad. Hagar called the well Beer Lahai Roi, "The well of the Living One who sees me."

When Hagar returned to Abraham's camp, Ishmael was born and accepted by Abraham as his son. But when Ishmael was 14, Isaac, the promised son, was born. The next year Ishmael mocked Isaac at the festival of Isaac's weaning. At Sarah's insistence and with God's approval, Hagar and Ishmael were expelled from Abraham's family. Abraham grieved for Ishmael, but God comforted him by revealing that a great nation would come out of Ishmael.

Hagar and Ishmael wandered in the wilderness until their water was gone. When Hagar laid her son under the shade of a bush to die, the angel of the Lord appeared to Hagar and showed her a well. This is a beautiful picture of God's concern for the outcast and helpless.

In Paul's allegory in Galatians 4, Hagar stands for Mount Sinai and corresponds to the earthly Jerusalem, while Isaac stands for the children of promise who are free in Christ.

HAGGAI [HAG eye] (festive)

An Old Testament prophet and author of the Book of Haggai. As God's spokesman, he encouraged the captives who had returned to Jerusalem to complete the reconstruction of the Temple. This work had started shortly after the first exiles returned from Babylon in 538 B.C. But the building activity was soon abandoned because of discouragement and oppression. Beginning in 520 B.C., Haggai and his fellow prophet, Zechariah, urged the people to resume the task. The Temple was completed five years later, about 515 B.C. (Ezra 5:1).

HAGGEDOLIM [HAH guh doe lihm] *(the great ones)*

The father of the priest Zabdiel (Neh. 11:14, NRSV, NIV).

HAGGERI [huh GHEE righ]

A form of HAGRI.

HAGGI [HAG eye] *(born on a feast day)*

A son of Gad and founder of a tribal family, the Haggites (Gen. 46:16).

HAGGIAH [hug EYE yuh] *(festival)*

A descendant of Merari, son of Levi (1 Chr. 6:30).

HAGGITH [HAG ith] *(festival)*

The fifth wife of David and the mother of Adonijah, who later claimed the throne (1 Chr. 3:2).

HAGRI [HAG righ]

The father of Mibhar, one of David's mighty men (1 Chr. 11:38; Haggeri, KJV; Hager, REB).

HAKKATAN [HAK uh tan] *(the small one)*

The father of Johanan, who returned from the Captivity with Ezra (Ezra 8:12).

HAKKOZ [HAK ahz]

A priest and chief of the seventh division of service in the sanctuary (1 Chr. 24:10; Ezra 2:61; Neh. 3:4, 21). Also see KOZ.

HAKUPHA [huh KOO fuh]

An ancestor of a family of Nethinim (Temple servants) who returned from Babylon with Zerubbabel (Ezra 2:51).

HALLOHESH [hah LOW hesh] *(the whisperer)*

The name of one or two men in the Book of Nehemiah:

1. The father of Shallum, who helped rebuild the walls of Jerusalem (Neh. 3:12; Halohesh, KJV).

2. A man who sealed the covenant with Nehemiah after the Captivity (Neh. 10:24). He may be the same person as No. 1.

H

HAM

Hayos

HALOHESH [ha LOW hesh]

A form of HALLOHESH.

HAM [hamm]

The youngest of Noah's three sons (Gen. 9:18, 24). Ham, along with the rest of Noah's household, was saved from the great Flood by entering the ark (Gen. 7:7). After the waters went down and Noah's household left the ark, Ham found his father, naked and drunk, asleep in his tent. Ham told his brothers, Shem and Japheth, who covered their father without looking on his nakedness. Noah was furious because Ham had seen him naked, and he placed a prophetic curse on Canaan, the son of Ham (Gen. 9:18, 25). The Canaanites were to serve the descendants of Shem and Japheth (Gen. 9:26–27; Josh. 9:16–27).

Ham had four sons: Cush, Mizraim, Put and Canaan (Gen. 10:6). The tribe of Mizraim settled in Egypt, while the tribes of Cush and Put settled in other parts of Africa. The tribe of Canaan populated Phoenicia and Palestine.

HAMAN [HAY mun]

The evil and scheming prime minister of Ahasuerus (Xerxes I), king of Persia (485–464 B.C.). When MORDECAI refused to bow to Haman, Haman plotted to destroy Mordecai and his family, as well as all of the Jews in the Persian Empire. But ESTHER intervened and saved her people. Haman was hanged on the very gallows he had constructed for Mordecai (Esth. 3:1—9:25). This shows that God is always in control of events, even when wickedness and evil seem to be winning out.

HAMMATH [HAM eth] (*hot spring*)

The founder of the house of Rechab, a family of the Kenites (1 Chr. 2:55).

HAMMEDATHA [ham ih DAY thuh]

The father of Haman the Agagite (Esth. 3:1).

HAMMELECH [HAM uh lek]

The father of Jerahmeel and Malchiah (Jer. 36:26; 38:6, KJV). The Hebrew word is probably not a proper name, but a general title that means "the king." Hence, the NKJV has "the king's son."

HAMMOLECHETH [huh MOH luh keth]

A form of HAMMOLEKETH.

HAMMOLEKETH [huh MOH luh keth] (*she who reigns*)

A daughter of Machir and sister of Gilead, the grandson of Manasseh (1 Chr. 7:18; Hammolecheth, NASB, NRSV).

HAMMUEL [HAM yoo el]

A form of HAMUEL.

HAMOR [HAY mohr] (*donkey*)

The father of SHECHEM. Hamor was killed with Shechem in revenge by Levi and Simon after Shechem raped their sister Dinah (Gen. 34:2–26). Jacob purchased land from the sons of Hamor and built an altar upon it (Gen. 33:19). Later, Joseph was buried on this land (Josh. 24:32).

HAMRAN [HAM ran]

A form of HEMDAN.

HAMUEL [HAM yoo el]

A son of Mishma, a descendant of Simeon (1 Chr. 4:26; Hammuel, NASB, NIV, NRSV).

HAMUL [HAY muhl]

A son of Perez, who was the son of Judah by Tamar (Gen. 46:12).

HAMUTAL [huh MYOO tuhl]

A daughter of Jeremiah of Libnah, one of King Josiah's wives, and the mother of Jehoahaz and Zedekiah (2 Kin. 23:31; 24:18).

HANAMEEL [huh NAM ih el]

A son of Shallum and a cousin of Jeremiah the prophet. Jeremiah purchased a field from Hanameel during the siege of Jerusalem by the Babylonians (Jer. 32:7–9, 12; Hanamel, NRSV, REB, NIV).

HANAN [HAY nuhn] (*merciful*)

The name of eight or nine Old Testament men:

1. A son of Shashak and a chief of the tribe of Benjamin (1 Chr. 8:23).
2. A son of Azel and a descendant of Saul and Jonathan (1 Chr. 8:38).
3. A son of Maachah and one of David's mighty men (1 Chr. 11:43).
4. The founder of a family of Nethinim (Temple servants) who returned from the Captivity with Zerubbabel (Ezra 2:46).
5. A Levite who helped Ezra interpret the law to the people (Neh. 8:7).
6. A Levite who sealed the covenant under Nehemiah (Neh. 10:10; 13:13). He may be the same person as No. 5.
7, 8. Two chiefs of the people who sealed the covenant under Nehemiah (Neh. 10:22, 26).
9. A son of Igdaliah and a prophet whose sons had a room in the Temple (Jer. 35:4).

HANANI [hah NAH nigh] (*gracious gift of the Lord*)

The name of six Old Testament men:
1. The father of Jehu (1 Kin. 16:1, 7).
2. A son of Heman and head of the 18th division of musicians appointed by David for the sanctuary (1 Chr. 25:4, 25).

3. A Seer who rebuked Asa for paying tribute money to Ben–Hadad, king of Syria (2 Chr. 16:7).
4. A priest who divorced his pagan wife after the Captivity (Ezra 10:20).
5. A brother of Nehemiah who brought news of Jerusalem to Susa and later was made governor of Jerusalem (Neh. 1:2; 7:2).
6. A Levite who played an instrument at the dedication of the repaired walls of Jerusalem (Neh. 12:36).

HANANIAH [han uh NIE uh] (*The Lord is gracious*)

The name of 15 men in the Old Testament:
1. An ancestor of Jesus in Luke's genealogy (1 Chr. 3:19, 21; Luke 3:27).
2. A son of Shashak (1 Chr. 8:24).
3. A leader of a division of priests in David's time (1 Chr. 25:4, 23).
4. A commander in the army of King Uzziah of Judah (2 Chr. 26:11).
5. A son of Bebai. Hananiah divorced his foreign wife following the Captivity (Ezra 10:28).
6. A perfumer who helped rebuild Jerusalem's walls during Nehemiah's time (Neh. 3:8).
7. The son of Shelemiah. Hananiah helped rebuild Jerusalem's walls during Nehemiah's time (Neh. 3:30).
8. An official in Jerusalem during Nehemiah's time (Neh. 7:2).
9. A clan leader who sealed the covenant in Nehemiah's time (Neh. 10:23).
10. A clan leader in the days of the high priest Joiakim after the Captivity (Neh. 12:12).
11. A priest who blew the trumpet at the dedication of Jerusalem's rebuilt wall (Neh. 12:41).
12. A false prophet in the prophet Jeremiah's time (Jeremiah 28).

13. A prince under King Jehoiakim of Judah (Jer. 36:12).

14. An ancestor of the guard who arrested the prophet Jeremiah (Jer. 37:13).

15. The Hebrew name of Shadrach (Dan. 1:6–7).

HANIEL [HAN ee uhl] (grace of God)

A leader and warrior-hero of the tribe of Asher (1 Chr. 7:39; Hanniel, NIV, NASB, NRSV). He was a son of Ulla.

HANNAH [HAN nuh] (gracious)

A wife of Elkanah, a Levite of the Kohathite branch of the priesthood (1 Sam. 1:1–2:21). Unable to bear children, Hannah suffered ridicule from Elkanah's other wife Peninnah, who bore him several children. Hannah vowed that if she were to give birth to a son, she would devote him to the Lord's service. The Lord answered her prayers, and to her was born the prophet Samuel.

Hannah was faithful to her promise. Making what must have been a heart-rending sacrifice, Hannah took Samuel to the Temple after he was weaned, there to "remain forever" (1:21). God rewarded Hannah's piety and faithfulness with three more sons and two daughters. Hannah's beautiful thanksgiving prayer (2:1–10) is similar to the song that Mary sang when she learned she would be the mother of Jesus (Luke 1:46–55).

HANNIEL [HAN ee uhl] (grace of God)

A son of Ephod, of the tribe of Manasseh (Num. 34:23). Hanniel was a leader who helped distribute the land west of the Jordan River after the Israelite conquest of the land of Canaan.

HANOCH [HAY nahk] (dedicated)

The name of two Old Testament men:
1. A son of Midian. Hanoch was a descendant of Abraham by Keturah (Gen. 25:4; 1 Chr. 1:33; Henoch, KJV).

2. The oldest son of Reuben and the founder of a tribal family, the Hanochites (1 Chr. 5:3).

HANUN [HAY nuhn] (gracious)

The name of three Old Testament men:

1. A son of Nahash, king of the Ammonites. When David sent ambassadors to console Hanun on the death of Nahash, Hanun dishonored David's ambassadors by shaving off their beards and cutting off their clothes. Upon hearing of this disgrace, David declared war against the Ammonites (2 Sam. 10:1–4).

2. A man who helped repair the walls of Jerusalem after the Captivity (Neh. 3:13).

3. A son of Zalaph who helped repair the walls of Jerusalem (Neh. 3:30).

HAPPIZZEZ [HAP uh zeez]

A descendant of Aaron whose family became the 18th of David's 24 divisions of priests (1 Chr. 24:15; Aphses, KJV, REB).

HARAN [HAIR uhn]

The name of three men in the Old Testament:

1. The third son of Terah, Abraham's father, and the younger brother of Abraham. Haran was the father of Lot, Milcah, and Iscah (Gen. 11:26–31).

2. A son of Caleb by Ephah, Caleb's concubine. Haran was the father of Gazez (1 Chr. 2:46).

3. A Levite from the family of Gershon and a son of Shimei. Haran lived during David's reign (1 Chr. 23:9).

HARBONA [hahr BOE nuh]

One of the eunuchs, or chamberlains, responsible for the harem of King

Ahasuerus (Xerxes I) of Persia (Esth. 1:10; 7:9).

HAREPH [HAIR ef]

A son of Caleb and the founder of Beth Gader, a town in Judah (1 Chr. 2:51).

HARHAIAH [hahr HIGH uh]

The father of Uzziel (Neh. 3:8).

HARHAS [HAHR hass]

A form of HASRAH.

HARHUR [HAHR hur]

An ancestor of a family of Nethinim (Temple servants) who returned from the Captivity (Ezra 2:51).

HARIM [HAIR em] (*dedicated* [to God])

The name of four Old Testament men:
1. A priest in charge of the third division of Temple duties (1 Chr. 24:8).
2. An ancestor of many Israelites who returned from the Captivity (Ezra 2:32). Harim's descendants divorced their pagan wives (Ezra 10:31).
3. The head of a priestly family who sealed the covenant with Nehemiah (Neh. 10:5).
4. Another Israelite who sealed the covenant with Nehemiah (Neh. 10:27).

HARIPH [HAIR if]

The name of two men in the time of Ezra and Nehemiah:
1. The founder of a family whose descendants returned from the Captivity (Neh. 7:24). He is also called Jorah (Ezra 2:18).
2. A leader who sealed the covenant, probably as a representative of his family (Neh. 10:19).

HARNEPHER [HAHR nuh fur]

A son of Zophah, of the tribe of Asher (1 Chr. 7:36).

HAROEH [huh ROE uh] (*the seer*)

A son of Shobal, descended from Judah through Hezron (1 Chr. 2:52). Haroeh may be the same person as REAIAH (1 Chr. 4:2).

HARSHA [HAHR shuh]

An ancestor of a family of Nethinim (Temple servants), some of whom returned from the Captivity (Ezra 2:52).

HARUM [HAIR uhm]

The father of Aharhel, a descendant of Koz (1 Chr. 4:8).

H

HARUMAPH [huh ROO mahf]

The father of Jedaiah (Neh. 3:10).

HARUZ [HAIR uz]

A man of Jotbah, a place in Judah (2 Kin. 21:19).

HASADIAH [hass uh DIGH uh] (*the Lord is faithful*)

A son of Zerubbabel and a descendant of Jehoiakim, king of Judah (1 Chr. 3:20).

HASENUAH [hass uh NOO uh]

A form of HASSENUAH.

HASHABIAH [hash uh BIGH uh] (*the Lord has taken account*)

The name of 14 men in the Old Testament:
1, 2. Two Levites of the family of Merari (1 Chr. 6:45; 9:14).
3. A son of Jeduthun (1 Chr. 25:3, 19).
4. A Levite of the family of Kohath and a descendant of Hebron (1 Chr. 26:30).
5. A son of Kemuel and chief of the tribe of Levi during David's reign (1 Chr. 27:17).
6. A chief of the Levites in the time of King Josiah of Judah (2 Chr. 35:9).

7. A Levite who returned from the Captivity with Ezra (Ezra 8:19).

8. One of the 12 priests appointed by Ezra to take care of the gold, the silver, and the dedicated vessels of the Temple after the Captivity (Ezra 8:24).

9. An Israelite who helped repair the walls of Jerusalem (Neh. 3:17).

10. A Levite who sealed the covenant with Nehemiah (Neh. 10:11).

11. A Levite, a son of Bunni, who lived in Jerusalem in Nehemiah's time (Neh. 11:15).

12. A Levite descended from Asaph (Neh. 11:22).

13. A priest who was head of the house of Hilkiah during the high priest Jehoiakim's time (Neh. 12:21).

14. A Levite after the Captivity (Neh. 12:24).

HASHABNAH [hah SHAHB nah]

One of the Israelites who sealed the covenant after the Captivity (Neh. 10:25).

HASHABNIAH [hah shahb nee EYE uh]

The name of two men in the Book of Nehemiah:

1. The father of Hattush (Neh. 3:10; Hashabneiah, NASB, NIV, NRSV).

2. A Levite who officiated at the feast under Ezra and Nehemiah when the covenant was sealed (Neh. 9:5).

HASHBADANA [hahsh buh DAH nuh] (thoughtful judge)

An Israelite who assisted Ezra in reading the Law (Neh. 8:4; Hashbaddanah, REB, NIV, NRSV).

HASHEM [HAY shem]

The father of several warriors who served in the bodyguard unit known as David's mighty men (1 Chr. 11:34).

HASHUB [HASH uhb] (considerate)

An Israelite who helped repair the wall of Jerusalem (Neh. 3:11; Hasshub, NRSV, NIV, NASB, REB).

HASHUBAH [huh SHOO buh] (considerate)

A son of Zerubbabel and a descendant of Jehoiakim, king of Judah (1 Chr. 3:20).

HASHUM [HASH uhm]

The name of three Old Testament men:

1. An Israelite whose descendants returned with Zerubbabel after the Captivity (Ezra 2:19).

2. A priest who helped Ezra read the Law to the returned captives (Neh. 8:4).

3. The head of a family that sealed the covenant with Nehemiah (Neh. 10:18).

HASHUPHA [huh SOO fuh]

A form of HASUPHA.

HASRAH [HASS rah]

The grandfather of Shallum (2 Chr. 34:22), who was also called Harhas (2 Kin. 22:14).

HASSENAAH [hass uh NAY uh]

An Israelite whose descendants helped rebuild Jerusalem's wall (Neh. 3:3).

HASSENUAH [hass uh NOO uh] (hated)

The father of Hodaviah (1 Chr. 9:7; Hasenuah, KJV; Hassenuah, NRSV).

HASSHUB [HASH uhb] (considerate)

The name of four men in the Old Testament:

1. The father of Shemaiah (1 Chr. 9:14).

2. An Israelite who helped repair the walls of Jerusalem after the Captivity (Neh. 3:23; Hashub, KJV).

3. A head of a family who sealed the covenant after the Captivity (Neh. 10:23).

4. A form of HASHUB (Neh. 3:11).

HASSOPHERETH [HASS soe FEAR eth]

A form of SOPHERETH.

HASUPHA [huh SOO fuh]

An ancestor of a family of Nethinim (Temple servants), some of whom returned with Zerubbabel from the Captivity (Ezra 2:43). The name is also spelled Hashupha (Neh. 7:46, KJV).

HATACH [HAY tak]

A form of HATHACH.

HATHACH [HAY thak]

A eunuch in the court of Ahasuerus (Xerxes), king of Persia, appointed to attend to Queen Esther (Esth. 4:5–6; Hatach, KJV).

HATHATH [HAY thath]

A son of Othniel (1 Chr. 4:13).

HATIPHA [huh TIGH fuh]

An ancestor of a family of Nethinim (Temple servants), some of whom returned with Zerubbabel from the Captivity (Ezra 2:54).

HATITA [huh TIGH tuh]

A Temple gatekeeper whose descendants returned from the Captivity (Ezra 2:42).

HATTIL [HAT uhl]

One of Solomon's servants. Members of Hattil's family returned from the Captivity with Zerubbabel (Neh. 7:59).

HATTUSH [HAT uhsh]

The name of three Old Testament men:

1. A descendant of David who returned with Ezra from the Captivity (Ezra 8:2).

2. An Israelite who helped rebuild the walls of Jerusalem under Nehemiah (Neh. 3:10).

3. A priest who returned from the Captivity with Zerubbabel and signed the covenant (Neh. 10:4).

HAVILAH [HAV uh luh]

The name of two:

1. A son of Cush and a grandson of Ham (Gen. 10:7).

2. A son of Joktan and a grandson of Eber (Gen. 10:29).

HAZAEL [HAZ a el] (God has seen)

A Syrian official whom the prophet Elijah anointed king over Syria at God's command (1 Kin. 19:15). Sometime between 845 and 843 B.C., Ben–Hadad, king of Syria, sent Hazael to the prophet Elisha to ask whether the king would recover from an illness. Elisha answered that Hazael himself was destined to become king. The next day Hazael assassinated Ben–Hadad and took the throne (2 Kin. 8:7–15). Hazael immediately attacked Ramoth Gilead, seriously wounding King Joram of Israel (2 Kin. 8:28–29).

At the end of Jehu's reign over Israel, Hazael attacked the Israelites east of the Jordan River (2 Kin. 10:32). During the reign of Jehu's successor, Jehoahaz, Hazael oppressed Israel because "the anger of the LORD was aroused against Israel" (2 Kin. 13:3). A gift of the dedicated treasures of the Temple from King Jehoash of Judah prevented Hazael from attacking Jerusalem (2 Kin. 12:17–18). When

Hazael died, his son Ben–Hadad II succeeded him.

As late as the first century A.D., Hazael was worshiped in Damascus because of the way in which he had adorned the city.

HAZAIAH [huh ZIGH uh] (*the Lord sees*)

A man of Judah, of the family of Shelah (Neh. 11:5).

HAZARMAVETH [HAY zur MAY veth]

The third son of Joktan and a descendant of Shem (Gen. 10:26). The descendants of Hazarmaveth (modern Hadhramaut) settled in the southern Arabian Peninsula.

HAZELELPONI [haz ih lehl POE nigh]

The daughter of Etam and the sister of Jezreel, Ishma, and Idbash in the genealogy of Judah (1 Chr. 4:3; Hazzelelponi, NASB, NIV, NRSV).

HAZIEL [HAY zee uhl] (*God sees*)

A Gershonite Levite of the family of Shimei in David's time (1 Chr. 23:9).

HAZO [HAY zoe] (*visionary*)

A son of Nahor and Milcah and a nephew of Abraham (Gen. 22:22).

HAZZELELPONI [haz ih lehl POE nigh]

A form of HAZELELPONI.

HEBER [HEE buhr] (*associate*)

The name of six men in the Bible:
1. A son of Beriah, of the tribe of Asher (Gen. 46:17).
2. The husband of Jael (Judg. 4:11–21).
3. A man of the tribe of Judah (1 Chr. 4:18).
4. The head of a family of Gadites (1 Chr. 5:13).

5. A Benjamite and a son of Elpaal (1 Chr. 8:17).
6. A Benjamite and a son of Shashak (1 Chr. 8:22; Eber, NASB, NIV, NKJV, NRSV).

HEGAI [HEG igh]

A eunuch under Ahasuerus (Xerxes), king of Persia, who had responsibility for the royal harem (Esth. 2:3; Hege, KJV).

HELAH [HEE luh]

A wife of Ashhur and the mother of Zereth, Zohar, and Ethan (1 Chr. 4:5, 7).

HELDAI [HEL digh]

The name of two men in the Old Testament:
1. A captain of the Temple service and one of David's mighty men (1 Chr. 27:15). Heldai is also called Heled (1 Chr. 11:30, NASB, NIV, KJV, NKJV, NRSV) and Heleb (2 Sam. 23:29, NASB, KJV, NRSV).
2. An Israelite who brought gold and silver from Babylon to help the exiles who returned to Jerusalem with Zerubbabel (Zech. 6:10). Heldai is also called Helem (Zech. 6:14, NAS, KJV).

HELEB [HEE leb]

A form of HELDAI No. 1.

HELED [HEE led]

A form of HELDAI No. 1.

HELEK [HEE lek] (*portion*)

A son of Gilead and founder of the Helekites (Num. 26:30).

HELEM [HEE lem]

The name of two Old Testament men:
1. A descendant of Asher (1 Chr. 7:35). Helem may be the same person as Hotham No. 1 (1 Chr. 7:32).
2. A man mentioned by the prophet Zechariah (Zech. 6:14). Helem may be

the same person as Heldai No. 2 (Zech. 6:10).

HELEZ [HEE lez]

The name of two Old Testament men:
1. One of David's mighty men (2 Sam. 23:26). He was a Pelonite or a Paltite.
2. A son of Azariah (1 Chr. 2:39).

HELI [HEE ligh] (*God is on high*)

The father of Joseph in Luke's genealogy of Jesus (Luke 3:23). Heli is the Greek form of Eli.

HELKAI [HEL kigh] (*the Lord is my portion*)

The head of a priestly house in the days of Joiakim the high priest (Neh. 12:15).

HELKATH [HEL kath] (*portion*)

A town of Asher assigned to the Levites of the family of Gershon (Josh. 19:25). Helkath is also called Hukok (1 Chr. 6:75).

HELON [HEE lahn]

A Zebulunite and the father of Eliab (Num. 1:9).

HEMAM [HEE mam]

A son of Lotan and grandson of Seir (Gen. 36:22). This name is also spelled Homam (1 Chr. 1:39).

HEMAN [HEE muhn] (*faithful*)

The name of two Old Testament men:
1. A son of Zerah and grandson of Jacob. Heman composed a meditative psalm, a prayer for deliverance from sadness (Psalm 88, title).
2. A son of Joel and a grandson of Samuel the prophet (1 Chr. 6:33; 15:17). Presented as "the singer" or "the musician," he was the first of three chief Levites to conduct the vocal and instrumental music of the tabernacle during the reign of David (1 Chr. 16:41–42).

HEMDAN [HEM dan] (*pleasant*)

A descendant of Seir the Horite and the oldest son of Dishon (Gen. 36:26). Hemdan is also spelled as Hamran (1 Chr. 1:41, NKJV, NASB, NRSV, REB) and Amram (1 Chr. 1:41, KJV).

HENADAD [HEN uh dad] (*grace of Hadad*)

A Levite whose descendants helped rebuild the walls of Jerusalem under Nehemiah (Neh. 10:9).

HENOCH [HEE nuhk]

A form of HANOCH.

HEPHER [HEE fur]

The name of three men:
1. The youngest son of Gilead and founder of the tribal family of Hepherites (Num. 26:32; 27:1).
2. A descendant of Judah and a son of Ashhur by Naarah (1 Chr. 4:6).
3. One of David's mighty men (1 Chr. 11:36).

HEPHZIBAH [HEF zih buh] (*my delight is in her*)

The wife of Hezekiah and the mother of Manasseh (2 Kin. 21:1).

HERESH [HEAR esh]

A Levite among the captives who returned to Jerusalem (1 Chr. 9:15).

HERMAS [HUR muhs]

A Christian in Rome to whom the apostle Paul sent greetings (Rom. 16:14).

HERMES [HUR meez] (*interpreter*)

A Christian to whom the apostle Paul sent greetings (Rom. 16:14).

HERMOGENES [hur MAH jih neez]
(offspring of Hermes)

An Asian Christian who deserted the apostle Paul at Ephesus (2 Tim. 1:15).

HEROD [HEHR ud]

The name of several Roman rulers in the Palestine region during Jesus' earthly ministry and the periods shortly before His birth and after His resurrection.

The Herodian dynasty made its way into Palestine through Antipater, an Idumean by descent. The Idumeans were of Edomite stock as descendants of Esau. Antipater was installed as procurator of Judea by Julius Caesar, the emperor of Rome, in 47 B.C. He appointed two of his sons to ruling positions. One of these was Herod, known as "Herod the Great," who was appointed governor of Judea.

Herod the Great

(37–4 B.C.) The title Herod the Great refers not so much to Herod's greatness as to the fact that he was the eldest son of Antipater. Nevertheless, Herod did show some unusual abilities. He was a ruthless fighter, a cunning negotiator, and a subtle diplomat. The Romans appreciated the way he subdued opposition and maintained order among the Jewish people. These qualities, combined with an intense loyalty to the emperor, made him an important figure in the life of Rome and the Jews of Palestine.

After Herod became governor of Galilee, he quickly established himself in the entire region. For 33 years he remained a loyal friend and ally of Rome. He was appointed as king of Judea, where he was in direct control of the Jewish people. This required careful diplomacy because he was always suspect by the Jews as an outsider (Idumean) and thus a threat to their national right to rule.

At first Herod was conscious of Jewish national and religious feelings. He moved slowly on such issues as taxation, Hellenism, and religion. He did much to improve his relationship with the Jews when he prevented the Temple in Jerusalem from being raided and defiled by invading Romans.

Herod the Great established his authority and influence through a centralized bureaucracy, well-built fortresses, and foreign soldiers. To assure his continued rule, he slaughtered all male infants who could possibly be considered legal heirs to the throne. His wife Mariamne also became a victim.

The territories under Herod's rule experienced economic and cultural growth. His business and organizational ability led to the erection of many important buildings. Hellenistic (Greek) ideas were introduced into Palestine through literature, art, and athletic contests. His major building project was the Temple complex in Jerusalem, which, according to John 2:20, had taken 46 years to build up to that time. From the Jewish perspective, this was his greatest achievement.

At times Herod implemented his policies with force and cruelty. His increasing fear of Jewish revolt led to suppression of any opposition. His personal problems also increased, and by 14 B.C. his kingdom began to decline. This decline was brought on mainly by his personal and domestic problems.

Herod's murder of his wife Mariamne apparently haunted him. This was compounded when his two sons from that marriage, Alexander and Aristobulus, realized that their father was responsible for their mother's death. By 7 B.C., Herod had both of these sons put to death. Of Herod it was said, "It is better to be Herod's pig (hys) than to be his son (huios)."

As Herod became increasingly ill, an intense struggle for succession to his throne emerged within the family. His 10 marriages and 15 children virtually guaranteed such a struggle. One son, Antipater, poisoned Herod's mind against two other eligible sons, Archelaus and Philip. This resulted in his initial choice of a younger son, Antipas, as sole successor. However, he later changed his will and made Archelaus king. Antipas and Philip received lesser positions as Tetrarchs, or rulers, over small territories.

After Herod died, his will was contested in Rome. Finally Archelaus was made ethnarch over Idumea, Judea, and Samaria—with a promise to be appointed king if he proved himself as a leader. Antipas became tetrarch over Galilee and Perea. Philip was made tetrarch over Gaulanitis, Trachonitis, Batanea, and Paneas in the northern regions.

Jesus was born in Bethlehem during the reign of Herod the Great. The wise men came asking, "Where is he that is born King of the Jews?" This aroused Herod's jealous spirit. According to Matthew's account, Herod tried to eliminate Jesus by having all the male infants of the Bethlehem region put to death (Matt. 2:13–16). But this despicable act failed. Joseph and Mary were warned by God in a dream to take their child and flee to Egypt. Here they hid safely until Herod died (Matt. 2:13–15).

Herod Archelaus

(4 B.C.–A.D. 6). Archelaus inherited his father Herod's vices without his abilities. He was responsible for much bloodshed in Judea and Samaria. Jewish revolts, particularly those led by the Zealots, were brutally crushed. Antipas and Philip did not approve of Archelaus' methods; so they complained to Rome. Their complaints were followed by a Jewish delegation that finally succeeded in having Archelaus stripped of power and banished to Rome.

The only biblical reference to Archelaus occurs in Matthew 2:22. Matthew recorded the fear that Mary and Joseph had about going through Judea on their way from Egypt to Galilee because Archelaus was the ruler.

Herod Philip the Tetrarch

(4 B.C.–A.D. 30). Philip, who inherited the northern part of his father Herod the Great's kingdom (Luke 3:1), must have been the best of Herod's surviving sons. During his long and peaceful rule, he was responsible for a number of building projects, including the city of Caesarea Philippi. He also rebuilt Bethsaida into a Greek city and renamed it Julias in honor of Augustus Caesar's daughter, Julia.

Herod Antipas

(4 B.C.–A.D. 39). Antipas, another of Herod the Great's sons, began as tetrarch over Galilee and Perea. He was the ruling Herod during Jesus' life and ministry. Herod Antipas was first married to the daughter of Aretas, a Nabatean king. But he became infatuated with Herodias, the wife of his half-brother, Philip I. The two eloped, although both were married at the time. This scandalous affair was condemned severely by John the Baptist (Matt. 14:4; Mark 6:17–18; Luke 3:19).

Although Antipas apparently had some respect for John the Baptist, he had John arrested and imprisoned for his outspokenness. Later, at a royal birthday party, Antipas granted Salome, the daughter of Herod Philip, a wish. Probably at the prodding of Herodias (Mark 6:19), Salome requested the head of John the Baptist (Matt. 14:6–12; Mark 6:21–29). Since he was under oath and did not want to lose face before his guests, Herod ordered John's execution.

Antipas' contacts with Jesus occurred at the same time as the ministry of John the Baptist. Because of Jesus' popularity and miraculous powers, Antipas may have been haunted by the possibility that Jesus was John the Baptist come back to life.

The New Testament record shows that the relationship between Jesus and Antipas must have been strained. Jesus' popularity and teachings may have threatened Antipas who, according to the Pharisees, sought to kill Him (Luke 13:31). By calling Herod a fox "Go, tell that fox," (Luke 13:32), Jesus showed His disapproval of his cunning and deceitful ways.

The next encounter between Antipas and Jesus occurred at the trial of Jesus (Luke 23:6–12). Luke indicated that Herod could not find anything in the charges against Jesus that deserved death; so he sent Jesus back to Pilate for a final decision.

During this time of his rule, Antipas was experiencing political problems of his own. Aretas, the Nabatean king whose daughter had been Antipas' wife before he became involved with Herodias, returned to avenge this insult. Antipas' troops were defeated. This, together with some other problems, led to his political downfall. Antipas was finally banished by the Roman emperor to an obscure section of France.

Herod Agrippa I

(A.D. 37–44). Agrippa took over Antipas' territory after Antipas fell from favor. Agrippa's power and responsibilities extended far beyond his ability. As a young person growing up in the imperial court, he developed an undisciplined and extravagant life-style. But Agrippa had enough charm and intelligence to stay on the good side of Rome.

After the Roman Emperor Caligula was murdered, Agrippa helped Claudius gain the throne. His loyalty was rewarded. Claudius confirmed Agrippa in his present position and added the territories of Judea and Samaria. This made Agrippa ruler of a kingdom as large as that of his grandfather, Herod the Great.

Very little about Agrippa I is recorded in Scripture. From the comments in Acts 12:1–23, we know that Agrippa sought to win the favor of his Jewish subjects by opposing the early Christian church and its leaders. The record of his death as recorded in Acts 12:20–23 shows the humiliating way he died. After his death, Palestine struggled through a number of chaotic years before Rome was able to establish order.

Herod Agrippa II

(A.D. 50–100). Agrippa II was judged to be too young to assume leadership over all the territory of his father, Agrippa I. Thus, Emperor Claudius appointed Cuspius Fadus procurator of Palestine. But in A.D. 53, Agrippa II was appointed as the legitimate ruler over part of this territory.

The only reference to Agrippa II in the New Testament occurs in Acts 25:13–26:32, which deals with Paul's imprisonment in Caesarea. Agrippa listened to Paul's defense, but the apostle appealed to Rome. Agrippa had no power to set him free.

Agrippa was caught in the Jewish revolts that preceded the destruction of Jerusalem in A.D. 70 under the Roman Emperor Titus. He continued to rule by appointment of Vespasian until his death in A.D. 100. His death marked the end of the Herodian dynasty in the affairs of the Jewish people in Palestine.

HERODIAS [heh ROE dee uhs]

The queen who demanded John the Baptist's head on a platter (Matt. 14:1–12). The granddaughter of Herod the Great, Herodias first married her father's brother, Herod Philip I. One child was born to this union. Philip's half-brother, the tetrarch Herod Antipas, wanted Herodias for his own wife, so he divorced his wife and married Herodias while Philip was still living.

When John the Baptist denounced their immorality, Herodias plotted John's death. She had her daughter Salome gain Herod's favor by dancing seductively for him at a banquet. As a result, Herod promised her anything she wanted. Following her mother's wishes, Salome asked for the head of John the Baptist.

HERODION [hih ROE dee uhn]

A Christian whom the apostle Paul called "my kinsman" (Rom. 16:11) and to whom he sent greetings.

HETH [heth]

The second son of Canaan, ancestor of the Hittites (Gen. 10:15; 1 Chr. 1:13). The Hittite Empire was centered in Anatolia, or Asia Minor.

HEZEKI [HEZ uh kigh]

A form of HIZKI.

HEZEKIAH [hez uh KIGH uh] (*the Lord is my strength*)

The name of three or four men in the Old Testament:

1. The 13th king of Judah. Born the son of Ahaz by Abi, daughter of Zechariah, Hezekiah became known as one of Judah's godly kings. That an ungodly man like Ahaz could have such a godly son can only be attributed to the grace of God. Hezekiah's father had given the kingdom over to idolatry; but upon his accession to the throne, Hezekiah decisively and courageously initiated religious reforms (2 Kin. 18:4).

In the first month of his reign, Hezekiah reopened the Temple doors that his father had closed. He also assembled the priests and Levites and commissioned them to sanctify themselves for service and to cleanse the Temple. Appropriate sacrifices were then offered with much rejoicing (2 Chr. 29:3–36).

Hezekiah faced a golden opportunity to reunite the tribes spiritually. In the north Israel had fallen to Assyria in 722 B.C. Hezekiah invited the remnant of the people to come to Jerusalem to participate in the celebration of the Passover. Although some northern tribes scorned the invitation, most responded favorably (2 Chr. 30:1–27).

Hezekiah's reformation reached beyond Jerusalem to include the cleansing of the land, extending even to the tribes of Benjamin, Ephraim, and Manasseh. High places, images, and pagan altars were destroyed. The bronze serpent that Moses had made in the wilderness centuries earlier (Num. 21:5–9) had been preserved, and people were worshiping it. Hezekiah had it destroyed also (2 Kin. 18:4; 2 Chr. 31:1). The land had never undergone such a thorough reform.

When Hezekiah experienced a serious illness, the prophet Isaiah informed the king that he would die. In response to Hezekiah's prayer for recovery, God promised him 15 additional years of life. God also provided a sign for Hezekiah as evidence that the promise would be fulfilled. The sign, one of the most remarkable miracles of the Old Testament, consisted of the sun's shadow moving backward ten degrees on the Sundial of Ahaz (Is. 38:1–8).

H

Shortly after he recovered from his illness (Is. 39:1), Hezekiah received visitors from the Babylonian king, Merodach–Baladan (2 Kin. 20:12). They came with letters to congratulate Hezekiah on his recovery and to inquire about the sign (2 Chr. 32:31) in the land. But their real reason for visiting may have been to gain an ally in their revolt against Assyria. When they lavished gifts upon Hezekiah, he in turn showed them his wealth—an action that brought stiff rebuke from Isaiah (2 Kin. 20:13–18).

There is no evidence to indicate that Hezekiah formed an alliance with Babylon. Neither is there any indication that he joined the rebellion in 711 B.C. led by Ashdod, the leading Philistine city. However, Scripture does reveal that he finally did rebel. Sargon II had died in 705 B.C.; and his successor, Sennacherib, was preoccupied with trying to consolidate the kingdom when Hezekiah rebelled. With that accomplished, however, Sennacherib was ready to crush Hezekiah's revolt.

Anticipating the Assyrian aggression, Hezekiah made extensive military preparations. He strengthened the fortifications of Jerusalem, produced weapons and shields for his army, and organized his fighting forces under trained combat commanders. Realizing the importance of an adequate water supply, Hezekiah constructed a tunnel that channeled water from the Spring of Gihon outside the city walls to the Pool of Siloam inside the walls (2 Kin. 20:20). This waterway (now known as Hezekiah's Tunnel) was cut through solid rock, extending more than 520 meters (1,700 feet).

As Sennacherib captured the fortified cities of Judah, Hezekiah realized that his revolt was a lost cause and he attempted to appease the Assyrian king. To send an apology and tribute, he emptied the palace treasuries and the Temple, even stripping the gold from the doors and pillars. But this failed to appease Sennacherib's anger.

At the height of the Assyrian siege, the Angel of the Lord struck the Assyrian camp, leaving 185,000 dead (2 Kin. 19:35). In humiliation and defeat, Sennacherib withdrew to his capital city of Nineveh.

Little more is said about Hezekiah's remaining years as king, but his achievements are recorded in 2 Chronicles 32:27–30. When he died, after reigning for 29 years, the people of Jerusalem "buried him in the upper tombs of the sons of David" (2 Chr. 32:33), a place of honor.

2. A descendant of David's royal line, a son of Neariah (1 Chr. 3:23).

3. A head of a family who returned from the Captivity in Babylon (Neh. 7:21).

4. The great-great-grandfather of the prophet Zephaniah (Zeph. 1:1; Hizkiah, KJV, perhaps the same as No. 1).

HEZION [HEE zih ahn]

The father of Tabrimmon and the grandfather of Ben–Hadad I, king of Syria in the time of King Asa of Judah (1 Kin. 15:18).

HEZIR [HEE zur] (*pig*)

The name of two Old Testament men:

1. A Levite in the time of David (1 Chr. 24:15).

2. A leader of the people who sealed the covenant after the Captivity (Neh. 10:20).

HEZRAI [HEZ righ]

A Carmelite and one of David's mighty men (2 Sam. 23:35; Hezro, NIV, NASB, NRSV).

HEZRO [HEZ roe]

A form of HEZRAI.

HEZRON [HEZ rahn] (*enclosure*)

The name of two men in the Old Testament:

1. A son of Reuben and founder of the Hezronites (Gen. 46:9).

2. A founder of a tribal family (Gen. 46:12) and an ancestor of Jesus (Matt. 1:3; Esrom, KJV).

HIDDAI [HID day eye]

One of David's mighty men (2 Sam. 23:30), also called Hurai (1 Chr. 11:32).

HIEL [HIGH uhl] (*God is living*)

A native of Bethel who fortified Jericho during the reign of Ahab (1 Kin. 16:34). Hiel also sacrificed his sons, in fulfillment of Joshua's curse (Josh. 6:26).

HILKIAH [hill KYE ah] (*the Lord is my portion*)

The name of seven or eight Old Testament men:

1. The father of Eliakim (2 Kin. 18:18, 26, 37).

2. A high priest during the reign of King Josiah of Judah (2 Kin. 22:4–14). Hilkiah assisted Josiah in reforming Judah's backslidden people.

3. A Levite and a son of Amzi (1 Chr. 6:45–46).

4. A son of Hosah (1 Chr. 26:11) and a tabernacle gatekeeper.

5. A priest who helped Ezra read the Book of the Law to the people (Neh. 8:4; 11:11). He may be the same person as No. 6.

6. A chief priest who returned from the Captivity with Zerubbabel (Neh. 12:7).

7. Father of Jeremiah the prophet (Jer. 1:1).

8. Father of Gemariah, a contemporary of Jeremiah (Jer. 29:3).

HILLEL [HILL el] (*he has praised*)

The father of Abdon (Judg. 12:13, 15). Abdon was one of the judges of Israel.

HINNOM [HIN ohm]

An unknown person, perhaps the original Jebusite owner, whose name appears only in the phrase, "the Valley of Hinnom" (Josh. 15:8; Neh. 11:30)—a valley outside Jerusalem.

HIRAH [HIGH ruh]

An Adullamite, the "friend" of Judah (Gen. 38:1, 12).

HIRAM [HIGH rum] (*my brother is exalted*)

The name of two Old Testament men:

1. A king of Tyre and friend of both David and Solomon (2 Sam. 5:11; 1 Kin. 10:11, 22; 2 Chr. 8:2, 18). The Jewish historian Josephus records that Hiram succeeded his father, Abibaal, and reigned for 34 years. Hiram greatly enhanced the city of Tyre, building an embankment on its east side and a causeway to connect the city with the island where the temple of Baal–Shamem stood.

Hiram appears throughout the reigns of David and Solomon. He sent representatives to David after David captured Jerusalem. When David built a palace, Hiram furnished cedar from Lebanon and workmen to assist with the project. In later years, when Solomon built the Temple in Jerusalem, Hiram again sent cedar and skilled laborers—this time in return for wheat and olive oil. Hiram also supplied ships and sailors for Solomon's trade interests, probably for a share of the profits.

2. A skilled laborer who worked on Solomon's Temple (1 Kin. 7:13, 40, 45).

H

He worked in bronze on the pillars, the laver, the basins, and the shovels. The title "father" given to him probably means he was a master workman. His name is also spelled Huram (2 Chr. 2:13–14; Huram–Abi, NIV).

HIZKI [HIZ kigh] ([the Lord is] *my strength*)

A son of Elpaal and a descendant of Benjamin (1 Chr. 8:17; Hezeki, KJV; Hizki, REB).

HIZKIAH [hiz KIGH uh]

A form of HEZEKIAH.

HOBAB [HOE bab]

The father-in-law of Moses (Num. 10:29; Judg. 4:11), apparently the same person as JETHRO.

HOBAIAH [hoe BIGH uh]

A form of HABAIAH.

HOD [hahd] (*glory*)

A son of Zophah and a descendant of Asher (1 Chr. 7:37).

HODAIAH [hoe DIGH uh]

A form of HODAVIAH.

HODAVIAH [hoe duh VIGH uh] (*give honor to the Lord*)

The name of four Old Testament men:
1. A son of Elioenai and a descendant of Zerubbabel and King David (1 Chr. 3:24; Hodaiah, KJV, REB).
2. A head of the half-tribe of Manasseh, east of the Jordan River (1 Chr. 5:24).
3. A son of Hassenuah (1 Chr. 9:7).
4. Founder of the family of the "sons of Hodaviah" (Ezra 2:40), also spelled Hodevah (Neh. 7:43).

HODESH [HOE desh] (*new moon*)

A wife of Shaharaim, of the tribe of Benjamin (1 Chr. 8:9), also called Baara (1 Chr. 8:8).

HODEVAH [HOE duh vuh]

A form of HODAVIAH.

HODIAH [hoe DIE uh] (*splendor of the Lord*)

A man who married Naham's sister (1 Chr. 4:19).

HODIJAH [hoe DIE juh] (*splendor of the Lord*)

The name of two men in the Old Testament:
1. A Levite in the time of Ezra and Nehemiah (Neh. 8:7).
2. A chief of the people who sealed the covenant after the Captivity (Neh. 10:18).

HOGLAH [HOG luh]

A daughter of Zelophehad of the tribe of Manasseh (Num. 26:33).

HOHAM [HOE ham]

One of five Amorite kings killed by Joshua near the cave at Makkedah (Josh. 10:1–27).

HOMAM [HOE mam]

A son of Lotan and grandson of Seir (1 Chr. 1:39), also called Hemam (Gen. 36:22).

HOPHNI [HOFF nigh] (*tadpole*)

A son of Eli the high priest who, along with his brother Phinehas, proved unworthy of priestly duties (1 Sam. 1:3; 2:34; 4:4–17). Their behavior was characterized by greed (1 Sam. 2:13–16) and lust (1 Sam. 2:22). Eli made only a half-

judgment was pronounced upon Eli and his household. Hophni and Phinehas were killed in a battle, and the Ark of the Covenant was captured by the Philistines (1 Sam. 4:1–11). When Eli heard the news, he fell backward and died of a broken neck (1 Sam. 4:12–18).

HOPHRA [HOFF ruh]

A king of Egypt who reigned 589–570 B.C. Early in his reign, Hophra marched against Nebuchadnezzar II who had besieged Jerusalem in 589 B.C. When the Babylonians turned from Jerusalem to challenge him, Hophra retreated to Egypt. Hophra's overthrow was foretold by the prophet Jeremiah (Jer. 44:30).

HORAM [HOHR em]

A king of Gezer defeated by Joshua (Josh. 10:33).

HORI [HOHR igh]

The name of two Old Testament men:
1. A son of Lotan and a descendant of Seir (Gen. 36:22).

2. The father of Shaphat, one of the 12 spies sent by Moses to spy out the land of Canaan (Num. 13:5).

HOSAH [HOE suh]

A Levite gatekeeper of the family of Merari in David's time (1 Chr. 16:38).

HOSEA [hoe ZAY uh] (*deliverance*)

An Old Testament prophet and author of the Book of Hosea. The son of Beeri (Hos. 1:1), Hosea ministered in the northern kingdom of Israel during the chaotic period just before the fall of this nation in 722 B.C. The literary features within Hosea's book suggest he was a member of the upper class. The tone and contents of the book also show he was a man of deep compassion, strong loyalty, and keen awareness of the political events taking place in the world at that time. As a prophet, he was also deeply committed to God and His will as it was being revealed to His Covenant People.

Hosea is one of the most unusual prophets of the Old Testament, since he was commanded by God to marry a pros-

HUR

titute (Hos. 1:2–9). His wife Gomer eventually returned to her life of sin, but Hosea bought her back from the slave market and restored her as his wife (Hos. 3:1–5). His unhappy family experience was an object lesson of the sin or "harlotry" of the nation of Israel in rejecting the one true God and serving pagan gods. Although the people deserved to be rejected because they had turned their backs on God, Hosea emphasized that God would continue to love them and use them as His special people.

In his unquestioning obedience of God, Hosea demonstrated he was a prophet who would follow his Lord's will, no matter what the cost. He was a sensitive, compassionate spokesman for righteousness whose own life echoed the message that God is love.

HOSHAIAH [hoe SHAY uh] (*the Lord has saved*)

The name of two Old Testament men:
1. An Israelite who participated in the dedication of the rebuilt wall of Jerusalem (Neh. 12:32).
2. The father of Jezaniah (Jer. 42:1) and Azariah (Jer. 43:2).

HOSHAMA [HOSH uh muh] (*the Lord has heard*)

A son of Jeconiah, king of Judah, who was carried away captive by Nebuchadnezzar (1 Chr. 3:18).

HOSHEA [hoe SHEE ah] (*salvation*)

The name of four men in the Old Testament:
1. Another name of Joshua the son of Nun (Num. 13:8, 16).
2. The last king of Israel (2 Kin. 15:30; 17:1–6; 18:1, 9–10). Hoshea became king after he assassinated the former king, Pekah. Hoshea did evil in God's sight, but not to the extent of former kings.

While he did not wipe out idolatrous worship, he at least did not give official approval to the practice. When Hoshea took the throne, he served as a puppet king under Assyria. But he eventually quit sending tribute money to Assyria and began negotiating an alliance with Egypt. When the Assyrian king, Shalmaneser V, learned of Hoshea's rebellion and conspiracy, he advanced toward Israel. The capital city of Samaria was besieged and Hoshea was captured and imprisoned. After two years, Assyria finally captured Samaria, and its inhabitants were carried away to new locations in the Assyrian Empire (2 Kin. 17:18–23).
3. A son of Azaziah (1 Chr. 27:20) and an Ephraimite ruler in David's time.
4. A resident of Jerusalem during the rebuilding of Jerusalem's wall under Nehemiah (Neh. 10:23); he signed a covenant to keep God's law.

HOTHAM [HOE tham] (*signet ring*)

The name of two men in the Old Testament:
1. A son of Heber (1 Chr. 7:32). Hotham is probably the same person as Helem (v. 35).
2. An Aroerite whose two sons Shama and Jeiel were among David's mighty men (1 Chr. 11:44; Hothan, KJV).

HOTHAN [HOE than]

A form of HOTHAM.

HOTHIR [HOE thur]

A Levite in charge of the 21st division of singers in the tabernacle service (1 Chr. 25:4).

HOZAI [HOE zay eye]

An unknown prophet who left a record of some of the events of King Manasseh's life (2 Chr. 33:19).

HUL [huhl]

The second son of Aram and a grandson of Shem (Gen. 10:23).

HULDAH [HUHL duh]

A prophetess consulted when the lost Book of the Law was found (2 Chr. 34:22–28). An indication of the esteem in which Huldah was held can be seen in Josiah's action. When the Book of the Law was found, he consulted her rather than Jeremiah. Huldah prophesied Jerusalem's destruction but added that because Josiah had done what was right in God's sight, it would not happen before Josiah died.

HUPHAM [HOO fuhm]

A descendant of Benjamin and the founder of a tribal family, the Huphamites (Num. 26:39). He is also called Huppim (Gen. 46:21).

HUPPAH [HUH puh] (*covering*)

A priest responsible for one of the divisions of service in the sanctuary in David's time (1 Chr. 24:13).

HUPPIM [HUH pim]

A form of Hupham.

HUR [her]

The name of six men in the Old Testament:

1. A leader who, with Aaron, held up Moses' hands at Rephidim so the army of Israel could defeat the forces of Amalek (Ex. 17:10, 12). Aaron and Hur were also left in charge of the people while Moses went up onto Mt. Sinai (Ex. 24:14).

2. A son of Caleb by Ephrath, grandfather of Bezaleel. Hur was filled with the Spirit by the Lord to work on the tabernacle (Ex. 38:22; 1 Chr. 2:19, 50; 2 Chr. 1:5).

3. One of the five kings of Midian. Hur was killed by the invading forces of Joshua (Num. 31:8; Josh. 13:21).

4. Father of Ben–Hur, an officer in Solomon's administration (1 Kin. 4:8).

5. A son of Judah (1 Chr. 4:1).

6. Father of Rephaiah, who helped repair Jerusalem's wall in Nehemiah's time (Neh. 3:9).

HURAI [HUR igh]

One of David's mighty men (1 Chr. 11:32), also called Hiddai (2 Sam. 23:30).

HURAM [HUR uhm] (*lofty brother*)

The name of three Old Testament men:

1. A descendant of Bela and grandson of Benjamin (1 Chr. 8:5).

2. A king of Tyre who formed an alliance with David and Solomon (2 Chr. 2:3), also called Hiram.

3. A master craftsman from Tyre employed by Solomon (2 Chr. 4:16; Huram–Abi, NIV), also called Hiram (1 Kin. 7:13).

HURI [HUR ree]

The father of Abihail (1 Chr. 5:14).

HUSHAH [HUH shah]

A son of Ezer and a member of the family of Judah (1 Chr. 4:4).

HUSHAI [HOO shigh]

A friend and wise counselor of King David (2 Sam. 15:32, 37). During Absalom's revolt, Hushai remained faithful to David and became a spy for him in Jerusalem. He probably was the father of Baana, one of Solomon's 12 officers (1 Kin. 4:16).

HUSHAM [HOO shuhm]

A king of Edom (Gen. 36:34–35).

HUSHIM [HOO shim]

The name of two men and one woman in the Old Testament:

1. A son of Dan (Gen. 46:23), also called Shuham (Num. 26:42).

2. A son of Aher, of the tribe of Benjamin (1 Chr. 7:12).

3. A Moabitess and one of the wives of Shaharaim (1 Chr. 8:11).

HUZ [huhz]

The oldest son of Nahor and Milcah (Gen. 22:21; Uz, NASB, REB, NIV).

HUZZAB [HUH zuhb]

The name of an Assyrian queen, or more likely, a poetic reference to Nineveh, the "queen" city of Assyria (Nah. 2:7, KJV).

HYMENAEUS [high muh NEE uhs]

An early Christian who denied the faith (1 Tim. 1:19–20; 2 Tim. 2:16–17). His message was heretical because he claimed the resurrection of the dead was already past. His "profane and vain babblings . . . spread like cancer" and destroyed the faith of believers.

HOLY SPIRIT

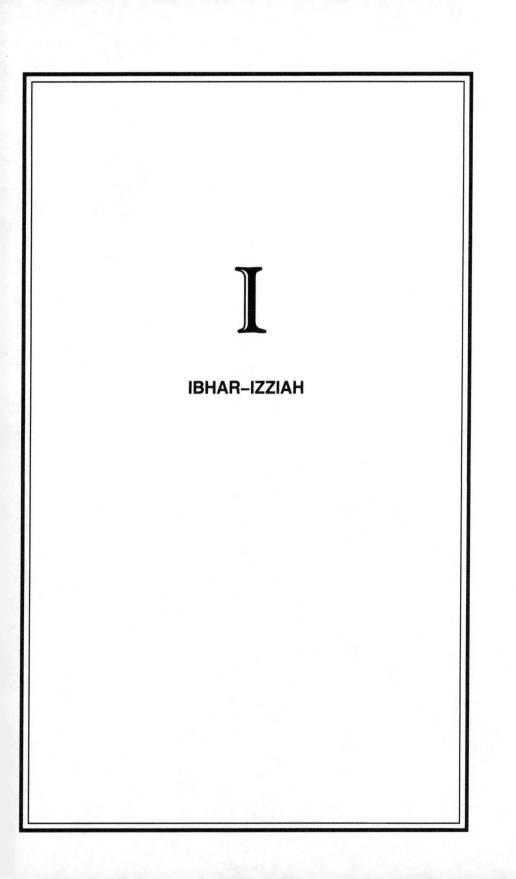

I

IBHAR–IZZIAH

IBHAR [IB hahr] (*[God] chooses*)

A son of David born at Jerusalem (2 Sam. 5:15).

IBNEIAH [ib NEE uh] (*the Lord builds*)

A son of Jeroham and the head of a Benjamite family that returned from the Captivity (1 Chr. 9:8).

IBNIJAH [ib NIGH juh] (*the Lord builds*)

A Benjamite and the father of Reuel (1 Chr. 9:8).

IBRI [IB righ]

A Levite during the reign of King David (1 Chr. 24:27).

IBSAM [IB sahm]

A form of JIBSAM.

IBZAN [IB zan]

A judge who ruled over Israel, or a portion of it (Judg. 12:8–10). He had 30 sons and 30 daughters and was a man of wealth and influence.

ICHABOD [IK uh bahd] (*inglorious*)

A son of Phinehas and grandson of Eli, the high priest. Several national and family tragedies prompted the wife of Phinehas to name her child Ichabod, declaring, "The glory has departed from Israel!" (1 Sam. 4:21).

IDBASH [ID bash]

One of the sons of the father of Etam (1 Chr. 4:3).

IDDO [IH doe]

The name of six or seven men in the Old Testament:

1. The father of Ahinadab, one of Solomon's 12 administrative officers (1 Kin. 4:14).

2. A Levite of the family of Gershon (1 Chr. 6:21; Gershom, KJV, NRSV, REB). He is also called Adaiah (1 Chr. 6:41).

3. A son of Zechariah. Iddo was a captain of the tribe of Manasseh in Gilead, east of the Jordan River, in David's time (1 Chr. 27:21).

4. A seer or prophet who wrote concerning three kings of Israel: Solomon (2 Chr. 9:29), Rehoboam (2 Chr. 12:15), and Abijah (2 Chr. 13:22).

5. A grandfather of the prophet Zechariah (Ezra 5:1; 6:14).

6. A leader of the Jews living at Casiphia in Babylonia (Ezra 8:17).

7. The head of a family of priests who returned to Jerusalem with Zerubbabel after the Captivity (Neh. 12:4, 16). He may be the same person as No. 5.

IGAL [EYE gal] (*the Lord redeems*)

The name of three men in the Old Testament:

1. One of the 12 spies sent by Moses to spy out the land of Canaan (Num. 13:7).

2. One of David's mighty men (2 Sam. 23:36).

3. A son of Shemaiah and a descendant of King David through King Jehoiachin (1 Chr. 3:22; Igeal, KJV; Igar, REB).

IGDALIAH [ig duh LIGH uh] (*great is the Lord*)

An ancestor of Hanan (Jer. 35:4).

IGEAL [IGH gih uhl]

A form of IGAL.

IKKESH [IK esh] (*subtle*)

A man of Tekoa and the father of Ira (2 Sam. 23:26).

ILAI [IGH ligh] (*elevated*)

One of David's mighty men (1 Chr. 11:29), also called Zalmon (2 Sam. 23:28).

IMLA [IM luh] (*God fulfills*)

The father of Micaiah the prophet (2 Chr. 18:7–8), also spelled as Imlah (1 Kin. 22:8–9).

IMMER [IM uhr]

A descendant of Aaron whose family had become a "father's house" by the time of David's reign (1 Chr. 24:14). The family was made the 16th of the 24 divisions of priests serving the tabernacle. Some members of this family returned from the Captivity (Ezra 2:37) and lived in Jerusalem (Neh. 11:13).

IMNA [IM nuh]

A son of Helem, of the tribe of Asher (1 Chr. 7:35).

IMNAH [IM nuh]

The name of two Old Testament men:
1. The oldest son of Asher (1 Chr. 7:30), also spelled Jimna (Num. 26:44) and Jimnah (Gen. 46:17).
2. The father of Kore, a Levite during the reign of King Hezekiah of Judah (2 Chr. 31:14).

IMRAH [IM ruh]

A descendant of Zophah, of the tribe of Asher (1 Chr. 7:36).

IMRI [IM righ]

The name of two Old Testament men:
1. A son of Bani (1 Chr. 9:4). Imri may be the same as Amariah (Neh. 11:4).
2. The father of Zaccur (Neh. 3:2).

IOB [IGH ahb]

A form of JASHUB No. 1.

IPHDEIAH [if DEE uh] (*the Lord redeems*)

A son of Shashak (1 Chr. 8:25; Iphedeiah, KJV, REB).

IR–NAHASH [ur NAY hash] (*city of the serpent*)

A person or a town of the tribe of Judah (1 Chr. 4:12).

IRA [IGH ruh]

The name of two or three men associated with David:
1. A "chief minister," or "priest" (NIV, NRSV), under David (2 Sam. 20:26).
2. One of David's mighty men (2 Sam. 23:26).
3. An Ithrite who was one of David's mighty men (2 Sam. 23:38). He may be the same person as Ira No. 1.

IRAD [IGH rad]

A grandson of Cain (Gen. 4:17–18).

IRAM [IGH ruhm]

An Edomite clan chief of the family of Esau (Gen. 36:43).

IRI [IGH righ]

A son of Bela (1 Chr. 7:7), possibly the same person as Ir (1 Chr. 7:12).

IRIJAH [igh RIGH juh] (*the Lord sees*)

A sentry who arrested the prophet Jeremiah while Jerusalem was under siege by the Babylonian army (Jer. 37:11–14).

IRU [IGH roo]

The oldest son of Caleb (1 Chr. 4:15).

ISAAC [EYE zik] (*[God] laughs*)

The only son of Abraham by his wife Sarah; father of Jacob and Esau. God promised to make Abraham's descendants a great nation that would become God's Chosen People. But the promised son was a long time in coming. Isaac was born when Abraham was 100 years old and Sarah was 90 (Gen. 17:17; 21:5). Both Abraham and Sarah laughed when they heard they would have a son in their old age (Gen. 17:17–19; 18:9–15). This partially explains why they named their son Isaac.

On the eighth day after his birth, Isaac was circumcised (Gen. 21:4). As he grew, his presence as Abraham's rightful heir brought him into conflict with Ishmael, Abraham's son by Sarah's handmaid Hagar. The strained relationship caused Sarah to send away Hagar and Ishmael (Gen. 21:9–21). God comforted Abraham by telling him that Ishmael would also become the father of a great nation (Gen. 21:13).

Birthright.

Isaac's birthright was an important part of his life. The blessings that God gave to Abraham were also given to his descendants. Thus, to inherit this cov-

enant with God was of far greater value than to inherit property or material goods.

Isaac's life gave evidence of God's favor. His circumcision was a sign of the covenant with God. God's favor toward him was also evident in Ishmael's disinheritance. The dismissal of the sons of Abraham's concubines to the "country of the east" is associated with the statement that Isaac inherited all that Abraham had, including God's blessing. Isaac was in a unique position historically because he would carry on the covenant.

When Isaac was a young man, God tested Abraham's faith by commanding him to sacrifice Isaac as an offering. But when Abraham placed Isaac upon the altar, an angel appeared and stopped the sacrifice, providing a ram instead (Genesis 22). This showed clearly that Isaac was God's choice to carry on the covenant.

ISAAC

Marriage.

Isaac married Rebekah when he was 40 years old. She became Isaac's wife when God directed one of Abraham's servants to her. The Bible reveals that Isaac loved Rebekah and that she was a comfort to him after his mother Sarah's death (Gen. 24:67). Isaac and Rebekah had twin sons, Jacob and Esau, who were born when Isaac was 60 years old (Gen. 25:20–26).

Famine prompted the family to move to Gerar, where God appeared to Isaac and reaffirmed the covenant. Moving through the Valley of Gerar, where he reopened the wells that Abraham had dug (Gen. 26:23; 28:10), Isaac made a camp at Beersheba. This place became his permanent home. There he built an altar just as his father had done (Gen. 26:24–25).

Jacob and Esau.

The older twin, Esau, was Isaac's favorite son, although God had declared that the older should serve the younger (Gen. 25:23). Jacob was Rebekah's favorite. Disagreement arose over which of the twins would receive the birthright and carry on the covenant that God had made with Abraham. Rebekah conspired with Jacob to trick the aging, blind Isaac into giving his blessing to Jacob rather than Esau.

Shortly thereafter, Isaac sent Jacob to Laban in Padan Aram to find a wife and to escape Esau's wrath. Esau soon left his father's household. Many years passed before the two brothers were at peace with each other. But they were united at last in paying last respects to their father after his death. Isaac lived to be 180 years old. He was buried alongside Abraham, Sarah, and Rebekah in the cave of Machpelah (Gen. 35:28–29; 49:30–31).

Isaac's Character.

The Bible contains many references to Isaac's good character. The Scripture gives evidence of his submission (Gen. 22:6, 9), meditation (Gen. 24:63), trust in God (Gen. 22:6, 9), devotion (Gen. 24:67), peaceful nature (Gen. 26:20–22), and his life of prayer and faith (Gen. 26:25; Heb. 11:11–17).

New Testament References.

In the New Testament, Isaac is called a child of promise (Gal. 4:22–23). The Book of Acts points to his significance as one who received circumcision on the eighth day (Acts 7:8). His position as the channel of the Abrahamic blessing is also emphasized (Rom. 9:7).

In a famous passage, Paul uses Isaac and his mother as historical examples when discussing those who are justified by faith in God's promise (Gal. 4:21–31).

ISAIAH [eye ZAY uh] (the Lord has saved)

A famous Old Testament prophet who predicted the coming of the Messiah; the author of the Book of Isaiah. Isaiah was probably born in Jerusalem of a family that was related to the royal house of Judah. He recorded the events of the reign of King Uzziah of Judah (2 Chr. 26:22). When Uzziah died (740 B.C.), Isaiah received his prophetic calling from God in a stirring vision of God in the Temple (Isaiah 6). The king of Judah had died; now Isaiah had seen the everlasting King in whose service he would spend the rest of his life.

Isaiah was married to a woman described as "the prophetess" (Is. 8:3). They had two sons whom they named Shear-Jashub, "A Remnant Shall Return" (Is. 7:3), and Maher-Shalal-Hash-Baz, "Speed the Spoil, Hasten the Booty" (Is. 8:3). These strange names portray two basic themes of the Book of Isaiah: God is about to bring judgment upon His people, hence Maher-Shalal-Hash-Baz; but after that there will be an outpouring of God's mercy and grace to the remnant of people who will remain faithful to God, hence Shear–Jashub.

After God called Isaiah to proclaim His message, He told Isaiah that most of his work would be a ministry of judgment. Even though the prophet would speak the truth, the people would reject his words (6:10). Jesus found in these words of Isaiah's call a prediction of the rejection of his message by many of the people (Matt. 13:14–15).

Isaiah's response to this revelation from the Lord was a lament: "Lord, how long?" (Isaiah 6:11). The Lord answered that Isaiah's ministry would prepare the people for judgment, but one day God's promises would be realized. Judah was to experience utter devastation, to be fulfilled with the destruction of the city of Jerusalem by the Babylonians in 586 B.C. (Is. 6:11). This destruction would be followed by the deportation of the people to Babylon (Is. 6:12). But although the tree of the house of David would be cut down, there would still be life in the stump (Is. 6:13). Out of the lineage of David would come a Messiah who would establish His eternal rule among His people.

Isaiah was a writer of considerable literary skill. The poetry of his book is magnificent in its sweep. A person of strong emotion and deep feelings, Isaiah also was a man of steadfast devotion to the Lord. His vision of God and His holiness in the Temple influenced his messages during his long ministry.

Isaiah's ministry extended from about 740 B.C. until at least 701 B.C. (Isaiah 37–39). His 40 years of preaching doom and promise did not turn the nation of Judah

from its headlong rush toward destruction. But he faithfully preached the message God gave him until the very end.

According to a popular Jewish tradition, Isaiah met his death by being sawn in half during the reign of the evil king Manasseh of Judah. This tradition seems to be supported by the writer of Hebrews (Heb. 11:37). Certainly Isaiah is one of the heroes of the faith "of whom the world was not worthy" (Heb. 11:38).

ISCAH [IZ kuh]

A daughter of Haran, Abraham's younger brother. Iscah was a sister of Milcah, the wife of Nahor (Gen. 11:29).

ISCARIOT [iss KER ee uht] (man of Kerioth)

The surname of Judas, one of the Twelve who betrayed Jesus (John 6:71; 12:4; 13:2, 26). Also see JUDAS ISCARIOT.

ISHBAH [ISH buh]

The father of Eshtemoa, of the tribe of Judah (1 Chr. 4:17).

ISHBAK [ISH bak]

A son of Abraham by Keturah (Gen. 25:2). Ishbak was probably the ancestor of a northern Arabian tribe.

ISHBI–BENOB [ISH bigh BEE nahb]

A descendant of the Philistine giants of Gath. Ishbi–Benob was killed by Abishai, one of David's mighty men (2 Sam. 21:16).

ISHBOSHETH [ihsh BOE sheth] (man of shame)

A son of Saul whom Abner proclaimed king after Saul's death (2 Sam. 2:8–10). The tribe of Judah proclaimed David king after the death of Saul and Jonathan at Gilboa, but the 11 other tribes remained loyal to Saul's family. Ishbosheth reigned two turbulent years from Mahanaim, east of the Jordan River, while David ruled Judah from Hebron. Throughout the period, each side attempted unsuccessfully to gain control of the entire kingdom (2 Sam. 2:12—3:1).

Ishbosheth made a grave error in charging Abner with having relations with Saul's concubine, Rizpah. In anger, Abner changed his allegiance to David (2 Sam. 3:6–21). When Joab murdered Abner in Hebron (2 Sam. 3:27), Ishbosheth became discouraged (2 Sam. 4:1). Two captains of his guard, Baanah and Rechab, assassinated Ishbosheth as he lay napping. They carried Ishbosheth's severed head to David, who ordered it buried in the tomb of Abner in Hebron. Then David put the assassins to death (2 Sam. 4:5–12). Saul's dynasty ended with Ishbosheth's death.

ISHHOD [ISH hahd]

A son of Hammoleketh, of the tribe of Manasseh (1 Chr. 7:18; Ishod, KJV).

ISHI [ISH igh]

The name of four men in the Old Testament:

1. A son of Appaim and a member of the family of Jerahmeel (1 Chr. 2:31).

2. A descendant of Judah through Caleb (1 Chr. 4:20).

3. The father of four men, who were captains of the tribe of Simeon (1 Chr. 4:42).

4. A chief of the half-tribe of Manasseh, east of the Jordan River (1 Chr. 5:24).

ISHIJAH [ish IGH juh]

A son of Harum who divorced his pagan wife (Ezra 10:31; Isshijah, NASB; Isshiah, REB, NRSV).

ISHMA [ISH muh] (may [God] hear)

A brother of Jezreel and Idbash, of the tribe of Judah (1 Chr. 4:3).

ISHMAEL [IHSH may ell] (God hears)

The name of six men in the Old Testament:

1. The first son of Abraham, by his wife's Egyptian maidservant, Hagar. Although God had promised Abraham an heir (Gen. 15:4), Abraham's wife, Sarah, had been unable to bear a child. When Abraham was 85, Sarah offered her maid to him in order to help fulfill God's promise (Gen. 16:1–2).

After Hagar learned that she was pregnant, she grew proud and began to despise Sarah. Sarah complained to Abraham, who allowed her to discipline Hagar. Sarah's harsh treatment of Hagar caused her to flee into the wilderness. There she met the angel of God, who told her to return to Sarah and submit to her authority. As an encouragement, the angel promised Hagar that her son, who would be named Ishmael, would have uncounted descendants. Hagar then returned to Abraham and Sarah and bore her son (Gen. 16:4–15).

When Ishmael was 13, God appeared to Abraham to tell him that Ishmael was not the promised heir. God made a covenant with Abraham that was to be passed down to the descendants of Isaac—a son who would be conceived by Sarah the following year. Because Abraham loved Ishmael, God promised to bless Ishmael and make him a great nation (Gen. 17:19–20).

At the customary feast to celebrate Isaac's weaning, Sarah saw 16-year-old Ishmael making fun of Isaac. She was furious and demanded that Abraham disown Ishmael and his mother so Ishmael could not share Isaac's inheritance.

ISAIAH

I TAKE IT THIS ISN'T GOING TO BE A MAGIC TRICK?

Hayes

Abraham was reluctant to cast out Ishmael and Hagar, but he did so when instructed by God (Gen. 21:8–13).

Hagar and Ishmael wandered in the wilderness of Beersheba. When their water was gone and Ishmael grew weary, Hagar placed him under a shrub to await death. The angel of God again contacted Hagar and showed her a well. After drawing water, she returned to Ishmael. Ishmael grew up in the wilderness of Paran and gained fame as an archer. Hagar arranged his marriage to an Egyptian wife (Gen. 21:14–21).

When Abraham died, Ishmael returned from exile to help Isaac with the burial (Gen. 25:9). As God promised, Ishmael became the father of 12 princes (Gen. 25:16), as well as a daughter, Mahalath, who later married Esau, son of Isaac (Gen. 28:9). Ishmael died at the age of 137 (Gen. 25:17).

Ishmael was the father of the Ishmaelites, a nomadic nation which lived in northern Arabia. Modern-day Arabs claim descent from Ishmael.

2. The son of Nethaniah and a member of the house of David. After the Babylonian conquest of Judah, King Nebuchadnezzar appointed a Jewish captive, Gedaliah, as governor. Gedaliah promised to welcome all Jews who came under his protection. Ishmael and several others accepted Gedaliah's offer with the intent of killing him (2 Kin. 25:22–24). Gedaliah was warned that Ishmael was allied with the Ammonite king in plotting to kill him, but he refused to believe it (Jer. 40:14–16). When Gedaliah invited Ishmael and ten others to a banquet, they murdered everyone in attendance. The killers fled toward the Ammonite country with several hostages, but they were overtaken by pursuers in Gibeon. The hostages were rescued, but Ishmael and eight men escaped to the Ammonites (Jer. 41:1–15).

3. A descendant of Jonathan, son of Saul (1 Chr. 8:38; 9:44).

4. The father of Zebadiah, ruler of the house of Judah and the highest civil authority under King Jehoshaphat (2 Chr. 19:11).

5. A son of Jehohanan. Ishmael was one of five army officers recruited by Jehoiada to help overthrow Queen Athaliah of Judah in favor of the rightful heir, Joash (2 Chr. 23:1).

6. A priest of the clan of Pashhur who divorced his foreign wife after the Babylonian Captivity (Ezra 10:22).

ISHMAIAH [ish MAY uh] (the Lord hears)

The name of two men in David's time:
1. A Gibeonite who was one of David's mighty men (1 Chr. 12:4).
2. A son of Obadiah and a chief of Zebulun in David's time (1 Chr. 27:19).

ISHMERAI [ISH muh righ] (the Lord protects)

A son of Elpaal (1 Chr. 8:18).

ISHOD [IGH shahd]

A form of ISHHOD.

ISHPAH [ISH puh]

A form of ISPAH.

ISHPAN [ISH pan]

A son of Shashak (1 Chr. 8:22).

ISHUAH [ISH yoo uh]

A form of ISHVAH.

ISHUAI [ISH yoo igh]

A form of ISHVI.

ISHUI [ISH yoo igh]

A form of ISHVI.

ISHVAH [ISH vuh] (he is like)

The second son of Asher, descended from Jacob and Zilpah (Gen. 46:17), also called Ishuah (KJV).

ISHVI [ISH vigh]

The name of two men in the Old Testament:
1. The third son of Asher and founder of the tribal family of the Ishvites, also spelled Isui (Gen. 46:17, KJV), Ishuai (1 Chr. 7:30, KJV), and Jesui (Num. 26:44, NKJV).
2. A son of King Saul by Ahinoam (1 Sam. 14:49; Ishui, KJV; Ishyo, REB; Jishui, NKJV). Some scholars believe Ishvi was the same person as ISHBOSHETH.

ISHYO [ISH yoe]

A form of ISHVI.

ISMACHIAH [is muh KIGH uh] (the Lord supports)

An overseer of the Temple in Hezekiah's time (2 Chr. 31:13; Ismakiah, NIV).

ISPAH [IS pah]

A son or descendant of Beriah, of the tribe of Benjamin (1 Chr. 8:16; Ishpah, NRSV).

ISRAEL [IS ray ell] (he strives with God)

The name given to JACOB after his great struggle with God at Peniel near the brook Jabbok (Gen. 32:28; 35:10). The name Israel has been interpreted by different scholars as "prince with God," "he strives with God," "let God rule," or "God strives." The name was later applied to the descendants of Jacob. The twelve tribes were called "Israelites," "children of Israel," and "house of Israel," identifying them as the descendants of Israel through his sons and grandsons.

ISSACHAR [IHZ ah car] (*there is hire or reward*)

The name of two men in the Old Testament:

1. The ninth son of Jacob; the fifth by his wife Leah (Gen. 30:17–18; 35:23). He fathered four sons: Tola, Puvah or Puah, Job or Jashub, and Shimron. He and his sons went with their father Jacob to Egypt to escape the famine (Gen. 46:13; Ex. 1:3; Num. 26:23–24; 1 Chr. 2:1; 7:1). Before his death, Jacob described Issachar as "a strong donkey lying down between two burdens" (Gen. 49:15). In other words, Jacob saw that Issachar could be a strong fighter but that his love of comfort could also cause him to settle for the easy way out.

2. A Levite gatekeeper in David's time (1 Chr. 26:5).

ISSHIAH [ih SHY ah]

The name of two men in the Old Testament:

1. A Levite, head of the house of Rehabiah (1 Chr. 24:21).

2. A Levite of the house of Uzziel (1 Chr. 24:25), also called Jesshiah (1 Chr. 23:20). Also see JISSHIAH.

ISSHIJAH [is SHIGH juh]

A form of ISHIJAH.

ISUI [ISS yoo igh]

A form of ISHVI.

ITHAMAR [ITH uh mahr]

The youngest of the four sons of Aaron and Elisheba (Ex. 6:23). Ithamar was consecrated for the priestly office, along with his father and his three older brothers (Ex. 28:1). His duty was to number the articles collected for the tabernacle (Ex. 38:21) and to supervise two

priestly families, the Gershonites and the Merarites (Num. 4:21–33). The priestly family founded by him included the high priest Eli and his descendants (1 Chr. 24:3–7). Although Ithamar's family eventually lost the high priesthood, it continued as a priestly family after the Captivity (Ezra 8:2).

ITHIEL [ITH ih el] (*God is with me*)

The name of two men in the Old Testament:

1. A Benjamite who returned from Babylon to Jerusalem after the Captivity (Neh. 11:7).

2. A person to whom AGUR addressed his oracle (Prov. 30:1).

ITHLAH [ITH luh]

A form of JETHLAH.

ITHMAH [ITH muh]

One of David's mighty men (1 Chr. 11:46).

ITHRA [ITH ruh]

A form of JITHRA.

ITHRAN [ITH ran] (*excellence*)

A son of Dishon and grandson of Seir the Horite (Gen. 36:26). Also see JITHRAN.

ITHREAM [ITH ree uhm] (*remnant of the people*)

The sixth son born to David and his wife Eglah at Hebron (2 Sam. 3:5).

ITTAI [IT uh eye]

The name of two of King David's supporters:

1. A native or inhabitant of the Philistine city of Gath who followed David during the dangerous period of Absalom's rebellion. Ittai, Abishai, and Joab each commanded a third of David's army in

the battle of the woods of Ephraim, during which Absalom was killed (2 Sam. 15:18–22; 18:2, 5, 12). Joab and Abishai are mentioned after this battle, but Ittai is not. Ittai may have been killed during the battle.

2. A son of Ribai, from Gibeah of Benjamin, and one of David's mighty men (2 Sam. 23:29), also called Ithai (1 Chr. 11:31).

IZHAR [IZ hahr]

A son of Kohath and the father of Korah (Ex. 6:18, 21). Izhar was the founder of a tribal family, the Izharites (Num. 3:27). His name is also spelled Izehar (Num. 3:19, NKJV, KJV).

IZRAHIAH [is ruh HIGH uh] (*the Lord will appear*)

A descendant of Issachar (1 Chr. 7:3). He may be the same person as Jezrahiah (Neh. 12:42).

IZRI [IZ righ]

A form of JIZRI.

IZZIAH [iz IGH uh]

A form of JEZIAH.

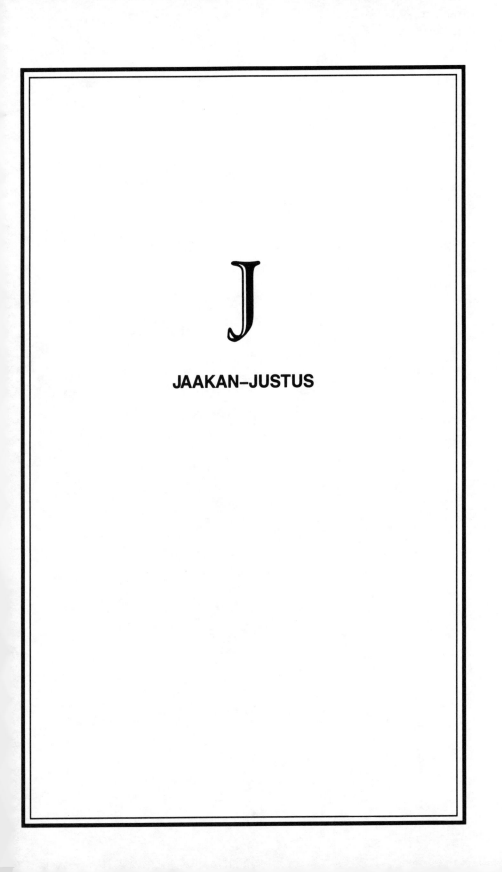

J

JAAKAN–JUSTUS

JAAKAN [JAY uh kan]

An ancestor of the "sons of Jaakan" around whose wells the Israelites camped during their wilderness wanderings (Deut. 10:6; Jakan, KJV). At the time of the Exodus, the "sons of Jaakan" lived on the borders of Edom near Mount Hor. Jaakan is also called Akan (Gen. 36:27).

JAAKOBAH [jay uh KOE buh]

A descendant of Simeon, the third son of Jacob (1 Chr. 4:36).

JAALA [JAY uh luh]

The founder of a tribal family whose descendants returned from the Captivity (Ezra 2:56; Jaalah, KJV, NRSV).

JAALAM [JAY uh luhm] (*he conceals*)

A son of Esau and Aholibamah, who became a chief of Edom (Gen. 36:18; Jalam, NRSV).

JAANAI [JAY uh nigh] (*the Lord answers*)

A chief of a family descended from Gad (1 Chr. 5:12; Janai, NRSV).

JAARE–OREGIM [JAY uh rih OHR uh jim]

The father of Elhanan (2 Sam. 21:19), also called Jair (1 Chr. 20:5).

JAARESHIAH [jar uh SHIGH uh]

A son of Jeroham (1 Chr. 8:27; Jaresiah, KJV).

JAASAI [JAY uh sigh] (*the Lord is maker*)

A man of the family of Bani who divorced his pagan wife after the Captivity (Ezra 10:37; Jaasu, NRSV; Jaasau, KJV, REB).

JAASAU [JAY uh saw]

A form of JAASAI.

JAASIEL [jay AY zih uhl] (*God is maker*)

The name of one or two people in the Old Testament:

1. One of David's mighty men (1 Chr. 11:47; Jasiel, KJV).

2. A leader of the tribe of Benjamin during David's reign (1 Chr. 27:21, possibly the same person as No. 1).

JAASU [JAY uh soo]

A form of JAASAI.

JAAZANIAH [jay az uh NIGH uh] (*the Lord hears*)

The name of four men in the Old Testament:

1. A son of Hoshaiah (2 Kin. 25:23), also called Jezaniah (Jer. 40:8; 42:1) and Azariah (Jer. 42:1, NRSV).

2. A chief Rechabite (Jer. 35:3).

3. A son of Shaphan and leader of elders who were offering incense to idols (Ezek. 8:11).

4. A prince who gave wicked counsel to his people (Ezek. 11:1).

JAAZIAH [jay uh ZIGH uh] (*may the Lord strengthen*)

A Levite, a descendant of Merari (1 Chr. 24:26–27).

JAAZIEL [jay AY zih uhl]

A Temple musician in the time of David (1 Chr. 15:18), also called Aziel (1 Chr. 15:20).

JABAL [JAY buhl]

A son of Lamech and Adah (Gen. 4:20).

JABESH [JAY besh] (*dry place*)

The father of Shallum (2 Kin. 15:10, 13–14), a king of Israel.

JABEZ [JAY biz]

The head of a family of the tribe of Judah noted for his honorable character (1 Chr. 4:9–10).

JABIN [JAY bin] (*he is perceptive*)

The name of two kings of the Canaanite kingdom of Hazor:

1. A king of Hazor defeated by Joshua at the waters of Merom (Josh. 11:1–14). Jabin organized a number of Canaanite princes against the Israelites.

2. A king of Hazor who oppressed Israel for 20 years. His army, led by SISERA, was defeated by DEBORAH and Barak at the River Kishon (Judg. 4:2).

JACHAN [JAY kan]

A clan leader of the tribe of Gad (1 Chr. 5:13; Jacan, NRSV).

JACHIN [JAY kin] (*he will establish*)

The name of two Old Testament men:

1. A founder of a tribal family, the Jachinites (Num. 26:12; Jakinites, NIV), also called Jarib (1 Chr. 4:24).

2. Head of the 21st division of priests during David's reign (1 Chr. 24:17; Jakin, NIV). Jachin is also used as a family name (1 Chr. 9:10), describing Jachin's descendants who returned from the Captivity.

JACOB [JAY cub] (*he supplants*)

One of the twin sons of Isaac and Rebekah. The brother of Esau, he was known also as Israel (Gen. 32:28).

Jacob was born in answer to his father's prayer (Gen. 25:21), but he became the favorite son of his mother (25:28). He was named Jacob because, at th birth of the twins, "his hand took hold of Esau's heel" (25:26). According to the accounts in Genesis, Jacob continued to "take hold of" the possessions of others—his brother's birthright (25:29–34), his fa-

ther's blessing (27:1–29), and his father-in-law's flocks and herds (30:25–43; 31:1).

The pattern of Jacob's life is found in his journeys, much like the travels of his grandfather ABRAHAM. Leaving his home in Beersheba, he traveled to Bethel (28:10–22); later he returned to Shechem (33:18–20), Bethel (35:6–7), and Hebron (35:27). At Shechem and Bethel he built altars, as Abraham had done (12:6–7; 12:8). Near the end of his life Jacob migrated to Egypt; he died there at an advanced age (Genesis 46—49).

The most dramatic moments in Jacob's life occurred at Bethel (Gen. 28:10–22), at the ford of the River Jabbok (32:22–32), and on his deathbed (49:1–33).

The experience at Bethel occurred when he left the family home at Beersheba to travel to Haran (a city in Mesopotamia), the residence of his uncle Laban (28:10). On the way, as he stopped for the night at Bethel, he had a dream of a staircase reaching from earth to heaven with angels upon it and the Lord above it. He was impressed by the words of the Lord, promising Jacob inheritance of the land, descendants "as the dust of the earth" in number, and His divine presence. Jacob dedicated the site as a place of worship, calling it Bethel (literally, "house of God"). More than 20 years later, Jacob returned to this spot, built an altar, called the place El Bethel (literally, "God of the house of God"), and received the divine blessing (35:6–15).

The experience at the ford of the River Jabbok occurred as Jacob returned from his long stay at Haran. While preparing for a reunion with his brother, Esau, of whom he was still afraid (32:7), he had a profound experience that left him changed in both body and spirit.

At the ford of the Jabbok, "Jacob was left alone" (32:24). It was night, and he found himself suddenly engaged in a wrestling match in the darkness. This match lasted until the breaking of the dawn. The socket of Jacob's hip was put out of joint as he struggled with this mysterious stranger, but he refused to release his grip until he was given a blessing. For the first time in the narrative of Genesis, Jacob had been unable to defeat an opponent. When asked to identify himself in the darkness, he confessed he was Jacob—the "heel-grabber."

But Jacob's struggling earned him a new name. For his struggle "with God and with men" in which he had prevailed, his name was changed to Israel (literally, "he struggles with God") [see Hos. 12:3]. In return, he gave a name to the spot that marked the change; it would be called Peniel—"For I have seen God face to face, and my life is preserved" (32:30).

In these first two instances, a deep spiritual sensitivity is evident in Jacob. He appears outwardly brash and grasping, always enriching himself and securing his future. Yet he responded readily to these night experiences—the dream and the wrestling contest—because he apparently sensed "the presence of the holy" in each of them. He also proved to be a man of his word in his dealings with Laban (Gen. 31:6), and in the fulfillment of his vow to return to Bethel (35:1–3).

At the end of his life, Jacob—now an aged man (47:28)—gathered his 12 sons about his bed to tell them what should befall them "in the last days" (49:1).

The harshest language came against Reuben, the firstborn, who was rejected by his father for his sin (49:3–4), and Simeon and Levi, who were cursed for their anger and cruelty (49:5–7). The loftiest language was applied to Judah, who would be praised by his brothers and whose tribe would be the source of roy-

alty, even the ruler of the people (49:8–12).

Words of warning were addressed to Dan, called "a serpent" and "a viper," a life that would be marked by violence (49:16–17). The two longest speeches were addressed to Judah and to Joseph, Jacob's favorite son (49:22–26).

Following this scene, Jacob died and was embalmed by the physicians (Gen. 49:33; 50:2). By his own request Jacob was carried back to the land of Canaan and was buried in the family burial ground in the cave of the field of Machpelah (Gen. 49:29–32; 50:13).

JADA [JAY duh] (*he cares*)

A son of Onam and grandson of Jerahmeel (1 Chr. 2:28, 32).

JADDAI [JAD eye]

An Israelite who divorced his pagan wife after the Captivity (Ezra 10:43; Jadau, KJV).

JADDUA [JAD oo uh] (*known*)

The name of two priests in the Book of Nehemiah:

1. A Levite who sealed the covenant with Nehemiah (Neh. 10:21).

2. A son of Jonathan and a descendant of the high priest Jeshua (Neh. 12:11, 22). Jaddua returned with Zerubbabel from the Captivity. He was the last High Priest mentioned in the Old Testament.

JADON [JAY dahn] (*he judges*)

An Israelite who helped repair the walls of Jerusalem after the Captivity (Neh. 3:7).

JAEL [JAY uhl] (*mountain goat*)

The woman who killed Sisera, Israel's mighty enemy, by driving a tent peg through his temple while he slept (Judg.

J

4:17–22). Sisera accepted Jael's invitation to seek refuge in her tent. She covered him with a mantle, gave him milk to quench his thirst, and promised to stand guard against intruders. Instead, Jael killed Sisera as he slept. In her famous song, the prophetess Deborah honored Jael: "Most blessed above women is Jael" (Judg. 5:24).

JAHALELEEL [juh HAH luh leel] *(may God shine forth)*

A descendant of Judah through Caleb (1 Chr. 4:16; Jehallelel, NIV, NRSV; Jehaleleel, KJV).

JAHATH [JAY hath]

The name of five men in the Old Testament:

1. A son of Reaiah (1 Chr. 4:2).
2. A son of Libni (1 Chr. 6:20, 43).
3. A son of Shimei (1 Chr. 23:10, 11).
4. A Levite of the family of Kohath (1 Chr. 24:22).
5. A Levite who helped repair the Temple during the reign of Josiah (2 Chr. 34:12).

JAHAZIAH [jay huh ZIGH uh] *(the Lord sees)*

A son of Tikvah and one of four men who opposed Ezra's condemnation of improper marriages (Ezra 10:15, 44).

JAHAZIEL [juh HAY zih uhl] *(God sees)*

The name of five men in the Old Testament:

1. A Benjamite warrior who joined David's army at Ziklag (1 Chr. 12:4).
2. A priest who blew a trumpet before the Ark of the Covenant as it was transported to Jerusalem (1 Chr. 16:6).
3. A Levite, the third son of Hebron (1 Chr. 23:19; 24:23).
4. A Levite who encouraged Jehoshaphat and his army to fight against the

Ammonite, Edomite, and Moabite invaders (2 Chr. 20:14–17).

5. The father of a clan leader who returned with Ezra from the Captivity (Ezra 8:5).

JAHDAI [JAH digh]

A man of Judah, apparently of the family of Caleb (1 Chr. 2:47).

JAHDIEL [JAH dih uhl] *(may God rejoice)*

A leader in the half-tribe of Manasseh who lived in Transjordan (1 Chr. 5:24).

JAHDO [JAH doe] *(may he rejoice)*

A son of Buz the Gadite (1 Chr. 5:14).

JAHLEEL [JAH lih uhl] *(God waits)*

The third son of Zebulun (Gen. 46:14) and ancestor of the Jahleelites (Num. 26:26).

JAHMAI [JAH migh]

A son of Tola and a clan leader of the tribe of Issachar (1 Chr. 7:2).

JAHZEEL [JAH zih uhl]

A son of Naphtali and ancestor of the Jahzeelites (Gen. 46:24), also spelled Jahziel (1 Chr. 7:13).

JAHZEIAH [jah ZEE uh]

A form of JAHAZIAH.

JAHZERAH [JAH zuh ruh]

A priest whose descendants lived in Jerusalem after the Captivity (1 Chr. 9:12), probably the same person as AHZAI (Neh. 11:13).

JAHZIEL [JAH zih uhl]

A form of JAHZEEL.

JAIR [JAY ur] *(may he shine forth)*

The name of four people in the Old Testament:

1. A descendant of Judah (Num. 32:41; Deut. 3:14).

2. A Gileadite who judged Israel for 22 years (Judg. 10:3, 5).

3. The father of Elhanan (1 Chr. 20:5), also called Jaare–Oregim (2 Sam. 21:19).

4. A Benjamite, the father of Mordecai, Esther's cousin (Esth. 2:5).

JAIRUS [jay EYE ruhs]

A ruler of a synagogue near Capernaum and the Sea of Galilee. Jairus' daughter was miraculously raised from the dead by Jesus (Mark 5:21–23, 35–43).

JAKAN [JAY kuhn]

A form of JAAKAN.

JAKEH [JAY kuh]

An ancestor of Agur, the wise man who wrote the 30th chapter of the Book of Proverbs (Prov. 30:1).

JAKIM [JAY kim] (*may he establish*)

The name of two men in the Old Testament:

1. A son of Shimei (1 Chr. 8:19).

2. A head of a family of priests (1 Chr. 24:12).

JAKIN [JAY kin]

A form of JACHIN.

JALAM [JAY luhm]

A form of JAALAM.

JALON [JAY lahn] (meaning unknown)

A son of Ezrah (1 Chr. 4:17).

JAMES

Five men in the New Testament:

1. James, the son of Zebedee, one of Jesus' twelve apostles. James' father was a fisherman; his mother, Salome, often cared for Jesus' daily needs (Matt. 27:56; Mark 15:40–41). In lists of the twelve apostles, James and his brother John always form a group of four with two other brothers, Peter and Andrew. The four were fishermen on the Sea of Galilee. Their call to follow Jesus is the first recorded event after the beginning of Jesus' public ministry (Matt. 4:18–22; Mark 1:16–20).

James is never mentioned apart from his brother John in the New Testament, even at his death (Acts 12:2). When the brothers are mentioned, James is always mentioned first, probably because he was the older. After the Resurrection, however, John became the more prominent, probably because of his association with Peter (Acts 3:1; 8:14). James was killed by Herod Agrippa I, the grandson of Herod the Great, sometime between A.D. 42–44. He was the first of the twelve apostles to be put to death and the only one whose martyrdom is mentioned in the New Testament (Acts 12:2).

James and John must have contributed a spirited and headstrong element to Jesus' band of followers, because Jesus nicknamed them "Sons of Thunder" (Mark 3:17). On one occasion (Luke 9:51–56), when a Samaritan village refused to accept Jesus, the two asked Jesus to call down fire in revenge, as Elijah had done (2 Kin. 1:10, 12). On another occasion, they earned the anger of their fellow disciples by asking if they could sit on Jesus' right and left hands in glory (Matt. 20:20–28; Mark 10:35–45).

James was one of three disciples—Peter, James, and John—whom Jesus took along privately on three special occasions. The three accompanied Him when He healed the daughter of Jairus (Mark 5:37; Luke 8:51); they witnessed His transfiguration (Matt. 17:1; Mark 9:2; Luke 9:28); and they were also with Him in His agony in Gethsemane (Matt. 26:37; Mark 14:33).

J

2. James, the son of Alphaeus. This James was also one of the twelve apostles. In each list of the apostles he is mentioned in ninth position (Matt. 10:3; Mark 3:18; Luke 6:15; Acts 1:13).

3. James the Less. This James is called the son of Mary (not the mother of Jesus), and the brother of Joses (Matt. 27:56; Mark 16:1; Luke 24:10). Mark 15:40 refers to him as "James the Less." The Greek word *mikros* can mean either "small" or "less." It could, therefore, mean James the smaller (in size), or younger (NIV), or James the less (well-known).

4. James, the father of Judas. Two passages in the New Testament refer to a James, the father of Judas (Luke 6:16; Acts 1:13). Judas was one of the twelve apostles; he was the last to be listed before his more infamous namesake, Judas Iscariot.

5. James, the brother of Jesus. James is first mentioned as the oldest of Jesus' four younger brothers (Matt. 13:55; Mark 6:3).

In the third and fourth centuries A.D., when the idea of the perpetual virginity of Mary gained ground, a number of church fathers argued that James was either a stepbrother to Jesus (by a former marriage of Joseph) or a cousin. But both options are forced. The New Testament seems to indicate that Mary and Joseph bore children after Jesus (Matt. 1:25; 12:47; Luke 2:7; John 2:12; Acts 1:14), and that the second oldest was James (Matt. 13:55–56; Mark 6:3). The Gospels reveal that Jesus' family adopted a skeptical attitude toward His ministry (Matt. 12:46–50; Mark 3:31–35; Luke 8:19–21; John 7:5). James apparently held the same attitude, because his name appears in no lists of the apostles, nor is he mentioned elsewhere in the Gospels.

After Jesus' crucifixion, however, James became a believer. Paul indicated that James was a witness to the resurrection of Jesus (1 Cor. 15:7). He called James an apostle (Gal. 1:19), though like himself, not one of the original Twelve (1 Cor. 15:5, 7).

In the Book of Acts, James emerges as the leader of the church in Jerusalem. His brothers also became believers and undertook missionary travels (1 Cor. 9:5). But James considered it his calling to oversee the church in Jerusalem (Gal. 2:9). He advocated respect for the Jewish law (Acts 21:18–25), but he did not use it as a weapon against Gentiles. Paul indicated that James endorsed his ministry to the Gentiles (Gal. 2:1–10).

The decree of the Council of Jerusalem (Acts 15:12–21) cleared the way for Christianity to become a universal religion. Gentiles were asked only "to abstain from things polluted by idols, from sexual immorality, from things strangled, and from blood" (Acts 15:20). The intent of this decree was practical rather than theological. It asked the Gentiles to observe certain practices that otherwise would offend their Jewish brothers in the Lord and jeopardize Christian fellowship with them.

Both Paul and Acts portray a James who was personally devoted to Jewish tradition but flexible enough to modify it to admit non-Jews into Christian fellowship. This James is probably the author of the Epistle of James in the New Testament.

JAMIN [JAY min] (*right hand; south*)

The name of three men in the Old Testament:

1. Founder of a tribal family, the Jaminites (Num. 26:12).

2. A son of Ram, of the tribe of Judah (1 Chr. 2:27).

3. A priest who helped interpret the law for the people after the Captivity (Neh. 8:7).

JAMLECH [JAM lek] (he rules)

A chief of the tribe of Simeon (1 Chr. 4:34, 41).

JANAI [JAN eye]

A form of JAANAI.

JANNA [JAN uh]

An ancestor of Jesus, "the son of Janna" (Luke 3:24; Jannai, NIV, NRSV).

JANNES AND JAMBRES [JAN iz, jam BREZ]

Two men who, according to the apostle Paul, "resisted Moses" (2 Tim. 3:8). Although Jannes and Jambres are not named in the Old Testament, they are common figures in late Jewish tradition. According to legend, they were two Egyptian magicians who opposed Moses' demand that the Israelites be freed. They sought to duplicate the miracles of Moses in an attempt to discredit him before Pharaoh "so the magicians of Egypt, they also did in like manner with their enhancement" (Ex. 7:11–12, 22).

JAPHETH [JAY fehth]

One of the three sons of Noah, usually mentioned after his two brothers Shem and Ham (Gen. 5:32; 6:10; 1 Chr. 1:4). Japheth and his wife were two of the eight people who entered the ark and were saved from the destructive waters of the Flood (Gen. 7:7; 1 Pet. 3:20).

Japheth's descendants spread over the north and west regions of the earth: "The sons of Japheth were Gomer, Magog, Madai, Javan, Tubal, Meshech, and Tiras" (1 Chr. 1:5). The Medes, Greeks, Romans, Russians, and Gauls are often referred to as his descendants.

JAPHIA [juh FIGH uh] (may he enlighten)

The name of two people in the Old Testament:

1. A king of Lachish, one of five Amorite kings who formed a military alliance to repel the Israelite invasion. They were defeated and executed by Joshua near the cave of Makkedah (Josh. 10:3).

2. A son of David, born during his reign in Jerusalem (2 Sam. 5:14–15).

JAPHLET [JAF lit] (may he deliver)

A son of Heber, an Asherite (1 Chr. 7:32–33).

JARAH [JAHR uh]

A form of JEHOADDAH.

JARED [JAY rid]

Father of Enoch and an ancestor of Abraham and Jesus (Gen. 5:15–16; 1 Chr. 1:2; Luke 3:37).

JARESIAH [jar uh SIGH uh]

A form of JAARESHIAH.

JARHA [JAHR huh]

An Egyptian servant of a man of Judah, Sheshan (1 Chr. 2:34–35). Sheshan gave his daughter in marriage to Jarha, and she later gave birth to Attai.

JARIB [JAY rib] (may he strive)

The name of three men in the Old Testament:

1. A son of Simeon (1 Chr. 4:24), also called Jachin (Ex. 6:15).

2. A clan leader in Ezra's time (Ezra 8:15–16).

3. A priest who divorced his pagan wife after the Captivity (Ezra 10:18).

JAROAH [juh ROE uh]

Father of Huri, of the tribe of Gad (1 Chr. 5:14).

JASHEN [JAY shuhn]

The father of one of David's mighty men (2 Sam. 23:32). Jashen was apparently the same person as Hashem (1 Chr. 11:34).

JASHOBEAM [juh SHOE bih uhm] (*the kinsman returns*)

The name of two of David's soldiers:
1. One of David's mighty men and a chief of his captains (1 Chr. 11:11; 27:2), also called Josheb–Basshebeth (2 Sam. 23:8).
2. A Benjamite who joined David's army at Ziklag (1 Chr. 12:6).

JASHUB [JAY shuhb] (*he turns back*)

The name of two men in the Old Testament:
1. A son of Issachar and founder of a tribal family, the Jashubites (Num. 26:24). Jashub is also called Job (Gen. 46:13).
2. A son of Bani who divorced his pagan wife after the Captivity (Ezra 10:29).

JASHUBI–LEHEM [juh SHOO bigh LEE hem]

A descendant of Judah, of the family of Shelah (1 Chr. 4:22).

JASIEL [JAY sih uhl]

A form of JAASIEL.

JASON [JAY suhn]

The name of one or two early Christians who worked with the apostle Paul:
1. A Christian of Thessalonica who gave lodging to Paul and Silas in his home during their visit to his city (Acts 17:5–7, 9). A mob of "evil men from the marketplace," incited by "the Jews who were not persuaded," attacked the house of Jason. When they could not find Paul and Silas, they dragged Jason before the rulers of the city on charges of disturbing the peace.
2. A "kinsman" or fellow countryman of the apostle Paul who sent greetings to Rome, "my kinsmen greet you" (Rom. 16:21). He may be the same person as Jason No. 1.

JATHNIEL [JATH nih uhl] (*God gives*)

A son of Meshelemiah and a gatekeeper of the sanctuary (1 Chr. 26:2).

JAVAN [JAY vuhn]

The fourth son of Japheth, son of Noah. Javan was the father of the Ionians, or Greeks (Gen. 10:2).

JAZIZ [JAY ziz]

Overseer of King David's flocks (1 Chr. 27:31).

JEATHERAI [jee ATH uh righ]

A Levite of the family of Gershon (1 Chr. 6:21; Jeaterai, KJV).

JEBERECHIAH [jeh bar uh KIGH uh] (*the Lord blesses*)

Father of Zechariah (Is. 8:2), not to be confused with Zechariah the prophet.

JECAMIAH [jek uh MIGH uh] (*may the Lord establish*)

A descendant of Jeconiah, king of Judah (1 Chr. 3:18; Jekamiah, NIV, NRSV).

JECHILIAH, JECOLIAH [jek ih LIGH uh]

Forms of JECHOLIAH.

JECHOLIAH [jek uh LIGH uh] (*the Lord is able*)

The mother of Azariah (or Uzziah), king of Judah (2 Kin. 15:2; 2 Chr. 26:3; Jechiliah, NASB; Jecoliah, NIV, REB, NRSV). She was the wife of King Amaziah of Judah, the father and predecessor of Azariah.

JECONIAH [JEK uh nigh uh]

A form of JEHOIACHIN.

JEDAIAH [juh DAY uh]

The name of seven men in the Old Testament:

1. A son of Shimri (1 Chr. 4:37).
2. A priest in Jerusalem (1 Chr. 9:10; 24:7).
3. A priest whose descendants returned from the Captivity (Neh. 7:39).
4. An Israelite who helped repair the wall of Jerusalem (Neh. 3:10).
5. A priest who returned from the Captivity with Zerubbabel (Neh. 11:10).
6. Another priest who returned with Zerubbabel (Neh. 12:7, 21).
7. One of the returned captives who brought gold and silver from Babylon to Jerusalem for the Temple (Zech. 6:10, 14).

JEDIAEL [juh DIGH uhl] (known by God)

The name of three or four men in the Old Testament:

1. A son of Benjamin and founder of a family (1 Chr. 7:6, 10–11).
2. One of David's mighty men (1 Chr. 11:45).
3. A Manassite warrior who joined David's army (1 Chr. 12:20). He may be identical with No. 2.
4. A gatekeeper of the tabernacle during David's reign (1 Chr. 26:2).

JEDIDAH [juh DIGH duh] (beloved)

The mother of King Josiah of Judah (2 Kin. 22:1–2). Jedidah was the wife of King Amon of Judah. Her son, Josiah, succeeded Amon as king.

JEDIDIAH [jed uh DIGH uh] (beloved by the Lord)

The name given to Solomon at his birth by Nathan the prophet (2 Sam.

12:25), symbolizing God's forgiveness of the wayward David.

JEDUTHUN [juh DOO thuhn]

The name of two men in the Old Testament:

1. A Levite of the family of Merari (1 Chr. 9:16; 16:41–42), appointed a sanctuary musician in David's time. Apparently he was the same person as ETHAN (1 Chr. 6:44).
2. The father of Obed–Edom (1 Chr. 16:38).

JEEZER [juh EE zur]

A form of ABIEZER.

JEHALELEEL [juh HAH luh leel]

A form of JAHALELEEL.

JEHALELEL [juh HAH lih lel] (may God shine forth)

A Levite who lived during the reign of King Hezekiah of Judah (2 Chr. 29:12; Jehallelel, NRSV).

JEHALLELEL [juh HAH lih lel]

A form of JAHALELEEL; JEHALELEL.

JEHDEIAH [juh DEE uh] (may the Lord rejoice)

The name of two men in the Old Testament:

1. A Levite, a son of Shubael (1 Chr. 24:20).
2. An official in charge of King David's donkeys (1 Chr. 27:30).

JEHEZEKEL [juh HEZ uh kel] (God strengthens)

A priest descended from Aaron (1 Chr. 24:16; Jehezkel, NIV, NRSV).

JEHEZKEL [juh HEZ kel]

A form of JEHEZEKEL.

JEHIAH [juh HIGH uh] (*the Lord lives*)

A Levite doorkeeper for the Ark of the Covenant in David's time (1 Chr. 15:24).

JEHIEL [juh HIGH uhl] (*God lives*)

The name of 10 or 11 men in the Old Testament:

1. A Levite who helped David transport the Ark of the Covenant to Jerusalem (1 Chr. 15:18, 20; 16:5).

2. A Levite of the family of Gershon. Jehiel supervised the treasury of the Temple (1 Chr. 23:8; 29:8).

3. A companion of David's sons (1 Chr. 27:32).

4. A son of King Jehoshaphat (2 Chr. 21:2).

5. A son of Heman the singer in the time of King Hezekiah of Judah (2 Chr. 29:14; Jehuel, NRSV).

6. A Levite in Hezekiah's time who presided over gifts in the Temple (2 Chr. 31:13).

7. A ruler of the Temple during Josiah's reformation (2 Chr. 35:8).

8. The father of Obadiah (Ezra 8:9).

9. The father of Shechaniah (Ezra 10:2).

10. A priest who divorced his pagan wife after the Captivity (Ezra 10:21).

11. A man of Elam's family who divorced his pagan wife after the Captivity (Ezra 10:26). He may be the same person as No. 8. Also see JEIEL.

JEHIELI [juh HIGH uh ligh] (*my God lives*)

A Levite and a son of Laadan the Gershonite (1 Chr. 26:21–22).

JEHIZKIAH [jee hiz KIGH uh] (*the Lord strengthens*)

A son of Shallum and one of the heads of the tribe of Ephraim during the reign of King Pekah of Israel (2 Chr. 28:12).

JEHOADDAH [juh HOE uh duh]

A descendant of King Saul of the tribe of Benjamin (1 Chr. 8:36; Jehoadah, KJV). He was also called Jarah (1 Chr. 9:42).

JEHOADDAN [juh HOE uh duhn]

The mother of Amaziah and the wife of Joash, kings of Judah (2 Kin. 14:1–2; Jehoaddin, NIV, NRSV).

JEHOAHAZ [juh HOE uh haz] (*the Lord sustains*)

The name of a king of Israel and two kings of Judah:

1. The son and successor of Jehu and the 12th king of Israel (2 Kin. 10:35). His 17-year reign (815–798 B.C.) was a disaster for the nation of Israel. By not renouncing the idolatry of the golden calves set up by Jeroboam I at Dan and Bethel, Jehoahaz "did evil in the sight of the Lord." Hazael of Syria and his son Ben–Hadad severely punished Israel during Jehoahaz's reign. This drove Jehoahaz to the Lord, who heard his prayer and granted temporary deliverance from Syria (2 Kin. 13:2–5). Unfortunately, after the danger passed, Jehoahaz quickly abandoned his faith. After his death, Jehoahaz was succeeded by his son Joash (or Jehoash).

2. A son of King Josiah and ruler of Judah for three months (609 B.C.). At the battle of Megiddo, King Josiah was defeated and slain by the powerful Pharaoh Necho of Egypt. Jehoahaz was appointed king in his place at the age of 23, but he was deposed after only three months by Pharaoh Necho (2 Kin. 23:30–34; 2 Chron. 36:1–4). Jehoahaz was also called Shallum (1 Chr. 3:15; Jer. 22:11).

3. The youngest son of Jehoram, king of Judah (2 Chr. 21:17; 25:23). The sixth

king of Judah, Jehoahaz was 42 years old at the beginning of his reign, which lasted only one year (842 or 841 B.C.). Jehoahaz is usually called Ahaziah (2 Kin. 8:24—14:13; 2 Chr. 22:1–11). Also, an inscription of the Assyrian king Tiglath-Pileser III refers to Ahaz, king of Judah, as Jehoahaz; this was evidently his full name, but the Bible always uses the abbreviated form AHAZ.

JEHOASH [juh HOE ash]

A form of JOASH.

JEHOHANAN [jee hoe HAY nuhn] (the Lord is gracious)

The name of eight men in the Old Testament:

1. A gatekeeper of the tabernacle in David's time (1 Chr. 26:3).

2. One of five captains in King Jehoshaphat's army (2 Chr. 17:15).

3. The father of Ishmael (2 Chr. 23:1).

4. A son of Eliashib (Ezra 10:6; Johanan, KJV).

5. A son of Bebai who divorced his pagan wife after the Captivity (Ezra 10:28).

6. A son of Tobiah the Ammonite, Nehemiah's opponent (Neh. 6:18; Johanan, KJV).

7. A priest who returned to Jerusalem with Zerubbabel after the Captivity (Neh. 12:13).

8. A priest who officiated at the dedication of the Jerusalem wall (Neh. 12:42).

JEHOIACHIN [juh HOI uh kin] (the Lord establishes)

The son and successor of Jehoiakim as king of Judah, about 598 or 597 B.C. (2 Chr. 36:8–9; Ezek. 1:2). Jehoiachin did evil in the sight of the Lord, like his father. But he had little opportunity to influence affairs of state, since he reigned

only three months. His brief reign ended when the armies of Nebuchadnezzar of Babylon besieged Jerusalem. When the city surrendered, Jehoiachin was exiled to Babylonia (2 Kin. 24:6–15).

Nebuchadnezzar then made Mattaniah, Jehoiachin's uncle, king in his place and changed Mattaniah's name to Zedekiah (v. 17). Zedekiah was destined to rule over a powerless land containing only poor farmers and laborers, while Jehoiachin was held a prisoner in Babylon.

In the 37th year of his captivity, Jehoiachin was finally released by a new Babylonian king, Evil-Merodach (Amel-Marduk). He must have been awarded a place of prominence in the king's court, since he ate his meals regularly in the presence of the king himself (2 Kin. 25:27–30).

Jehoiachin is also called Jeconiah (1 Chr. 3:16–17) and Coniah (Jer. 22:24). In the New Testament he is listed by Matthew as an ancestor of Jesus (Matt. 1:11–12).

JEHOIADA [juh HOI uh duh] (the Lord knows)

The name of six men in the Old Testament:

1. The father of Benaiah (2 Sam. 8:18).

2. A priest during the reigns of Ahaziah, Athaliah, and Joash of Judah (2 Kin. 11:1—12:16) who helped hide the young king Joash from the wrath of Queen Athaliah (2 Chr. 22:10–12). By his courageous action, Jehoiada was instrumental in preserving the line of David, since Joash was a descendant of David and an ancestor of Jesus. Jehoiada married Jehoshabeath, daughter of King Jehoram (2 Chr. 22:11). Even after Joash became king, Jehoiada was a powerful influence for good in his kingdom. Under his over-

J

sight, the temple of Baal was torn down and the influence of Baalism over the people was reduced. Under the prompting of the young king Joash, the Temple of the Lord was restored to its former glory (2 Kings 12; 2 Chronicles 24). Jehoiada lived to be 130 years old. When he died, he was awarded the honor of burial in the royal tombs "because he had done good in Israel, both toward God and His house" (2 Chr. 24:15–16).

3. A leader of the Aaronites who joined David at Ziklag (1 Chr. 12:27).

4. One of David's aides, or counselors (1 Chr. 27:34).

5. A son of Paseah (Neh. 3:6; Joiada, NIV, NRSV). After the Captivity, Jehoiada helped repair a gate in Jerusalem's wall.

6. A priest in Jerusalem in the prophet Jeremiah's time (Jer. 29:26).

JEHOIAKIM [juh HOI uh kim] (*the Lord raises up*)

An evil king of Judah whose downfall was predicted by the prophet Jeremiah.

A son of the good king Josiah, Jehoiakim was 25 years old when he succeeded to the throne. He reigned 11 years in Jerusalem, from 609 B.C. to 598 B.C. During his reign Pharaoh Necho of Egypt exacted heavy tribute from the people of Judah (2 Chr. 36:3, 5). Jehoiakim was forced to levy a burdensome tax upon his people to pay this tribute.

The prophet Jeremiah described the arrogance of Jehoiakim in great detail (Jer. 1:3; 24:1; 27:1, 20; 37:1; 52:2). He censured Jehoiakim for exploiting the people to build his own splendid house with expensive furnishings (Jer. 22:13–23). Unlike his father Josiah, Jehoiakim ignored justice and righteousness. Jehoiakim had no intention of obeying the Lord; he "did evil in the sight of the Lord" (2 Kin. 23:37). His 11-year reign was filled with abominable acts against God (2 Chr. 36:8). Because of this evil, Jeremiah predicted that no one would lament the death of Jehoiakim.

Jeremiah also told of Jehoiakim's execution of Urijah, a prophet of the Lord (Jer. 26:20–23). Perhaps Jehoiakim's most cynical act was his burning of Jeremiah's prophecies (Jer. 36:22–23). Jeremiah wrote a scroll of judgment against the king, but as this scroll was read, Jehoiakim sliced it into pieces and threw them into the fire.

Jehoiakim could burn the Word of God, but he could not destroy its power. Neither could he avoid Jeremiah's prophecy of his approaching destruction. Recognizing the power of the Babylonians, he made an agreement with Nebuchadnezzar to serve as his vassal king on the throne of Judah. After three years of subjection, he led a foolish rebellion to regain his nation's independence. The rebellion failed and Jerusalem was destroyed by the Babylonians. Jehoiakim was bound and carried away as a captive (2 Chr. 36:6).

JEHOIARIB [juh HOI uh rib] (*the Lord contends*)

A descendant of Aaron whose name was given to a priestly house identified with the reign of King David. When David divided the priests into 24 divisions for the service of the tabernacle, the family of Jehoiarib was made responsible for the first course (1 Chr. 24:7). He is also called Joiarib (Neh. 11:10).

JEHONADAB [juh HAHN uh dab] (*the Lord gives*)

A son of Rechab (2 Kin. 10:15, 23). He was a zealous supporter of JEHU in the ruthless extermination of the house of Ahab and the violent suppression of Baal worship in Samaria. He is also called Jonadab (Jer. 35:6–19).

JEHONATHAN [juh HAHN uh thuhn] (*the Lord gives*)

The name of three men in the Old Testament:

1. An overseer of the storehouses in the days of David (1 Chr. 27:25; Jonathan, NIV, NRSV).

2. A Levite sent by Jehoshaphat to teach the law in the cities of Judah (2 Chr. 17:8).

3. Head of the family of Shemaiah in the days of the high priesthood of Joiakim (Neh. 12:18). He is also called Jonathan (Neh. 12:35).

JEHORAM [juh HOHR uhm] (*the Lord is exalted*)

The name of three men in the Old Testament:

1. The fifth king of Judah, Jehoram was also called Joram. See JORAM No. 2.

2. The ninth king of Israel, Jehoram was also called Joram. See JORAM No. 3.

3. A priest sent by King Jehoshaphat to instruct the people in the law (2 Chr. 17:8).

JEHOSHABEATH [jee hoe SHAB ih ath]

A form of JEHOSHEBA.

JEHOSHAPHAT [juh HAH shuh fat] (*the Lord is judge*)

The name of five men in the Old Testament:

1. An official under David and Solomon (2 Sam. 8:16).

2. A son of Paruah and an official responsible for supplying food for King Solomon's table (1 Kin. 4:17).

3. A son of Asa who succeeded his father as king of Judah (1 Kin. 15:24). Jehoshaphat was 35 years old when he became king, and he reigned 25 years in Jerusalem (2 Chr. 20:31), from about 873 B.C. to about 848 B.C.

Jehoshaphat received an excellent heritage from his father Asa, who in the earlier years of his reign showed a reforming spirit in seeking God (2 Chr. 15:1–19). Jehoshaphat's faith in God led him to "delight in the ways of the LORD" (2 Chr. 17:6). He attacked pagan idolatry and he sent teachers to the people to teach them more about God (2 Chr. 17:6–9). In affairs of state, Jehoshaphat also showed a willingness to rely on the Lord. In a time of danger he prayed for God's help (2 Chr. 20:6–12).

Jehoshaphat showed a high regard for justice in his dealings (2 Chr. 19:4–11). He reminded the judges whom he appointed that their ultimate loyalty was to God. His attitude toward impartial justice is reflected in these words: "Behave courageously, and the LORD will be with the good" (2 Chr. 19:11).

But in his dealings with Ahab, king of Israel, Jehoshaphat made some serious mistakes. Through the marriage of his son, Jehoram, to Ahab's daughter, Jehoshaphat allied himself with Ahab (2 Chr. 21:5–6). This alliance led to even further dealings with the wicked king of Israel (2 Chr. 18:1–34), which the prophet Jehu rebuked (2 Chr. 19:1–3).

Jehoshaphat and his father Asa are bright lights against the dark paganism that existed during their time. Both father and son had certain weaknesses, but their faith in the Lord brought good to themselves as well as God's people during their reigns.

4. A son of Nimshi and father of Jehu, king of Israel (2 Kin. 9:2, 14).

5. A priest who helped move the Ark of the Covenant from the house of Obed-Edom to Jerusalem (1 Chr. 15:24; Joshaphat, NIV, NRSV).

JEHOSHEBA, JEHOSHABEATH [juh HAH shuh buh, jee hoe SHAB ih ath] (*the Lord is her oath*)

The courageous woman who rescued her nephew Joash from certain death at the hands of Athaliah, the wicked queen of Judah (2 Kin. 11:1–3; 2 Chr. 22:10–12). Jehosheba was the half-sister of King Ahaziah. When Ahaziah was killed in battle, his mother, Athaliah, attempted to kill all her grandsons and took the throne for herself. But Jehosheba rescued the youngest of Ahaziah's sons (2 Kin. 11:2) and hid him in the Temple for six years—until he was old enough to be proclaimed king.

Jehosheba's courageous act preserved "the house and lineage of David" (Luke 2:4), from which Jesus was descended.

JEHOSHUA [juh HAH shoo uh]

A form of JOSHUA.

JEHOZABAD [juh HOE zuh bad] (*the Lord bestows*)

The name of three men in the Old Testament:

1. A servant of Joash who conspired against his master and assisted in his assassination (2 Kin. 12:21).

2. A son of Obed–Edom (1 Chr. 26:4).

3. A Benjamite chief who was one of Jehoshaphat's military officers (2 Chr. 17:18).

JEHU [JEE hyoo] (*the Lord is He*)

The name of five men in the Old Testament:

1. A prophet who announced a message of doom against Baasha, king of Israel (1 Kin. 16:12). Jehu also rebuked Jehoshaphat, king of Judah (2 Chr. 19:2).

2. The 11th king of Israel (2 Chr. 22:7–9). Jehu was anointed by Elisha the prophet as king; he later overthrew Joram (Jehoram), King Ahab's son and successor, and reigned for 28 years (841–813 B.C.). His corrupt leadership weakened the nation. He is known for his violence against all members of the "house of Ahab" as he established his rule throughout the nation.

At Jehu's command, Jezebel, the notorious wife of Ahab, was thrown out of the window of the palace to her death, as prophesied by Elijah (1 Kin. 21:23). Ahab's murder of Naboth and the subversion of the religion of Israel had brought terrible vengeance, but more blood was to be shed by Jehu. Next to feel the new king's wrath were the 70 sons of Ahab who lived in Samaria (2 Kings 10). Jehu ordered them killed by the elders of Samaria. Jehu's zeal extended even further, commanding the death of Ahab's advisors and close acquaintances. This excessive violence led the prophet Hosea to denounce Jehu's bloodthirstiness (Hos. 1:4).

Jehu continued his slaughter against the family of Ahaziah, king of Judah (2 Kin. 10:12–14). Then he made an alliance with Jehonadab, the chief of the Rechabites, to destroy the followers of Baal. Jehu and Jehonadab plotted to conduct a massive assembly in honor of Baal. After assuring the Baal worshipers of their sincerity and gathering them into the temple of Baal, Jehu had them all killed (2 Kin. 10:18–28). So complete was this destruction that Baalism was wiped out in Israel, and the temple of Baal was torn down and made into a garbage dump.

Although Jehu proclaimed his zeal for the Lord (2 Kin. 10:16), he failed to follow the Lord's will completely (2 Kin. 10:31). He did not completely eliminate worship of the golden calves at Dan and Bethel, and his disobedience led to the conquest of many parts of Israel by the Syrians (2 Kin. 10:32–33).

3. A son of Obed and a descendant of Hezron (1 Chr. 2:38). Jehu was descended from the family of Jerahmeel and the tribe of Judah.

4. A son of Joshibiah, of the tribe of Simeon (1 Chr. 4:35).

5. A Benjamite of Anathoth (1 Chr. 12:3) who joined David's army at Ziklag.

JEHUBBAH [juh HUH buh] *(he is hidden)*

A son of Shemer, of the tribe of Asher (1 Chr. 7:34).

JEHUCAL [juh HOO kuhl]

A messenger sent to the prophet Jeremiah to ask for his prayers when the Babylonians besieged Jerusalem (Jer. 37:3), also called Jucal (Jer. 38:1).

JEHUDI [juh HOO digh] *(Judahite)*

An officer of Jehoiakim, king of Judah (Jer. 36:14, 21, 23). Jehudi read Jeremiah's prophecies to the king, who destroyed the scroll.

JEHUDIJAH [jee huh DIGH juh] *(the woman from Judah)*

One of the two wives of Mered and the mother of Jered, Heber, and Jekuthiel (1 Chr. 4:18; his Judean wife, NIV).

JEHUEL [juh HOO uhl]

A form of JEHIEL No. 5.

JEHUSH [JEE huhsh]

A form of JEUSH No. 3.

JEIEL [jih EYE uhl]

The name of nine or ten men in the Old Testament:

1. A chief of the tribe of Reuben (1 Chr. 5:7).

2. An ancestor of King Saul (1 Chr. 9:35; Jehiel, KJV, REB).

3. One of David's mighty men (1 Chr. 11:44; Jehiel, KJV). He may be the same person as No. 1.

4. A Levite gatekeeper of the tabernacle during David's reign (1 Chr. 15:18, 21; Jehiel, KJV, NRSV, REB).

5. A Levite of the sons of Asaph (2 Chr. 20:14).

6. A scribe who helped prepare the roll of military personnel for King Uzziah (2 Chr. 26:11).

7. A Levite of the family of Elizaphan in the time of King Hezekiah of Judah (2 Chr. 29:13; Jeuel, NRSV).

8. A chief Levite at King Josiah's great Passover feast (2 Chr. 35:9).

9. A son of Adonikam who returned with Ezra from the Captivity (Ezra 8:13; Jeuel, NRSV).

10. A member of the family of Nebo who divorced his pagan wife after the Captivity (Ezra 10:43).

JEKAMEAM [jek uh MEE uhm]

The fourth son of Hebron and the head of a priestly house (1 Chr. 23:19; 24:23).

JEKAMIAH [jek uh MIGH uh] *(may the Lord establish)*

A son of Shallum, of the tribe of Judah (1 Chr. 2:41). See also JECAMIAH.

JEKUTHIEL [juh KOO thih uhl]

A descendant of Caleb the spy and the father of Zanoah (1 Chr. 4:18).

JEMIMAH [juh MIGH muh]

The first of Job's three daughters born after his great trial of suffering was over and his prosperity was restored (Job 42:14; Jemima, KJV).

J

JEMUEL [JEM yoo uhl]

The oldest son of Simeon and a grandson of Jacob (Ex. 6:15), also called Nemuel (Num. 26:12).

JEPHTHAH [JEF thuh]

The ninth judge of Israel, who delivered God's people from the Ammonites (Judg. 11:1—12:7).

An illegitimate child, Jephthah was cast out of the family by his half-brothers, to prevent him from sharing in the inheritance. He fled to "the land of Tob," where he gathered a group of "worthless men" and soon engaged in raids throughout the surrounding countryside. When Israel was threatened by the Ammonites, the elders of Gilead asked Jephthah to free them from oppression by organizing a counterattack on Ammon. Jephthah showed shrewd foresight by insisting on a position of leadership in Gilead if he should succeed against the Ammonites. After this assurance (Judg. 11:10–11), he began his campaign.

Jephthah first tried the diplomatic approach, but Ammon wanted war. So Jephthah launched an attack through Mizpah of Gilead (Judg. 11:29) and defeated the Ammonites "with a very great slaughter" (Judg. 11:33). At this point, Jephthah made a rash vow, promising God that in exchange for victory in battle he would offer up as a sacrifice the first thing that should come out of his house to meet him on his return (Judg. 11:31).

The Lord delivered Ammon's army into Jephthah's hands. When he returned home, his daughter—his only child—came out to meet him (Judg. 11:34). Jephthah tore his clothing in distress as he realized the terrible rashness of his vow. The text seems to indicate that Jephthah followed through on his vow (Judg. 11:39), although a few scholars believe the verse means she was kept as a virgin dedicated to special service to the Lord for the rest of her life.

After this incident, Jephthah punished an arrogant group of Ephraimites at the Jordan River by using a clever strategy to confuse the enemy. He asked the soldiers to say "shibboleth." If they were Ephraimites, they would not be able to pronounce the word correctly and would say "sibboleth." Their accent would betray them as the enemy.

Jephthah was a man with remarkable abilities of leadership. In spite of rejection by his family, he exercised his many talents and rose to a position of great authority. His greatest weakness was his rash, thoughtless behavior. After his death, he was buried in a city of Gilead. The Book of Hebrews lists him as one of the heroes of faith (Heb. 11:32).

JEPHUNNEH [juh FUH nuh]

The name of two men in the Old Testament:

1. The father of CALEB the spy (Num. 13:6).

2. A son of Jether, of the tribe of Asher (1 Chr. 7:38).

JERAH [JIHR uh] (*moon*)

The fourth son of Joktan, of the family of Shem (1 Chr. 1:20).

JERAHMEEL [jih RAH mih uhl] (*God is compassionate*)

The name of three men in the Old Testament:

1. A son of Hezron of the tribe of Judah. Jerahmeel had many descendants, called Jerahmeelites (1 Chr. 2:9, 25–27, 33, 42).

2. A son of Kish, of the tribe of Levi (1 Chr. 24:29).

3. An official of King Jehoiakim of Judah (Jer. 36:26) sent to arrest Baruch the scribe and Jeremiah the prophet. Jerahmeel is called "the king's son" (Jer. 36:26). A clay impression of his official seal was recently found in a burnt archive in the Jerusalem area.

JERED [JEE red]

A man of the tribe of Judah and the father of Gedor (1 Chr. 4:18).

JEREMAI [JER uh migh] (the Lord hurls)

A son of Hashum who divorced his pagan wife after the Captivity (Ezra 10:33).

JEREMIAH [jer uh MIGH uh] (the Lord hurls)

The name of nine men in the Old Testament:

1. The father of Hamutal (Jer. 52:1).
2. The head of a family of the tribe of Manasseh (1 Chr. 5:23–24).
3. A Benjamite who joined David at Ziklag (1 Chr. 12:4).
4. A Gadite who joined David at Ziklag (1 Chr. 12:10).
5. Another Gadite who joined David at Ziklag (1 Chr. 12:13).
6. A priest who sealed Nehemiah's covenant after the Captivity (Neh. 10:2).
7. A priest who returned from the Captivity with Zerubbabel (Neh. 12:1, 12, 34).
8. A son of Habazziniah and father of Jaazaniah, of the house of the Rechabites (Jer. 35:3).
9. The major prophet during the decline and fall of the southern kingdom of Judah and author of the Book of Jeremiah. He prophesied during the reigns of the last five kings of Judah.

Jeremiah was born in Anathoth, situated north of Jerusalem in the territory of Benjamin (Jer. 1:1–2). He was called to the prophetic ministry in the 13th year of Josiah's reign, about 627 B.C. He must have been a young man at the time, since his ministry lasted for about 40 years—through the very last days of the nation of Judah when the capital city of Jerusalem was destroyed in 586 B.C.

Jeremiah's call is one of the most instructive passages in his book. God declared that he had sanctioned him as a prophet even before he was born (Jer. 1:5). But the young man responded with words of inadequacy: "Ah, Lord GOD!" (Jer. 1:6). These words actually mean "No, Lord GOD!" Jeremiah pleaded that he was a youth and that he lacked the ability to speak. But God replied that he was being called not because of age or ability but because God had chosen him.

Immediately Jeremiah saw the hand of God reaching out and touching his mouth. "Behold, I have put My words in your mouth," God declared (Jer. 1:9). From that moment, the words of the prophet were to be the words of God. And his ministry was to consist of tearing down and rebuilding, uprooting and replanting: "See, I have this day set you over the kingdoms, to root out and to pull down, to destroy and to throw down, to build and to plant" (Jer. 1:10).

Because of the negative nature of Jeremiah's ministry, judgmental texts abound in his book. Jeremiah was destined from the very beginning to be a prophet of doom. He was even forbidden to marry so he could devote himself fully to the task of preaching God's judgment (Jer. 16:1–13). A prophet of doom cannot be a happy man. All of Jeremiah's life was wrapped up in the knowledge that God was about to bring an end to the holy city and cast off His Covenant People.

J

Jeremiah is often called "the weeping prophet" because he wept openly about the sins of his nation (Jer. 9:1). He was also depressed at times about the futility of his message. As the years passed and his words of judgment went unheeded, he lamented his unfortunate state: "O LORD, You induced me, and I was persuaded; You are stronger than I, and have prevailed. I am in derision daily; everyone mocks me" (Jer. 20:7).

At times Jeremiah tried to hold back from his prophetic proclamation. But he found that the word of the Lord was "like a burning fire shut up in my bones" (Jer. 20:9). He had no choice but to proclaim the harsh message of God's judgment.

Jeremiah did not weep and lament because of weakness, nor did he proclaim evil because of a dark and gloomy personality. He cried out because of his love for his people and his God. This characteristic of the prophet is actually a tribute to his sensitivity and deep concern. Jeremiah's laments remind us of the weeping of the Savior (Matt. 23:37–39).

As Jeremiah predicted, the nation of Judah was eventually punished by God because of its sin and disobedience. In 586 B.C. Jerusalem was destroyed and the leading citizens were deported to Babylonia. Jeremiah remained in Jerusalem with a group of his fellow citizens under the authority of a ruling governor appointed by the Babylonians. But he was forced to seek safety in Egypt after the people of Jerusalem revolted against Babylonian rule. He continued his preaching in Egypt (Jeremiah 43—44). This is the last we hear of Jeremiah. There is no record of what happened to the prophet during these years of his ministry.

In the New Testament (KJV) Jeremiah was referred to as Jeremy (Matt. 2:17; 27:9) and Jeremias (Matt. 16:14).

JEREMIAS, JEREMY [jer uh MIGH ass, JER uh mee]

Forms of JEREMIAH.

JEREMOTH [JER e moth]

The name of eight men in the Old Testament:

1. A son of Becher, of the tribe of Benjamin (1 Chr. 7:8, NIV, NRSV, and REB).

2. A son of Beriah, of the tribe of Benjamin (1 Chr. 8:14). Jeremoth is probably the same person as Jeroham No. 2.

3. A Levite of the family of Merari and house of Mushi (1 Chr. 23:23), also called Jerimoth (1 Chr. 24:30).

4. A descendant of Heman. Jeremoth was the head of the 15th division of musicians during David's reign (1 Chr. 25:22). He is also called Jerimoth (1 Chr. 25:4).

5. A son of Azriel and chief officer of the tribe of Naphtali during David's reign (1 Chr. 27:19, NRSV; Jerimoth, KJV, NKJV, and NIV).

6, 7, 8. Three Jews who, after the Captivity, divorced their pagan wives (Ezra 10:26, 27, 29). The name is spelled Ramoth in Ezra 10:29 (KJV and NKJV) instead of Jeremoth (NIV, NRSV, and REB).

JERIAH [juh RIGH uh]

A Levite in the time of David (1 Chr. 23:19), also Jerijah (1 Chr. 26:31).

JERIBAI [JER uh bigh] (*the Lord contends*)

One of David's mighty men (1 Chr. 11:46).

JERIEL [JER ih uhl] (*God sees*)

A man of the tribe of Issachar (1 Chr. 7:2).

JERIJAH [juh RIGH juh]

A form of JERIAH.

JERIMOTH [JER ih mahth]

The name of eight men in the Old Testament:

1. A son of Bela (1 Chr. 7:7).

2. A son of Becher (1 Chr. 7:8; Jeremoth, NIV, NRSV).

3. A Benjamite who became one of David's mighty men (1 Chr. 12:5).

4. A Levite of the family of Merari (1 Chr. 24:30), also called Jeremoth (1 Chr. 23:23).

5. A descendant of Heman (1 Chr. 25:4), also called Jeremoth (1 Chr. 25:22).

6. A ruler of the tribe of Naphtali in the days of David (1 Chr. 27:19; Jeremoth, NRSV).

7. A son of David (2 Chr. 11:18).

8. A Levite overseer in the Temple during the reign of King Hezekiah of Judah (2 Chr. 31:13).

JERIOTH [JER ih ahth] (*tent curtains*)

The second wife, or perhaps a concubine, of Caleb, son of Hezron (1 Chr. 2:18).

JEROBOAM [jehr uh BOE ahm] (*let the kinsman plead*)

The name of two kings of the northern kingdom of Israel:

1. Jeroboam I, the first king of Israel (the ten northern tribes, or the Northern Kingdom), a state established after the death of Solomon (1 Kin. 11:26—14:20). The son of Nebat and Zeruah, Jeroboam reigned over Israel for 22 years (1 Kin. 14:20), from 931/30 to 910/09 B.C.

Jeroboam I first appears in the biblical record as Solomon's servant: "the officer over all the labor force of the house of Joseph" (1 Kin. 11:28). One day as Jeroboam went out of Jerusalem, the prophet Ahijah the Shilonite met him on the road and confronted him with an enacted parable. Ahijah, who was wearing a new garment, took hold of the garment and tore it into 12 pieces. He then said to Jeroboam, "Take for yourself ten pieces, for thus says the Lord, the God of Israel: 'Behold, I will tear the kingdom out of the hand of Solomon and will give ten tribes to you'" (1 Kin. 11:31).

When Solomon learned of Ahijah's words, he sought to kill Jeroboam. But Jeroboam fled to Egypt, where he was granted political asylum by Shishak I, the king of Egypt. Only after the death of Solomon did Jeroboam risk returning to his native Palestine (1 Kin. 11:40; 12:2–3).

Solomon's kingdom was outwardly rich, prosperous, and thriving. But the great building projects he undertook were accomplished by forced labor, high taxes, and other oppressive measures. Discontent and unrest existed throughout Solomon's kingdom. When the great king died, the kingdom was like a powder keg awaiting a spark.

The occasion for the explosion, the tearing of the ten northern tribes from Solomon's successor, came because of the foolish insensitivity of Solomon's son Rehoboam. Rehoboam had gone to Shechem to be anointed as the new king. A delegation led by Jeroboam, who had returned from Egypt following Solomon's death, said to Rehoboam, "Your father made our yoke heavy; now therefore, lighten the burdensome service of your father, and his heavy yoke which he put on us, and we will serve" (1 Kin. 12:4).

But Rehoboam followed the advice of his inexperienced companions and replied, "Whereas my father laid a heavy yoke on you, I will add to your yoke; my father chastised you with whips, but I will chastise you with scourges!" (1 Kin. 12:11). After this show of Rehoboam's foolishness, the ten northern tribes re-

J

volted against Rehoboam and appointed Jeroboam as their king (1 Kin. 12:16–20).

Jeroboam was concerned that the people of Israel might return to the house of David if they continued to journey to Jerusalem for the festivals and observances at the Temple of Solomon. So he proposed an alternative form of worship that was idolatrous. He made two calves of gold that bore a close resemblance to the mounts of the Canaanite pagan god Baal. The king told his countrymen: "It is too much for you to go up to Jerusalem. Here are your gods, O Israel, which brought you up from the land of Egypt!" (1 Kin. 12:28). One calf was erected in Bethel and one in Dan.

Once committed to this sinful direction, Jeroboam's progress was downhill. He next appointed priests from tribes other than Levi. He offered sacrifices to these images and gradually polluted the worship of Israel. The Lord confronted Jeroboam by sending him an unnamed prophet who predicted God's judgment on the king and the nation.

Although outwardly he appeared to be repentant, Jeroboam would not change his disastrous idolatry. His rebellious, arrogant attitude set the pattern for rulers of Israel for generations to come. Eighteen kings sat on the throne of Israel after his death, but not one of them gave up his pagan worship.

2. Jeroboam II, the 14th king of Israel, who reigned for 41 years (793–753 B.C.). Jeroboam was the son and successor of Joash (or Jehoash); he was the grandson of Jehoahaz and the great-grandson of Jehu (2 Kin. 13:1, 13; 1 Chr. 5:17). The Bible declares that Jeroboam "did evil in the sight of the LORD" (2 Kin. 14:24).

Jeroboam was successful in his military adventures. His aggressive campaigns "recaptured for Israel, from Damascus and Hamath, what had be-

longed to Judah" (2 Kin. 14:28). The boundaries of Israel expanded to their greatest extent since the days of David and Solomon: "He restored the territory of Israel from the entrance of Hamath to the Sea of the Arabah" (2 Kin. 14:25).

Jeroboam II was king during the prosperous interval between the economic reverses of other rulers. Hosea, Amos, and Jonah lived during his reign (Hos. 1:1; Amos 1:1–2; 2 Kin. 14:25). During this time of superficial prosperity, the prophet Amos especially spoke out against the many social abuses in Israel. A severe oppression of the poor had been instituted by the newly prosperous class. Justice was in the hands of lawless judges; dishonest merchants falsified the balances by deceit; and worship was little more than a pious smokescreen that covered the terrible abuses of the poor. Amos prophesied that the destructive fury of God would fall upon the house of Jeroboam (Amos 7:9).

After Jeroboam's death, his son Zechariah succeeded him on the throne of Israel (2 Kin. 14:29). Zechariah reigned in Samaria only six months before he was assassinated by Shallum (2 Kin. 15:10).

JEROHAM [juh ROE ham]

The name of several men in the Old Testament:

1. A Levite, the grandfather of the prophet Samuel (1 Sam. 1:1).

2. The head of a Benjamite family (1 Chr. 8:27). Jeroham may be the same person as Jeremoth No. 2.

3. A Benjamite (1 Chr. 9:8). He may be the same person as No. 2.

4. A priest of Jerusalem (1 Chr. 9:12).

5. A Benjamite of Gedor (1 Chr. 12:7).

6. The father of Azarel (1 Chr. 27:22).

7. The father of Azariah (2 Chr. 23:1).

8. The father of Adaiah the priest (Neh. 11:12). He may be the same person as No. 4.

JERUBBAAL [jer uh BAY uhl] (*let Baal plead*)

A name given to GIDEON, one of the judges of Israel, by his father after Gideon destroyed the altar of Baal at Ophrah (Judg. 6:32).

JERUBBESHETH [juh RUHB uh sheth] (*let "shame" plead*)

A name given to JERUBBAAL (or GIDEON) by those who wanted to avoid pronouncing the name of Baal, who was associated with the shameful idol worship of the Canaanites (2 Sam. 11:21).

JERUSHA [juh ROO shuh] (*taken in marriage*)

The wife of Uzziah, king of Judah, and the mother of Jotham, who became king of Judah when Uzziah died (2 Kin. 15:33). The name is also spelled Jerushah (2 Chr. 27:1).

JERUSHAH [juh ROO shuh]

A form of JERUSHA.

JESAIAH [juh SIGH uh]

A form of JESHAIAH.

JESHAIAH [juh SHAY uh] (*salvation of the Lord*)

The name of six men in the Old Testament:

1. A son of Hananiah (1 Chr. 3:21; Jesaiah, KJV).

2. A son of Jeduthun (1 Chr. 25:3, 15).

3. A Levite and a son of Rehabiah (1 Chr. 26:25).

4. A son of Athaliah who returned from the Babylonian Captivity (Ezra 8:7).

5. A Levite who returned from Babylon with Ezra (Ezra 8:19).

6. The father of Ithiel whose descendants lived in Jerusalem (Neh. 11:7; Jesaiah, KJV).

JESHARELAH [jesh uh REE luh]

A musician who presided over the service of song during the reign of King David (1 Chr. 25:14; Asarelah, REB).

JESHEBEAB [juh SHEB ih ab]

Head of the 14th division of priests in the sanctuary service in David's time (1 Chr. 24:13).

JESHER [JEE shur] (*uprightness*)

A son of Caleb (1 Chr. 2:18).

JESHIAH [jih SHY uh]

A form of JESSHIAH.

JESHISHAI [juh SHISH eye]

A son of Jahdo (1 Chr. 5:14).

JESHOHAIAH [jesh oe HAY uh] (*the Lord humbles*)

A leader of the tribe of Simeon (1 Chr. 4:36).

JESHUA [JESH oo uh] (*the Lord is salvation*)

The name of eight men in the Old Testament:

1. Head of the ninth division of priests in David's time (Neh. 7:39; Jeshuah, KJV).

2. A Levite in the days of King Hezekiah of Judah (2 Chr. 31:15).

3. A priest who returned to Jerusalem from the Captivity (Ezra 2:2). Jeshua and his fellow priests and kinsmen built the altar of God to restore the burnt offerings and also began work on the restored temple. He opposed the Samaritans in their efforts to discourage work on the temple (Ezra 4:3–5). In Zechariah 3:1–9 and 6:11 he is called Joshua.

4. The father of Jozabad (Ezra 8:33).

J

5. A son of Pahath-Moab, whose descendants returned from the Captivity with Zerubbabel (Neh. 7:11).

6. The father of Ezer (Neh. 3:19).

7. A Levite who helped Ezra explain the Law to the people (Neh. 8:7).

8. A son of Azaniah (Ezra 2:40).

JESHUAH [jih SHOO uh]

A form of JESHUA No. 1.

JESIAH [jih SIGH uh]

A form of JISSHIAH.

JESIMIEL [juh SIM ih uhl] (God establishes)

A leader of the tribe of Simeon (1 Chr. 4:36).

JESSE [JES ee] (meaning unknown)

The father of King David (1 Sam. 16:18–19) and an ancestor of Jesus. Jesse was the father of eight sons—Eliab, Abinadab, Shimea (Shammah), Nethanel, Raddai, Ozem, Elihu, and David—and two daughters, Zeruiah and Abigail (1 Chr. 2:13–16). He is called a "Bethlehemite" (1 Sam. 16:1, 18).

On instructions from the Lord, the prophet Samuel went to Bethlehem to select a new king from among Jesse's eight sons. After the first seven were rejected, David was anointed by Samuel to replace Saul as king of Israel (1 Sam. 16:1–13). Later King Saul asked Jesse to allow David to visit his court and play soothing music on the harp. Jesse gave his permission and sent Saul a present (1 Sam. 16:20).

The title "son of Jesse" soon became attached to David. It was sometimes used in a spirit of insult and ridicule, mocking David's humble origins (1 Sam. 20:27; 1 Kin. 12:16). But the prophet Isaiah spoke of "a Rod from the stem of Jesse" (11:1) and of "a Root of Jesse" (11:10)—prophecies of the Messiah to come. For the apostle Paul, the "root of Jesse" (Rom. 15:12) was a prophecy fulfilled in Jesus Christ.

JESSHIAH [jesh EYE uh] (the Lord exists)

The second son of Uzziel and the father of Zechariah (1 Chr. 23:20; Jesiah, KJV; Isshiah, NIV), also called Isshiah (1 Chr. 24:25).

JESUI [JES yoo igh]

The third son of Asher and founder of a tribal family, the Jesuites (Num. 26:44). He is also called Isui (Gen. 46:17) and Ishvi (1 Chr. 7:30; Ishuai, KJV).

JESUS [GEE zus] (the Lord is salvation)

The name of five men in the Bible:

1. Jesus BARABBAS, a prisoner released by the Roman governor Pontius Pilate before Jesus was crucified (Matt. 27:16–17, REB; some manuscripts omit the word Jesus and have simply Barabbas).

2. An ancestor of Christ (Luke 3:29; Jose, KJV, NKJV; Joshua, NASB, REB, NIV).

3. The KJV rendering of Joshua, the son of Nun, in the New Testament (Acts 7:45; Heb. 4:8).

4. Jesus Justus, a Jewish Christian who, with the apostle Paul, sent greetings to the Colossians (Col. 4:11).

5. Jesus, the son of Mary. Also see JESUS CHRIST.

JESUS CHRIST

The human-divine Son of God born of the Virgin Mary; the great High Priest who intercedes for His people at the right hand of God; founder of the Christian church and central figure of the human race.

To understand who Jesus was and what He accomplished, students of the New Testament must study: (1) His life, (2) His teachings, (3) His person, and (4) His work.

The Life of Jesus.

The twofold designation Jesus Christ combines the personal name "Jesus" and the title "Christ," meaning "anointed" or "Messiah." The significance of this title became clear during the scope of His life and ministry.

Birth and Upbringing. Jesus was born in Bethlehem, a town about ten kilometers (six miles) south of Jerusalem, toward the end of Herod the Great's reign as king of the Jews (37–4 B.C.). Early in His life He was taken to Nazareth, a town of Galilee. There He was brought up by His mother, Mary, and her husband, Joseph, a carpenter by trade. Hence He was known as "Jesus of Nazareth" or, more fully, "Jesus of Nazareth, the son of Joseph" (John 1:45).

Jesus was His mother's firstborn child; He had four brothers (James, Joses, Judas, and Simon) and an unspecified number of sisters (Mark 6:3). Joseph apparently died before Jesus began His public ministry. Mary, with the rest of the family, lived on and became a member of the church of Jerusalem after Jesus' death and resurrection.

The only incident preserved from Jesus' first 30 years (after his infancy) was His trip to Jerusalem with Joseph and Mary when He was 12 years old (Luke 2:41–52). Since He was known in Nazareth as "the carpenter" (Mark 6:3), He may have taken Joseph's place as the family breadwinner at an early age.

The little village of Nazareth overlooked the main highway linking Damascus to the Mediterranean coast and Egypt. News of the world outside Galilee probably reached Nazareth quickly. During His boyhood Jesus probably heard of the revolt led by Judas the Galilean against the Roman authorities. This happened when Judea, to the south, became a Roman province in A.D. 6 and its inhabitants had to pay tribute to Caesar. Jews probably heard also of the severity with which the revolt was crushed.

Galilee, the province in which Jesus lived, was ruled by Herod Antipas, youngest son of Herod the Great. So the area where He lived was not directly involved in this revolt. But the sympathies of many Galileans were probably stirred. No doubt the boys of Nazareth discussed this issue, which they heard their elders debating. There is no indication of what Jesus thought about this event at the time. But we do know what he said about it in Jerusalem 24 years later (Mark 12:13–17).

Sepphoris, about six kilometers (four miles) northwest of Nazareth, had been the center of an anti-Roman revolt during Jesus' infancy. The village was destroyed by the Romans, but it was soon rebuilt by Herod Antipas. Antipas lived there as tetrarch of Galilee and Perea until he founded a new capital for his principality at Tiberias, on the western shore of the Lake of Galilee (A.D. 22). Reports of happenings at his court, while he lived in Sepphoris, were probably carried to Nazareth. A royal court formed the setting for several of Jesus' parables.

Scenes from Israel's history could be seen from the rising ground above Nazareth. To the south stretched the Valley of Jezreel, where great battles had been fought in earlier days. Beyond the Valley of Jezreel was Mount Gilboa, where King Saul fell in battle with the Philistines. To the east Mount Tabor rose to 562 meters (1,843 feet), the highest elevation in that part of the country. A growing boy would readily find his mind moving back and forth between the stirring events of former days and the realities of the contemporary situation: the all-pervasive presence of the Romans.

Beginnings of Jesus' Ministry. Jesus began His public ministry when He sought baptism at the hands of John the Baptist. John preached between A.D. 27 and 28 in the lower Jordan Valley and baptized those who wished to give expression to their repentance (Matt. 3:13–17; Mark 1:9–11; Luke 3:21–22; John 1:29–34). The descent of the dove as Jesus came up out of the water was a sign that He was the One anointed by the Spirit of God as the Servant-Messiah of His people (Is. 11:2; 42:1; 61:1).

A voice from heaven declared, "You are My beloved Son; in You I am well pleased" (Luke 3:22). This indicated that He was Israel's anointed King, destined to fulfill His kingship as the Servant of the Lord described centuries earlier by the prophet Isaiah (Is. 42:1; 52:13).

In the Gospels of Matthew, Mark, and Luke, Jesus' baptism is followed immediately by His temptation in the wilderness (Matt. 4:1–11; Mark 1:12–13; Luke 4:1–13). This testing confirmed His understanding of the heavenly voice and His acceptance of the path that it marked out for Him. He refused to use His power as God's Son to fulfill His personal desires, to amaze the people, or to dominate the world by political and military force.

Apparently, Jesus ministered for a short time in southern and central Palestine, while John the Baptist was still preaching (John 3:22—4:42). But the main phase of Jesus' ministry began in Galilee after John's imprisonment by Herod Antipas. This was the signal, according to Mark 1:14–15, for Jesus to proclaim God's Good News in Galilee:

"The time is fulfilled, and the kingdom of God is at hand. Repent, and believe in the gospel." What is the character of this kingdom? How was it to be established?

A popular view was that the kingdom of God meant throwing off the oppressive yoke of Rome and establishing an independent state of Israel. JUDAS MACCABEUS and his brothers and followers had won independence for the Jewish people in the second century B.C. by guerrilla warfare and diplomatic skill. Many of the Jewish people believed that with God's help, the same thing could happen again. Other efforts had failed, but the spirit of revolt remained. If Jesus had consented to become the military leader, which the people wanted, many would gladly have followed Him. But in spite of His temptation, Jesus resisted taking this path.

Jesus' proclamation of the kingdom of God was accompanied by works of mercy and power, including the healing of the sick, particularly those who were demon-possessed. These works also proclaimed the arrival of the kingdom of God. The demons that caused such distress to men and women were signs of the kingdom of Satan. When they were cast out, this proved the superior strength of the kingdom of God.

For a time, Jesus' healing aroused great popular enthusiasm throughout Galilee. But the religious leaders and teachers found much of Jesus' activity disturbing. He refused to be bound by their religious ideas. He befriended social outcasts. He insisted on understanding and applying the law of God in the light of its original intention, not according to the popular interpretation of the religious establishment. He insisted on healing sick people on the Sabbath day. He believed that healing people did not profane the Sabbath but honored it, because it was established by God for the rest and relief of human beings (Luke 6:6–11).

This attitude brought Jesus into conflict with the scribes, the official teachers of the law. Because of their influence, He was soon barred from preaching in the synagogues. But this was no great inconvenience. He simply gathered larger congregations to listen to Him on the hillside or by the lakeshore. He regularly illustrated the main themes of His preaching by parables. These were simple stories from daily life that would drive home some special point and make it stick in the hearer's understanding.

The Mission of the Twelve and Its Sequel. From among the large number of His followers, Jesus selected 12 men to remain in His company for training that would enable them to share His preaching and healing ministry. When He judged the time to be ripe, Jesus sent them out two by two to proclaim the kingdom of God throughout the Jewish districts of Galilee. In many places, they found an enthusiastic hearing.

Probably some who heard these disciples misunderstood the nature of the kingdom they proclaimed. Perhaps the disciples themselves used language that could be interpreted as stirring political unrest. News of their activity reached Herod Antipas, ruler of Galilee, arousing His suspicion. He had recently murdered John the Baptist. Now he began to wonder if he faced another serious problem in Jesus.

On the return of His 12 apostles, they withdrew under Jesus' leadership from the publicity that surrounded them in Galilee to the quieter territory east of the Lake of Galilee. This territory was ruled

J

JESUS

EXCUSE ME! I ORDERED THE STEAK!

Hayes

by Antipas' brother Philip—"Philip the te-trarch"—who had only a few Jews among his subjects. Philip was not as likely to be troubled by Messianic excite-ment.

But even here Jesus and His disciples found themselves pursued by enthusias-tic crowds from Galilee. He recognized them for what they were, "sheep without a shepherd," aimless people who were in danger of being led to disaster under the wrong kind of leadership.

Jesus gave these people further teach-ing, feeding them also with loaves and fishes. But this only stimulated them to try to compel Him to be the king for whom they were looking. He would not be the kind of king they wanted, and they had no use for the only kind of king He was prepared to be. From then on, His popularity in Galilee began to decline. Many of His disciples no longer followed Him.

He took the Twelve farther north, into Gentile territory. Here He gave them spe-cial training to prepare them for the cri-sis they would have to meet shortly in Jerusalem. He knew the time was ap-proaching when He would present His challenging message to the people of the capital and to the Jewish leaders.

At the city of Caesarea Philippi, Jesus decided the time was ripe to encourage the Twelve to state their convictions about His identity and His mission. When Peter declared that He was the Messiah, this showed that He and the other apos-tles had given up most of the traditional ideas about the kind of person the Mes-siah would be. But the thought that Jesus would have to suffer and die was some-thing they could not accept. Jesus recog-nized that He could now make a beginning with the creation of a new community. In this new community of

God's people, the ideals of the kingdom He proclaimed would be realized.

These ideals that Jesus taught were more revolutionary in many ways than the insurgent spirit that survived the overthrow of Judas the Galilean. The Jewish rebels against the rule of Rome developed into a party known as the Zealots. They had no better policy than to counter force with force, which, in Jesus' view, was like invoking Satan to drive out Satan. The way of nonresis-tance that He urged upon the people seemed impractical. But it eventually proved to be more effective against the might of Rome than armed rebellion.

Jerusalem: The Last Phase. At the Feast of Tabernacles in the fall of A.D. 29, Jesus went to Jerusalem with the Twelve. He apparently spent the next six months in the southern part of Palestine. Jerusa-lem, like Galilee, needed to hear the mes-sage of the kingdom. But Jerusalem was more resistant to it even than Galilee. The spirit of revolt was in the air; Jesus' way of peace was not accepted. This is why He wept over the city. He realized the way that so many of its citizens pre-ferred was bound to lead to their de-struction. Even the magnificent temple, so recently rebuilt by Herod the Great, would be involved in the general over-throw.

During the week before Passover in A.D. 30, Jesus taught each day in the tem-ple area, debating with other teachers of differing beliefs. He was invited to state His opinion on a number of issues, in-cluding the question of paying taxes to the Roman emperor. This was a test question with the Zealots. In their eyes, to acknowledge the rule of a pagan king was high treason against God, Israel's true King.

Jesus replied that the coinage in which these taxes had to be paid belonged to the Roman emperor because his face and name were stamped on it. Let the emperor have what so obviously belonged to him, Jesus declared; it was more important to make sure that God received what was due Him.

This answer disappointed those patriots who followed the Zealot line. Neither did it make Jesus popular with the priestly authorities. They were terrified by the rebellious spirit in the land. Their favored position depended on maintaining good relations with the ruling Romans. If revolt broke out, the Romans would hold them responsible for not keeping the people under control. They were afraid that Jesus might provoke an outburst that would bring the heavy hand of Rome upon the city.

The enthusiasm of the people when Jesus entered Jerusalem on a donkey alarmed the religious leaders. So did his show of authority when he cleared the temple of traders and moneychangers. This was a "prophetic action" in the tradition of the great prophets of Israel. Its message to the priestly establishment came through loud and clear. The prophets' vision of the temple—"My house shall be called a house of prayer for all nations" (Is. 56:7)—was a fine ideal. But any attempt to make it measure up to reality would be a threat to the priestly privileges. Jesus' action was as disturbing as Jeremiah's speech foretelling the destruction of Solomon's temple had been to the religious leaders six centuries earlier (Jer. 26:1–6).

To block the possibility of an uprising among the people, the priestly party decided to arrest Jesus as soon as possible. The opportunity came earlier than they expected when one of the Twelve, Judas Iscariot, offered to deliver Jesus into their power without the risk of a public disturbance. Arrested on Passover Eve, Jesus was brought first before a Jewish court of inquiry, over which the high priest Caiaphas presided.

The Jewish leaders attempted first to convict Him of being a threat to the temple. Protection of the sanctity of the temple was the one area in which the Romans still allowed the Jewish authorities to exercise authority. But this attempt failed. Then Jesus accepted their charge that He claimed to be the Messiah. This gave the religious leaders an occasion to hand Him over to Pilate on a charge of treason and sedition.

While "Messiah" was primarily a religious title, it could be translated into political terms as "king of the Jews." Anyone who claimed to be king of the Jews, as Jesus admitted He did, presented a challenge to the Roman emperor's rule in Judea. On this charge Pilate, the Roman governor, finally convicted Jesus. This was the charge spelled out in the inscription fixed above His head on the cross. Death by crucifixion was the penalty for sedition by one who was not a Roman citizen.

With the death and burial of Jesus, the narrative of His earthly career came to an end. But with His resurrection on the third day, He lives and works forever as the exalted Lord. His appearances to His disciples after His resurrection assured them He was "alive after His suffering" (Acts 1:3). These appearances also enabled them to make the transition in their experience from the form in which they had known Him earlier to the new way in which they would be related to Him by the Holy Spirit.

The Teachings of Jesus.

Just as Jesus' life was unique, so His teachings are known for their fresh and new approach. Jesus taught several distinctive spiritual truths that set Him apart from any other religious leader who ever lived.

The Kingdom of God. The message Jesus began to proclaim in Galilee after John the Baptist's imprisonment was the good news of the kingdom of God. When He appeared to His disciples after the Resurrection, He continued "speaking of the things pertaining to the kingdom of God" (Acts 1:3). What did Jesus mean by the kingdom of God?

When Jesus announced that the kingdom of God was drawing near, many of His hearers must have recognized an echo of those visions recorded in the Book of Daniel. These prophecies declared that one day "the God of heaven will set up a kingdom which shall never be destroyed" (Dan. 2:44). Jesus' announcement indicated the time had come when the authority of this kingdom would be exercised.

The nature of this kingdom is determined by the character of the God whose kingdom it is. The revelation of God lay at the heart of Jesus' teaching. Jesus called Him "Father" and taught His disciples to do the same. But the term that He used when He called God "Father" was *Abba* (Mark 14:36), the term of affection that children used when they addressed their father at home or spoke about him to others. It was not unusual for God to be addressed in prayer as "my Father" or "our Father." But it was most unusual for Him to be called *Abba*. By using this term, Jesus expressed His sense of nearness to God and His total trust in Him. He taught His followers to look to God with the trust that children show when they expect their earthly fathers to provide them with food, clothes, and shelter.

This attitude is especially expressed in the Lord's Prayer, which may be regarded as a brief summary of Jesus' teaching. In this prayer the disciples were taught to pray for the fulfillment of God's eternal purpose (the coming of His kingdom) and to ask Him for daily bread, forgiveness of sins, and deliverance from temptation.

In Jesus' healing of the sick and proclamation of good news to the poor, the kingdom of God was visibly present, although it was not yet fully realized. Otherwise, it would not have been necessary for Him to tell His disciples to pray, "Your kingdom come" (Matt. 6:10). One day, He taught, it would come "with power" (Mark 9:1), and some of them would live to see that day.

In the kingdom of God the way to honor is the way of service. In this respect, Jesus set a worthy example, choosing to give service instead of receiving it.

The death and resurrection of Jesus unleashed the kingdom of God in full power. Through proclamation of the kingdom, liberation and blessing were brought to many more than could be touched by Jesus' brief ministry in Galilee and Judea.

The Way of the Kingdom. The ethical teaching of Jesus was part of His proclamation of the kingdom of God. Only by His death and resurrection could the divine rule be established. But even while the kingdom of God was in the process of inauguration during His ministry, its principles could be translated into action in the lives of His followers. The most familiar presentation of these principles is found in the Sermon on the Mount (Matthew 5—7), which was addressed to His disciples. These principles showed how those who were already children of the kingdom ought to live.

Jesus and the Law of Moses. The people whom Jesus taught already had a large body of ethical teaching in the Old Testament law. But a further body of oral interpretation and application had grown up around the Law of Moses over the centuries. Jesus declared that He had come to fulfill the law, not to destroy it (Matt. 5:17). But He emphasized its ethical quality by summarizing it in terms of what He called the two great commandments: "You shall love the LORD your God" (Deut. 6:5) and "You shall love your neighbor as yourself" (Lev. 19:18). "On these two commandments," He said, "hang all the Law and the Prophets" (Matt. 22:40).

Jesus did not claim uniqueness or originality for His ethical teaching. One of His purposes was to explain the ancient law of God. Yet there was a distinctiveness and freshness about His teaching, as He declared His authority: "You have heard that it was said . . . But I say to you" (Matt. 5:21–22). Only in listening to His words and doing them could people build a secure foundation for their lives (Matt. 7:24–27; Luke 6:46–49).

In His interpretation of specific commandments, Jesus did not use the methods of the Jewish rabbis. He dared to criticize their rulings, which had been handed down by word of mouth through successive generations of scribes. He even declared that these interpretations sometimes obscured the original purpose of the commandments. In appealing to that original purpose, He declared that a commandment was most faithfully obeyed when God's purpose in giving it was fulfilled. His treatment of the Sabbath law is an example of this approach.

In a similar way, Jesus settled the question of divorce by an appeal to the original marriage ordinance (Gen. 1:26–27; 2:24–25). Since husband and wife were made one by the Creator's decree, Jesus pointed out, divorce was an attempt to undo the work of God. If the law later allowed for divorce in certain situations (Deut. 24:1–4), that was a concession to people's inability to keep the commandment. But it was not so in the beginning, He declared, and it should not be so for those who belong to the kingdom of God.

Jesus actually injected new life into the ethical principles of the Law of Moses. But He did not impose a new set of laws that could be enforced by external sanctions; He prescribed a way of life for His followers. The act of murder, forbidden in the sixth commandment, was punishable by death. Conduct or language likely to provoke a breach of the peace could also bring on legal penalties. No human law can detect or punish the angry thought; yet it is here, Jesus taught, that the process that leads to murder begins. Therefore, "whoever is angry with his brother . . . shall be in danger of the judgment" (Matt. 5:22). But He was careful to point out that the judgment is God's, not man's.

The law could also punish a person for breaking the seventh commandment, which forbade adultery. But Jesus maintained that the act itself was the outcome of a person's internal thought. Therefore, "whoever looks at a woman to lust for her has already committed adultery with her in his heart" (Matt. 5:28).

Jesus' attitude and teaching also made many laws about property irrelevant for His followers. They should be known as people who give, not as people who get. If someone demands your cloak (outer garment), Jesus said, give it to him, and give him your tunic (undergarment) as well (Luke 6:29). There is more to life than abundance of possessions (Luke 12:15); in fact, He pointed out, material wealth is a hindrance to one's spiritual life. The wise man therefore will get rid of it: "It is easier for a camel to go through the eye of a needle than for a rich man to enter the kingdom of God"

(Mark 10:25). In no area have Jesus' followers struggled more to avoid the uncompromising rigor of his words than in His teaching about the danger of possessions.

Jesus insisted that more is expected of His followers than the ordinary morality of decent people. Their ethical behavior should exceed "the righteousness of the scribes and Pharisees" (Matt. 5:20). "If you love [only] those who love you," He asked, "what credit is that to you? For even sinners love those who love them" (Luke 6:32). The higher standard of the kingdom of God called for acts of love to enemies and words of blessing and goodwill to persecutors. The children of the kingdom should not insist on their legal rights but cheerfully give them up in response to the supreme law of love.

The Way of Nonviolence. The principle of nonviolence is deeply ingrained in Jesus' teaching. In His references to the "men of violence" who tried to bring in the kingdom of God by force, Jesus gave no sign that He approved of their ideals or methods. The course He called for was the way of peace and submission. He urged His hearers not to strike back against injustice or oppression but to turn the other cheek, to go a second mile when their services were demanded for one mile, and to take the initiative in returning good for evil.

But the way of nonviolence did not appeal to the people. The crowd chose the militant Barabbas when they were given the opportunity to have either Jesus or Barabbas set free. But the attitude expressed in the shout, "Not this man, but Barabbas!" (Matt. 27:15–26) was the spirit that would one day level Jerusalem and bring misery and suffering to the Jewish nation.

The Supreme Example. In the teaching of Jesus, the highest of all incentives is the example of God. This was no new principle. The central section of Leviticus is called "the law of holiness" because of its recurring theme: "I am the LORD your God . . . Be holy; for I am holy" (Lev. 11:44). This bears a close resemblance to Jesus' words in Luke 6:36, "Be merciful, just as your Father also is merciful." The children of God should reproduce their Father's character. He does not discriminate between the good and the evil in bestowing rain and sunshine; likewise, His followers should not discriminate in showing kindness to all. He delights in forgiving sinners; His children should also be marked by a forgiving spirit.

The example of the heavenly Father and the example shown by Jesus on earth are one and the same, since Jesus came to reveal the Father. Jesus' life was the practical demonstration of His ethical teaching. To His disciples He declared, "I have given you an example, that you should do as I have done to you" (John 13:15).

This theme of the imitation of Christ pervades the New Testament letters. It is especially evident in the writings of Paul, who was not personally acquainted with Jesus before he met Him on the Damascus Road. Paul instructed his converts to follow "the meekness and gentleness of Christ" (2 Cor. 10:1). He also encouraged them to imitate him as he himself imitated Christ (1 Cor. 11:1). When he recommended to them the practice of all the Christian graces, he declared, "Put on the Lord Jesus Christ" (Rom. 13:14). Throughout the New Testament, Jesus is presented as the One who left us an example, that we should follow in His steps (1 Pet. 2:21).

The Person of Christ.

The doctrine of the person of Christ, or Christology, is one of the most important concerns of Christian theology. The various aspects of the person of Christ are best seen by reviewing the titles that are applied to Him in the Bible.

Son of Man. The title "Son of Man" was Jesus' favorite way of referring to Himself. He may have done this because this was not a recognized title already known by the people and associated with popular ideas. This title means essentially "The Man." But as Jesus used it, it took on new significance.

Jesus applied this title to Himself in three distinct ways:

First, He used the title in a general way, almost as a substitute for the pronoun "I." A good example of this usage occurred in the saying where Jesus contrasted John the Baptist, who "came neither eating bread nor drinking wine," with the Son of Man, who "has come eating and drinking" (Luke 7:33–34). Another probable example is the statement that "the Son of Man has nowhere to lay His head" (Luke 9:58). In this instance He warned a would-be disciple that those who wanted to follow Him must expect to share His homeless existence.

Second, Jesus used the title to emphasize that "the Son of Man must suffer" (Mark 8:31). The word "must" implies that His suffering was foretold by the prophets. It was, indeed, "written concerning the Son of Man, that He must suffer many things and be treated with contempt" (Mark 9:12). So when Jesus announced the presence of the betrayer at the Last Supper, He declared, "The Son of Man indeed goes just as it is written of Him" (Mark 14:21). Later the same evening He submitted to His captors with the words, "The Scriptures must be fulfilled" (Mark 14:49).

Finally, Jesus used the title "Son of Man" to refer to Himself as the one who exercised exceptional authority—authority delegated to Him by God. "The Son of Man has power [authority] on earth to forgive sins" (Mark 2:10), He declared. He exercised this authority in a way that made some people criticize Him for acting with the authority of God: "The Son of Man is also Lord of the Sabbath" (Mark 2:28).

The Son of Man appeared to speak and act in these cases as the representative human being. If God had given people dominion over all the works of His hands, then He who was the Son of Man in this special representative sense was in a position to exercise that dominion.

Near the end of His ministry, Jesus spoke of His authority as the Son of Man at the end of time. Men and women "will see the Son of Man coming in the clouds with great power and glory," He declared (Mark 13:26). He also stated to the high priest and other members of the supreme court of Israel: "You will see the Son of Man sitting at the right hand of Power, and coming with the clouds of heaven" (Mark 14:62). He seemed deserted and humiliated as He stood there awaiting their verdict. But the tables would be turned when they saw Him vindicated by God as Ruler and Judge of all the world.

Only once was Jesus referred to as the Son of Man by anyone other than Himself. This occurred when Stephen, condemned by the Jewish Sanhedrin, saw "the Son of Man standing at the right hand of God" (Acts 7:56). In Stephen's vision the Son of Man stood as his heavenly advocate, in fulfillment of Jesus' words: "Whoever confesses Me before men, him the Son of Man also will confess before the angels of God" (Luke 12:8).

Messiah. When Jesus made His declaration before the high priest and His colleagues, He did so in response to the

J

question: "Are You the Christ, the Son of the Blessed?" (Mark 14:61). He replied, "I am" (Mark 14:62). "It is as you said" (Matt. 26:64).

The Christ was the Messiah, the Son of David—a member of the royal family of David. For centuries the Jewish people had expected a Messiah who would restore the fortunes of Israel, liberating the nation from foreign oppression and extending His rule over Gentile nations.

Jesus belonged to the family of David. He was proclaimed as the Messiah of David's line, both before His birth and after His resurrection. But He Himself was slow to make messianic claims. The reason for this is that the ideas associated with the Messiah in the minds of the Jewish people were quite different from the character and purpose of His ministry. Thus, He refused to give them any encouragement.

When, at Caesarea Philippi, Peter confessed Jesus to be the Messiah, Jesus directed him and his fellow disciples to tell no one that He was the Christ. After His death and resurrection, however, the concept of messiahship among His followers was transformed by what He was and did. Then He could safely be proclaimed as Messiah, God's Anointed King, resurrected in glory to occupy the throne of the universe.

Son of God. Jesus was acclaimed as the Son of God at His baptism (Mark 1:11). But He was also given this title by the angel Gabriel at the annunciation: "That Holy One who is to be born will be called the Son of God" (Luke 1:35). The Gospel of John especially makes it clear that the Father-Son relationship belongs to eternity—that the Son is supremely qualified to reveal the Father because He has His eternal being "in the bosom of the Father" (John 1:18).

At one level the title "Son of God" belonged officially to the Messiah, who personified the nation of Israel. "Israel is My son, My firstborn," said God to Pharaoh (Ex. 4:22). Of the promised prince of the house of David, God declared, "I will make him My firstborn" (Ps. 89:27).

But there was nothing merely official about Jesus' consciousness of being the Son of God. He taught His disciples to think of God and to speak to Him as their Father.

But He did not link them with Himself in this relationship and speak to them of "our Father"—yours and mine. The truth expressed in His words in John 20:17 is implied throughout His teaching: "My Father and your Father . . . My God and your God."

As the Son of God in a special sense, Jesus made Himself known to the apostle Paul on the Damascus Road. Paul said, "It pleased God . . . to reveal His Son in me" (Gal. 1:15–16). The proclamation of Jesus as the Son of God was central to Paul's preaching (Acts 9:20; 2 Cor. 1:19).

When Jesus is presented as the Son of God in the New Testament, two aspects of His person are emphasized: His eternal relation to God as His Father and His perfect revelation of the Father to the human race.

Word and Wisdom. Jesus' perfect revelation of the Father is also expressed when He is described as the Word (*logos*) of God (John 1:1–18). The Word is the self-expression of God; that self-expression has personal status, existing eternally with God. The Word by which God created the world (Ps. 33:6) and by which He spoke through the prophets "became flesh" in the fullness of time (John 1:14), living among men and women as Jesus of Nazareth.

Much that is said in the Old Testament about the Word of God is paralleled by what is said of the Wisdom of God: "The LORD by wisdom founded the earth" (Prov. 3:19). In the New Testament Christ is portrayed as the personal Wisdom of God (1 Cor. 1:24, 30)—the one through whom all things were created (1 Cor. 8:6; Col. 1:16; Heb. 1:2).

The Holy One of God. This title was given to Jesus by Peter (John 6:69, NIV, NRSV) and remarkably, by a demon-possessed man (Mark 1:24). In their preaching, the apostles called Jesus "the Holy One and the Just" (Acts 3:14). This was a name belonging to Him as the Messiah, indicating He was especially set apart for God. This title also emphasized His positive goodness and His complete dedication to the doing of His Father's will. Mere "sinlessness," in the sense of the absence of any fault, is a pale quality in comparison to the unsurpassed power for righteousness that filled His life and teaching.

The Lord. "Jesus is Lord" is the ultimate Christian creed. "No one can say that Jesus is Lord except by the Holy Spirit" (1 Cor. 12:3). A Christian, therefore, is a person who confesses Jesus as Lord.

Several words denoting lordship were used of Jesus in the New Testament. The most frequent, and the most important in relation to the doctrine of His person, was the Greek word *kyrios.* It was frequently given to Him as a polite term of address, meaning "Sir." Sometimes the title was used of Him in the third person, when the disciples and others spoke of Him as "The Lord" or "The Master."

After His resurrection and exaltation, however, Jesus was given the title "Lord" in its full, Christological sense. Peter, concluding his address to the crowd in Jerusalem on the Day of Pentecost, declared, "Let all the house of Israel know assuredly that God has made this Jesus, whom you crucified, both Lord and Christ" (Acts 2:36).

The title "Lord" in the Christological sense must have been given to Jesus before the church moved out into the Gentile world. The evidence for this is the invocation "Maranatha" (KJV) or "O Lord, come!" (1 Cor. 16:22). The apostle Paul, writing to a Gentile church in the Greek-speaking world, assumed that its members were familiar with this Aramaic phrase. It was an early Christian title for Jesus which was taken over untranslated. It bears witness to the fact that from the earliest days of the church, the One who had been exalted as Lord was expected to return as Lord.

Another key New Testament text that shows the sense in which Jesus was acknowledged as Lord is Philippians 2:5–11. In these verses Paul may be quoting an early confession of faith. If so, he endorsed it and made it his own. This passage tells how Jesus did not regard equality with God as something that He should exploit to His own advantage. Instead, He humbled Himself to become a man, displaying "the form of God" in "the form of a servant." He became "obedient to the point of death, even the death of the cross. Therefore God also has highly exalted Him and given Him the name which is above every name, that at the name of Jesus every knee should bow, . . . and that every tongue should confess that Jesus Christ is Lord" (Phil. 2:8–11).

The "name which is above every name" is probably the title "Lord" in the highest sense that it can bear. The words echo Isaiah 45:23, where the God of Israel swears, "To Me every knee shall bow, every tongue shall take an oath [or, make confession]." In the Old Testament passage the God of Israel denies to any other being the right to receive the worship that belongs to Him alone. But in the pas-

J

sage from Philippians He readily shares that worship with the humiliated and exalted Jesus. More than that, He shares His own name with Him. When human beings honor Jesus as Lord, God is glorified.

God. If Jesus is called "Lord" in this supreme sense, it is not surprising that He occasionally is called "God" in the New Testament. Thomas, convinced that the risen Christ stood before him, abandoned his doubts with the confession, "My Lord and my God!" (John 20:28).

But the classic text is John 1:1. John declared that the Word existed not only "in the beginning," where He was "with God," but also actually "was God." This is the Word that became incarnate as real man in Jesus Christ, without ceasing to be what He had been from eternity. The Word was God in the sense that the Father shared with Him the fullness of His own nature. The Father remained, in a technical phrase of traditional theology, "the fountain of deity." But from that fountain the Son drew in unlimited measure.

The Bible thus presents Christ as altogether God and altogether man—the perfect mediator between God and mankind because He partakes fully of the nature of both.

The Work of Christ. The work of Christ has often been stated in relation to His threefold office as prophet, priest, and king. As prophet, He is the perfect spokesman of God to the world, fully revealing God's character and will. As priest, Jesus has offered to God by His death a sufficient sacrifice for the sins of the world. Now, on the basis of that sacrifice, He exercises a ministry of intercession on behalf of His people. As king, He is "the ruler over the kings of the earth" (Rev. 1:5)—the One to whose rule the whole world is subject.

The work of Jesus can be discussed in terms of past, present, and future.

The Finished Work of Christ. By the "finished" work of Christ is meant the work of atonement or redemption for the human race that He completed by His death on the cross. This work is so perfect in itself that it requires neither repetition nor addition. Because of this work, He is called "Savior of the world" (1 John 4:14) and "the Lamb of God who takes away the sin of the world" (John 1:29).

In the Bible sin is viewed in several ways: as an offense against God, which requires a pardon; as defilement, which requires cleansing; as slavery, which cries out for emancipation; as a debt, which must be canceled; as defeat, which must be reversed by victory; and as estrangement, which must be set right by reconciliation. However sin is viewed, it is through the work of Christ that the remedy is provided. He has procured the pardon, the cleansing, the emancipation, the cancellation, the victory, and the reconciliation.

When sin is viewed as an offense against God, it is also interpreted as a breach of His law. The law of God, like law in general, involves penalties against the lawbreaker. So strict are these penalties that they appear to leave no avenue of escape for the lawbreaker. The apostle Paul, conducting his argument along these lines, quoted one uncompromising declaration from the Old Testament: "Cursed is everyone who does not continue in all things which are written in the book of the law, to do them" (Deut. 27:26; Gal. 3:10).

But Paul goes on to say that Christ, by enduring the form of death on which a divine curse was expressly pronounced in the Law, absorbed in His own person the curse invoked on the lawbreaker:

"Christ has redeemed us from the curse of the law, having become a curse for us (for it is written, 'Cursed is everyone who hangs on a tree')" (Deut. 21:23; Gal. 3:13).

Since Christ partakes of the nature of both God and humanity, He occupies a unique status with regard to them. He represents God to humanity, and He also represents humanity to God. God is both Lawgiver and Judge; Christ represents Him. The human family has put itself in the position of the lawbreaker; Christ has voluntarily undertaken to represent us. The Judge has made Himself one with the guilty in order to bear our guilt. It is ordinarily out of the question for one person to bear the guilt of others. But when the one person is the representative human being, Jesus Christ, bearing the guilt of those whom He represents, the case is different.

In the hour of His death, Christ offered His life to God on behalf of mankind. The perfect life that He offered was acceptable to God. The salvation secured through the giving up of that life is God's free gift to mankind in Christ.

When the situation is viewed in terms of a law court, one might speak of the accused party as being acquitted. But the term preferred in the New Testament, especially in the apostle Paul's writings, is the more positive word "justified." Paul goes on to the limit of daring in speaking of God as "Him who justifies the ungodly" (Rom. 4:5). God can be so described because "Christ died for the ungodly" (Rom. 5:6). Those who are united by faith to Him are "justified" in Him. As Paul explained elsewhere, "He made Him who knew no sin to be sin for us, that we might become the righteousness of God in Him" (2 Cor. 5:21). The work of Christ, seen from this point of view, is to set humanity in a right relationship with God.

When sin is considered as defilement that requires cleansing, the most straightforward affirmation is that "the blood of Jesus Christ His Son cleanses us from all sin" (1 John 1:7). The effect of His death is to purify a conscience that has been polluted by sin. The same thought is expressed by the writer of the Book of Hebrews. He speaks of various materials that were prescribed by Israel's ceremonial law to deal with forms of ritual pollution, which was an external matter. Then he asks, "How much more shall the blood of Christ, who through the eternal Spirit offered Himself without spot to God, purge your conscience from dead works to serve the living God?" (Heb. 9:14). Spiritual defilement calls for spiritual cleansing, and this is what the death of Christ has accomplished.

When sin is considered as slavery from which the slave must be set free, then the death of Christ is spoken of as a ransom or a means of redemption. Jesus Himself declared that He came "to give His life a ransom for many" (Mark 10:45). Paul not only spoke of sin as slavery; he also personified sin as a slaveowner who compels his slaves to obey his evil orders. When they are set free from his control by the death of Christ to enter the service of God, they find this service, by contrast, to be perfect freedom.

The idea of sin as a debt that must be canceled is based on the teaching of Jesus. In Jesus' parable of the creditor and the two debtors (Luke 7:40–43), the creditor forgave them both when they could make no repayment. But the debtor who owed the larger sum, and therefore had more cause to love the forgiving creditor, represented the woman whose "sins, which are many, are forgiven" (Luke 7:47). This is similar to Paul's reference to God as "having canceled the bond which stood against us with its legal demands" (Col. 2:14, NRSV).

Paul's words in Colossians 2:15 speak of the "principalities and powers" as a personification of the hostile forces in the world that have conquered men and women and held them as prisoners of war. There was no hope of successful resistance against them until Christ confronted them. It looked as if they had conquered Him too, but on the cross He conquered death itself, along with all other hostile forces. In His victory all who believe in Him have a share: "Thanks be to God, who gives us the victory through our Lord Jesus Christ" (1 Cor. 15:57).

Sin is also viewed as estrangement, or alienation, from God. In this case, the saving work of Christ includes the reconciliation of sinners to God. The initiative in this reconciling work is taken by God: "God was in Christ reconciling the world to Himself" (2 Cor. 5:19). God desires the well-being of sinners; so He sends Christ as the agent of His reconciling grace to them (Col. 1:20).

Those who are separated from God by sin are also estranged from one another. Accordingly, the work of Christ that reconciles sinners to God also brings them together as human beings. Hostile divisions of humanity have peace with one another through Him. Paul celebrated the way in which the work of Christ overcame the mutual estrangement of Jews and Gentiles: "For He Himself is our peace, who has made both one, and has broken down the middle wall of division between us" (Eph. 2:14).

When the work of Christ is pictured in terms of an atoning sacrifice, it is God who takes the initiative. The word "propitiation," used in this connection in older English versions of the Bible (Rom. 3:25; 1 John 2:2; 4:10), does not mean that sinful men and women have to do something to appease God or turn away His anger; neither does it mean that Christ died on the cross to persuade God to be merciful to sinners. It is the nature of God to be a pardoning God. He has revealed His pardoning nature above all in the person and work of Christ. This saving initiative is equally and eagerly shared by Christ: He gladly cooperates with the Father's purpose for the redemption of the world.

The Present Work of Christ. The present work of Christ begins with His exaltation by God, after the completion of His "finished" work in His death and resurrection.

The first aspect of His present work was the sending of the Holy Spirit to dwell in His people. "If I do not go away," He had said to his disciples in the Upper Room, "the Helper will not come to you; but if I depart, I will send Him to you" (John 16:7). The fulfillment of this promise was announced by Peter on the Day of Pentecost: "Therefore being exalted to the right hand of God, and having received from the Father the promise of the Holy Spirit, He poured out this which you now see and hear" (Acts 2:33).

The promise of the Holy Spirit can be traced back to John the Baptist, who prophesied that the One who was to come after him, mightier than himself, would "baptize you with the Holy Spirit" (Mark 1:8).

But the present work of Christ that receives the main emphasis in the New Testament is His intercession. Paul, quoting what appears to be an early Christian confession of faith, spoke of "Christ who died, and furthermore is also risen, who is even at the right hand of God, who also makes intercession for us" (Rom. 8:34). So too, the writer to the Hebrews says that "He ever lives to make intercession" for His people (Heb. 7:25). He describes in detail Jesus' exceptional qualifications to be their high priest.

Jesus' presence with God as His people's representative provides the assurance that their requests for spiritual help are heard and granted. To know that He is there is a powerful incentive for His followers. No good thing that Jesus seeks for them is withheld by the Father.

The exaltation of Christ is repeatedly presented in the New Testament as the fulfillment of Psalm 110:1: "Sit at My right hand, till I make Your enemies Your footstool." This means that Christ reigns from His present place of exaltation and must do so until all His enemies are overthrown. Those enemies belong to the spiritual realm: "The last enemy that will be destroyed is death" (1 Cor. 15:26). With the destruction of death, which occurred with the resurrection of Jesus, the present phase of Christ's work gives way to His future work.

The Future Work of Christ. During His earthly ministry, Jesus declared that He had even greater works to do in the future. He specified two of these greater works: the raising of the dead and the passing of final judgment. To raise the dead and to judge the world are prerogatives of God, but He delegated these works to His Son. While the Son would discharge these two functions at the time of the end, they were not unrelated to the events of Jesus' present ministry. Those who were spiritually dead received new life when they responded in faith to the Son of God. In effect, they were passing judgment on themselves as they accepted or rejected the life He offered.

The raising of the dead and the passing of judgment are associated with the second coming of Christ. When Paul dealt with this subject, he viewed Christ's

appearing in glory as the occasion when His people would share His glory and be displayed to the universe as the sons and daughters of God, heirs of the new order. He added that all creation looks forward to that time, because then it "will be delivered from the bondage of corruption into the glorious liberty of the children of God" (Rom. 8:21).

Both the present work of Christ and His future work are dependent on His "finished" work. That "finished" work was the beginning of God's "good work" in His people. This work will not be completed until "the day of Jesus Christ" (Phil. 1:6), when the entire universe will be united "in Christ" (Eph. 1:10).

JESUS JUSTUS

(see JUSTUS).

JESUS, SON OF SIRACH

The author of the Book of Ecclesiasticus, also called The Wisdom of Jesus, Son of Sirach—one of the longer books of the Apocrypha.

JETHER [JEE thur] (*abundance*)

The name of five men in the Old Testament:

1. A son of Gideon, called his "firstborn" (Judg. 8:20–21).

2. An Ishmaelite (1 Chr. 2:17), also called "Jithra, an Israelite" (2 Sam. 17:25). He was the father of Amasa (1 Kin. 2:5).

3. One of the sons of Jada, a descendant of Judah through Jerahmeel (1 Chr. 2:32).

4. A son of Ezrah and a descendant of Caleb the spy (1 Chr. 4:17).

5. An Asherite and the father of Jephunneh, Pispah, and Ara (1 Chr. 7:38). Also see JITHRAN.

JETHETH [JEE theth]

A chief of Esau (Gen. 36:40), or Edom (1 Chr. 1:51).

JETHRO [JETH roe] (*his excellency*)

The father-in-law of Moses (Ex. 3:1), also called Reuel (Ex. 2:18), Hobab (Judg. 4:11), and Raguel (Num. 10:29; Reuel, NIV).

After Moses fled from Egypt into the region of the Sinai Peninsula, he married one of Jethro's daughters, Zipporah (Ex. 2:21). Then Moses tended Jethro's sheep for 40 years (Acts 7:30) before his experience at the burning bush (Exodus 3), when he was called to lead the Israelites from bondage in Egypt.

During the Exodus, Jethro and the rest of Moses' family joined Moses in the wilderness near Mount Sinai (Ex. 18:5). During this visit, Jethro taught Moses to delegate his responsibilities. He noted that Moses was doing all the work himself and advised Moses to decide the difficult cases and to secure able men to make decisions in lesser matters (Ex. 18:13–23). Following this meeting, Jethro departed from the Israelites.

JETUR [JEE tuhr]

A son of Ishmael (Gen. 25:15). His tribe warred against the tribes of Reuben and Gad and the half-tribe of Manasseh (1 Chr. 5:19).

JEUEL [JOO uhl]

A descendant of Zerah. Jeuel and his clan lived in Jerusalem after the Captivity (1 Chr. 9:6). Also see JEIEL.

JEUSH [JEE uhsh]

The name of five men in the Old Testament:

1. A son of Esau and Aholibamah (Gen. 36:5, 14, 18).

2. A Benjamite, son of Bilhan (1 Chr. 7:10).

3. A son of Eshek and a descendant of King Saul (1 Chr. 8:39; Jehush, KJV).

4. A son of Shimei and a Gershonite Levite (1 Chr. 23:10–11).

5. A son of King Rehoboam and grandson of King Solomon (2 Chr. 11:19).

JEUZ [JEE uhz] (*he counsels*)

A son of Shaharaim and Hodesh (1 Chr. 8:10).

JEZANIAH [jez uh NIGH uh] (*the Lord hears*)

One of the Judahite "captains" who allied himself with Gedaliah and remained at Mizpah after Judah was deported to Babylon. He was a son of Hoshaiah the Maachathite (Jer. 40:8; 42:1). He is also called Jaazaniah (2 Kin. 25:23).

JEZEBEL [JEZ uh bel] (*there is no prince*)

The name of two women in the Bible:

1. The wife of Ahab, king of Israel, and mother of Ahaziah, Jehoram, and Athaliah (1 Kin. 16:31). Jezebel was a tyrant who corrupted her husband, as well as the nation, by promoting pagan worship.

She was reared in Sidon, a commercial city on the coast of the Mediterranean Sea, known for its idolatry and vice. When she married Ahab and moved to Jezreel, a city that served the Lord, she decided to turn it into a city that worshiped Baal, a Phoenician god.

The wicked, idolatrous queen soon became the power behind the throne. Obedient to her wishes, Ahab erected a sanctuary for Baal and supported hundreds of pagan prophets (1 Kin. 18:19).

When the prophets of the Lord opposed Jezebel, she had them "massacred" (1 Kin. 18:4, 13). After Elijah defeated her prophets on Mount Carmel, she swore revenge. She was such a fearsome figure that the great prophet was afraid and "ran for his life" (1 Kin. 19:3).

After her husband Ahab was killed in battle, Jezebel reigned for 10 years through her sons Ahaziah and Joram (or Jehoram). These sons were killed by Jehu, who also disposed of Jezebel by having her thrown from the palace window. In fulfillment of the prediction of the prophet Elijah, Jezebel was trampled by the horses and eaten by the dogs (1 Kin. 21:19). Only Jezebel's skull, feet, and the palms of her hands were left to bury when the dogs were finished (2 Kin. 9:30–37).

One truth that emerges from Jezebel's life is that God balances the scales of justice. Wickedness may prevail for a season, but His righteousness will eventually triumph over the forces of evil.

2. A prophetess of Thyatira who enticed the Christians in that church "to commit sexual immorality and to eat things sacrificed to idols" (Rev. 2:20). John probably called this woman "Jezebel" because of her similarity to Ahab's idolatrous and wicked queen.

JEZER [JEE zur]

A son of Naphtali (Gen. 46:24) and founder of a tribal family, the Jezerites (Num. 26:49).

JEZIAH [juh ZIGH uh]

A son of Parosh who divorced his pagan wife (Ezra 10:25; Izziah, NIV, NRSV).

JEZIEL [JEE zih uhl]

A son of Azmaveth who, with his brother Pelet, joined David's army at Ziklag (1 Chr. 12:1–3).

JEZLIAH [jez LIGH uh]

A form of JIZLIAH.

JEZRAHIAH [jez ruh HIGH uh] (*the Lord is shining*)

Director of the singers at the rededication of the walls of Jerusalem (Neh. 12:42). He may have been the same person as IZRAHIAH (1 Chr. 7:3).

JEZREEL [JEZ reel] (*God scatters*)

The name of two people in the Old Testament:

1. A man of the tribe of Judah (1 Chr. 4:3).

2. A symbolic name given by the prophet Hosea to his oldest son (Hos. 1:4). The name Jezreel signified the great slaughter that God would bring on the house of Jehu because of the violent acts he had committed (2 Kings 9).

JIBSAM [JIB suhm]

A son of Tola and a warrior in David's army (1 Chr. 7:2; Ibsam, NIV, NRSV).

JIDLAPH [JID laf]

A son of Nahor (Gen. 22:22).

JIMNAH [JIM nuh]

The firstborn son of Asher (Gen. 46:17) and the founder of the Jimnites (Num. 26:44; Jimna). He is also called Imnah (1 Chr. 7:30) and Imna (Num. 26:44, REB).

JISHUI [JISH yoo eye]

A son of King Saul by his wife Ahinoam (1 Sam. 14:49). Other spellings are Ishui, KJV; Ishvi, NIV, NRSV; and Ishyo, REB.

JISSHIAH [jish EYE uh]

One of David's mighty men (1 Chr. 12:6; Jesiah, KJV; Isshiah, NIV, NRSV, REB).

JITHRA [JITH ruh] (excellence)

An Israelite who fathered Amasa by Abigail, David's sister or half-sister (2 Sam. 17:25; Ithra, KJV, NRSV, REB; Jether, NIV). Amasa later became the commander of Absalom's rebel army (2 Sam. 19:13; 20:4–12).

JITHRAN [JITH ran] (abundance)

A son of Zophah, of the tribe of Asher (1 Chr. 7:37; Ithran, KJV, NIV, NRSV). Apparently, he is the same person as Jether (1 Chr. 7:38).

JIZLIAH [jiz LIGH uh] (the Lord delivers)

A son of Elpaal (1 Chr. 8:18; Jezliah, KJV, REB; Izliah, NRSV, NIV, NASB).

JIZRI [JIZ righ]

A Levite and head of the fourth course of musicians for the sanctuary (1 Chr. 25:11; Izri, KJV). He is also called Zeri (1 Chr. 25:3), a son of Jeduthun.

JOAB [JO ab] (the Lord is father)

The name of three men in the Old Testament:

1. One of the three sons of Zeruiah (2 Sam. 2:13; 8:16; 14:1; 17:25; 23:18, 37; 1 Kin. 1:7; 2:5, 22; 1 Chr. 11:6, 39; 18:15; 26:28; 27:24) who was David's sister (or half sister). Joab was the "general" or commander-in-chief of David's army (2 Sam. 5:8; 1 Chr. 11:6; 27:34).

Joab's father is not mentioned by name, but his tomb was at Bethlehem (2 Sam. 2:32). Joab's two brothers were Abishai and Asahel. When Asahel was killed by Abner (2 Sam. 2:18–23), Joab got revenge by killing Abner (2 Sam. 3:22–27).

When David and his army went to Jerusalem, in an attempt to capture that city (then called Jebus), he said, "Whoever attacks the Jebusites first shall be chief and captain" (1 Chr. 11:6). Joab led the assault at the storming of the Jebusite stronghold on Mount Zion, apparently climbing up into the city by way of a water shaft. The city was captured and Joab was made the general of David's army (2 Sam. 5:8).

Other military exploits by Joab were achieved against the Edomites (2 Sam. 8:13–14; 1 Kin. 11:15) and the Ammonites (2 Sam. 10:6–14; 11:1–27; 1 Chr. 19:6–15; 20:1–3). His character was deeply stained, as was David's, by his participation in the death of Uriah the Hittite (2 Sam. 11:14–25). In putting Absalom to death (2 Sam. 18:1–14), he apparently acted from a sense of duty.

When Absalom revolted against David, Joab remained loyal to David. Soon afterward, however, David gave command of his army to Amasa, Joab's cousin (2 Sam. 19:13; 20:1–13). Overcome by jealous hate, Joab killed Amasa (2 Sam. 20:8–13).

Another of David's sons, Adonijah, aspired to the throne, refusing to accept the fact that Solomon was not only David's choice but also the Lord's choice as the new king. Joab joined the cause of Adonijah against Solomon. Joab was killed by Benaiah, in accordance with Solomon's command and David's wishes. Joab fled to the tabernacle of the Lord, where he grasped the horns of the altar. Benaiah then struck him down with a sword. Joab was buried "in his own house in the wilderness" (1 Kin. 2:34).

2. A son of Seraiah and grandson of Kenaz (1 Chr. 4:13–14). He was the "father of Ge–Harashim" (1 Chr. 4:14), or the founder of a place in Judah called the "Valley of Craftsmen."

3. A man of the house of Pahath-Moab, some of whose descendants returned from the Exile with Zerubbabel (Ezra 2:6; 8:9; Neh. 7:11).

JOAH [JOE uh] (*the Lord is brother*)

The name of four men in the Old Testament:

1. A recorder in the time of King Hezekiah (Is. 36:3).

2. A descendant of Gershon, of the tribe of Levi (1 Chr. 6:21).

3. A gatekeeper in the tabernacle during David's time (1 Chr. 26:4).

4. A son of Joahaz who served as recorder in the time of King Josiah (2 Chr. 34:8).

JOAHAZ [JOE uh haz] (*the Lord helps*)

The father of JOAH (2 Chr. 34:8).

JOANNA [joe AN uh] (*the Lord has been gracious*)

The wife of Chuza, the steward of Herod Antipas. Along with Mary Magdalene, Susanna, and others, she provided for the material needs of Jesus and His disciples from her own funds (Luke 8:3). Joanna was one of the women who witnessed the empty tomb and announced Christ's resurrection to the unbelieving apostles (Luke 24:1–10).

JOANNAS [joe AN us]

A son of Rhesa and the father of Judah in the genealogy of Jesus (Luke 3:27; Joanan, NIV, NRSV; Joanna, KJV; Johanan, REB).

JOASH, JEHOASH [JOE ash, juh HOE ash] (*the Lord supports*)

The name of eight men in the Old Testament:

1. The father of Gideon (Judg. 6:11). Apparently Joash was an idolater who built an altar to Baal on his land. Gideon pulled down his father's altar, and the men of the city of Ophrah demanded that Joash put his son to death. But Joash refused, saying, "If he [Baal] is a god, let him plead for himself" (Judg. 6:31). After this event, Joash called his son Jerubbaal, which means "Let Baal plead" (Judg. 6:32).

2. A man who was commanded by Ahab, king of Israel, to imprison the prophet Micaiah (1 Kin. 22:26).

3. The eighth king of Judah; he was a son of King Ahaziah (2 Kin. 11:2) by Zibiah of Beersheba (2 Kin. 12:1). Joash was seven years old when he became king, and he reigned 40 years in Jerusalem (2 Chr. 24:1), from about 835 B.C. until 796 B.C. He is also called Jehoash (2 Kin. 11:21).

After Ahaziah died, Athaliah killed all the royal heirs to the throne. But God spared Joash through his aunt, Jehosheba, who hid him for six years in the house of the Lord (2 Kin. 11:2–3). When Joash reached the age of seven, Jehoiada the priest arranged for his coronation as king (2 Kin. 11:4–16).

Early in his reign, Joash repaired the Temple and restored true religion to Judah, destroying Baal worship (2 Kin. 11:18–21). But the king who began so well faltered upon the loss of his advisor, Jehoiada. After Jehoiada died, Joash allowed idolatry to grow (2 Chr. 24:18). He even went so far as to have Zechariah, the son of Jehoiada, stoned to death for rebuking him (2 Chr. 24:20–22). God's judgment came quickly in the form of a Syrian invasion, which resulted in the wounding of Joash (2 Chr. 24:23–24). He was then killed by his own servants.

4. The 13th king of Israel; he was the son and successor of Jehoahaz, king of Israel, and was the grandson of Jehu, king of Israel. He is also called Jehoash (2 Kin. 13:10, 25; 14:8–17). Joash reigned in Samaria for 16 years (2 Kin. 13:9–10), from about 798 B.C. to 782/81 B.C.

Israel was revived during the reign of Joash (2 Kin. 13:7), following a long period of suffering at the hands of the Syrians. But while achieving political success, Joash suffered spiritual bankruptcy: "He did evil in the sight of the LORD; he did not depart from all the sins of Jeroboam the son of Nebat, who had made Israel sin; but he walked in them" (2 Kin. 13:11). He was succeeded by his son Jeroboam II.

5. A descendant of Shelah, of the family of Judah (1 Chr. 4:22).

6. A descendant of Becher, of the family of Benjamin (1 Chr. 7:8).

7. A commander of the warriors who left Saul and joined David's army at Ziklag (1 Chr. 12:3).

8. An officer in charge of David's olive oil supplies (1 Chr. 27:28).

JOATHAM [JOE uh tham]

A form of JOTHAM.

JOB [jobe]

The name of two men in the Old Testament:

1. The third son of Issachar, and founder of a tribal family, the Jashubites (Gen. 46:13). He is also called Jashub (Num. 26:24; 1 Chr. 7:1).

2. The central personality of the Book of Job. He was noted for his perseverance (James 5:11) and unwavering faith in God, in spite of his suffering and moments of frustration and doubt. All the facts known about Job are contained in the Old Testament book that bears his name. He is described as "a man in the land of Uz" (Job 1:1) and "the greatest of all the people of the East" (Job 1:3). Uz is probably a name for a region in Edom (Jer. 25:20; Lam. 4:21).

A prosperous man, Job had 7,000 sheep, 3,000 camels, 500 yoke of oxen, 500 female donkeys, and a large house-

hold, consisting of seven sons and three daughters. He was also "blameless and upright, and one who feared God and shunned evil" (Job 1:1).

Satan suggested to God that Job would remain righteous as long as it was financially profitable for him to do so. Then the Lord permitted Satan to test Job's faith in God. Blow after blow fell upon Job: his children, his servants, and his livestock were taken from him and he was left penniless. Nevertheless, "In all this Job did not sin nor charge God with wrong" (Job 1:22).

Satan continued his assault by sneering, "Touch his bone and his flesh, and he will surely curse You to Your face!" (Job 2:5). The Lord allowed Satan to afflict Job with painful boils from the soles of his feet to the crown of his head, so that Job sat in the midst of ashes and scraped his sores with a piece of pottery. "Do you still hold fast to your integrity?" his wife asked him. "Curse God and die!" (Job 2:9). But Job refused to curse God. "Shall we indeed accept good from God," he replied, "and shall we not accept adversity?" (Job 2:10).

Job's faith eventually triumphed over all adversity, and he was finally restored to more than his former prosperity. He had 14,000 sheep, 6,000 camels, 1,000 yoke of oxen, and 1,000 female donkeys. He also had seven sons and three daughters. He died at a ripe old age (Job 42:12–13, 16–17).

Job is a model of spiritual integrity—a person who held fast to his faith, without understanding the reason behind his suffering. He serves as a continuing witness to the possibility of authentic faith in God in the most troubling of circumstances.

JOBAB [JOE bab]

The name of five men in the Old Testament:

JOB

1. A son of Joktan the Shemite (Gen. 10:29; 1 Chr. 1:23).

2. A king of Edom (1 Chr. 1:44–45).

3. A king of Madon, a royal city of the Canaanites (Josh. 11:1).

4. A son of Shaharaim and Hodesh (1 Chr. 8:9).

5. A son of Elpaal (1 Chr. 8:18).

JOCHEBED [JAH kuh bed] (*the Lord honors*)

A daughter of Levi and the mother of Aaron, Moses, and Miriam. To protect Moses from Pharaoh's command that every male Hebrew child be killed, she placed him in an ark of bulrushes on the river. After Pharaoh's daughter discovered the baby, Jochebed became his nurse. She is noted among the heroes of the faith (Heb. 11:23).

JOED [JOE ed] (*the Lord is witness*)

A Benjamite who lived in Jerusalem after the Captivity (Neh. 11:7).

JOEL [JOE uhl] (*the Lord is God*)

The name of 14 men in the Old Testament:

1. The oldest son of Samuel the prophet (1 Sam. 8:2; 1 Chr. 6:28; Vashni, KJV) and the father of Heman the singer (1 Chr. 6:33).

2. A leader of the tribe of Simeon (1 Chr. 4:35).

3. The father of Shemaiah, of the tribe of Reuben (1 Chr. 5:4).

4. A man of the tribe of Gad and a chief in the land of Bashan (1 Chr. 5:12).

5. A Levite ancestor of Samuel the prophet (1 Chr. 6:36).

6. A chief of the tribe of Issachar (1 Chr. 7:3).

7. One of David's mighty men (1 Chr. 11:38).

8. A Levite who helped bring the ark of the covenant from the house of Obed–Edom to Jerusalem (1 Chr. 15:7).

9. A keeper of the temple treasuries in David's time (1 Chr. 26:22).

10. A son of Pedaiah who lived during the time of David (1 Chr. 27:20).

11. A Levite who helped cleanse the temple during the reign of King Hezekiah of Judah (2 Chr. 29:12).

12. A son of Nebo who divorced his pagan wife after the Captivity (Ezra 10:43).

13. Overseer of the Benjamites in Jerusalem in Nehemiah's government (Neh. 11:9).

14. An Old Testament prophet and author of the Book of Joel. A citizen of Jerusalem, he spoke often of the priests and their duties (Joel 1:9, 13–14, 16). For this reason, many scholars believe he may have been a temple prophet. He also had an ear for nature (Joel 1:4–7), and included imagery from agriculture and the natural world in his messages.

JOELAH [joe EE luh]

A son of Jeroham of Gedor (1 Chr. 12:7).

JOEZER [joe EE zur] (*the Lord is help*)

A warrior who joined David's army at Ziklag (1 Chr. 12:6).

JOGLI [JAHG ligh] (*may he reveal*)

The father of BUKKI (Num. 34:22).

JOHA [JOE uh] (*the Lord is living*)

The name of two men in the Old Testament:

1. A son of Beriah (1 Chr. 8:16).

2. A son of Shimri (1 Chr. 11:45).

JOHANAN [joe HAY nuhn] (*the Lord is gracious*)

The name of eight or nine men in the Old Testament:

1. A captain of the Jews who joined forces with Gedaliah after the fall of Jerusalem (2 Kin. 25:23). When Gedaliah was murdered, Johanan pursued the assassin. He rescued several people, whom the assassin had taken as captives, including Jeremiah (Jeremiah 41–43). Against Jeremiah's protests, Johanan took all of them to Egypt.

2. The oldest son of Josiah, king of Judah (1 Chr. 3:15).

3. A son of Elioenai, of the family of Jeconiah (1 Chr. 3:24).

4. A grandson of Ahimaaz and father of Azariah (1 Chr. 6:9–10).

5. A Benjamite soldier who joined David's army at Ziklag (1 Chr. 12:4).

6. A Gadite soldier who joined David's forces at Ziklag (1 Chr. 12:12).

7. Father of Azariah (2 Chr. 28:12).

8. A son of Hakkatan, of the clan of Azgad (Ezra 8:12).

9. A son of Eliashib the high priest (Neh. 12:22–23; Ezra 10:6; Jehohanen, NKJV, NIV), also called Jonathan (Neh. 12:11). See also JEHOHANAN No. 6.

JOHN THE APOSTLE

One of Jesus' disciples, the son of Zebedee, and the brother of James. Before his call by Jesus, John was a fisherman, along with his father and brother (Matt. 4:18–22; Mark 1:16–20). His mother was probably Salome (Matt. 27:56; Mark 15:40), who may have been a sister of Mary (John 19:25), the mother of Jesus.

Although it is not certain that Salome and Mary were sisters, if it were so it would make James and John cousins of Jesus. This would help explain Salome's forward request of Jesus on behalf of her sons (Matt. 20:20–28). The Zebedee family apparently lived in Capernaum on the north shore of the Sea of Galilee (Mark 1:21). The family must have been prosperous, because the father owned a boat and hired servants (Mark 1:19–20). Salome the mother provided for Jesus out of her substance (Mark 15:40–41; Luke 8:3). John must have been the younger of the two brothers, for he is always mentioned second to James in the Gospels of Matthew, Mark, and Luke.

The brothers Zebedee were called by Jesus after His baptism (Mark 1:19–20). This happened immediately after the call of two other brothers, Simon Peter and Andrew (Mark 1:16–18), with whom they may have been in partnership (Luke 5:10). Three of the four—Peter, James, and John—eventually became Jesus' most intimate disciples. They were present when Jesus healed the daughter of Jairus (Mark 5:37; Luke 8:51). They witnessed His Transfiguration (Matt. 17:1–2; Mark 9:2; Luke 9:28–29), as well as His agony in Gethsemane (Matt. 26:37; Mark 14:33). Along with Peter, John was entrusted by Jesus with preparations for the Passover supper (Luke 22:8).

James and John must have contributed a headstrong element to Jesus' band of followers, because Jesus nicknamed them "Sons of Thunder" (Mark 3:17). On one occasion (Luke 9:51–56); when a Samaritan village refused to accept Jesus, the two offered to call down fire in revenge, as the prophet Elijah had once done (2 Kin. 1:10, 12). On another occasion, they earned the anger of their fellow disciples by asking if they could sit on Jesus' right and left hands in glory (Mark 10:35–45).

Following the ascension of Jesus, John continued in a prominent position of leadership among the disciples (Acts 1:13). He was present when Peter healed the lame man in the Temple. Together with Peter he bore witness before the Sanhedrin to his faith in Jesus Christ. The boldness of their testimony brought the hostility of the Sanhedrin (Acts 3—4). When the apostles in Jerusalem received word of the evangelization of Samaria, they sent Peter and John to investigate whether the conversions were genuine (Acts 8:14–25). This was a curious thing to do. The Samaritans had long been suspect in the eyes of the Jews (John 4:9). John himself had once favored the destruction of a Samaritan village (Luke 9:51–56). That he was present on this mission suggests he had experienced a remarkable change.

In these episodes Peter appears as the leader and spokesman for the pair, but John's presence on such errands indicates his esteem by the growing circle of disciples. After the execution of his brother James by Herod Agrippa I, between A.D. 42–44 (Acts 12:1–2), John is not heard of again in Acts. Paul's testimony to John as one of the "pillars," along with Peter and James (the Lord's brother, Gal. 2:9), however, reveals that John continued to hold a position of respect and leadership in the early church.

As might be expected of one of Jesus' three closest disciples, John became the subject of an active and varied church tradition. Tertullian (about A.D. 160–220) said that John ended up in Rome, where he was "plunged, unhurt, into boiling oil." A much later tradition believed that both James and John were martyred. The dominant tradition, however, was that the apostle John moved to Ephesus in Asia Minor, and that from there he was banished to the Island of Patmos (during Domitian's reign, A.D. 81–96). Tradition also held that he returned later to Ephesus, where he died some time after Trajan became emperor in A.D. 98.

J

Stories that John reclaimed a juvenile delinquent, raised a dead man, and opposed the Gnostic heretic Cerinthus survive from this era in his life. It was also the general opinion of the time that from Ephesus John composed the five writings that bear his name in the New Testament (Gospel of John; 1, 2, and 3 John; and Revelation).

Only Revelation identifies its author as John (1:1, 9). The second and third epistles of John identify the author as "the elder" (2 John 1; 3 John 1). Although 1 John and the Gospel of John do not name their author, he can be none other than "the elder," because style and content in these writings are unmistakably related. It may be, as tradition asserts, that the apostle John wrote all five documents. It appears more likely, however, that four of the five writings were actually penned not by John the apostle but by John the elder, a disciple and friend of John's who relied directly on the apostle's testimony as he wrote the documents. This would explain those passages in the Gospel that speak about the beloved disciple (who presumably is John the apostle; John 19:35; 21:24), as well as the reference to "the elder" in 2 and 3 John. Revelation, however, was probably written directly by the apostle John himself.

JOHN THE BAPTIST

Forerunner of Jesus; a moral reformer and preacher of messianic hope. According to Luke 1:36, Elizabeth and Mary, the mothers of John and Jesus, were either blood relatives or close kinswomen. Luke adds that both John and Jesus were announced, set apart, and named by the angel Gabriel even before their birth.

As is true of Jesus, practically nothing is known of John's boyhood, except that he "grew and became strong in spirit"

(Luke 1:80). The silence of his early years, however, was broken by his thundering call to repentance some time around A.D. 28–29, shortly before Jesus began His ministry. Matthew reports that the place where John preached was the wilderness of Judea (3:1). It is likely that he also preached in Perea, east of the Jordan River. Perea, like Galilee, lay within the jurisdiction of Herod Antipas, under whom John was later arrested.

The four gospels are unanimous in their report that John lived "in the wilderness." There he was raised (Luke 1:80) and was called by God (Luke 3:2), and there he preached (Mark 1:4) until his execution. The wilderness—a vast badland of crags, wind, and heat—was the place where God had dwelled with His people after the Exodus. Ever since, it had been the place of religious hope for Israel. John called the people away from the comforts of their homes and cities and out into the wilderness, where they might meet God.

The conviction that God was about to begin a new work among this unprepared people broke upon John with the force of a desert storm. He was called to put on the prophet's hairy mantle with the resolve and urgency of Elijah himself. Not only did he dress like Elijah, in camel's hair and leather belt (2 Kin. 1:8; Mark 1:6); he understood his ministry to be one of reform and preparation, just as Elijah did (Luke 1:17). In the popular belief of the time, it was believed that Elijah would return from heaven to prepare the way for the Messiah (Mal. 4:5–6). John reminded the people of Elijah because of his dress and behavior (Matt. 11:14; Mark 9:12–13).

John was no doubt as rugged as the desert itself. Nevertheless, his commanding righteousness drew large crowds to hear him. What they encountered from this "voice . . . crying in the wilderness" (Mark 1:3) was a call to moral renewal, baptism, and a messianic hope.

The bite of John's moral challenge is hard for us to appreciate today. His command to share clothing and food (Luke 3:11) was a painful jab at a society that was hungry to acquire material objects. When he warned the tax collectors not to take more money than they had coming to them (Luke 3:12–13), he exposed the greed that had drawn persons to such positions in the first place. And the soldiers, whom he told to be content with their wages, must have winced at the thought of not using their power to take advantage of the common people (Luke 3:14).

John's baptism was a washing, symbolizing moral regeneration, administered to each candidate only once. He criticized the people for presuming to be righteous and secure with God because they were children of Abraham (Matt. 3:9). John laid an ax to the root of this presumption. He warned that they, the Jews, would be purged and rejected unless they demonstrated fruits of repentance (Matt. 3:7–12).

John's effort at moral reform, symbolized by baptism, was his way of preparing Israel to meet God. He began his preaching with the words, "Prepare the way of the Lord, make His paths straight" (Mark 1:3). He had a burning awareness of one who was to come after him who would baptize in fire and Spirit (Mark 1:7–8). John was a forerunner of this mightier one, a herald of the messianic hope that would dawn in Jesus.

John was a forerunner of Jesus not only in his ministry and message (Matt. 3:1; 4:17) but also in his death. Not until John's arrest did Jesus begin His ministry (Mark 1:14), and John's execution foreshadowed Jesus' similar fate. Im-

J

JOHN THE BAPTIST

prisoned by Antipas in the fortress of Machaerus on the lonely hills east of the Dead Sea, John must have grown disillusioned by his own failure and the developing failure he sensed in Jesus' mission. He sent messengers to ask Jesus, "Are You the Coming One, or do we look for another?" (Matt. 11:3). John was eventually killed by a functionary of a puppet king who allowed himself to be swayed by a scheming wife, a loose daughter-in-law, and the people around him (Mark 6:14–29).

Josephus records that Herod arrested and executed John because he feared his popularity might lead to a revolt. The Gospels reveal it was because John spoke out against Herod's immoral marriage to Herodias, the wife of his brother Philip (Mark 6:17–19). The accounts are complementary, because John's moral righteousness must have fanned many a smoldering political hope to life.

Jesus said of John, "Among those born of women there has not risen one greater than John the Baptist" (Matt. 11:11). He was the last and greatest of the prophets (Matt. 11:13–14). Nevertheless, he stood, like Moses, on the threshold of the Promised Land. He did not enter the kingdom of God proclaimed by Jesus; and consequently, "he who is least in the kingdom of heaven is greater than he" (Matt. 11:11).

John's influence continued to live on after his death. When Paul went to Ephesus nearly 30 years later, he found a group of John's disciples (Acts 19:1–7). Some of his disciples must have thought of John in messianic terms. This compelled the author of the Gospel of John, writing also from Ephesus some 60 years after the Baptist's death, to emphasize Jesus' superiority (John 1:19–27; 3:30).

JOHN MARK

(See MARK, JOHN.)

JOIADA [JOY uh duh] (the Lord knows)

A high priest after the Captivity. He was succeeded by his son Jonathan (Neh. 12:10–11, 22). See also JEHOIADA No. 5.

JOIAKIM [JOY uh kim] (the Lord raises)

A high priest after the Captivity, and the father of Eliashib (Neh. 12:10, 12, 26).

JOIARIB [JOY uh rib] (the Lord contends)

The name of three men in the Old Testament:

1. A teacher sent by Ezra to Iddo to request ministers for Temple service (Ezra 8:16).

2. An ancestor of a family in Jerusalem in Nehemiah's time (Neh. 11:5).

3. A priest who returned from the Captivity and the father of Jedaiah (Neh. 11:10; 12:6, 19). He is also called JEHOIARIB (1 Chr. 24:7).

JOKIM [JOE kim] (the Lord sets up)

A descendant of Shelah, of the tribe of Judah (1 Chr. 4:22).

JOKSHAN [JAHK shan]

A son of Abraham by his concubine Keturah (1 Chr. 1:32).

JOKTAN [JAHK tan] (little)

A son of Eber, of the family of Shem (Gen. 10:25–26, 29).

JONADAB [JOE nuh dab] (the Lord gives)

The name of two men in the Old Testament:

1. A son of Shimeah. Described as "a very crafty man" (2 Sam. 13:3), Jonadab suggested the plan that Amnon used to

seduce Tamar. Later, when Absalom murdered Amnon, he reassured David that his other sons were still alive (2 Sam. 13:32–33). This suggests a prior knowledge of the crime.

2. A son of Rechab the Kenite and apparently the founder of the Rechabites (Jer. 35:1–19), also called JEHONADAB (2 Kin. 10:15, 23). When Jehu suppressed Baal worship, Jonadab became his zealous supporter in exterminating the house of Ahab. Accompanying Jehu to Samaria, Jonadab assisted him in clearing the temple of Baal of all who were not priests of Baal. In this way Jonadab prepared the way for Jehu's massacre of the Baal worshipers (2 Kin. 10:15–28).

JONAH [JOE nuh] (*a dove*)

The prophet who was first swallowed by a great fish before he obeyed God's command to preach repentance to the Assyrian city of Nineveh. Jonah was not always a reluctant spokesman for the Lord. He is the same prophet who pre-

dicted the remarkable expansion of Israel's territory during the reign of Jeroboam II (ruled about 793–753 B.C.; 2 Kin. 14:25). This passage indicates that Jonah, the son of Amittai, was from Gath Hepher, a town in Zebulun in the northern kingdom of Israel.

While Jonah is described as a servant of the Lord in 2 Kings 14:25, he is a sad and somewhat tragic figure in the book bearing his name. It is a mark of the integrity and reliability of the Bible that a prophet like Jonah is described in such a candid manner. The natural tendency of human writers would be to obscure and hide such a character. But the Spirit of God presents valiant heroes along with petty people to illustrate truth, no matter how weak and unpleasant these characters may have been. We know nothing of Jonah after he returned to Israel from his preaching venture in Nineveh.

JONAM [JOE nuhm]

A form of JONAN.

JONAH

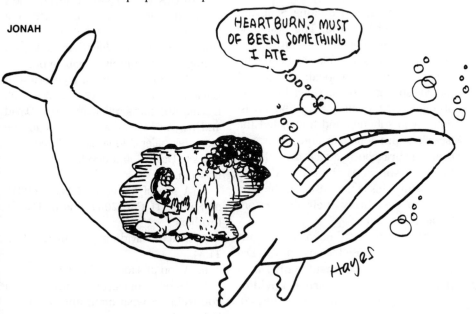

HEARTBURN? MUST OF BEEN SOMETHING I ATE

Hayes

JONAN [JOE nuhn] (*the Lord has been gracious*)

An ancestor of Joseph in Luke's genealogy of Jesus (Luke 3:30; Jonam, NIV, NRSV, REB).

JONAS [JOE nuhs]

Greek form of JONAH.

JONATHAN [JAHN uh thuhn] (*the Lord has given*)

The name of 14 men in the Old Testament:

1. A Levite from Bethlehem in Judah (Judg. 17:7–9) who was employed by Micah. Jonathan became the priest at Micah's idol shrine in the mountains of Ephraim. When the tribe of the Danites took Micah's graven image, ephod, household idols, and molded image (Judg. 18:18), Jonathan went with them. Jonathan and the Danites settled in the newly captured city of Dan (formerly Laish), and he became their priest (Judges 17—18).

2. The oldest son of King Saul and a close friend of David. The first time Jonathan is mentioned in Scripture he is described as a commander of 1,000 men (1 Sam. 13:2). When Jonathan attacked the Philistine garrison at Geba, his action brought swift retaliation by the Philistines, who subdued and humiliated the Israelites. But Jonathan and his armorbearer courageously attacked the Philistine garrison at Michmash and were successful. This action inspired the Israelites to overthrow their oppressors (1 Sam. 14:1–23).

Perhaps the best-known fact about Jonathan is his close friendship with David. He made a covenant with David (1 Sam. 18:3–4) and warned David of Saul's plot against his life (1 Sam. 19:1–2). When Saul sought David's life, Jonathan interceded on behalf of David, and Saul reinstated David to his good favor (1 Sam. 19:1–7). Jonathan's loyalty to David was proven time after time as he warned David of Saul's threats of vengeance (1 Samuel 20) and encouraged David in times of danger (1 Sam. 23:16, 18).

The tragic end for Jonathan came at Mount Gilboa when he, his father Saul, and two of his brothers were slain by the Philistines (1 Sam. 31:1–2; 1 Chr. 10:1–6). When David heard of this, he mourned and fasted (2 Sam. 1:12). He then composed a lamentation, the "Song of the Bow," in which he poured out his grief over the death of Saul and Jonathan (2 Sam. 1:17–27).

Because David loved Jonathan, he treated Jonathan's lame son, Mephibosheth, kindly (2 Sam. 9:1–13). As a final act of love and respect, David brought the bones of Saul and Jonathan from Jabesh Gilead and buried them "in the country of Benjamin in Zelah, in the tomb of Kish his father" (2 Sam. 21:12–14). In this way David honored God's anointed king, Saul, and recognized the loyal, unselfish love of his friend. The story of David and Jonathan is a good example of the unselfish nature of love.

3. A son of Abiathar, a high priest in David's time (2 Sam. 15:27, 36; 17:17, 20). During Absalom's rebellion, when David and his supporters were forced to flee from Jerusalem, Jonathan relayed messages to David about developments in Jerusalem.

4. A son of Shimeah (2 Sam. 21:21), or Shimea (1 Chr. 20:7), one of David's brothers.

5. One of David's mighty men (1 Chr. 11:34).

6. A son of Jada (1 Chr. 2:32).

7. An uncle of David. Jonathan was "a counselor, a wise man, and a scribe" (1 Chr. 27:32).

8. The father of Ebed (Ezra 8:6).

9. A son of Asahel who opposed Ezra's proposal that pagan wives should be divorced (Ezra 10:15).

10. A descendant of Jeshua the high priest (Neh. 12:10–11), also called Johanan (Neh. 12:22).

11. A priest descended from Melichu (Neh. 12:14).

12. A priest descended from Shemaiah (Neh. 12:35), also called Jehonathan (Neh. 12:18).

13. A scribe in whose house Jeremiah the prophet was imprisoned (Jer. 37:15; 38:26).

14. A son of Kareah who joined Gedaliah after the fall of Jerusalem (Jer. 40:8).

See also JEHONATHAN.

JORAH [JOHR uh]

An Israelite whose descendants returned with Zerubbabel from the Captivity (Ezra 2:18). Jorah is also called Hariph (Neh. 7:24).

JORAI [JOHR eye]

A chief of the tribe of Gad (1 Chr. 5:13).

JORAM [JOHR uhm] (the Lord is exalted)

The name of four men in the Old Testament:

1. A son of Toi, king of Hamath (2 Sam. 8:9–10). When David defeated the army of Hadadezer, Toi sent Joram—with gifts of gold, silver, and bronze—to greet and bless David.

2. The son and successor of Jehoshaphat as king of Judah (1 Chr. 3:10–11), also called Jehoram (1 Kin. 22:50). Joram reigned eight years (2 Kin. 8:17) while his brother-in-law, also named Joram, reigned in Israel. His marriage to Athaliah, Ahab's daughter, marked the beginning of Joram's downfall. Athaliah influenced Joram to promote Baal wor-

ship in Judah. This illustrates the perils of an ungodly marriage.

In addition to promoting religious atrocities (2 Chr. 21:11), Joram is remembered for murdering his six brothers and chief nobles. This mass murder assured his position as king and probably added to his wealth (2 Chr. 21:4). Little else is noted of his reign, with the exception of revolts by Edom and Libnah (2 Chr. 21:8–10).

In spite of Joram's evil ways, "The LORD would not destroy the house of David, because of the covenant that He had made with David." But through a letter from Elijah, the Lord did warn Joram of coming judgment (2 Chr. 21:7, 12–15). The king soon lost nearly all his possessions, wives, and children at the hands of Philistine and Arabian raiders as Elijah had prophesied. Joram also contracted an excruciating intestinal disease. After two years of suffering, "he died in severe pain," for "his intestines came out because of his sickness" (2 Chr. 21:19).

Because of Joram's moral and religious depravity, no one mourned his death, and he was not buried in the tombs of the kings. Thus, at the age of 40, his reign was ended prematurely. Within a year, his wife had all of his descendants executed, except one grandson, Joash (2 Kin. 11:1–3).

3. The tenth king of Israel, slain by Jehu (2 Kin. 8:16–29; 9:14–29). The son of Ahab and Jezebel, Joram succeeded his brother, Ahaziah, as king. He was also called Jehoram (2 Kin. 1:17). His 12-year reign was characterized as an evil time, although he did manage to restrain Baal worship (2 Kin. 3:3).

One of Joram's first major projects was to enlist Jehoshaphat, king of Judah, and the king of Edom in a campaign against Moab. Joram also defended Israel against Syria. Through the aid of the prophet Elisha, Joram defeated the Syrian invaders. Later, however, Ben–Hadad of Syria besieged Samaria, leading to severe famine and even cannibalism (2 Kin. 6:8–29). In the darkest hour of the siege, however, the Lord miraculously delivered His people, just as Elisha had prophesied (2 Kin. 7:1–20).

When Hazael replaced Ben–Hadad as king of Syria, Joram made an alliance with his nephew Ahaziah, king of Judah, to occupy the city of Ramoth Gilead by force. Joram was wounded in the battle, and he went back to Jezreel to recover. Jehu, the leader of his army, came to Jezreel and assassinated Joram. Joram's body was then thrown upon the very property that Ahab and Jezebel had stolen from Naboth, thus fulfilling Elijah's prophecy that the house of Ahab would come to an end (1 Kin. 21:21–29; 2 Kin. 9:21–29).

4. A Levite who worked as a treasury official in the tabernacle in David's time (1 Chr. 26:25).

Also see JEHORAM.

JORIM [JOHR im] (the Lord is exalted)

An ancestor of Jesus in Luke's genealogy (Luke 3:29).

JORKOAM [johr KOE uhm]

A son of Raham (1 Chr. 2:44; Jorkeam, NIV, NRSV).

JOSABAD [JAHS uh bad]

A form of JOZABAD.

JOSE [JOE see] (the Lord is salvation)

An ancestor of Jesus in Luke's genealogy (Luke 3:29; Joshua, NIV, REB, NRSV).

JOSECH [JOE sek]

An ancestor of Jesus in Luke's genealogy (Luke 3:26).

JOSEPH [JOE zeph] (may he add)

The name of several men in the Bible:

1. The 11th son of Jacob (Gen. 30:24). Joseph was sold into slavery and later rose to an important position in the Egyptian government. The account of Joseph's life is found in Genesis 37—50.

Joseph was the first child of Rachel (30:24) and his father's favorite son (37:31). This is most clearly shown by the special coat that Jacob gave to Joseph. This favoritism eventually brought serious trouble for the whole family. Joseph's ten older brothers hated him because he was Jacob's favorite and because Joseph had dreams that he interpreted to his brothers in a conceited way. It is no surprise that Joseph's brothers hated him enough to kill him (37:4).

Joseph's brothers were shepherds in the land of Canaan. One day Jacob sent Joseph to search for his brothers, who were tending the flocks in the fields. When Joseph found them, they seized upon the chance to kill him. The only opposing voice was Reuben's, but they finally sold Joseph into slavery to passing merchants.

To hide the deed from their father Jacob, Joseph's brothers took his coat and dipped it in animal blood. When Jacob saw the coat, he was convinced that Joseph had been killed by a wild animal (37:34–35).

Joseph was taken to Egypt, where he was sold to POTIPHAR, an officer of the ruling pharaoh of the nation. His good conduct soon earned him the highest position in the household. Potiphar's wife became infatuated with Joseph and tempted him to commit adultery with her. When he refused, she accused him of the crime and Joseph was sent to prison.

While in prison, Joseph's behavior earned him a position of responsibility over the other prisoners. Among the prisoners Joseph met were the pharaoh's baker and his butler. When each of them had a dream, Joseph interpreted their dreams. When the butler left prison, he failed to intercede on Joseph's behalf, and Joseph spent two more years in prison.

When the pharaoh had dreams that none of his counselors could interpret, the butler remembered Joseph and mentioned him to the pharaoh. Then Joseph was called to appear before the pharaoh. He interpreted the pharaoh's dreams, predicting seven years of plentiful food, followed by seven years of famine. He also advised the pharaoh to appoint a commissioner to store up supplies during the plentiful years.

To Joseph's surprise, the pharaoh appointed him as food commissioner. This was a position of great prestige. Under Joseph's care, many supplies were stored and the land prospered (41:37–57). Joseph was given many comforts, including servants and a wife. He was called Zaphenath–Paneah. When the famine struck, Joseph was second only to the pharaoh in power. People from all surrounding lands came to buy food from him.

Many years passed between Joseph's arrival in Egypt as a slave and his rise to power in the nation during the famine. The famine also struck Canaan, and Joseph's brothers eventually came to Egypt to buy grain. When they met Joseph, they did not recognize him. He recognized them, however, and decided to test them to see if they had changed. He accused them of being spies. Then he sold them grain only on the condition that Simeon stay as a hostage until they brought Benjamin, the youngest brother, to Egypt with them.

Upon returning to Canaan, the brothers told Jacob of their experiences. He vowed not to send Benjamin to Egypt. But the continuing famine forced him to change his mind. On the next trip Benjamin went with his brothers to Egypt.

When they arrived, Joseph treated them royally, weeping openly at the sight of his youngest brother. Simeon was returned to them. After purchasing their grain, they started home. On their way home, however, they were stopped by one of Joseph's servants, who accused them of stealing Joseph's silver cup. The cup was found in Benjamin's bag, where Joseph had placed it. The brothers returned to face Joseph, who declared that Benjamin must stay in Egypt. At this point Judah pleaded with Joseph, saying that it would break their father Jacob's heart if Benjamin failed to return with them. Judah's offer to stay in Benjamin's place is one of the most moving passages in the Old Testament.

Joseph was overcome with emotion. He revealed himself to them as their brother, whom they had sold into slavery years earlier. At first Joseph's brothers were afraid that Joseph would take revenge against them, but soon they were convinced that Joseph's forgiveness was genuine. Judah's plea on Benjamin's behalf was evidence of the change that Joseph had hoped to find in his brothers. He sent them back to Canaan with gifts for his father and invited the family to come live in Egypt.

The grace of God working in the family of Jacob is evident in the way Joseph dealt with his brothers. Joseph did not want revenge against them. He realized that his personal suffering had preserved the family as an instrument of God's will. Joseph also was aware that his rise to power was for the good of his family, not for his own glory (45:7–8).

J

Other men named Joseph include:

2. The father of one of the spies sent into Canaan (Num. 13:7).

3. A son of Asaph (1 Chr. 25:2, 9).

4. One who married a foreign wife during the Exile (Ezra 10:42).

5. A priest of the family of Shebaniah (Neh. 12:14).

6. The husband of Mary, mother of Jesus (Matt. 1:16–24; 2:13; Luke 1:27; 2:4).

7. A converted Jew of Arimathea in whose tomb Jesus was laid (Matt. 27:57, 59; Luke 23:50–53).

8–10. Three different ancestors of Christ, about whom little is known (Luke 3:24, 26, 30).

11. A disciple (known also as Barsabas and Justus) considered to take the place of Judas Iscariot (Acts 1:23). Also see JOSES.

JOSEPHUS, FLAVIUS [joe SEE fis, FLAY vih us]

A Jewish historian and a general of the Galilean Jewish army in the war against Rome (A.D. 66–70). The historical works of Josephus provide important background information for the New Testament and the late intertestamental period. They include information on agriculture, geography, politics, religion, social traditions and practices, and insights into outstanding personalities such as HEROD, and FELIX. Josephus also refers to John the Baptist, James the Lord's brother, and Jesus.

JOSES [JOE seez]

The name of three men in the New Testament:

1. One of the four brothers of Jesus (Matt. 13:55; Mark 6:3), also called Joseph.

2. The brother of James the Less (Mark 15:40, 47), also called Joseph.

3. The original name of BARNABAS (Acts 4:36), also called Joseph.

JOSHAH [JOE shuh]

A son of Amaziah, of the tribe of Simeon (1 Chr. 4:34).

JOSHAPHAT [JAHSH uh fat] (the Lord judges)

The name of two men in the Old Testament:

1. One of David's mighty men (1 Chr. 11:43).

2. A priest who preceded the Ark of the Covenant when it was moved to Jerusalem (1 Chr. 15:24; Jehoshaphat, KJV).

JOSHAVIAH [jahsh uh VIGH uh]

One of David's mighty men (1 Chr. 11:46).

JOSHBEKASHAH [jahsh buh KAY shuh]

A son of Heman appointed by David as a singer (1 Chr. 25:4, 24).

JOSHEB–BASSHEBETH [JOE sheb bash EE beth]

A form of JASHOBEAM.

JOSHIBIAH [jah shuh BIGH uh]

A son of Seraiah (1 Chr. 4:35).

JOSHUA [JAHSH oo uh] (the Lord is salvation)

The successor to Moses and the man who led the nation of Israel to conquer and settle the Promised Land.

Joshua was born in Egypt. He went through the great events of the Passover and the Exodus with Moses and all the Hebrew people who escaped from slavery in Egypt at the hand of their Redeemer God. In the Wilderness of Sinai, Moses took his assistant Joshua with him when he went into the mountains to talk with God (Ex. 24:13). Moses also gave

JOSEPH

Joshua a prominent place at the Tabernacle. As Moses' servant, Joshua would remain at the tabernacle as his representative while the great leader left the camp to fellowship with the Lord (Ex. 33:11).

When Moses sent spies to scout out the land of Canaan, Joshua was selected as the representative of the tribe of Ephraim (Num. 13:8). Only Joshua and Caleb returned to the camp with a report that they could conquer the land with God's help. The other ten spies complained that they were "like grasshoppers" in comparison to the Canaanites (Num. 13:33). Because of their show of faith, Joshua and Caleb were allowed to enter the land at the end of their years of wandering in the wilderness. But all the other Israelites who lived at that time died before the nation entered the Promised Land (Num. 14:30).

At Moses' death, Joshua was chosen as his successor (Josh. 1:1–2). He led the Israelites to conquer the land (Joshua 1–2), supervised the division of the territory among the 12 tribes, and led the people to renew their covenant with God (Joshua 13–22).

When Joshua died at the age of 110, he was buried in the land of his inheritance at Timnath Serah (Josh. 24:30). As Moses' successor, Joshua completed the work that this great leader had begun. Moses led Israel out of Egypt; Joshua led Israel into Canaan. Joshua's name, an Old Testament form of Jesus, means "the Lord is salvation." By his name and by his life, he demonstrated the salvation that comes from God.

JOSIAH [joe SIGH uh]

The name of two men in the Old Testament:

1. The 16th king of Judah, the son of AMON, and the grandson of Manasseh (2 Kin. 21:23—23:30). The three decades of Josiah's reign were characterized by

peace, prosperity, and reform. Hence, they were among the happiest years experienced by Judah. King Josiah devoted himself to pleasing God and reinstituting Israel's observance of the Mosaic Law. That a wicked king like Amon could have such a godly son and successor is a tribute to the grace of God. The Bible focuses almost exclusively on Josiah's spiritual reform, which climaxed in the 18th year of his reign with the discovery of the Book of the Law.

Josiah's reform actually occurred in three stages. Ascending to the throne at age eight, he apparently was blessed with God-fearing advisors who resisted the idolatrous influence of his father. More importantly, however, at the age of 16 (stage one), Josiah personally "began to seek the God of his father David" (2 Chr. 34:3).

At the age of 20 (stage two), Josiah began to cleanse Jerusalem and the land of Judah of idolatrous objects (2 Chr. 34:3–7). His reform was even more extensive than that of his predecessor, HEZE-KIAH (2 Kin. 18:4; 2 Chr. 29:3–36). Josiah extended his cleansing of the land into the territory of fallen Israel; at the time Israel was nominally controlled by Assyria. Josiah personally supervised the destruction of the altars of the Baals, the incense altars, the wooden images, the carved images, and the molded images as far north as the cities of Naphtali. Josiah's efforts were aided by the death of the great Assyrian king, Ashurbanipal, which brought about a serious decline in Assyria's power and allowed Josiah freedom to pursue his reforms.

At the age of 26 (stage three), Josiah ordered that the Temple be repaired under the supervision of Hilkiah, the high priest. In the process, a copy of the Book of the Law was discovered (2 Chr. 34:14–15). When it was read to Josiah, he was horrified to learn how far Judah had departed from the law of God. This discovery provided a new momentum for the reformation that was already in progress.

In 609 B.C. Josiah attempted to block Pharaoh Necho II of Egypt as he marched north to assist Assyria in her fight with Babylon for world supremacy. Despite the pharaoh's assurance to the contrary, Josiah saw Necho's northern campaign as a threat to Judah's security. When he engaged Necho in battle at Megiddo, Josiah was seriously injured. He was returned to Jerusalem, where he died after reigning 31 years. His death was followed by widespread lamentation (2 Chr. 35:20–27). In the New Testament, Josiah is referred to as Josias (Matt. 1:10, KJV).

2. A captive who returned to Jerusalem from Babylon in Zechariah's day (Zech. 6:10), also called Hen (Zech. 6:14).

JOSIAS [joe SIGH us]

A form of JOSIAH.

JOTHAM [JOE thum] (the Lord is perfect)

The name of three men in the Old Testament:

1. The youngest son of Gideon (Judg. 9:1–21). He escaped death at the hands of Abimelech, another son of Gideon. When the Shechemites made Abimelech king, Jotham stood on Mount Gerizim and pronounced judgment on Abimelech and the Shechemites by telling a parable of the trees (vv. 7–20). In fear for his life, Jotham fled to Beer. No more is recorded of him, except that his curse was fulfilled three years later (Judg. 9:57).

2. A son of Uzziah (or Azariah) and the 11th king of Judah (2 Kin. 15:32–38; 2 Chr. 26:21–23), who reigned from about 750–732 B.C. Jotham ruled as co-regent with his father when it was dis-

covered that Uzziah had leprosy. His 18-year reign was a godly one, although the people persisted in idolatry. He was undoubtedly encouraged by the prophets Isaiah, Hosea, and Micah, who ministered during his reign (Is. 1:1; Hos. 1:1; Mic. 1:1).

Jotham built the Upper Gate of the Temple and strengthened the Jerusalem wall of Ophel. He also built cities and fortified buildings throughout the countryside to further strengthen Judah. He fought and defeated the Ammonites and exacted tribute from them for three years (2 Chr. 27:3–5).

Jotham's strength and prosperity were attributed to the fact that "he prepared his ways before the LORD his God" (2 Chr. 27:6). Jotham was an ancestor of Jesus (Matt. 1:9; Joatham, KJV).

3. A son of Jahdai and a descendant of Caleb (1 Chr. 2:47).

JOZABAD [JAHZ uh bad] (the Lord bestows)

The name of several men in the Old Testament:

1. A Gederathite who joined David at Ziklag (1 Chr. 12:4; Josabad, KJV).

2, 3. Two captains of the tribe of Manasseh who defected from Saul to join David's forces at Ziklag (1 Chr. 12:20).

4. A Levite overseer in the Temple during the reign of Hezekiah (2 Chr. 31:13).

5. A chief Levite during the reign of Josiah (2 Chr. 35:9).

6. A son of Jeshua (Ezra 8:33). He may be the same person as Jozabad No. 8, 9, or 10.

7. A descendant of Pashhur who divorced his pagan wife after the Captivity (Ezra 10:22).

8. A Levite who divorced his pagan wife after the Captivity (Ezra 10:23).

9. A Levite who helped Ezra interpret the Law to the people (Neh. 8:7–8).

10. A chief Levite in Jerusalem after the Captivity (Neh. 11:16).

Also see JOSABAD; JOZACHAR.

JOZACHAR [JAHZ uh kahr] (the Lord remembers)

A son of Shimeath and one of two servants of Joash (Jehoash), king of Judah, who formed a conspiracy against Joash. Together they assassinated Joash (2 Kin. 12:20–21; Jozabad, NIV).

JOZADAK [JAHZ uh dak] (the Lord is just)

The father of Jeshua (or Joshua), the high priest in Zerubbabel's time. Jozadak was among those who were carried into Babylonian captivity by Nebuchadnezzar.

JUBAL [JOO buhl]

A descendant of Cain, called "the father of all those who play the harp and the flute" (Gen. 4:21).

JUCAL [JOO kal]

A form of JEHUCAL.

JUDA [JOO duh]

A form of JUDAS.

JUDAEA [joo DEE uh]

A form of JUDEA.

JUDAH [JOO duh] (praise)

The name of seven men in the Old Testament:

1. The fourth son of Jacob and Leah and the founder of the family out of which the messianic line came (Gen. 29:35; Num. 26:19–21; Matt. 1:2).

Judah was one of the most prominent of the 12 sons of Jacob. He saved Joseph's life by suggesting that his brothers sell

Joseph to Ishmaelite merchants rather than kill him (Gen. 37:26–28). In Egypt it was Judah who begged Joseph to detain him rather than Benjamin, Jacob's beloved son. In an eloquent speech Judah confessed what he and his brothers had done to Joseph; shortly thereafter, Joseph identified himself to his brothers (Gen. 44:14—45:1).

It appears that Judah was the leader of Jacob's sons who remained at home. Even though he was not the oldest son, Judah was sent by Jacob to precede him to Egypt (Gen. 46:28). Also Judah, rather than his older brothers, received Jacob's blessing (Gen. 49:3–10). In that blessing, Jacob foretold the rise of Judah: "Your father's children shall bow down before you. . . . The scepter shall not depart from Judah . . . until Shiloh comes" (Gen. 49:8, 10).

Judah had three sons: Er, Onan, and Shelah (Gen. 38:3–5). Er and Onan were killed by divine judgment because of their sins (Gen. 38:7–10). Judah also fathered twin sons, Perez and Zerah, by TAMAR, Er's widow (Gen. 38:29–30). The line of Judah ran through Perez to David and thus became the messianic line (Luke 3:30; Judas, KJV).

2. An ancestor of certain Israelites who helped rebuild the Temple after the Captivity (Ezra 3:9).

3. A Levite who divorced his pagan wife after returning from the Captivity (Ezra 10:23).

4. A son of Senuah (Neh. 11:9).

5. A Levite who returned from the Captivity with Zerubbabel (Neh. 12:8).

6. A leader of Judah who participated in the dedication of the Jerusalem wall (Neh. 12:34).

7. A musician and son of a priest (Neh. 12:36).

JUDAS [JOO duhs] (*praise*)

The name of five men in the New Testament:

1. One of the four brothers of Jesus (Matt. 13:55; Mark 6:3; Juda, KJV). Some scholars believe he was the author of the Epistle of Jude.

2. One of the twelve apostles of Jesus. John is careful to distinguish him from Judas Iscariot (John 14:22). He is called "Judas the son of James" (Luke 6:16; Acts 1:13). In the list of the Twelve given in Mark, instead of "Judas . . . of James" a Thaddaeus is mentioned (Mark 3:18). Matthew has Lebbaeus, whose surname was Thaddaeus (Matt. 10:3). He was also called Judas the Zealot. Tradition says he preached in Assyria and Persia and died a martyr in Persia.

3. Judas of Galilee (Acts 5:37). In the days of the census (Luke 2:2), he led a revolt against Rome. He was killed, and his followers were scattered. According to the Jewish historian Josephus, Judas founded a sect whose main belief was that their only ruler and lord was God.

4. A man with whom the apostle Paul stayed in Damascus after his conversion (Acts 9:11).

5. A disciple surnamed Barsabas who belonged to the church in Jerusalem. The apostles and elders of that church chose Judas and Silas to accompany Paul and Barnabas to Antioch; together they conveyed to the church in that city the decree of the Jerusalem Council about circumcision.

Also see JUDAH.

JUDAS ISCARIOT [JOO duhs iss KAR ih uht]

The disciple who betrayed Jesus. Judas was the son of Simon (John 6:71), or of Simon Iscariot (NRSV). The term Iscariot, which is used to distinguish Judas from the other disciple named Judas (Luke 6:16; John 14:22; Acts 1:13), refers to his hometown of Kerioth, in southern Judah (Josh. 15:25). Thus, Judas was a Judean, the only one of the Twelve who was not from Galilee.

The details of Judas' life are sketchy. Because of his betrayal of Jesus, Judas, however, is even more of a mystery. It must be assumed that Jesus saw promise in Judas, or He would not have called him to be a disciple.

Judas' name appears in three of the lists of the disciples (Matt. 10:2–4; Mark 3:16–19; Luke 6:14–16), although it always appears last. His name is missing from the list of the 11 disciples in Acts 1:13; by that time Judas had already committed suicide. Judas must have been an important disciple, because he served as their treasurer (John 12:6; 13:29).

During the week of the Passover festival, Judas went to the chief priests and offered to betray Jesus for a reward (Matt. 26:14–16; Mark 14:10–11). At the Passover supper, Jesus announced that He would be betrayed and that He knew who His betrayer was—one who dipped his hand with him in the dish (Mark 14:20), the one to whom He would give the piece of bread used in eating (John 13:26–27). Jesus was saying that a friend, one who dipped out of the same dish as He, was His betrayer. These verses in John indicate that Judas probably was reclining beside Jesus, evidence that Judas was an important disciple.

Jesus said to Judas, "What you do, do quickly" (John 13:27). Judas left immediately after he ate (John 13:30). The first observance of the Lord's Supper was probably celebrated afterward, without Judas (Matt. 26:26–29).

Judas carried out his betrayal in the Garden of Gethsemane. By a prear-

ranged sign, Judas singled out Jesus for the soldiers by kissing him. The gospels do not tell us why Judas was needed to point out Jesus, who had become a well-known figure. It is possible that Judas disclosed where Jesus would be that night, so that He could be arrested secretly without the knowledge of His many supporters (Matt. 26:47–50).

Matthew reports that, realizing what he had done, Judas attempted to return the money to the priests. When the priests refused to take it, Judas threw the money on the Temple floor, went out, and hanged himself. Unwilling to use "blood money" for the Temple, the priests bought a potter's field, which became known as the "Field of Blood" (Matt. 27:3–10). This field is traditionally located at the point where the Kidron, Tyropoeon, and Hinnom valleys come together.

It is difficult to understand why Judas betrayed Jesus. Since he had access to the disciples' treasury, it seems unlikely that he did it for the money only; 30 pieces of silver is a relatively small amount. Some have suggested that Judas thought that his betrayal would force Jesus into asserting His true power and overthrowing the Romans. Others have suggested that Judas might have become convinced that Jesus was a false messiah, and that the true Messiah was yet to come, or that he was upset over Jesus' apparent indifference to the law and His association with sinners and his violation of the Sabbath. Whatever the reason, Judas' motive remains shrouded in mystery.

Acts 1:20 quotes Psalm 109:8 as the basis for electing another person to fill the place vacated by Judas: "Let another take his office." When the 11 remaining apostles cast lots for Judas' replacement, "the lot fell on Matthias. And he was

J

numbered with the eleven apostles" (Acts 1:26).

JUDAS MACCABAEUS [JOO duhs mak uh BEE uhs]

The title Maccabeus was first given to Judas, the third son of Mattathias, but it was soon transferred to the entire family. Some scholars believe the term is derived from a Hebrew or Aramaic word meaning "hammer," probably in allusion to the crushing blows inflicted by Judas and his successors upon their enemies. Thus, Judas may have been called "the Hammer" or "the Hammerer," or, as some scholars prefer, "Extinguisher" or "Quencher" (of the enemy).

Antiochus had sent commissioners throughout the entire country of Judea to enforce his decree. Appalled by the sacrilegious acts committed in Judea and Jerusalem and moved by his fervent zeal for the law of Moses, Mattathias killed one of the officers of the king sent to enforce pagan sacrifice. He and his five sons then fled from Modein, taking refuge in the rugged hills nearby. Joined by a growing number of sympathizers who detested the "abomination of desolation" (Dan. 11:31; 12:11; see Dan. 9:27) set up on the altar by Antiochus, the Maccabees carried on guerilla warfare against the Syrians and the Jewish collaborators.

In December 164 B.C. Judas Maccabeus recaptured most of Jerusalem. Then he forced the loyal priests, those who had not collaborated with Antiochus, to cleanse the Holy Place and erect a new altar. On the 25th of Kislev, 164 B.C., precisely three years after Antiochus had defiled it, Judas rededicated the temple.

According to Jewish tradition, only one undefiled jar of oil could be found. This jar contained oil for only one day. Miraculously, however, the oil kept burning for eight days. The Hebrew word *Hanukkah,* which means "dedication," is the name still used today for the Jewish Festival of Lights that commemorates this event. Celebrated for eight days from the 25th day of the month of Kislev to the second day of Adar, Hanukkah occurs near or at the same time as the Christian celebration of Christmas. The Feast of Dedication is mentioned in the New Testament (John 10:22).

After a short time of peace, warfare broke out again between the Jews and the Syrians. Leadership of the Maccabees passed from Judas to Jonathan and then to Simon. (The two other brothers had been killed without assuming leadership.) After the death of Simon, the last remaining son of Mattathias, the succession of the Maccabees was maintained by Simon's son John, known later as John Hyrcanus or Hyrcanus I.

JUDE [jood] (*praise*)

The author of the Epistle of Jude, in which he is described as "a servant of Jesus Christ, and brother of James" (Jude 1). Jude is an English form of the name Judas. Many scholars believe that the James mentioned in this passage is James the brother of Jesus. In Matthew 13:55 the people said concerning Jesus, "Is this not the carpenter's son? Is not His mother called Mary? And His brothers James, Joses, Simon, and Judas?" (Mark 6:3).

If Jude (Judas) was the brother of James and of Jesus, Jude did not believe in Him (John 7:5) until after Jesus' resurrection (Acts 1:14).

JUDITH [JOO dith] (*the praised one*)

One of the two Hittite wives of Esau (Gen. 26:34). Although she was a Hittite, her name is pure Hebrew, the feminine form of Judah.

KADMIEL [KAD mih uhl] (*God is foremost*)

The name of three men in the Old Testament:

1. A Levite whose descendants returned from the Captivity with Zerubbabel (Ezra 2:40).

2. A Levite who helped rebuild the Temple after the Captivity (Ezra 3:9).

3. A Levite who sealed the covenant after the Captivity (Neh. 9:4–5).

KALLAI [KAL eye]

A priest who returned from the Captivity with Zerubbabel (Neh. 12:20).

KAREAH [kuh REE uh] (*bald*)

The father of Johanan and Jonathan (Jer. 41:11–16; Careah, 2 Kin. 25:23, KJV).

KEDAR [KEE dur]

The second son of Ishmael (Gen. 25:13).

KEDEMAH [KED eh muh] (*eastern*)

The youngest son of Ishmael and the name of an Arabian tribe (1 Chr. 1:31).

KEDORLAOMER

A form of CHEDORLAOMER.

KEILAH [kee EYE luh]

A descendant of Caleb, of the family of Judah (1 Chr. 4:19).

KELAIAH [kih LAY uh]

A priest who divorced his pagan wife after the Captivity (Ezra 10:23).

KELAL

A form of CHELAL.

KELITA [kih LIGH tuh]

The name of one or two men in the Old Testament:

1. A priest who interpreted the Law to the people when it was read by Ezra (Neh. 8:7).

2. A Levite who sealed the covenant made by Nehemiah (Neh. 10:10). He may be the same person as No. 1.

KELUB

A form of CHELUB.

KELUHI [keh LOU high]

A form of CHELUH.

KEMUEL [KEM yoo uhl]

The name of three men in the Old Testament:

1. The father of Aram (Gen. 22:21).

2. A leader of the tribe of Ephraim (Num. 34:24).

3. The father of Hashabiah (1 Chr. 27:17).

KENAANAH

A form of CHENAANAH.

KENAN [KEE nuhn]

A form of CAINAN.

KENANI

A form of CHENANI.

KENANIAH

A form of CHENANIAH.

KENAZ [KEE naz]

The name of three men in the Old Testament:

1. A son of Eliphaz (Gen. 36:11, 15).

2. The father of Othniel the judge (Judg. 1:13).

3. A son of Elah and grandson of Caleb (1 Chr. 4:15).

KERAN

A form of CHERAN.

KEREN–HAPPUCH [KER uhn HAP uhk] (horn of antimony)

The youngest of Job's three daughters, apparently born after his restoration to prosperity and health (Job 42:14). Also see JEMIMAH and KEZIAH.

KEROS [KIR ahs]

One of the Temple servants whose descendants returned from the Captivity with Zerubbabel (Ezra 2:44).

KESED

A form of CHESED.

KETURAH [keh TUR uh]

A wife of Abraham (Gen. 25:1, 4), also called Abraham's concubine (1 Chr. 1:32–33). Some suggest that Keturah had been Abraham's "concubine-wife," before the death of Sarah. After Sarah died, Keturah was then elevated to the full status of Abraham's wife. Keturah bore to Abraham six sons: Zimran, Jokshan, Medan, Midian, Ishbak, and Shuah (Gen. 25:1–4). These men were the founders or ancestors of six Arabian tribes in southern and eastern Palestine. Late Arabian genealogies mention a tribe by the name of Katura dwelling near Mecca.

Keturah's sons were not on the same level as Abraham's promised son, Isaac. Through Isaac God would carry out His promise to Abraham to make of his descendants a Chosen People. While he was still alive, therefore, Abraham gave Keturah's sons gifts and sent them to "the country of the east" (Gen. 25:6).

Abraham was already advanced in years when he married Keturah. She brought him both companionship and children in his old age. Keturah apparently outlived Abraham (Gen. 25:7).

KEZIAH [kih ZIE uh] (cinnamon)

A daughter of Job born after his restoration to prosperity and health (Job. 42:14; Kezia, KJV).

KILION

A form of CHILION.

KIMHAM

A form of CHIMHAM.

KISH [kish]

The name of four men in the Old Testament:

1. The father of King Saul (1 Chr. 12:1).

2. A Levite who lived in David's time (1 Chr. 23:21–22; 24:29). He was a son of Mahli and a grandson of Merari.

3. A Levite who helped cleanse the Temple during the reign of King Hezekiah of Judah (2 Chr. 29:12).

4. A Benjamite ancestor of MORDECAI (Esth. 2:5).

KISHI [KISH eye]

A Levite of the Merari family (1 Chr. 6:44), also called Kushaiah (1 Chr. 15:17).

KOHATH [KOE hath]

The second son of Levi (Gen. 46:11). Kohath went to Egypt with Levi and Jacob (Gen. 46:11) and lived to the age of 133 (Ex. 6:18). He was the founder of the Kohathites.

KOLAIAH [koe LAY uh]

The name of two men in the Old Testament:

1. A son of Maaseiah whose descendants lived in Jerusalem after the Captivity (Neh. 11:7).

2. The father of AHAB, the false prophet condemned by Jeremiah (Jer. 29:21–23).

KORAH

The name of four men in the Old Testament:

1. The third son of Esau by his wife Aholibamah (Gen. 36:5, 14). Born in Canaan, Korah became a chief of an Edomite tribe (Gen. 36:18).

2. The grandson of Esau through Eliphaz. Korah was an Edomite chief (Gen. 36:16).

3. The Levite who, along with Dathan, Abiram, and On of the tribe of Reuben, led a revolt against the leadership of Moses and Aaron (Num. 16:1–49). Korah was the son of Izhar and a first cousin of Moses and Aaron (Ex. 6:21). He was equal in rank with Aaron within the tribe of Levi.

Korah apparently was jealous that Aaron held the position of high priest. The Reubenites were the descendants of Jacob's oldest son. They thought the responsibility for leading Israel should rest with their tribe rather than the Levites. The four ringleaders gathered 250 leaders of the congregation, publicly charging Moses and Aaron with abusing their power. They claimed that all members of the congregation should have equal access to the Lord.

Moses placed the dispute in the hands of the Lord, directing Korah and his company to bring containers of incense as an offering to the Lord. Korah complied with this and went with his congregation to the door of the tabernacle where the Lord appeared, threatening to "consume them in a moment" (Num. 16:21). Moses and Aaron interceded, saving the nation of Israel from destruction. The decision of leadership was again placed before the Lord as Moses instructed the congregation to "depart from the tents of these wicked men" (Num. 16:26). The decision in favor of Moses was dramatized as "the earth opened its mouth" and swallowed all the men of Korah (Num. 16:32).

Apparently some of the descendants of Korah survived to become ministers of music in the tabernacle during the time of David (1 Chr. 6:31–37).

4. The oldest son of Hebron, a descendant of Caleb and Judah (1 Chr. 2:43).

KORE [KOR ih] (one who proclaims)

The name of two men in the Old Testament:

1. The father of Shallum and Meshelemiah, who were gatekeepers at the tabernacle (1 Chr. 9:19).

2. A son of Imnah the Levite. Kore was the keeper of the East Gate of the Temple (2 Chr. 31:14).

KOZ [kahz]

The name of three men in the Old Testament:

1. A descendant of Caleb, of the tribe of Judah (1 Chr. 4:8; Coz, KJV).

2. The ancestor of a priestly family that returned from the Captivity (Ezra 2:61). HAKKOZ (1 Chr. 24:10) may be the same person.

3. An ancestor of a person who helped repair the walls of Jerusalem (Neh. 3:4, 21).

KUSHAIAH [koo SHAY uh]

A form of KISHI (1 Chr. 15:17).

LAADAH–CLAUDIUS LYSIAS

LAADAH [LAY uh duh]

A son of Shelah and grandson of Judah (1 Chr. 4:21).

LAADAN [LAY uh dan]

The name of two men in the Old Testament:

1. A descendant of Ephraim and an ancestor of Joshua (1 Chr. 7:26; Ladan, NIV, NRSV).

2. A Levite of the family of Gershon (1 Chr. 23:7–9; Ladan, NIV, NRSV), also called Libni (Ex. 6:17).

LABAN [LAY bihn] (*white*)

Father-in-law of Jacob. Laban lived in the city of Nahor in Padan Aram where Abraham sent his servant to find a wife for Isaac. Laban, brother of Rebekah, is introduced when he heard of the servant's presence, saw the golden jewelry given Rebekah, and eagerly invited Abraham's emissary into their home (Gen. 24:29–60). Laban played an important role in the marriage arrangements. His stubbornness and greed characterized his later dealings with Rebekah's son, Jacob.

Many years later, Jacob left home to escape Esau's wrath. At the well of Haran he met Rachel, Laban's daughter. Laban promised her to his nephew Jacob in return for seven years of labor from Jacob. Laban consequently dealt with Jacob with deception and greed; he gave him the wrong wife and then forced him to work seven more years for Rachel. Then he persuaded Jacob to stay longer, but the wages he promised were changed ten times in six years (Genesis 29–30).

When family situations became tense, Jacob quietly left with his wives, children, and possessions, only to be pursued by Laban (Genesis 31). Laban and Jacob eventually parted on peaceful terms, but they heaped up stones as a mutual testimony that they would have no further dealings with one another. They called upon God as their witness that they would not impose upon one another again (Gen. 31:43–55).

LADAN [LAY duhn]

A form of LAADAN.

LAEL [LAY uhl] (*belonging to God*)

A Levite of the family of Gershon (Num. 3:24).

LAHAD [LAY had]

Son of Jahath (1 Chr. 4:2).

LAHMI [LAH migh] (*warrior*)

A brother of Goliath, the Philistine giant killed by David (1 Chr. 20:5).

LAISH [LAY ish] (*lion*)

Father of Palti (1 Sam. 25:44), or Paltiel (2 Sam. 3:15).

LAMECH [LAY mik]

The name of two men in the Old Testament:

1. A son of Methushael and a descendant of Cain (Gen. 4:18–24). Lamech is the first man mentioned in the Bible as having two wives (Gen. 4:19). By Adah he had two sons, Jabal and Jubal; and by Zillah he had a son, Tubal–Cain, and a daughter, Naamah.

2. The first son of Methuselah, and the father of Noah (Gen. 5:25–26, 28–31). Lamech lived to be 777 years old (Gen. 5:31). He is mentioned in the genealogy of Jesus (Luke 3:36).

LAPIDOTH, LAPPIDOTH [LAP uh doth] (*flames*)

The husband of Deborah the prophetess, whose home appears to have been "between Ramah and Bethel in the mountains of Ephraim" (Judg. 4:4–5).

LAZARUS [LAZ ah russ] (God has helped)

The name of two men in the New Testament:

1. The beggar in Jesus' story about a rich man and a poor man (Luke 16:19–25). The wealthy man despised the beggar, paying no attention to his needs when he passed him each day. After the death of Lazarus, the poor man, he was carried by angels to Abraham's bosom, where he found comfort. But the rich man at death found himself in Hades, in eternal torment.

This story was not intended to praise the poor and condemn the rich. It shows the dangers of turning away from the needs of others. It teaches that our attitude on earth will result in an eternal destiny that parallels our attitude. This note is sounded frequently in the teaching of Jesus (Matt. 7:24–27; Luke 16:9).

2. The brother of Martha and Mary of Bethany (John 11:1). One long account in the Gospel of John tells about his death and resurrection at the command of Jesus (John 11). A second account in the same gospel describes him as sitting with Jesus in the family home after the resurrection miracle (John 12:1–2). Because of the publicity surrounding this event, the chief priest plotted to kill Lazarus (John 12:9–11).

Twice John's gospel records Jesus' love for Lazarus (John 11:3, 5). Yet, upon hearing of the sickness of his friend, Jesus delayed in returning to Bethany. When He finally arrived, both Martha and Mary rebuked Jesus for not coming sooner. Jesus showed His impatience at their unbelief (11:33) as well as His personal sorrow ("Jesus wept"). Then he brought Lazarus back to life (11:43).

LEAH [LEE uh]

The older daughter of Laban, who deceitfully gave her in marriage to Jacob instead of her younger sister Rachel

LAZARUS

DOES ANYBODY HAVE A BREATH MINT?

(Gen. 29:16–30). Although Rachel was the more beautiful of the two daughters of Laban and obviously was Jacob's favorite wife, the Lord blessed Leah and Jacob with six sons—Reuben, Simeon, Levi, Judah (Gen. 29:31–35), Issachar, and Zebulun (Gen. 30:17–20)—and a daughter, Dinah (Gen. 30:21). Leah's maid, Zilpah, added two more sons: Gad and Asher (Gen. 30:9–13).

Leah was the less-favored of the two wives of Jacob, and she must have been painfully conscious of this during all the years of her marriage. But it was Leah rather than Rachel who gave birth to Judah, through whose line Jesus the Messiah was eventually born.

Apparently Leah died in the land of Canaan before the migration to Egypt (Gen. 46:6). She was buried in the Cave of Machpelah in Hebron (Gen. 49:31).

LEBANA [leh BAY nuh]

A form of LEBANAH.

LEBANAH [lih BAY nuh] (*whiteness*)

The head of a family of Nethinim (temple servants). Some of his descendants returned from the Captivity with Zerubbabel (Ezra 2:45). The name is also spelled Lebana (Neh. 7:48).

LEBBAEUS [leh BEE uhs] (*man of heart*)

One of the 12 apostles, also called THADDAEUS (Matt. 10:3). According to a church tradition, Lebbaeus is the same person as "Judas the son [or brother] of James" (Luke 6:16).

LECAH [LEE kuh]

A son of Er, descended from Judah (1 Chr. 4:21).

LEHABIM [lih HAY bim]

A son of Mizraim (Gen. 10:13).

LEMUEL [LEM yoo uhl]

An unknown king who records "the utterance which his mother taught him" (Prov. 31:1). Some of the early Jewish rabbis identified Lemuel with Solomon. Other scholars believe he was Hezekiah, or even an Arabian prince.

LESHEM [LESH uhm]

A form of LAISH.

LETUSHIM [lih TOO shuhm]

A son of Dedan (Gen. 25:3).

LEUMMIM [LEE uh mim] (*people*)

A son of Dedan (Gen. 25:3).

LEVI [LEE vigh] (*joined*)

The name of four men in the Bible:

1. The third son of Jacob and Leah (Gen. 29:34). His three sons were ancestors of the three main divisions of the Levitical priesthood: the Gershonites, the Kohathites, and the Merarites (Gen. 46:11). Levi participated in the plot against Joseph (Gen. 37:4) and later took his family to Egypt with Jacob. On his deathbed Jacob cursed Simeon and Levi because of their "cruelty" and "wrath," and foretold that their descendants would be divided and scattered (Gen. 49:5–7). Levi died in Egypt at the age of 137 (Ex. 6:16).

2. Another name for MATTHEW, one of the twelve apostles (Mark 2:14). Levi was formerly a tax collector.

3. An ancestor of Jesus Christ (Luke 3:24). Levi was a son of Melchi and the father of Matthat.

4. Another ancestor of Jesus Christ (Luke 3:29). This Levi was a son of Simeon and the father of Matthat.

LIBNI [LIB nigh] (*white*)

The name of one or two men in the Old Testament:

1. A son of Gershon and a grandson of Levi (Ex. 6:17), also called Laadan (1 Chr. 23:7–9).

2. A Levite descended from Merari (1 Chr. 6:29). He may be the same person as No. 1.

LIKHI [LIK high]

A son of Shemida, of the tribe of Manasseh (1 Chr. 7:19).

LINUS [LIE nuhs]

A Christian man at Rome who joined the apostle Paul in sending greetings to Timothy (2 Tim. 4:21).

LO–AMMI [loe AM eye] (not my people)

The name given by the prophet Hosea to his second son (Hos. 1:9–10; 2:23) to symbolize God's rejection of the nation of Israel (Rom. 9:25–26).

LO–RUHAMAH [low roo HAY muh] (not pitied)

A daughter born to Gomer, the prophet Hosea's wife (Hos. 1:6, 8; no longer have pity, NRSV). The name symbolized God's anger and His rejection of the nation of Israel. The faithful remnant of Israel is called Ruhamah, which means "pitied" (Hos. 2:1, 23).

LOIS [LOE iss]

The mother of Eunice and the grandmother of Timothy. A devout Jewess, Lois instructed both her daughter and her grandson in the Old Testament. Paul gave Lois and her daughter Eunice credit for Timothy's spiritual instruction (2 Tim. 3:15). Also see Acts 1.

LOT [laht]

Abraham's nephew. Lot accompanied Abraham from Mesopotamia to Canaan and to and from Egypt (Gen. 11:27–31; 12:4–5; 13:1). Both Lot and Abraham had large herds of cattle, and their herdsmen quarreled over their pasturelands. At Abraham's suggestion, the two decided to separate.

Abraham gave Lot his choice of land; and Lot chose the more fertile, well-watered site—the Jordan River valley—as opposed to the rocky hill country. Failing to take into account the character of the inhabitants, Lot "pitched his tent toward Sodom" (Gen. 13:12, KJV).

When the Elamite king Chedorlaomer invaded Canaan with his allies, Lot was taken captive. Abraham attacked Chedorlaomer's forces by night and rescued his nephew (Gen. 13:1—14:16).

When two angels were sent to warn Lot that God intended to destroy Sodom, Lot could not control the Sodomites, who wished to abuse the two visitors carnally. The angels struck the Sodomites blind to save Lot (Gen. 19:1–11), and Lot and his family fled the doomed city. Lot's wife, however, did not follow the angels' orders and looked back at Sodom. Because of her disobedience she was turned into a "pillar of salt" (Gen. 19:26). Our Lord Jesus warned, "Remember Lot's wife" (Luke 17:32), as a reminder of the disastrous results of disobedience.

Following his escape from Sodom, Lot lived in a cave near Zoar (Gen. 19:30–38). His two daughters served their father wine and enticed him into incest. They did this because "there is no man on the earth to come in to us as is the custom of all the earth" (Gen. 19:31). Out of that union came two sons, Moab and Ben-Ammi, the ancestors of the Moabites and the Ammonites respectively.

Lot's character is revealed by the major decisions he made throughout his life. He chose to pitch his tent with the worldly Sodomites, seeking riches and a life of ease rather than a path of obedience to God. He prospered for a while,

LOT

but this decision eventually led to his humiliation and the tragic loss of his wife and other members of his family.

LOTAN [LOE tan]

A son of Seir the Horite and a clan chief of a tribe of Horites in the land of Edom (Gen. 36:20, 22, 29).

LUCAS [LOO kuhs]

A form of LUKE.

LUCIUS [LOO shuhs]

The name of one or two men in the New Testament:

1. Lucius of Cyrene, a teacher in the church in Antioch of Syria (Acts 13:1). Lucius and other church leaders laid their hands on Barnabas and Paul and sent them forth on their first missionary journey.

2. A Jewish Christian, a kinsman of the apostle Paul, who sent greetings from Corinth to Rome (Rom. 16:21). He may be the same person as Lucius No. 1.

LUD [luhd]

The fourth son of SHEM (Gen. 10:22; 1 Chr. 1:17) and the ancestor of a people known as the Ludim (1 Chr. 1:11).

LUDIM [LOU deam]

The first son of MIZRAIM, who was the second son of Ham (Gen. 10:13; 1 Chr. 1:11). Some scholars, however, believe this term refers not to an individual but to a people; in both passages the NEB translates Lydians and the NIV translates Ludites. Some scholars attempt to identify the Ludim with the Lubim (2 Chr. 12:3; 16:8; Nah. 3:9), the plural of Libyan, a people of North Africa west of Egypt bordering the Mediterranean Sea.

There is no textual authority, however, for identifying Ludim with Lubim. Some confusion also exists because of the ambiguous way the Ludim are associated with both African and Asiatic nations.

LUKE

A "fellow laborer" of the apostle Paul (Philem. 24) and the author of the Gospel of Luke and the Acts of the Apostles. By profession he was a physician (Col. 4:14). During one of Paul's imprisonments, probably in Rome, Luke's faithfulness was recorded by Paul when he declared, "Only Luke is with me" (2 Tim. 4:11). These three references are our only direct knowledge of Luke in the New Testament.

A bit more of Luke's life and personality can be pieced together with the aid of his writings (Luke and Acts) and some outside sources. Tradition records that he came from Antioch in Syria. This is possible, because Antioch played a significant role in the early Gentile mission that Luke described in Acts (Acts 11; 13; 14; 15; 18). Luke was a Gentile (Col. 4:10–17) and the only non-Jewish author of a New Testament book. A comparison of 2 Corinthians 8:18 and 12:18 has led some to suppose that Luke and Titus were brothers, but this is a guess.

Luke accompanied Paul on parts of his second, third, and final missionary journeys. At three places in Acts, the narrative changes to the first person ("we"). This probably indicates that Luke was personally present during those episodes. On the second journey (A.D. 49–53), Luke accompanied Paul on the short voyage from Troas to Philippi (Acts 16:10–17). On the third journey (A.D. 54–58), Luke was present on the voyage from Philippi to Jerusalem (Acts 20:5—21:18). Whether Luke had spent the intervening time in Philippi is uncertain, but his connection with Philippi has led some to favor it (rather than Antioch) as Luke's home.

Once in Palestine, Luke probably remained close by Paul during his two-year imprisonment in Caesarea. During this time, Luke probably drew together material, both oral and written, which he later used in the composition of his Gospel (Luke 1:1–4). A third "we" passage describes in masterful suspense the shipwreck during Paul's voyage to Rome for his trial before Caesar. Each of the "we" passages involves Luke on a voyage, and the description of the journey from Jerusalem to Rome is full of observations and knowledge of nautical matters (Acts 27).

Luke apparently was a humble man, with no desire to sound his own horn. More than one-fourth of the New Testament comes from his pen, but not once does he mention himself by name. He had a greater command of the Greek language and was probably more broadminded and urbane than any New Testament writer. He was a careful historian, both by his own admission (Luke 1:1–4) and by the judgment of later history.

Luke's gospel reveals his concern for the poor, sick, and outcast, thus offering a clue to why Paul called him "the beloved physician" (Col. 4:14). He was faithful not only to Paul, but to the greater cause he served—the publication of "good tidings of great joy" (Luke 2:10).

LYDIA [LID ih uh]

A prosperous businesswoman from the city of Thyatira who became a convert to Christianity after hearing the apostle Paul speak (Acts 16:12–15, 40). Thyatira was noted for its "purple"—its beautifully dyed cloth. Lydia, who lived in Philippi, sold dyes or dyed goods from as far away as Thyatira. Already a worshiper of God, the usual designation for a Proselyte to Judaism, Lydia believed the gospel when Paul preached in Philippi. She became the first convert to Christianity in Macedonia and, in fact, in all of Europe. Lydia is a good example for Christians in the business world today. A devout Christian and a conscientious businesswoman, she used her work to help further God's purpose.

LYSANIAS [lih SAY nih uhs]

The tetrarch or governor of the region of Abilene in the 15th year of the reign of Tiberius Caesar, emperor of Rome (Luke 3:1). Lysanias was a contemporary of John the Baptist and Jesus.

LYSIAS, CLAUDIUS [LIS ih uhs, KLAW dih uhs]

The commander of the Roman garrison at Jerusalem who rescued the apostle Paul from an angry mob (Acts 21:31–38). Claudius Lysias sent Paul to Caesarea by night under military escort to the Roman governor, Felix (Acts 22:24—23:35). His letter to Felix (Acts 23:25–30) is an example of Roman military correspondence.

Claudius Lysias was a commander (commandant, REB; tribune, NRSV). The Greek noun is *chiliarchos*, which means "ruler of a thousand." A tribune was a Roman military officer commanding a cohort, a unit of from 600 to 1,000 men.

L

M

MAACAH–MUSHI

MAACAH [MAY ah kah]

The name of four women and one man in the Old Testament:

1. One of David's wives and the mother of Absalom (2 Sam. 3:3; 1 Chr. 3:2).

2. Apparently, an Aramean king from whom the Ammonites hired a thousand men to fight David's army (2 Sam. 10:6; the king of Maacah, NIV).

3. A wife of Rehoboam and the mother of Abijah, kings of Judah (1 Kin. 15:2; 2 Chr. 11:20–22). Maacah was the favorite wife of Rehoboam and she bore him Abijah, Attai, Ziza, and Shelomith (2 Chr. 11:20–21). Abijah, or Abijam (1 Kin. 14:31—15:8), her oldest son, succeeded Rehoboam as king of Judah. A strong-willed woman, Maacah maintained her position as queen mother until her grandson Asa (1 Kin. 15:8; 2 Chr. 14:1) removed her from that position. Maacah fell from favor "because she had made an obscene image of Asherah (a Canaanite goddess)" (1 Kin. 15:13; 2 Chr. 15:16).

4. The grandmother of Asa, king of Judah (2 Chr. 15:16; Maachah, 1 Kin. 15:10, 13).

5. A wife of Jeiel, the father of Gibeon (1 Chr. 8:29; 9:35). Maacah is mentioned in the genealogy of King Saul.

MAACHAH [MAY ah kah]

The name of four men and two women in the Old Testament:

1. A son of Nahor by Reumah (Gen. 22:24) and a brother of Abraham.

2. The father of Achish (1 Kin. 2:39). Achish was king of Gath during the reign of Solomon. Also see MAOCH.

3. A concubine of Caleb, son of Hezron (1 Chr. 2:48).

4. The sister of Huppim and Shuppim and the wife of Machir of the tribe of Manasseh (1 Chr. 7:15–16).

5. The father of Hanan (1 Chr. 11:43).

6. The father of Shephatiah (1 Chr. 27:16).

MAADAI [may uh DIE]

A son of Bani who divorced his pagan wife after the Captivity (Ezra 10:34).

MAADIAH [may uh DYE uh]

A priest who returned with Zerubbabel from the Captivity (Neh. 12:5). Maadiah may be the same person as Moadiah (Neh. 12:17) or Maaziah No. 2 (Neh. 10:8).

MAAI [may AY eye]

A priest who participated in the celebration after the walls of Jerusalem were rebuilt (Neh. 12:36).

MAASAI [MAY uh sye] (work of the Lord)

An Aaronite priest whose family lived in Jerusalem after the Captivity (1 Chr. 9:12; Maasiai, KJV). He may be the same person as Amashai (Neh. 11:13).

MAASEIAH [may uh SYE uh]

The name of several men in the Old Testament:

1. A Levite who was a member of the second division of priests during David's reign (1 Chr. 15:18, 20).

2. A commander who helped Jehoiada overthrow Queen Athaliah and bring JOASH to the throne of Judah (2 Chr. 23:1).

3. An officer under King UZZIAH of Judah (2 Chr. 26:11).

4. A son of Judah's royal line (2 Chr. 28:7). Maaseiah was probably the son of Jotham.

5. The governor of Jerusalem during the reign of King Josiah of Judah (2 Chr. 34:8).

M

6. A priest who divorced his pagan wife after the Captivity (Ezra 10:18).

7. Another priest of the family of Harim, who divorced his pagan wife (Ezra 10:21).

8. A priest of the family of Pashhur who divorced his wife after the Captivity (Ezra 10:22).

9. A son of Pahath–Moab (Ezra 10:30).

10. The father of Azariah (Neh. 3:23).

11. A priest who helped Ezra read the Law to the people (Neh. 8:4).

12. A priest who explained the Law to the people after Ezra's reading (Neh. 8:7). He may be the same person as Maaseiah No. 11.

13. A leader of the Israelites who sealed the covenant after the Captivity (Neh. 10:25).

14. A man of Judah descended through Perez (Neh. 11:5).

15. A man from the tribe of Benjamin whose descendants lived in Jerusalem after the Captivity (Neh. 11:7).

16. A priest who assisted at the dedication of Jerusalem's rebuilt wall (Neh. 12:41).

17. Another priest who took part in the dedication of the Jerusalem walls (Neh. 12:42).

18. The father of Zephaniah (Jer. 21:1).

19. The father of Zedekiah (Jer. 29:21).

20. The grandfather of Baruch (Jer. 32:12, KJV; Mahseiah, NKJV, NIV), Jeremiah's scribe.

21. A gatekeeper during the reign of King Jehoiakim of Judah (Jer. 35:4).

MAASIAI [may uh SYE eye]

A form of MAASAI.

MAATH [MAY ath]

An ancestor of Jesus, listed in Luke's genealogy (Luke 3:26).

MAAZ [MAY az]

The oldest son of Ram, of the tribe of Judah (1 Chr. 2:27).

MAAZIAH [may uh ZYE uh]

The name of two men in the Old Testament:

1. Head of the 24th division of priests in David's time (1 Chr. 24:18).

2. A priest who sealed the covenant after the Captivity (Neh. 10:8), perhaps the same person as Maadiah (Neh. 12:5).

MACBANNAI [MAK buh nye]

A form of MACHBANAI.

MACHBANAI [MAK buh nye]

A warrior who joined David at Ziklag (1 Chr. 12:13; Machbannai, NRSV, NASB; Macbannai, NIV).

MACHBENAH [mak BEE nuh]

A son of Sheva mentioned in the genealogy of Judah. Machbenah was of the family of Caleb (1 Chr. 2:49).

MACHI [MAY kye]

One of 12 men sent by Moses to spy out the land of Canaan (Num. 13:15).

MACHIR [MAY kir] (*sold*)

The name of two men in the Old Testament:

1. The firstborn son of Manasseh (Gen. 50:23). The Machirites descended from Machir and were the only family of the tribe of Manasseh. They defeated the city of Gilead, which Moses gave to the Machirites as an inheritance (Josh. 17:1). In Judges 5:14 "Machir" is used poetically to refer to the whole tribe of Manasseh.

2. A son of Ammiel who lived in Lo Debar, east of the Jordan River (2 Sam. 9:4–5; 17:27). Machir provided for Saul's

only surviving son, MEPHIBOSHETH, after David became king. He also brought provisions and supplies to David during Absalom's rebellion.

MACHNADEBAI [mak NAD eh bye]

A son of Bani who divorced his pagan wife after the Captivity (Ezra 10:34, 40).

MADAI [MAY dye]

The third son of Japheth and a grandson of Noah (Gen. 10:2). He was probably the ancestor of the Medes.

MADMANNAH [mad MAN nuh]

A son of Shaaph, of the tribe of Judah (1 Chr. 2:49).

MAGDALENE [mag de LEE nih] (from Magdala)

The designation given to a woman named Mary, one of Jesus' most prominent Galilean female disciples, to distinguish her from the other Marys. The first appearance of Mary Magdalene in the Gospels is in Luke 8:2, which mentions her among those who were ministering to Jesus. Mary Magdalene has sometimes mistakenly been described as a woman of bad character and loose morals, simply because Mark 16:9 states that Jesus had cast seven demons out of her. Nor is there any reason to conclude that she was the same person as the sinful woman whom Simon the Pharisee treated with such disdain and contempt (Luke 7:36–50).

Mary Magdalene was among the "many women who followed Jesus from Galilee, ministering to Him" (Matt. 27:55). She was one of the women at Calvary who were "looking on from afar" (Mark 15:40) when Jesus died on the cross (also John 19:25). She was at Joseph's tomb when the body of Jesus was wrapped in a fine linen cloth and a large stone was rolled against the door of the tomb (Matt. 27:61; Mark 15:47). And she was a witness of the risen Christ (Matt. 28:1; Mark 16:1; Luke 24:10; John 20:1). In fact, she was the first of any of Jesus' followers to see Him after His resurrection (Mark 16:9; John 20:11–18).

Apparently Mary is called "Magdalene" because she was a native or inhabitant of Magdala.

MAGDIEL [MAG deh el]

An Edomite clan chief, descended from Esau (1 Chr. 1:54).

MAGI [MAY jie]

(See WISE MEN.)

MAGOG [MAY gog] (land of Gog)

The second son of Japheth and a grandson of Noah (Gen. 10:2).

MAGOR-MISSABIB [MAY gore meh SAY bib] (fear on every side)

A symbolic name given by the prophet Jeremiah to PASHHUR, the chief governor of the temple (Jer. 20:3). Jeremiah prophesied that Pashhur and his family would be taken captive to Babylon (Jer. 20:1–6).

MAGPIASH [MAG peh ash]

An Israelite chief who sealed the covenant after the Captivity (Neh. 10:20).

MAHALAH [muh HAY luh]

A form of MAHLAH.

MAHALALEEL [muh HAY luh lee el] (God shines forth)

The name of two men in the Bible:
1. A son of Cainan (1 Chr. 1:2), also spelled Maleleel.
2. An Israelite of the tribe of Judah (Neh. 11:4).

M

MAHALATH [MAY huh lath]

The name of two women in the Old Testament:

1. A daughter of Ishmael and one of Esau's wives (Gen. 28:9), perhaps the same person as BASEMATH (Gen. 36:3-4).

2. A daughter of Jerimoth (2 Chr. 11:18).

MAHALI [MAY huh lye]

A form of MAHLI.

MAHARAI [muh HAR ay eye]

One of David's mighty men. Maharai was captain over 24,000 men (2 Sam. 23:28; 1 Chr. 11:30; 27:13).

MAHATH [MAY hath]

The name of two Temple servants in the Old Testament:

1. A priest who helped purify the sanctuary (1 Chr. 6:35).

2. A Levite overseer of Temple offerings in Hezekiah's time (2 Chr. 31:13). He may be identical with Mahath No. 1.

MAHAZIOTH [muh HAY zeh ahth]
    (*visions*)

Chief of the 23rd division of musicians in the Temple during David's reign (1 Chr. 25:4, 30).

MAHER-SHALAL-HASH-BAZ [MAY her SHAL al HASH baz] (*hasten the booty, speed the plunder*)

The symbolic name of the second son of the prophet Isaiah (Is. 8:1, 3), signifying the doom of Damascus and Samaria and the destruction of Syria and Israel, who had formed a military alliance against Jerusalem (Is. 7:1).

MAHLAH [MAH luh] (*weak one*)

The name of two people in the Old Testament:

1. The oldest of the five daughters of Zelophehad (Num. 26:33). Because Zelophehad had no sons, his daughters were allowed to inherit their father's estate (Num. 36:1-13).

2. The third child of Hammoleketh (1 Chr. 7:18; Mahalah, KJV).

MAHLI [MAH leh] (*weak*)

The name of two men in the Old Testament:

1. The oldest son of Merari and founder of the Mahlites (Num. 3:33), also called Mahali (Ex. 6:19).

2. A son of Mushi (1 Chr. 23:23).

MAHLON [MAH lahn] (*sickly*)

The husband of Ruth the Moabitess who died childless in the land of Moab (Ruth 1:1-5).

MAHOL [MAY hall] (*dance*)

An ancestor of Ethan, Heman, Chalcol, and Darda (1 Kin. 4:31), men known for their wisdom during the reign of King Solomon.

MAHSEIAH [muh SIGH yuh] (*the Lord is a refuge*)

The father of Neriah (Jer. 32:12; 51:59; Maaseiah, KJV).

MALACHI [MAL ah kie] (*my messenger*)

Old Testament prophet and author of the prophetic book that bears his name. Nothing is known about Malachi's life except the few facts that may be inferred from his prophecies. He apparently prophesied after the Captivity, during the time when NEHEMIAH was leading the people to rebuild Jerusalem's wall and recommit themselves to following God's Law. The people's negligence in paying tithes to God was condemned by both Nehemiah and Malachi (Neh. 13:10-14; Mal. 3:8-10).

MALCAM [MAL kam] (*their king*)

A Benjamite, the fourth of the seven sons of Shaharaim by his wife Hodesh (1 Chr. 8:9; Malcham, KJV, REB).

MALCHAM [MAL kam]

A form of MALCAM. Also used (Zeph. 1:5, KJV) as a form of Milcom.

MALCHIAH [mal KYE ah] (*the Lord is my king*)

The name of two or three men in the Old Testament:

1. A son of Parosh (Ezra 10:25). He divorced his pagan wife after the Captivity.

2. The father of Pashhur (Jer. 38:1; Malkijah, NIV). King Zedekiah of Judah sent Pashhur to inquire of the Lord concerning the military situation with Nebuchadnezzar, king of Babylon. Malchiah is also called Melchiah (Jer. 21:1).

3. A royal prince—"the king's son" (Jer. 38:6)—in the time of Zedekiah, king of Judah. Jeremiah was cast into the dungeon of Malchiah. This is probably the same person as Malchiah No. 2.

MALCHIEL [MAL keh el] (*God is my king*)

Younger son of Beriah (Gen. 46:17) and founder of a tribal family, the Malchielites (Num. 26:45).

MALCHIJAH [mal KIE jah] (*the Lord is my king*)

The name of nine men in the Old Testament:

1. A Gershonite Levite and descendant of Asaph (1 Chr. 6:40).

2. A Levite descended from Aaron. Malchijah's descendants formed the fifth division of priests during David's time (1 Chr. 24:9).

3. A son of Parosh (Ezra 10:25). After the Captivity Malchijah divorced his pagan wife.

4. A son of Harim who divorced his pagan wife after the Captivity (Ezra 10:31).

5. A son of Rechab (Neh. 3:14).

6. A member of the guild of goldsmiths who helped repair the Jerusalem wall after the Captivity (Neh. 3:31).

7. One who helped Ezra explain the Law to the people (Neh. 8:4).

8. One of those who sealed the covenant in Nehemiah's time (Neh. 10:3).

9. A priest who officiated at the dedication of Jerusalem's wall (Neh. 12:42).

MALCHIRAM [mal KYE ram] (*my king is exalted*)

A son of King Jeconiah (Jehoiachin) of Judah and grandson of King Jehoiakim (1 Chr. 3:18).

MALCHISHUA [mal kye SHOO uh] (*my king is salvation*)

One of the four sons of King Saul killed by the Philistines at Mount Gilboa (1 Sam. 14:49; 31:2; Melchishua, KJV).

MALCHUS [MAL kus] (*ruler*)

A servant of the high priest who was present at the arrest of Jesus in the Garden of Gethsemane. Simon Peter struck Malchus with a sword and cut off his ear (John 18:10).

MALELEEL [muh LEE leh el]

A form of MAHALALEEL No. 1.

MALKIJAH [mal KIE juh]

A form of MALCHIAH No. 2.

MALLOTHI [MAL oh thigh]

A son of Heman who served in the temple sanctuary during David's reign (1 Chr. 25:4, 26).

M

MALLUCH [MAL uhk]

The name of six men in the Old Testament:

1. A Levite of the family of Merari (1 Chr. 6:44).

2, 3. A son of Babi (Ezra 10:29) and a son of Harim (Ezra 10:32), each of whom divorced his pagan wife after the Captivity.

4, 5. A priest (Neh. 10:4) and a chief of the people (Neh. 10:27), both of whom sealed the covenant with Nehemiah after the Captivity.

6. A priest who returned to Jerusalem after the Captivity (Neh. 12:1–2). In Nehemiah 12:14, Malluch is also spelled Malluchi, NASB, NRSV; Melichu, NKJV and Melicu, KJV.

MALLUCHI [mal LOU kih]

A form of MALLUCH No. 6.

MAMRE [MAM reh]

An Amorite chief who formed an alliance with Abraham against CHEDORLAOMER (Gen. 14:13, 24).

MANAEN [MAN uh en] (comforter)

A man listed as one of the "prophets and teachers" (Acts 13:1) in the church of Antioch of Syria. Luke records that Manaen "had been brought up with" Herod the tetrarch. Some scholars believe Manaen may have been a playmate of the young Herod, or may have been educated with him at Rome. In any case, his past association with Herod marked Manaen as a man of distinction.

MANAHATH [MAN uh hath] (resting place)

A son of Shobal and a grandson of Seir the Horite (Gen. 36:23).

MANASSEH [muh NASS uh] (causing to forget)

The name of five men in the Old Testament:

1. Joseph's firstborn son who was born in Egypt to Asenath the daughter of Poti–Pherah, priest of On (Gen. 41:50–51). Like his younger brother EPHRAIM, Manasseh was half Hebrew and half Egyptian. Manasseh's birth caused Joseph to forget the bitterness of his past experiences. Manasseh and Ephraim were both adopted by Jacob and given status as sons just like Jacob's own sons Reuben and Simeon (Gen. 48:5).

2. The grandfather of the Jonathan who was one of the priests of the graven image erected by the tribe of Dan (Judg. 18:30).

3. The 14th king of Judah, the son of HEZEKIAH born to Hephzibah (2 Kin. 21:1–18). Manasseh reigned longer (55 years) than any other Israelite king and had the dubious distinction of being Judah's most wicked king. He came to the throne at the age of 12, although he probably co-reigned with Hezekiah for ten years. His father's godly influence appears to have affected Manasseh only negatively, and he reverted to the ways of his evil grandfather, Ahaz.

Committed to idolatry, Manasseh restored everything Hezekiah had abolished. Manasseh erected altars to Baal; he erected an image of Asherah in the Temple; he worshiped the sun, moon, and stars; he recognized the Ammonite god Molech and sacrificed his son to him (2 Kin. 21:6); he approved Divination; and he killed all who protested his evil actions. It is possible that he killed the prophet Isaiah; rabbinical tradition states that Manasseh gave the command that Isaiah be sawn in two (see also Heb. 11:37). Scripture summarizes Manasseh's reign by saying he "seduced them [Judah] to do more evil than the nations whom the Lord had destroyed before the children of Israel" (2 Kin. 21:9).

Manasseh was temporarily deported to Babylon where he humbled himself before God in repentance (2 Chr. 33:11–13). Upon Manasseh's return to Jerusalem, he tried to reverse the trends he had set; but his reforms were quickly reversed after his death by his wicked son Amon.

4. A descendant, or resident, of Pahath–Moab (Ezra 10:30). After the Captivity he divorced his pagan wife.

5. An Israelite of the family of Hashum. Manasseh divorced his pagan wife after the Captivity (Ezra 10:33).

MANOAH [muh NOH uh] (quiet)

Father of Samson the judge (Judg. 13:2–23). A Danite of the city of Zorah, Manoah and his wife tried to persuade Samson not to marry a Philistine woman, but he was determined to do so. They accompanied Samson to Timnah, where the ceremonies took place. Samson was buried "between Zorah and Eshtaol in the tomb of his father Manoah" (Judg. 16:31).

MAOCH [MAY ahk]

The father of Achish, king of Gath (1 Sam. 27:2). Maoch may be the same person as Maachah (1 Kin. 2:39).

MAON [MAY ahn] (dwelling)

A son of Shammai (1 Chr. 2:45).

MARA [MAY ruh] (bitter)

The name that Naomi chose for herself after the death of her husband and sons to express her sadness and bereavement (Ruth 1:20).

MARCUS [MAR kus]

Greek form of MARK (1 Pet. 5:13, KJV).

MARESHAH [muh REE shuh] (summit)

The name of two men in the Old Testament:

1. The founder of Hebron (1 Chr. 2:42).

2. A son of Laadah, of the tribe of Judah (1 Chr. 4:21).

MARK, JOHN

An occasional associate of Peter and Paul, and the probable author of the second Gospel. Mark's lasting impact on the Christian church comes from his writing rather than his life. He was the first to develop the literary form known as the "gospel" and is rightly regarded as a creative literary artist.

John Mark appears in the New Testament only in association with more prominent personalities and events. His mother, Mary, was an influential woman of Jerusalem who possessed a large house with servants. The early church gathered in this house during Peter's imprisonment under Herod Agrippa I (Acts 12:12). Barnabas and Saul (Paul) took John Mark with them when they returned from Jerusalem to Antioch after their famine-relief visit (Acts 12:25). Shortly thereafter, Mark accompanied Paul and Barnabas on their first missionary journey as far as Perga. He served in the capacity of "assistant" (Acts 13:5), which probably involved making arrangements for travel, food, and lodging; he may have done some teaching, too.

At Perga John Mark gave up the journey for an undisclosed reason (Acts 13:13); this departure later caused a rift between Paul and Barnabas when they chose their companions for the second missionary journey (Acts 15:37–41). Paul

M

was unwilling to take Mark again and chose Silas; they returned to Asia Minor and Greece. Barnabas persisted in his choice of Mark, who was his cousin (Col. 4:10), and returned with him to his homeland of Cyprus (Acts 15:39; also Acts 4:36).

This break occurred about A.D. 49–50, and John Mark is not heard from again until a decade later. He is first mentioned again, interestingly enough, by Paul— and in favorable terms. Paul asks the Colossians to receive Mark with a welcome (Col. 4:10), no longer as an assistant but as one of his "fellow laborers" (Philem. 24). And during his imprisonment in Rome, Paul tells Timothy to bring Mark with him to Rome, "for he is useful to me for ministry" (2 Tim. 4:11). One final reference to Mark comes also from Peter in Rome; Peter affectionately refers to him as "my son" (1 Pet. 5:13). Thus, in the later references to Mark in the New Testament, he appears to be reconciled to Paul and laboring with the two great apostles in Rome.

Information about Mark's later life is dependent on early church tradition. Writing at an early date, Papias (A.D. 60–130), whose report is followed by Clement of Alexandria (A.D. 150–215), tells us that Mark served as Peter's interpreter in Rome and wrote his Gospel from Peter's remembrances. Of his physical appearance we are only told, rather oddly, that Mark was "stumpy fingered." Writing at a later date (about A.D. 325), the church historian Eusebius says that Mark was the first evangelist to Egypt, the founder of the churches of Alexandria, and the first bishop of that city. So great were his converts, both in number and sincerity of commitment, says Eusebius, that the great Jewish philosopher, Philo, was amazed.

MARSENA [mar SEE nuh]

A high Persian official at Shushan, or Susa. Marsena was one of seven princes "who had access to the king's presence" (Esth. 1:14).

MARTHA [MAR thuh] (*lady, mistress*)

The sister of Mary and Lazarus of Bethany (Luke 10:38–41; John 11:1–44; 12:1–3). All three were sincere followers of Jesus, but Mary and Martha expressed their love for Him in different ways. The account of the two women given by Luke reveals a clash of temperaments between Mary and Martha. Martha "was distracted with much serving" (Luke 10:40); she was an activist busy with household chores. Her sister Mary "sat at Jesus' feet and heard His word" (Luke 10:39); her instinct was to sit still, meditate, and receive spiritual instruction.

While Martha busied herself making Jesus comfortable and cooking for Him in her home, Mary listened intently to His teaching. When Martha complained that Mary was not helping her, Jesus rebuked Martha. "You are worried and troubled about many things," He declared. "But one thing is needed, and Mary has chosen that good part, which will not be taken away from her" (Luke 10:41–42). He told her, in effect, that Mary was feeding her spiritual needs. This was more important than Martha's attempt to feed His body.

Jesus recognized that Martha was working for Him, but He reminded her that she was permitting her outward activities to hinder her spiritually. Because of her emphasis on work and her daily chores, her inner communion with her Lord was being hindered.

MARY [MAIR ee]

The name of six women in the New Testament:

3. A priest in the days of Joiakim the high priest (Neh. 12:19).

MATTHAN [MAT than] (*gift* [of God])

The grandfather of Joseph listed in Matthew's genealogy of Jesus Christ (Matt. 1:15).

MATTHAT [MAT that] (*gift* [of God])

The name of two men in the New Testament:

1. An ancestor of Jesus listed in Luke's genealogy (Luke 3:24).

2. Another ancestor of Jesus listed in Luke's genealogy (Luke 3:29).

MATTHEW [MA thue] (*gift of the Lord*)

A tax collector who became one of the twelve apostles of Jesus (Matt. 9:9). Matthew's name appears seventh in two lists of apostles (Mark 3:18; Luke 6:15), and eighth in two others (Matt. 10:3; Acts 1:13).

In Hebrew, Matthew's name means "gift of the Lord," but we know from his trade that he delighted in the gifts of others as well. He was a tax collector (Matt. 9:9–11) who worked in or around Capernaum under the authority of Herod Antipas. In Jesus' day, land and poll taxes were collected directly by Roman officials, but taxes on transported goods were contracted out to local collectors. Matthew was such a person, or else he was in the service of one. These middlemen paid an agreed-upon sum in advance to the Roman officials for the right to collect taxes in an area. Their profit came from the excess they could squeeze from the people.

The Jewish people hated these tax collectors not only for their corruption, but also because they worked for and with the despised Romans. Tax collectors were ranked with murderers and robbers, and a Jew was permitted to lie to them if necessary. The attitude found in the Gospels is similar. Tax collectors are lumped together with harlots (Matt. 21:31), Gentiles (Matt. 18:17), and, most often, sinners (Matt. 9:10). They were as offensive to Jews for their economic and social practices as lepers were for their uncleanness; both were excluded from the people of God.

It is probable that the Matthew mentioned in Matthew 9:9–13 is identical with the Levi of Mark 2:13–17 and Luke 5:27–32; the stories obviously refer to the same person and event. The only problem in the identification is that Mark mentions Matthew rather than Levi in his list of apostles (Mark 3:18), thus leading one to assume two different persons. It is possible, however, that the same person was known by two names (compare "Simon" and "Peter"), or, less likely, that Levi and James the son of Alphaeus are the same person, since Mark calls Alphaeus the father of both (Mark 2:14; 3:18). Following his call by Jesus, Matthew is not mentioned again in the New Testament.

MATTHIAS [muh THIGH us] (*gift of the Lord*)

A disciple chosen to succeed Judas Iscariot as an apostle (Acts 1:23, 26). Matthias had been a follower of Jesus from the beginning of His ministry until the day of His ascension and had been a witness of His resurrection. In this way he fulfilled the requirements of apostleship (Acts 1:21–22). Probably he was one of the "seventy" (Luke 10:1, 17). The New Testament makes no further mention of him after his election. One tradition says that Matthias preached in Judea and was stoned to death by the Jews. Another tradition holds that he worked

M

in Ethiopia and was martyred by crucifixion.

MATTITHIAH [mat uh THIGH uh] (*gift of the Lord*)

The name of four or five men in the Old Testament:

1. A son of Shallum the Korahite (1 Chr. 9:31).

2. A Levite musician and gatekeeper during the reign of David (1 Chr. 15:18).

3. A son of Jeduthun. Mattithiah was appointed to the service of song during the reign of David (1 Chr. 25:3, 21). He was probably the same person as No. 2.

4. A son of Nebo who divorced his pagan wife after the Captivity (Ezra 10:43).

5. An Israelite who helped Ezra read the Book of the Law to the people (Neh. 8:4).

MEBUNNAI [meh BUN eh]

A Hushathite, one of David's mighty men (2 Sam. 23:27). The name is probably a textual corruption of Sibbechai (2 Sam. 21:18). Also see SIBBECHAI.

MEDAD [ME dad]

An Israelite who prophesied in the wilderness camp (Num. 11:26–27). When 70 elders assembled in the "tabernacle of meeting," the Spirit rested on them and they prophesied. Medad and Eldad had not gone to the tabernacle, but had remained in the camp. Nevertheless, the Spirit rested upon them also and they, too, prophesied. A young man ran and told Moses. Joshua asked Moses to forbid them; but Moses replied, "Oh, that all the LORD's people were prophets and that the LORD would put His Spirit upon them!" (Num. 11:29).

This story emphasizes the truth that God's Spirit can fill any person at any place at any time.

MEDAN [MEE dan]

A son of Abraham and Keturah, Abraham's concubine (1 Chr. 1:32).

MEHETABEEL [meh HET uh beel]

Father of Delaiah and grandfather of Shemaiah (Neh. 6:10; Mehetabel, NRSV, NASB, REB, NIV).

MEHETABEL [meh HET uh bel]

The wife of Hadar (Gen. 36:39), or Hadad (1 Chr. 1:50), king of Edom. Mehetabel was a daughter of Matred.

Also see MEHETABEEL.

MEHIDA [meh HIGH duh] (*renowned*)

Founder of a family of Nethinim (Temple servants) whose descendants returned from the Captivity with Zerubbabel (Ezra 2:52).

MEHIR [MEE hur] (*price*)

A son of Chelub, of the tribe of Judah (1 Chr. 4:11).

MEHUJAEL [meh HUE jay el]

A son of Irad, of the family of Cain (Gen. 4:18).

MEHUMAN [meh HUE man]

A eunuch or chamberlain who had charge of the harem of King Ahasuerus (Xerxes) of Persia (Esth. 1:10).

MELATIAH [mel uh TYE uh] (*the Lord sets free*)

A Gibeonite who helped repair the wall of Jerusalem in Nehemiah's time (Neh. 3:7).

MELCHI [mel KYE] (*my king*)

The name of two men in Luke's genealogy of Jesus Christ:

1. A son of Janna and the father of Levi (Luke 3:24).

2. A son of Addi and the father of Neri (Luke 3:28).

MELCHIAH [mell KIE ah]

A form of MALCHIAH NO. 2.

MELCHISEDEC [mel KIZ uh dek]

A form of MELCHIZEDEK.

MELCHI-SHUA [mel kye SHU uh]

A form of MALCHISHUA.

MELCHIZEDEK [mel KIZ eh deck] (*king of righteousness*)

A king of Salem (Jerusalem) and priest of the Most High God (Gen. 14:18–20; Ps. 110:4; Heb. 5:6–11; 6:20—7:28). Melchizedek's appearance and disappearance in the Book of Genesis are somewhat mysterious. Melchizedek and Abraham first met after Abraham's defeat of Chedorlaomer and his three allies. Melchizedek presented bread and wine to Abraham and his weary men, demonstrating friendship and religious kinship. He bestowed a blessing on Abraham in the name of El Elyon ("God Most High"), and praised God for giving Abraham a victory in battle (Gen. 14:18–20).

Abraham presented Melchizedek with a tithe (a tenth) of all the booty he had gathered. By this act Abraham indicated that he recognized Melchizedek as a fellow-worshiper of the one true God as well as a priest who ranked higher spiritually than himself. Melchizedek's existence shows that there were people other than Abraham and his family who served the true God.

In Psalm 110, a messianic psalm written by David (Matt. 22:43), Melchizedek is seen as a type of Christ. This theme is repeated in the Book of Hebrews, where both Melchizedek and Christ are considered kings of righteousness and peace.

By citing Melchizedek and his unique priesthood as a type, the writer shows that Christ's new priesthood is superior to the old Levitical order and the priesthood of Aaron (Heb. 7:1–10; Melchisedec, KJV).

Attempts have been made to identify Melchizedek as an imaginary character named Shem, an angel, the Holy Spirit, Christ, and others. All are products of speculation, not historical fact; and it is impossible to reconcile them with the theological argument of Hebrews. Melchizedek was a real, historical king-priest who served as a type for the greater King-Priest who was to come, Jesus Christ.

MELEA [MEE lee uh]

An ancestor of Jesus (Luke 3:31).

MELECH [MEE lek] (*king*)

A Benjamite, the son of Micah and a descendant of King Saul (1 Chr. 8:35; 9:41).

MELICHU, MELICU [MEL eh kue]

Forms of MALLUCH NO. 6.

MENAHEM [MEN ah him] (*comforter*)

A son of Gadi and 17th king of Israel (2 Kin. 15:14–23). Some scholars believe Menahem probably was the military commander of King Zechariah. When Shallum took the throne from Zechariah by killing him in front of the people, Menahem determined that Shallum himself must be killed. After Shallum had reigned as king of Israel for a month in Samaria, Menahem "went up from Tirzah, came to Samaria, and struck Shallum . . . and killed him; and he reigned in his place" (2 Kin. 15:14).

When the city of Tiphsah refused to recognize Menahem as the lawful ruler of Israel, Menahem attacked it and inflicted terrible cruelties upon its people (2 Kin. 15:16). This act apparently secured his position, because Menahem remained king for ten years (752–742 B.C.). His reign was evil, marked by cruelty, oppression, and idolatrous worship.

During his reign Menahem faced a threat from the advancing army of Pul (Tiglath-pileser III), king of Assyria. To strengthen his own position as king and to forestall a war with Assyria, he paid tribute to the Assyrian king by exacting "from each man fifty shekels of silver" (2 Kin. 15:20). After Menahem's death, his son Pekahiah became king of Israel (2 Kin. 15:22).

MENAN [MEE nan]

An ancestor of Jesus (Luke 3:31; Menna, NIV, NRSV).

MENNA [MEN uh]

A form of MENAN.

MEONOTHAI [meh AHN oh thigh]
(*habitations of the Lord*)

The father of Ophrah and a descendant of Judah (1 Chr. 4:14).

MEPHIBOSHETH [meh FIB oh shehth]
(meaning unknown)

The name of two men in the Old Testament:

1. A son of Jonathan and grandson of Saul. Mephibosheth was also called Merib–Baal (1 Chr. 8:34; 9:40), probably his original name, meaning "a striver against Baal." His name was changed because the word "Baal" was associated with idol worship.

Mephibosheth was only five years old when his father, Jonathan, and his grandfather, Saul, died on Mount Gilboa in the Battle of Jezreel (2 Sam. 4:4). When

the child's nurse heard the outcome of the battle, she feared for Mephibosheth's life. As she fled for his protection, "he fell and became lame" (2 Sam. 4:4). For the rest of his life he was crippled.

After David consolidated his kingdom, he remembered his covenant with Jonathan to treat his family with kindness (1 Samuel 20). Through Ziba, a servant of the house of Saul, David found out about Mephibosheth. The lame prince had been staying "in the house of Machir the son of Ammiel, in Lo Debar" (2 Sam. 9:4). David then summoned Mephibosheth to his palace, restored to him the estates of Saul, appointed servants for him, and gave him a place at the royal table (2 Sam. 9:7–13).

When David's son Absalom rebelled, the servant Ziba falsely accused Mephibosheth of disloyalty to David (2 Sam. 16:1–4). David believed Ziba's story and took Saul's property from Mephibosheth. Upon David's return to Jerusalem, Mephibosheth cleared himself. David in turn offered Mephibosheth half of Saul's estates (2 Sam. 19:24–30), but he refused. David's return to Jerusalem as king was the only reward Mephibosheth desired.

Although Mephibosheth was often wronged and his life was filled with tragedy, he never grew angry or embittered. Even material possessions had little appeal to him—an important lesson for all followers of the Lord.

2. A son of King Saul and Rizpah (2 Sam. 21:8).

MERAB [MEE rab] (*increase*)

The older daughter of King Saul (1 Sam. 14:49). When GOLIATH defied and taunted the Israelites, Saul promised that the man who killed him would be given great riches as well as Merab in marriage (1 Sam. 17:25). When David killed the giant, however, Saul changed his mind. David then married MICHAL, the younger daughter of Saul.

MERAIAH [meh RYE uh]

Head of the priestly family of Seraiah after the return from the Captivity (Neh. 12:12).

MERAIOTH [meh RAY yawth]

The name of two men in the Old Testament:
1. A son of Zerahiah and the father of Amariah (1 Chr. 6:6–7).
2. A son of Ahitub and a priest of Jerusalem (Neh. 11:11).

MERARI [meh RAY eye] (bitter)

The third and youngest son of Levi and the founder of the Merarites, one of the three Levitical families. Merari was the father of MAHLI and MUSHI (Ex. 6:16–19), who, in turn, were the founders of the Mahlites and the Mushites (Num. 3:33; 26:58).

MERED [MEE red]

A son of Ezrah, of the tribe of Judah (1 Chr. 4:17).

MEREMOTH [MER eh moth] (heights)

The name of three or four men in the Old Testament:
1. A son of Uriah the priest who was assigned the task of weighing the gold and silver articles that Ezra brought back from Babylon (Ezra 8:33).
2. One of the "sons of Bani" (Ezra 10:34, 36) who divorced his pagan wife after the Captivity.
3. A priest who, with Nehemiah, sealed the covenant (Neh. 10:5). He may be the same person as Meremoth No. 1.
4. A priest who returned with Zerubbabel from the Captivity (Neh. 12:3).

MERES [MEE ress]

A high Persian official at Shushan (Susa), one of seven princes "who had access to the king's presence" (Esth. 1:14).

MERIB-BAAL [MER ib BAY uhl]
(contender against Baal)

A son of Jonathan (1 Chr. 8:34) and grandson of King Saul. Merib-Baal is the same person as MEPHIBOSHETH NO. 1 (2 Sam. 9:6).

MERODACH-BALADAN [MEHR oh dack BAL ah dahn] (the god Marduk has given an heir)

The king of Babylon (721–710 and 704 B.C.) who sent emissaries to King Hezekiah of Judah (Is. 39:1; Berodach-Baladan, 2 Kin. 20:12).

To the Assyrians, Merodach-Baladan was a persistent rebel king. He appeared on the political scene during the days of TIGLATH-PILESER III of Assyria. He rallied the support of the Aramean tribes in Babylonia and arranged an alliance with Elam. In 721 B.C., when SARGON II came to power in Assyria, Merodach-Baladan entered Babylon and claimed kingship to the country.

In 710 B.C., Sargon made a determined effort to expel Merodach-Baladan and make himself king. After submitting to Sargon, Merodach-Baladan was reinstated as king of the tribe of Bit-Yakin, a district near the mouth of the Euphrates River. Merodach-Baladan remained faithful to Sargon; but when Sennacherib came to power in 705 B.C., he grew restless. In 703 B.C., Merodach-Baladan returned to Babylon, killed the ruler there, and prepared to fight Assyria. Sennacherib reacted energetically and drove Merodach-Baladan into exile once again.

M

Merodach–Baladan sent ambassadors to Jerusalem to visit King Hezekiah of Judah, who had just recovered miraculously from a serious illness. He sent letters and presents (2 Kin. 20:12; Is. 39:1) and inquired of the "wonder that was done in the land" (2 Chr. 32:31). This probably was a reference to the sun's shadow moving backward ten degrees on the Sundial of Ahaz (2 Kin. 20:8–11). The real reason for his visit may have been to gain an ally in Hezekiah and to involve him in revolt against Assyria.

There is no indication that Hezekiah formed an alliance, but he showed the Babylonian ambassadors his wealth and arsenal—an act that brought stiff rebuke from the prophet Isaiah (2 Kin. 20:13–18). Hezekiah later revolted from Assyria, a move that resulted in Sennacherib's invasion of Judah in 701 B.C.

Merodach–Baladan was never successful in his bid for Babylonian independence. The task was left for NABOPOLASSAR (626–605 B.C.), who was able to succeed where Merodach–Baladan had failed.

MESECH [MEE sek]

A form of MESHECH.

MESHA [MEE shuh]

The name of three men in the Old Testament:

1. A king of Moab who "regularly paid the king of Israel [Ahab] one hundred thousand lambs and the wool of one hundred thousand rams" (2 Kin. 3:4). After Ahab's death at Ramoth Gilead, Mesha refused to pay the tribute to Ahab's successor, Ahaziah (2 Kin. 1:1).

Mesha led the Moabites, Ammonites, and Edomites in an invasion of Judah after Jehoshaphat, Judah's king, began his religious reform. Mesha and his allies were defeated when the Lord caused them to turn on one another; Judah and Jehoshaphat won without a battle (2 Chr. 20).

When King Ahaziah died, Jehoram became king of Israel. Jehoram wanted Mesha to resume the tribute, and he asked Jehoshaphat to help him force Mesha to pay it (2 Kin. 3). The two kings, along with a king of Edom, moved around the southern end of the Dead Sea to attack Mesha. The armies nearly died of thirst, but the prophet Elisha instructed them to dig trenches to reach water.

In the glare of the early-morning sun, Mesha mistook the water for blood. He carelessly moved to attack the armies of Israel and Judah. His army was beaten, and the cities of Moab were destroyed. In a last-ditch effort to avert total defeat, Mesha offered his oldest son as a burnt offering upon the wall of Kir Haraseth as a sacrifice to the god Chemosh. The human sacrifice apparently frightened or shocked the armies of Israel and Judah, so they pulled back from the city, lifting the siege and failing to capture Kir Haraseth.

Mesha is the king of whom the famous Moabite Stone declares: "I am Mesha, son of Chemosh [Yat] . . . king of Moab, the Dibonite." Thus, he is the one who caused the Moabite Stone to be written and had it erected.

2. A man of the tribe of Judah (1 Chr. 2:42).

3. An ancestor of King Saul (1 Chr. 8:8–9).

MESHACH [MEE shak]

The Chaldean name given to Mishael, one of Daniel's companions (Dan. 1:7). Along with SHADRACH and ABED–NEGO, Meshach would not bow down and worship the pagan image of gold set up by Nebuchadnezzar. They were cast into "the burning fiery furnace," but were preserved from harm by the power of God.

MESHECH [MEE shek]

The name of two men in the Old Testament:

1. A son of Japheth (1 Chr. 1:5).

2. A son of Shem (1 Chr. 1:17), or possibly an unknown Aramean tribe, also spelled Mash (Gen. 10:23).

MESHELEMIAH [meh SHEL uh mye uh]
(the Lord repays)

A Levite gatekeeper of the tabernacle during David's reign (1 Chr. 9:21). He is also called Shelemiah (1 Chr. 26:14).

MESHEZABEEL [meh SHEZ uh beel]

The name of three men in the Book of Nehemiah:

1. An ancestor of Meshullam (Neh. 3:4).

2. One of the leaders of the people who sealed the covenant with Nehemiah (Neh. 10:21).

3. A descendant of Judah through Zerah (Neh. 11:24).

Any two or perhaps all three of these men may be identical. The NIV, NASB, REB, and NRSV spell the name Meshezabel.

MESHEZABEL [meh SHEZ uh bell]

A form of MESHEZABEEL.

MESHILLEMITH [meh SHILL uh meth]

A form of MESHILLEMOTH No. 2.

MESHILLEMOTH [meh SHILL uh moth]
(acts of repayment)

The name of two men in the Old Testament:

1. A man of the tribe of Ephraim (2 Chr. 28:12).

2. A priest of the family of Immer (Neh. 11:13), also called Meshillemith (1 Chr. 9:12).

MESHOBAB [meh SHOH bab] (restored)

A leader of the tribe of Simeon in the days of Hezekiah, king of Judah (1 Chr. 4:34).

MESHULLAM [meh SHUHL um]
(friendship)

The name of twenty-one men in the Old Testament:

1. An ancestor of Shaphan (2 Kin. 22:3).

2. A son of Zerubbabel and descendant of King Jehoiakim's son, Jeconiah (1 Chr. 3:19).

3. A leader of the tribe of Gad during the reign of Jotham of Judah (1 Chr. 5:13).

4. A man of the tribe of Benjamin listed in the family tree of King Saul (1 Chr. 8:17).

5. The father of Sallu of the tribe of Benjamin (Neh. 11:7).

6. A son of Shephatiah, of the tribe of Benjamin (1 Chr. 9:8).

7. A priest and member of an important priestly family (Neh. 11:11).

8. A priest of the house of Immer (1 Chr. 9:12).

9. A Levite of the Kohathite family who helped oversee temple repairs under King Josiah of Judah (2 Chr. 34:12).

10. A man whom Ezra sent to find Levites willing to go to Jerusalem after the Captivity (Ezra 8:16).

11. A man who opposed Ezra in the matter of divorcing pagan wives married during the Captivity (Ezra 10:15).

12. A descendant of Bani who divorced his pagan wife after the Captivity (Ezra 10:29).

M

13. A son of Berechiah who helped repair two sections of the Jerusalem wall (Neh. 3:4, 30).

14. A son of Besodeiah who helped repair the Jerusalem wall (Neh. 3:6).

15. A leader of the people who helped Ezra read the Law of Moses (Neh. 8:4).

16. A priest who sealed the covenant with Nehemiah (Neh. 10:7).

17. A leader of the people who sealed the covenant with Nehemiah (Neh. 10:20).

18. A priest of the family of Ezra in the time of the high priest Joiakim (Neh. 12:13).

19. A priest in the time of Joiakim (Neh. 12:16).

20. A gatekeeper during the time of Joiakim (Neh. 12:25).

21. A prince of Judah who participated in the dedication of the Jerusalem wall (Neh. 12:33).

MESHULLEMETH [meh SHUHL uh meth] (*restitution*)

The wife of Manasseh, king of Judah (2 Kin. 21:19). Meshullemeth was the mother of Amon, Manasseh's son who succeeded him to the throne of Judah.

MESSIAH [meh SIGH uh] (*anointed one*)

The one anointed by God and empowered by God's spirit to deliver His people and establish His kingdom. In Jewish thought, the Messiah would be the king of the Jews, a political leader who would defeat their enemies and bring in a golden era of peace and prosperity. In Christian thought, the term Messiah refers to Jesus' role as a spiritual deliverer, setting His people free from sin and death.

The word Messiah comes from a Hebrew term that means "anointed one." Its Greek counterpart is *Christos*, from which the word Christ comes. Messiah

was one of the titles used by early Christians to describe who Jesus was.

In Old Testament times, part of the ritual of commissioning a person for a special task was to anoint him with oil. The phrase "anointed" one was applied to a person in such cases. In the Old Testament, Messiah is used more than 30 times to describe kings (2 Sam. 1:14, 16), priests (Lev. 4:3, 5, 16), the patriarchs (Ps. 105:15), and even the Persian king Cyrus (Is. 45:1). The word is also used in connection with King David, who became the model of the messianic king who would come at the end of the age (2 Sam. 22:51; Ps. 2:2). But it was not until the time of Daniel (sixth century B.C.) that Messiah was used as an actual title of a king who would come in the future (Dan. 9:25–26). Still later, as the Jewish people struggled against their political enemies, the Messiah came to be thought of as a political, military ruler.

From the New Testament we learn more about the people's expectations. They thought the Messiah would come soon to perform signs (John 7:31) and to deliver His people, after which He would live and rule forever (John 12:34). Some even thought that John the Baptist was the Messiah (John 1:20). Others said that the Messiah was to come from Bethlehem (John 7:42). Most expected the Messiah to be a political leader, a king who would defeat the Romans and provide for the physical needs of the Israelites.

According to the Gospel of John, a woman of Samaria said to Jesus, "I know that Messiah is coming." Jesus replied, "I who speak to you am He" (John 4:25–26). In the Gospels of Matthew, Mark, and Luke, however, Jesus never directly referred to Himself as the Messiah, except privately to His disciples, until the crucifixion (Matt. 26:63–64; Mark 14:61–62; Luke 22:67–70). He did accept the title and function of messiahship privately (Matt. 16:16–17). Yet Jesus constantly avoided being called "Messiah" in public (Mark 8:29–30). This is known as Jesus' "messianic secret." He was the Messiah, but He did not want it known publicly.

The reason for this is that Jesus' kingdom was not political but spiritual (John 18:36). If Jesus had used the title "Messiah," people would have thought he was a political king. But Jesus understood that the Messiah, God's Anointed One, was to be the Suffering Servant (Is. 52:13—53:12). The fact that Jesus was a suffering Messiah—a crucified deliverer—was a "stumbling block" to many of the Jews (1 Cor. 1:23). They saw the cross as a sign of Jesus' weakness, powerlessness, and failure. They rejected the concept of a crucified Messiah.

But the message of the early church centered around the fact that the crucified and risen Jesus is the Christ (Acts 5:42; 17:3; 18:5). They proclaimed the "scandalous" gospel of a crucified Messiah as the power and wisdom of God (1 Cor. 1:23–24). John wrote, "Who is a liar but he who denies that Jesus is the Christ [the Messiah]?" (1 John 2:22).

By the time of the apostle Paul, "Christ" was in the process of changing from a title to a proper name. The name is found mostly in close association with the name "Jesus," as in "Christ Jesus" (Rom. 3:24) or "Jesus Christ" (Rom. 1:1). When the church moved onto Gentile soil, the converts lacked the Jewish background for understanding the title, and it lost much of its significance. Luke wrote, "The disciples were first called Christians [those who belong to and follow the Messiah] in Antioch" (Acts 11:26).

As the Messiah, Jesus is the divinely appointed king who brought God's kingdom to earth (Matt. 12:28; Luke 11:20).

His way to victory was not by physical force and violence, but through love, humility, and service.

MESSIAS [muh SYE uhs]

Greek form of MESSIAH.

METHUSELAH [meh THUE zuh luh]

A son of Enoch and the grandfather of Noah. At the age of 187, Methuselah became the father of Lamech. After the birth of Lamech, Methuselah lived 782 years and died at the age of 969. He lived longer than any other human. He was an ancestor of Jesus (Luke 3:37; Mathusala, KJV).

METHUSHAEL [meh THUE sheh el] (*man of God*)

A son of Mehujael and the father of Lamech (Gen. 4:18).

MEZAHAB [MEZ uh hab] (*waters of gold*)

The father of Matred and grandfather of Mehetabel. Mehetabel was the wife of Hadar (Gen. 36:39), or Hadad (1 Chr. 1:50), king of Edom.

MIAMIN [MYE uh min]

A form of MIJAMIN Nos. 2 and 4.

MIBHAR [MIB har] (*elite*)

A "son of Hagri," probably meaning a Hagrite—one of the nomadic peoples of Gilead. Mibhar was one of David's mighty men (1 Chr. 11:38).

MIBSAM [MIB sam] (*fragrance*)

The name of two men in the Old Testament:

1. A son of Ishmael (Gen. 25:13).
2. A descendant of Simeon (1 Chr. 4:25).

MIBZAR [MIB zar] *(fortress)*

An Edomite clan chief descended from Esau (Gen. 36:42).

MICAH [MIE kuh] *(Who is like the Lord)*

The name of six men in the Old Testament:

1. A man from the mountains of Ephraim during the period of the judges in Israel's history. Micah's worship of false gods led the Danites into idolatry (Judges 17—18).

2. A descendant of Reuben (1 Chr. 5:5).

3. A son of Merib–Baal listed in the family tree of King Saul of Benjamin (1 Chr. 8:34–35; 9:40–41). Micah was the father of Pithon, Melech, Tarea (or Tahrea), and Ahaz. His father Merib–Baal (also called Mephibosheth, 2 Sam. 4:4) was a son of Jonathan and a grandson of Saul.

4. A son of Zichri and grandson of Asaph (1 Chr. 9:15). Micah is also called "Micha, the son of Zabdi" (Neh. 11:17; also Neh. 11:22) and "Michaiah, the son of Zaccur" (Neh. 12:35).

5. The father of Abdon (2 Chr. 34:20) or Achbor (2 Kin. 22:12). Abdon was one of five men whom King Josiah of Judah sent to inquire of Huldah the prophetess when Hilkiah the priest found the Book of the Law. Micah is also called Michaiah (2 Kin. 22:12).

6. An Old Testament prophet and author of the Book of Micah. A younger contemporary of the great prophet Isaiah, Micah was from Moresheth Gath (Mic. 1:1, 14), a town in southern Judah. His prophecy reveals his country origins; he uses many images from country life (Mic. 7:1).

Micah spoke out strongly against those who claimed to be prophets of the Lord but who used this position to lead the people of Judah into false hopes and further errors: "The sun shall go down on the prophets, and the day shall be dark for them" (Mic. 3:6). Micah's love for God would not allow him to offer false hopes to those who were under His sentence of judgment.

Little else is known about this courageous spokesman for the Lord. He tells us in his book that he prophesied during the reigns of three kings in Judah: Jotham, Ahaz, and Hezekiah (Mic. 1:1). This would place the time of his ministry from about 750 to 687 B.C.

MICAIAH [mie KAY yah] *(who is like the Lord?)*

The prophet who predicted the death of King Ahab of Israel in the battle against the Syrians at Ramoth Gilead (1 Kin. 22:8–28; 2 Chr. 18:7–27). Ahab gathered about 400 prophets, apparently all in his employment. They gave their unanimous approval to Ahab's proposed attack against the Syrian king, Ben–Hadad.

King Jehoshaphat of Judah was unconvinced by this display. He asked, "Is there not still a prophet of the LORD here, that we may inquire of Him?" (1 Kin. 22:7; 2 Chr. 18:6). Ahab replied, "There is still one man, Micaiah the son of Imlah, by whom we may inquire of the LORD; but I hate him, because he does not prophesy good concerning me, but evil" (1 Kin. 22:8; 2 Chr. 18:7). The prophet Micaiah was then summoned.

When Ahab asked this prophet's advice, Micaiah answered, "Go and prosper, for the LORD will deliver it into the hand of the king!" (1 Kin. 22:15; 2 Chr. 18:14).

Micaiah's answer was heavy with sarcasm, irony, and contempt. Ahab realized he was being mocked; so he commanded him to speak nothing but the truth. Micaiah then said, "I saw all Israel scattered on the mountains as sheep that have no shepherd" (1 Kin. 22:17; 2 Chr. 18:16). Ahab turned to Jehoshaphat and said, "Did I not tell you that he would not prophesy good concerning me, but evil?" (1 Kin. 22:18; 2 Chr. 18:17).

Zedekiah then struck Micaiah on the cheek and accused him of being a liar. Ahab commanded that Micaiah be put in prison until the king's victorious return from Ramoth Gilead. Then Micaiah said, "If you ever return . . . the LORD has not spoken by me" (1 Kin. 22:28; 2 Chr. 18:27).

Ahab did not return; he died at Ramoth Gilead, just as Micaiah had predicted.

MICHA [MY kuh] (*who is like the Lord?*)

The name of three men in the Old Testament:

1. A son of Mephibosheth (2 Sam. 9:12).

2. A Levite who sealed the covenant with Nehemiah (Neh. 10:11).

3. A Levite descended from Asaph (Neh. 11:17, 22), also called Micah (1 Chr. 9:15).

METHUSELAH

M

MICHAEL [MIE kay el] (*who is like God?*)

The name of ten men in the Bible:

1. The father of Sethur (Num. 13:13). Sethur was a representative of the tribe of Asher among the 12 spies sent by Moses to spy out the land of Canaan.

2. A descendant of Gad who settled in Bashan (1 Chr. 5:11–13).

3. Another descendant of Gad (1 Chr. 5:14).

4. A Levite of the family of Gershon (1 Chr. 6:40). He was an ancestor of Asaph the singer.

5. A chief man of the tribe of Issachar, family of Tola, house of Uzzi (1 Chr. 7:3).

6. One of the sons of Beriah (1 Chr. 8:16). Michael is mentioned in the family tree of King Saul of Benjamin.

7. A warrior from the tribe of Manasseh. He joined David at Ziklag (1 Chr. 12:20).

8. The father of Omri (1 Chr. 27:18).

9. A son of Jehoshaphat, king of Judah (2 Chr. 21:2). Michael was a brother of Jehoram, king of Judah.

10. The father of Zebadiah, of the family of Shephatiah (Ezra 8:8).

MICHAH [MY kuh] (*who is like the Lord?*)

A Levite during David's reign (1 Chr. 23:20).

MICHAIAH [my KYE uh] (*who is like the Lord?*)

The name of four men and one woman in the Old Testament:

1. An officer of King Josiah of Judah (2 Kin. 22:12), also called Micah (2 Chr. 34:20).

2. The wife of King Rehoboam and mother of King Abijah (2 Chr. 13:1–2).

3. A leader sent by Jehoshaphat, king of Judah, to teach the Law in the cities of Judah (2 Chr. 17:7).

4. A priest who blew a trumpet during the celebration after Jerusalem's walls were rebuilt (Neh. 12:35, 41), also called Micah (1 Chr. 9:15).

5. A son of Gemariah (Jer. 36:11, 13).

MICHAL [MY kul] (*who is like God?*)

The younger daughter of King Saul who became David's wife. After David had become a hero by slaying GOLIATH, Saul offered to give Michal to David as his wife. But instead of a dowry, Saul requested of David "one hundred foreskins of the Philistines" (1 Sam. 18:25), hoping that David would be killed by the Philistines.

Instead, David won an impressive victory. He and his warriors killed 200 Philistines and brought their foreskins to the king. Then Saul presented Michal to David to become his wife (1 Sam. 18:27–28).

After their marriage, the Ark of the Covenant was brought from the house of Obed–Edom to the City of David. Caught up in an inspired frenzy of religious fervor, David was filled with joy at being able to bring the ark back to Jerusalem. "Then David danced before the LORD with all his might; and David was wearing [only] a linen ephod [loincloth, kilt, or apron]" (2 Sam. 6:14). Whatever garment David was wearing, it apparently scandalized Michal, who accused him of lewd, base behavior—of "uncovering himself in the eyes of the maids" (2 Sam. 6:20).

Michal's withering sarcasm was met by David's devastating response. In effect he said, "My dance was a dance of joy, faith, and happiness in the Lord. Where is your joy in the Lord? Why do you not dance also?" By judging and condemning David, Michal had revealed a lack of love in her soul—quite a contrast to her earlier attitude (1 Sam. 18:20). Michal died barren (2 Sam. 6:21–23), one of the most terrible fates that could befall a Hebrew woman.

MICHRI [MICK rye] (*purchase price*)

A descendant of Benjamin and an ancestor of Elah (1 Chr. 9:8).

MIDIAN [MID ee un]

A son of Abraham by his concubine Keturah (Gen. 25:1–6). Midian had four sons (1 Chr. 1:33).

MIJAMIN [MIJ uh min] (*on the right hand*)

The name of several men in the Old Testament:

1. A descendant of Aaron and leader of a course of priests in David's time (1 Chr. 24:9).

2. A son of Parosh (Ezra 10:25; Miamin, KJV) who divorced his pagan wife after the Captivity.

3. A priest who sealed the covenant (Neh. 10:7). Perhaps he was the Minjamin (Neh. 12:41) who was one of the trumpeters at the dedication of the wall of Jerusalem.

4. A chief of the priests who returned with Zerubbabel from Babylon (Neh. 12:5; Miamin, KJV), also called Minjamin (Neh. 12:17).

MIKLOTH [MICK lawth]

The name of two men in the Old Testament:

1. A descendant of Jeiel, of the tribe of Benjamin (1 Chr. 8:32).

2. An officer who served under Dodai in David's army (1 Chr. 27:4).

MIKNEIAH [mick NYE uh] (*possession of the Lord*)

A Levite harpist during the reign of David (1 Chr. 15:18, 21).

MILALAI [MILL uh lye] (*eloquent*)

A musician who participated in the dedication of the wall of Jerusalem in Nehemiah's time (Neh. 12:36).

MILCAH [MILL kuh] (*queen*)

The name of two women in the Old Testament:

1. A daughter of Haran and the wife of Nahor (Gen. 22:20–22).

2. One of the five daughters of Zelophehad, of the tribe of Manasseh. Zelophehad had no sons. When he died, his daughters asked Moses for permission to share their father's inheritance. Their request was granted, providing they married within their own tribe in order to keep the inheritance within Manasseh (Num. 36:11–12).

MINIAMIN [meh NYE uh min] (*on the right hand*)

A form of MINJAMIN.

MINJAMIN [MIN juh men] (*on the right-hand side*)

The name of two or three men in the Old Testament:

1. One who helped Kore the Levite distribute the freewill offerings collected in the reign of Hezekiah (2 Chr. 31:15; Miniamin, NKJV, KJV, NRSV, NIV, NASB).

2. A priest who returned with Zerubbabel from the Captivity (Neh. 12:17; Miniamin, KJV, NRSV, NASB, REB, NIV). He is also called Mijamin (Neh. 12:5).

3. A priest who played the trumpet at the dedication of the rebuilt wall in Jerusalem (Neh. 12:41; Miniamin, KJV, NRSV, NASB, REB). He may be the same person as No. 2. Also see MIJAMIN.

MIRIAM [MER eh um]

The name of two women in the Old Testament:

M

1. A sister of Aaron and Moses (Num. 26:59; 1 Chr. 6:3). Called "Miriam the prophetess" (Ex. 15:20), she is described as one of the leaders sent by the Lord to guide Israel (Mic. 6:4). Although the Bible does not specifically say so, Miriam was probably the sister who watched over the infant Moses in the ark of bulrushes (Ex. 2:4–8). Miriam's song of victory after the Israelites' successful crossing of the Red Sea (Ex. 15:20–21) is one of the earliest poems.

Miriam was involved in a rebellion against Moses when he married an Ethiopian woman (Num. 12:1–2). Both she and Aaron claimed to be prophets, but God heard their claims and rebuked them. Because of her part in the rebellion against Moses' leadership, Miriam was struck with leprosy. However, Moses interceded for her, and she was quickly healed (Num. 12:1–16). She is not mentioned again until her death and burial at Kadesh in the Wilderness of Zin (Num. 20:1).

2. A daughter of Ezrah of the tribe of Judah (1 Chr. 4:17).

MIRMAH [MUR muh] (*height*)

A son of Shaharaim and Hodesh (1 Chr. 8:10; Mirma, KJV).

MISHAEL [MISH eh uhl] (*who is what God is?*)

The name of three men in the Old Testament:

1. A son of Uzziel and grandson of Kohath, of the tribe of Levi (Lev. 10:4).

2. An Israelite who helped Ezra read the Book of the Law to the people (Neh. 8:4).

3. One of the three friends of Daniel who were cast into the fiery furnace. "Now from among those of the sons of Judah were Daniel, Hananiah, Mishael,

and Azariah." The Babylonians changed his name to MESHACH (Dan. 1:6–7).

MISHAM [MY sham]

A son of Elpaal, of the tribe of Benjamin (1 Chr. 8:12).

MISHMA [MISH muh]

The name of two men in the Old Testament:

1. A son of Ishmael (Gen. 25:14). Mishma's name probably became the name of an Arabian tribe.

2. A descendant of Simeon (1 Chr. 4:25–26).

MISHMANNAH [mish MAN uh]

A warrior who joined David at Ziklag (1 Chr. 12:10).

MISPAR [MISS par]

An Israelite who returned with Zerubbabel from the Captivity (Ezra 2:2; Mizpar, KJV). The feminine form of the name, Mispereth, is used in Nehemiah 7:7.

MISPERETH [MISS puh reth]

The feminine form of MISPAR.

MITHREDATH [MITH reh dath]

The name of two men in the Book of Ezra:

1. The treasurer of King Cyrus of Persia. Mithredath delivered the Temple vessels that were to be returned to Jerusalem (Ezra 1:8).

2. A man who protested the rebuilding of the walls of Jerusalem by the Israelites (Ezra 4:7).

MIZRAIM [MIZ ray im] (*two Egypts*)

The second son of Ham as well as the name of his descendants and the country where they lived. Mizraim apparently was the ancestor of the Egyptians. In the

Old Testament the nation of Egypt is sometimes called Mizraim, perhaps referring to the fact that Egypt was divided into two parts (Upper and Lower Egypt). (Gen. 10:6, 13; 1 Chr. 1:8, 11).

MIZZAH [MIZ uh]

A son of Reuel and chief of a clan in the land of Edom (1 Chr. 1:37).

MNASON [NAY sohn]

A Christian with whom the apostle Paul stayed on his final visit to Jerusalem (Acts 21:16). A native of Cyprus, Mnason was "an early disciple"—perhaps meaning that he was converted to Christianity on the Day of Pentecost or shortly thereafter. He may have been an acquaintance of Barnabas, who also was from Cyprus (Acts 4:36).

MOAB [MOE abb] (*of my father*)

A son of Lot by an incestuous union with his older daughter (Gen. 19:37). Moab became an ancestor of the Moabites.

MOADIAH [moh uh DYE uh]

A priest and the head of a father's house in the time of the high priest Joiakim (Neh. 12:17). Moadiah may be the same person as Maadiah (Neh. 12:5).

MOLID [MOH lid] (*begetter*)

A son of Abishur and a descendant of Judah through Perez (1 Chr. 2:3, 29).

MORDECAI [MAWR deh kie] (*related to Marduk*)

The name of two men in the Old Testament:

1. One of the Jewish captives who returned with Zerubbabel from Babylon (Ezra 2:2; Neh. 7:7).

2. The hero of the Book of Esther. Mordecai was probably born in Babylo-

nia during the years of the Captivity of the Jewish people by this pagan nation. He was a resident of Susa (Shushan), the Persian capital during the reign of Ahasuerus (Xerxes I), the king of Persia (ruled 486–465 B.C.).

When Mordecai's uncle, Abihail, died (Esth. 2:5), Mordecai took his orphaned cousin, Hadassah (Esther), into his home as her adoptive father (Esth. 2:7). When two of the king's eunuchs, Bigthan and Teresh, conspired to assassinate King Ahasuerus, Mordecai discovered the plot and exposed it, saving the king's life (Esth. 2:21–22). Mordecai's good deed was recorded in the royal chronicles of Persia (Esth. 2:23).

Mordecai showed his loyalty to God by refusing to bow to Haman, the official second to the king (Esth. 3:2, 5). According to the Greek historian Herodotus, when the Persians bowed before their king, they paid homage as to a god. Mordecai, a Jew, would not condone such idolatry.

Haman's hatred for Mordecai sparked his plan to kill all the Jews in the Persian Empire (Esth. 3:6). Mordecai reminded his cousin, who had become Queen Esther, of her God-given opportunity to expose Haman to the king and to save her people (Esth. 3:1—4:17). The plot turned against Haman, who ironically was impaled on the same stake that he had prepared for Mordecai (Esth. 7:10).

Haman was succeeded by Mordecai, who now was second in command to the most powerful man in the kingdom. He used his new position to encourage his people to defend themselves against the scheduled massacre planned by Haman. Persian officials also assisted in protecting the Jews, an event celebrated by the annual Feast of Purim (Esth. 9:26–32).

M

MOSES [MOE zez]

The Hebrew prophet who delivered the Israelites from Egyptian slavery and who was their leader and lawgiver during their years of wandering in the wilderness. He was from the family line of Amram and Jochebed (Ex. 6:18, 20; Num. 26:58–59), Kohath and Levi. He was also the brother of Aaron and Miriam.

Moses was a leader so inspired by God that he was able to build a united nation from a race of oppressed and weary slaves. In the covenant ceremony at Mount Sinai, where the Ten Commandments were given, he founded the religious community known as Israel. As the interpreter of these covenant laws, he was the organizer of the community's religious and civil traditions. His story is told in the Old Testament—in the books of Exodus, Leviticus, Numbers, and Deuteronomy.

Moses' life is divided into three major periods:

The Forty Years in Egypt.

The Hebrew people had been in slavery in Egypt for some 400 years. This was in accord with God's words to Abraham that his seed, or descendants, would be in a foreign land in affliction for 400 years (Gen. 15:13). At the end of this time, God began to set His people free from their bondage by bringing Moses

to birth. He was a child of the captive Hebrews, but one whom the Lord would use to deliver Israel from her oppressors.

Moses was born at a time when the pharaoh, the ruler of Egypt, had given orders that no more male Hebrew children should be allowed to live. The Hebrew slaves had been reproducing so fast that the king felt threatened by a potential revolt against his authority. To save the infant Moses, his mother made a little vessel of papyrus waterproofed with asphalt and pitch. She placed Moses in the vessel, floating among the reeds on the bank of the Nile River.

By God's providence, Moses—the child of a Hebrew slave—was found and adopted by an Egyptian princess, the daughter of the pharaoh himself. He was reared in the royal court as a prince of the Egyptians: "And Moses was learned in all the wisdom of the Egyptians, and was mighty in words and deeds" (Acts 7:22). At the same time, the Lord determined that Moses should be taught in his earliest years by his own mother. This meant that he was founded in the faith of his fathers, although he was reared as an Egyptian (Ex. 2:1–10).

One day Moses became angry at an Egyptian taskmaster who was beating a Hebrew slave; he killed the Egyptian and buried him in the sand (Ex. 2:12). When this became known, however, he feared for his own life and fled from Egypt to the land of Midian. Moses was 40 years old when this occurred (Acts 7:23–29).

The Forty Years in the Land of Midian.

Moses' exile of about 40 years was spent in the land of Midian (mostly in northwest Arabia), in the desert between Egypt and Canaan. In Midian Moses became a shepherd and eventually the son-in-law of Jethro, a Midianite priest.

Jethro gave his daughter Zipporah to Moses in marriage (Ex. 2:21); and she bore him two sons, Gershom and Eliezer (Ex. 18:3–4; Acts 7:29). During his years as a shepherd, Moses became familiar with the wilderness of the Sinai Peninsula, learning much about survival in the desert. He also learned patience and much about leading sheep. All of these skills prepared him to be the shepherd of the Israelites in later years when he led them out of Egypt and through the Wilderness of Sinai.

Near the end of his 40-year sojourn in the land of Midian, Moses experienced a dramatic call to ministry. This call was given at the Burning Bush in the wilderness near Mount Sinai. The Lord revealed to Moses His intention to deliver Israel from Egyptian captivity into a "land flowing with milk and honey" that He had promised centuries before to Abraham, Isaac, and Jacob. The Lord assured Moses that He would be with him, and that by God's presence, he would be able to lead the people out.

God spoke to Moses from the midst of a burning bush, but Moses doubted that it was God who spoke. He asked for a sign. Instantly his rod, which he cast on the ground, became a serpent (Ex. 4:3).

In spite of the assurance of this miraculous sign, Moses was still hesitant to take on this task. He pleaded that he was "slow of speech and slow of tongue" (Ex. 4:10), perhaps implying that he was a stutterer or a stammerer. God countered Moses' hesitation by appointing his brother Aaron to be his spokesman. Moses would be God's direct representative, and Aaron would be his mouthpiece and interpreter to the people of Israel. Finally Moses accepted this commission from God and returned to Egypt for a confrontation with Pharaoh.

M

Soon after his return, Moses stirred the Hebrews to revolt and demanded of Pharaoh, "Let My people go, that they may hold a feast to Me in the wilderness" (Ex. 5:1). But Pharaoh rejected the demand of this unknown God of whom Moses and Aaron spoke: "Who is the LORD, that I should obey His voice to let Israel go? I do not know the LORD, nor will I let Israel go" (Ex. 5:2). He showed his contempt of this God of the Hebrews by increasing the oppression of the slaves (Ex. 5:5–14). As a result, the people grumbled against Moses (Ex. 5:20–21).

But Moses did not waver in his mission. He warned Pharaoh of the consequences that would fall on his kingdom if he should refuse to let the people of Israel go. Then followed a stubborn battle of wills with Pharaoh hardening his heart and stiffening his neck against God's commands. Ten terrible plagues were visited upon the land of Egypt (Ex. 7:14—12:30), the tenth plague being the climax of horrors.

The ultimate test of God's power to set the people free was the slaying of the firstborn of all Egypt, on the night of the Passover feast of Israel (Ex. 11:1—12:30). That night Moses began to lead the slaves to freedom, as God killed the firstborn of Egypt and spared the firstborn of Israel through the sprinkling of the blood of the Passover lamb. This pointed to the day when God's own Lamb would come into the world to deliver, by His own blood, all of those who put their trust in Him, setting them free from sin and death "but with the precious blood of Christ, as of a lamb without blemish and without spot" (1 Pet. 1:19).

After the Hebrews left, Pharaoh's forces pursued them to the Red Sea (or Sea of Reeds), threatening to destroy them before they could cross. A Pillar, however, stood between the Israelites and the Egyptians, protecting the Israelites until they could escape. When Moses stretched his hand over the sea, the waters were divided and the Israelites passed to the other side. When the Egyptians attempted to follow, Moses again stretched his hand over the sea, and the waters closed over the Egyptian army (Ex. 14:19–31).

The Forty Years in the Wilderness.

Moses led the people toward Mount Sinai, in obedience to the word of God spoken to him at the burning bush (Ex. 3:1–12). During the long journey through the desert, the people began to murmur because of the trials of freedom, forgetting the terrible trials of Egyptian bondage. Through it all, Moses was patient, understanding both the harshness of the desert and the blessings of God's provision for them.

In the Wilderness of Shur the people murmured against Moses because the waters of Marah were bitter. The Lord showed Moses a tree. When Moses cast the tree into the waters, the waters were made sweet (Ex. 15:22–25). In answer to Moses' prayers, God sent bread from heaven—manna and quail to eat (Exodus 16). In the Wilderness of Sin, when they again had no water, Moses performed a miracle by striking a rock, at a place called Massah (Testing) and Meribah (Contention), and water came out of the rock (Ex. 17:1–7). When they reached the land of Midian, Moses' father-in-law Jethro came to meet them. He gave Moses sound advice on how to exercise his leadership and authority more efficiently by delegating responsibility to subordinate rulers who would judge the people in small cases (Exodus 18).

When the Israelites arrived at Mount Sinai, Moses went up onto the mountain for 40 days (Ex. 24:18). The Lord appeared in a terrific storm—"thunderings and lightnings, and a thick cloud" (Ex. 19:16). Out of this momentous encounter came the covenant between the Lord and Israel, including the Ten Commandments (Ex. 20:1–17).

In giving the Law to the Hebrew people, Moses taught the Israelites what the Lord expected of them—that they were to be a holy people separated from the pagan immorality and idolatry of their surroundings. Besides being the lawgiver, Moses was also the one through whom God presented the Tabernacle and

instructions for the holy office of the priesthood. Under God's instructions, Moses issued ordinances to cover specific situations, instituted a system of judges and hearings in civil cases, and regulated the religious and ceremonial services of worship.

When Moses delayed in coming down from Mount Sinai, the faithless people became restless. They persuaded Aaron to take their golden earrings and other articles of jewelry and to fashion a golden calf for worship. When he came down from the mountain, Moses was horrified at the idolatry and rebellion of his people. The sons of Levi were loyal to Moses, however; and he ordered them

M

to punish the rebels (Ex. 32:28). Because of his anger at the golden calf, Moses cast down the two tablets of stone with the Ten Commandments and broke them at the foot of the mountain (Ex. 32:19). After the rebellion had been put down, Moses went up onto Mount Sinai again and there received the Ten Commandments a second time (Ex. 34:1, 29).

After leaving Mount Sinai, the Israelites continued their journey toward the land of Canaan. They arrived at Kadesh Barnea, on the border of the Promised Land. From this site, Moses sent 12 spies, one from each of the 12 tribes of Israel, into Canaan to explore the land. The spies returned with glowing reports of the fruitfulness of the land. They brought back samples of its figs and pomegranates and a cluster of grapes so large that it had to be carried between two men on a pole (Num. 13:1–25). The majority of the spies, however, voted against the invasion of the land. Ten of them spoke fearfully of the huge inhabitants of Canaan (Num. 13:31–33).

The minority report, delivered by Caleb and Joshua, urged a bold and courageous policy. By trusting the Lord, they said, the Israelites would be able to attack and overcome the land (Num. 13:30). But the people lost heart and rebelled, refusing to enter Canaan and clamoring for a new leader who would take them back to Egypt (Num. 14:1–4). To punish them for their lack of faith, God condemned all of that generation, except Caleb and Joshua, to perish in the wilderness (Num. 14:26–38).

During these years of wandering in the wilderness, Moses' patience was continually tested by the murmurings, grumblings, and complaints of the people. At one point, Moses' patience reached its breaking point and he sinned against the Lord, in anger against the people. When the people again grumbled against Moses, saying they had no water, the Lord told Moses to speak to the rock and water would flow forth. Instead, Moses lifted his hand and struck the rock twice with his rod. Apparently because he disobeyed the Lord in this act, Moses was not permitted to enter the Promised Land (Num. 20:1–13). That privilege would belong to his successor, Joshua.

When Moses had led the Israelites to the borders of Canaan, his work was done. In "the Song of Moses" (Deut. 32:1–43), Moses renewed the Sinai Covenant with the survivors of the wanderings, praised God, and blessed the people, tribe by tribe (Deut. 33:1–29). Then he climbed Mount Nebo to the top of Pisgah and viewed the Promised Land from afar and died. The Hebrews never saw him again, and the circumstances of his death and burial remain shrouded in mystery (Num. 34:1–8).

After his death, Moses continued to be viewed by Israel as the servant of the Lord (Josh. 1:1–2) and as the one through whom God spoke to Israel (Josh. 1:3; 9:24; 14:2). For that reason, although it was truly the Law of God, the Law given at Mount Sinai was consistently called the Law of Moses (Josh. 1:7; 4:10). Above all, Joshua's generation remembered Moses as the man of God (Josh. 14:6).

This high regard for Moses continued throughout Israelite history. Moses was held in high esteem by Samuel (1 Sam. 12:6, 8), the writer of 1 Kings (1 Kin. 2:3), and the Jewish people who survived in the times after the Captivity (1 Chr. 6:49; 23:14).

The psalmist also remembered Moses as the man of God and as an example of a great man of prayer (Ps. 99:6). He recalled that God worked through Moses (Ps. 77:20; 103:7), realizing that the consequence of his faithfulness to God was to suffer much on behalf of God's people (Ps. 106:16, 32).

The prophets of the Old Testament also remembered Moses as the leader of God's people (Is. 63:12), as the one by whom God brought Israel out of Egypt (Mic. 6:4), and as one of the greatest of the interceders for God's people (Jer. 15:1). Malachi called the people to remember Moses' Law and to continue to be guided by it, until the Lord Himself should come to redeem them (Mal. 4:4).

Jesus showed clearly, by what He taught and by how He lived, that He viewed Moses' Law as authoritative for the people of God (Matt. 5:17–18). To the two disciples on the road to Emmaus, Jesus expounded the things concerning Himself written in the Law of Moses, the Prophets, and the other writings of the Old Testament (Luke 24:27). At the Transfiguration, Moses and Elijah appeared to Jesus and talked with Him (Matt. 17:1–4; Mark 9:2–5; Luke 9:28–33).

In his message before the Jewish Council, Stephen included a lengthy reference to how God delivered Israel by Moses and how Israel rebelled against God and against Moses' leadership (Acts 7:20–44).

The writer of the Book of Hebrews spoke in glowing terms of the faith of Moses (Heb. 11:24–29). These and other passages demonstrate how highly Moses was esteemed by various writers of the Old and New Testaments.

The New Testament, however, shows that Moses' teaching was intended only to prepare humanity for the greater teaching and work of Jesus Christ (Rom. 1:16–3:31). What Moses promised, Jesus fulfilled: "For the law was given through Moses, but grace and truth came through Jesus Christ" (John 1:17).

MOZA [MOH zuh]

The name of two men in the Old Testament:

1. A son of Ephah, of the family of Hezron and the tribe of Judah (1 Chr. 2:46).

2. A descendant of King Saul (1 Chr. 8:36–37).

MUPPIM [MUP em]

A descendant of Benjamin (Gen. 46:21), also called Shupham (Num. 26:3 Shephupham, NRSV) and Shuppim (1 Chr. 7:12, 15; Shuppites, NIV).

MUSHI [MUE shy]

A son of Merari and founder of the Mushites (Num. 3:20, 33).

N

NAAM–NYMPHAS

NAAM [NAY am] (*pleasantness*)

A descendant of Caleb, of the tribe of Judah (1 Chr. 4:15).

NAAMAH [NAY a mah] (*pleasant*)

The name of two women in the Old Testament:

1. A sister of Tubal–Cain (Gen. 4:22), one of only four women who lived before the Flood whose names have been preserved.

2. The mother of Rehoboam, king of Judah (2 Chr. 12:13).

NAAMAN [NAY a man] (*pleasant*)

The name of three or four men in the Old Testament:

1. A son of Benjamin (Gen. 46:21).

2. A son of Bela and the founder of a family, the Naamites (Num. 26:40). He may be the same person as No. 1.

3. A commander of the Syrian army who was cured of leprosy by the Lord through the prophet Elisha. Naaman was a "great and honorable man in the eyes of his master [Ben–Hadad, king of Syria] . . . but he was a leper" (2 Kin. 5:1–27). Although leprosy was a despised disease in Syria, as in Israel, those who suffered from the disease were not outcasts.

On one of Syria's frequent raids of Israel, a young Israelite girl was captured and became a servant to Naaman's wife. The girl told her mistress about the prophet Elisha, who could heal Naaman of his leprosy. Ben–Hadad sent a letter about Naaman to the king of Israel. Fearing a Syrian trick to start a war, the king of Israel had to be assured by Elisha that Naaman should indeed be sent to the prophet. To demonstrate to Naaman that it was God, not human beings, who healed, Elisha refused to appear to Naaman. Instead, he sent the commander a

message, telling him to dip himself in the Jordan River seven times.

Naaman considered such treatment an affront and angrily asked if the Syrian rivers, the Abana and the Pharpar, would not do just as well. His servants, however, persuaded him to follow Elisha's instructions. Naaman did so and was healed. In gratitude, Naaman became a worshiper of God and carried two mule-loads of Israelite earth back to Syria in order to worship the Lord "on Israelite soil," even though he lived in a heathen land.

Before he departed for Damascus, however, Naaman asked Elisha's understanding and pardon for bowing down in the temple of Rimmon when he went there with Ben–Hadad (2 Kin. 5:18). Elisha said to him, "Go in peace" (v. 19), thus allowing Naaman to serve his master, the king.

4. A son of Ehud, of the tribe of Benjamin (1 Chr. 8:7).

NAARAH [NAY a rah] (*girl*)

A wife of Ashhur, a man of the tribe of Judah (1 Chr. 4:5–6).

NAARAI [NAY a rye] (*attendant of the Lord*)

A son of Ezbai and one of David's mighty men (1 Chr. 11:37), also called Paarai the Arbite (2 Sam. 23:35).

NAASSON [nay AS on]

A form of NAHSHON.

NABAJOTH [nab ah JOHTH]

The firstborn son of Ishmael (1 Chr. 1:29), also called NEBAJOTH.

NABAL [NAY bal]

A wealthy sheepmaster of Maon and a member of the house of Caleb (1 Sam. 25:2–39). Nabal pastured his sheep near

N

the Judahite town of Carmel on the edge of the wilderness. Nabal was "harsh and evil in his doings" and was "such a scoundrel" that no one could reason with him (1 Sam. 25:3, 17).

While David was hiding from Saul, he sent ten men to Nabal to ask for food for himself and his followers. Nabal refused. David, who had protected people in the area from bands of marauding Bedouin, was so angered by Nabal's refusal that he determined to kill Nabal and every male in his household (1 Sam. 25:4–22).

Nabal's wife Abigail was "a woman of good understanding and beautiful appearance" (v. 3). She realized the danger threatening her family because of her husband's stupidity. "Then Abigail made haste and took two hundred loaves of bread, two skins of wine, five sheep already dressed, five seahs of roasted grain, one hundred clusters of raisins, and two hundred cakes of figs, and loaded them on donkeys" (1 Sam. 25:18). She took these gifts of food to David, fell to the ground, and apologized for her husband's behavior. Her quick action soothed David's anger.

When Abigail returned home, she found a great feast in progress. Oblivious to his narrow brush with death, "Nabal's heart was merry within him, for he was very drunk" (1 Sam. 25:36). Abigail waited until the next morning to tell him of the destruction and death that he almost brought upon his household. Immediately, Nabal's "heart died within him, and he became like a stone" (1 Sam. 25:37). He died about ten days later.

When David heard that Nabal was dead, he proposed to Abigail; and she later became one of his wives. She is referred to as "Abigail the Carmelitess, Nabal's widow" (1 Sam. 27:3).

What a contrast they are—Abigail with her beauty and wisdom and Nabal with his beastly behavior and foolishness. Not only did her wisdom save her life and the lives of her family; it caught the heart of David so that he provided her with his love and protection.

NABONIDUS [nab oh NIE duss] (the god Nabu is exalted)

The last king of the Neo-Babylonian, or Chaldean, Empire (556–539 B.C.). He is not mentioned in the Bible.

Nabonidus' wife Nitocris was the daughter of Nebuchadnezzar II. Their son, Belshazzar, was the king who saw the handwriting on the wall (Dan. 5:1–31). Belshazzar was co-regent with Nabonidus from the third year of Nabonidus' reign until the empire fell to the Persians in 539 B.C. During a major portion of that time, Nabonidus stayed away from the capital city of Babylon; thus little is known of his activities.

Among the Dead Sea Scrolls discovered at Qumran was a fragmentary document containing the "Prayer of Nabonidus." This document tells how Nabonidus was struck by a "dread disease of the most high God" and for seven years was "set apart from men." Apparently he was struck with a severe skin disease. Some scholars suggest that a nervous disorder, or psychological disturbance, may also have been involved. Nabonidus' mysterious illness has been compared with the madness of Nebuchadnezzar (Dan. 4:23–33).

NABOPOLASSAR [nay boh puh LASS ur] (may the god Nabu protect the son)

A king of Babylon (626–605 B.C.) who founded the Chaldean dynasty. He was the father of NEBUCHADNEZZAR II, the

Babylonian king who defeated Jerusalem and carried the Jewish people into captivity (2 Kin. 25:1-7). Nabopolassar brought Babylon to greatness by defeating the Assyrians. Nebuchadnezzar continued his father's policies by capturing other surrounding nations.

NABOTH [NAY bahth]

An Israelite of Jezreel who owned a vineyard next to the summer palace of Ahab, king of Samaria (1 Kin. 21:1). Ahab coveted this property. He wanted to turn it into a vegetable garden to furnish delicacies for his table. He offered Naboth its worth in money or a better vineyard. But Naboth refused to part with his property, explaining that it was a family inheritance to be passed on to his descendants.

Jezebel obtained the property for Ahab by bribing two men to bear false witness against Naboth and testify that he blasphemed God and the king. Because of their lies, Naboth was found guilty; and both he and his sons (2 Kin. 9:26) were stoned to death. Elijah the prophet pronounced doom upon Ahab and his house for this disgusting act of false witness (1 Kin. 21:1-29; 2 Kin. 9:21-26).

NACHOR [NAY kor]

A form of NAHOR.

NADAB [NAY dab] (liberal or willing)

The name of four men in the Old Testament:

1. A son of Aaron and Elisheba (Ex. 6:23). Nadab is always mentioned in association with ABIHU, Aaron's second son. Nadab was privileged to accompany Moses, Aaron, Abihu, and 70 elders of Israel as they ascended Mount Sinai to be near the Lord (Ex. 24:1-10). Along with his father and brothers—Abihu, Eleazar, and Ithamar—he was consecrated a priest to minister at the tabernacle (Ex. 28:1).

Later, Nadab and Abihu were guilty of offering "profane fire before the LORD" in the Wilderness of Sinai; and both died when "fire went out from the LORD and devoured them" (Lev. 10:1-2).

2. A king of Israel (about 910-909 B.C.). Nadab was the son and successor of Jeroboam I (1 Kin. 14:20; 15:25). About the only noteworthy event that happened during Nadab's reign was the siege of Gibbethon by the Israelites. During the siege, Nadab was assassinated by his successor, Baasha (1 Kin. 15:27-28).

3. A son of Shammai, of the family of Jerahmeel.

4. A Benjamite, son of Jeiel and Maacah (1 Chr. 8:30).

NAGGAI [NAG eye]

An ancestor of Jesus Christ (Luke 3:25; Nagge, KJV).

NAGGE [NAG eh]

A form of NAGGAI.

NAHAM [NAY ham] (consolation)

A chieftain of the tribe of Judah (1 Chr. 4:19).

NAHAMANI [nay huh MAY nigh] (comforter)

A leader of the tribe of Judah who returned with Zerubbabel from the Captivity (Neh. 7:7).

NAHARAI [NAY ha righ]

The armorbearer of Joab, commander-in-chief of David's army (2 Sam. 23:37; Nahari, KJV).

NAHARI [NAY ha rye]

A form of NAHARAI.

NAHASH [NAY hash] (*serpent*)

The name of two or three men in the Old Testament:

1. A king of the Ammonites who besieged Jabesh Gilead and was defeated by Saul (1 Sam. 12:12). When Nahash's men surrounded the city, the inhabitants of Jabesh Gilead sought peace (1 Sam. 11:1). Nahash refused to accept the tribute tax and threatened to put out all their right eyes. He allowed the people of Jabesh Gilead one week to appeal for help from the rest of Israel; after that they were to surrender to him. When Saul, the newly proclaimed king of Israel, heard about this, he was enraged. He quickly assembled an army and defeated the Ammonites (1 Sam. 11:4–11). The Nahash mentioned in 2 Samuel 10:2 and 1 Chronicles 19:1–2 was either this same Nahash or one of his descendants, probably a son.

2. Probably the father of Abigail and Zeruiah, David's half-sisters (2 Sam. 17:25). Some scholars feel that Nahash was a woman, one of Jesse's wives. But it is more likely that Nahash was a man whose widow married Jesse and bore him David.

3. A man of Rabbah of the Ammonites (2 Sam. 17:27), perhaps the same person as No. 1.

NAHATH [NAY hath] (*quietness*)

The name of three men in the Old Testament:

1. An Edomite clan chief (Gen. 36:17).

2. A descendant of Elkanah, of the tribe of Levi (1 Chr. 6:26). Nahath probably is the same person as Toah (1 Chr. 6:34) and Tohu (1 Sam. 1:1).

3. An overseer of Temple tithes and offerings during the reign of Hezekiah of Judah (2 Chr. 31:13).

NAHBI [NAH buy]

One of the 12 spies sent by Moses to investigate the land of Canaan (Num. 13:14).

NAHOR [NAY hor]

The name of two men in the Old Testament:

1. Father of Terah, grandfather of Abraham (Gen. 11:22–25), and an ancestor of Jesus Christ (Luke 3:34; Nachor, KJV).

2. A son of Terah and a brother of Abraham and Haran (Gen. 11:26–29). Nahor had 12 children, 8 by his wife Milcah and 4 by his concubine Reumah. One of his children was Bethuel, who became the father of Rebekah and LABAN (Gen. 28:5).

NAHSHON [NAH shun]

A son of Amminadab and a leader of the tribe of Judah during the wilderness wanderings (Num. 2:3). Nahshon was an ancestor of Boaz and of King David (Ruth 4:20–22) and, therefore, of Jesus Christ (Matt. 1:4; Luke 3:32–33; Naasson, KJV).

NAHUM [NAY hum] (*compassionate*)

The name of two men in the Bible:

1. An Old Testament prophet and author of the Book of Nahum whose prophecy pronounced God's judgment against the mighty nation of Assyria.

Very little is known about Nahum. His hometown, Elkosh in the nation of Israel (Nah. 1:1), has not been located. But he must have lived some time shortly before 612 B.C., the year when Assyria's capital city, Nineveh, was destroyed by the Babylonians. Nahum announced that the judgment of God would soon be visited upon this pagan city.

The Book of Nahum is similar to the Book of Obadiah, since both these prophecies were addressed against neighboring nations. Obadiah spoke the word of the Lord against Edom, while Nahum prophesied against Assyria. Both messages contained a word of hope for God's Covenant People, since they announced that Israel's enemies would soon be overthrown.

While little is known about Nahum the man, his prophetic writing is among the most colorful in the Old Testament. The Book of Nahum is marked by strong imagery, a sense of suspense, and vivid language, with biting puns and deadly satire. Nahum was a man who understood God's goodness, but he could also describe the terror of the Lord against His enemies.

2. An ancestor of Jesus (Luke 3:25).

NAOMI [nay OH mee] (*my joy*)

The mother-in-law of Ruth. After her husband and two sons died, Naomi returned to her home in Bethlehem, accompanied by Ruth. Naomi advised Ruth to work for a near kinsman, Boaz (Ruth 2:1), and to seek his favor. When Boaz and Ruth eventually married, they had a son, whom they named Obed. This child became the father of Jesse, the grandfather of David, and an ancestor of Jesus Christ (Ruth 4:21–22; Matt. 1:5).

NAPHISH [NAY fish]

A son of Ishmael (1 Chr. 1:31) and the founder of a clan against which the Israelite tribes east of the Jordan River were victorious (1 Chr. 5:19; Nephish, KJV).

NAPHTALI [NAF tuh lie] (*my wrestling*)

The sixth son of Jacob (Gen. 35:25). Because Jacob's wife Rachel was barren and her sister Leah had borne four sons to Jacob, Rachel was distraught. She gave her maidservant Bilhah to Jacob. Any offspring of this union were regarded as Rachel's. When Bilhah gave birth to Dan and Naphtali, Rachel was joyous. "With great wrestlings I have wrestled with my sister," she said, "and indeed I have prevailed" (Gen. 30:8). So she called his name Naphtali, which means "my wrestling."

NAPHTUHIM [naf TOO heem]

A son of Mizraim, who was one of the four sons of Ham (Gen. 10:13). Some scholars, however, believe that the name Naphtuhim describes a tribal family that settled in the Egyptian Delta or west of Egypt.

NARCISSUS [narr SIS us]

A man to whose household the apostle Paul sent greetings (Rom. 16:11). Paul does not indicate if Narcissus was a Christian. Some scholars suggest he was a prominent freedman who served as secretary to the Emperor Claudius.

NATHAN [NAY thun] (*he gave*)

The name of several men in the Old Testament:

1. A son of David and Bathsheba and an older brother of Solomon. Nathan was David's third son born in Jerusalem (2 Sam. 5:14). Six sons had been born to David earlier, while he was at Hebron. Through Nathan the line of descent passed from David to Jesus Christ (Luke 3:31).

2. A prophet during the reign of David and Solomon. Nathan told David that he would not be the one to build the Temple (1 Chr. 17:1–15). Using the parable of the "one little ewe lamb," Nathan confronted David ("You are the man!") with his double sin, the murder of Uriah the Hittite and his adultery with Bathsheba, Uriah's wife (2 Sam. 12:1–15). Nathan, as the Lord's official prophet, named Solomon Jedidiah, which means "Beloved of the Lord" (2 Sam. 12:25).

Nathan was also involved in David's arrangement of the musical services of the sanctuary (2 Chr. 29:25).

When David was near death, Nathan advised Bathsheba to tell David of the plans of David's son Adonijah to take the throne. Bathsheba related the news to David, who ordered that Solomon be proclaimed king (1 Kin. 1:8–45). Nathan apparently wrote a history of David's reign (1 Chr. 29:29) and a history of Solomon's reign (2 Chr. 9:29).

3. A man from Zobah, an Aramean, or Syrian, kingdom between Damascus and the Euphrates River (2 Sam. 23:36).

4. Father of two of Solomon's officials (1 Kin. 4:5), perhaps the same person as No. 1 or No. 2.

5. A descendant of Jerahmeel, of the tribe of Judah (1 Chr. 2:36).

6. A brother of Joel (1 Chr. 11:38) and probably the same man as No. 3.

7. A leader sent by Ezra to find Levites for the Temple (Ezra 8:15–16).

8. A son of Bani (Ezra 10:34) who divorced his pagan wife after returning from the Captivity in Babylon (Ezra 10:39), probably the same person as No. 7.

NATHAN–MELECH [NAY thun MEH leck] (*the king has given*)

A Judahite officer before whose chamber King Josiah removed the horses that previous "kings of Judah had dedicated to the sun" (2 Kin. 23:11).

NATHANAEL [nuh THAN ih el] (*God has given*)

A native of Cana in Galilee (John 21:2) who became a disciple of Jesus (John 1:45–49). Nathanael was introduced to Jesus by his friend Philip, who claimed Jesus was the MESSIAH. This claim troubled Nathanael. He knew that Nazareth, the town where Jesus grew up, was not

mentioned in the Old Testament prophecies. He considered Nazareth an insignificant town, hardly the place where one would look to find the Redeemer of Israel. "Can anything good come out of Nazareth?" he asked. Philip did not argue with him, but simply said, "Come and see." After Nathanael met Jesus, he acknowledged Him to be the Messiah, calling Him "the Son of God" and "the King of Israel" (John 1:46, 49).

Nathanael was one of those privileged to speak face to face with Jesus after His resurrection (John 21:1–14). Some scholars see Nathanael as a type, or symbol, of a true Israelite—"an Israelite indeed" (John 1:47)—who accepts Jesus as Lord and Savior by faith.

Many scholars believe Nathanael is the same person as BARTHOLOMEW (Matt. 10:3), one of the twelve apostles of Christ.

NEARIAH [nee uh RYE uh] (*attendant of the Lord*)

The name of two men in the Old Testament:

1. A son of Shemaiah (1 Chr. 3:22–23).

2. A son of Ishi, of the tribe of Simeon, who lived in the days of King Hezekiah of Judah (1 Chr. 4:42).

NEBAI [NEE buy]

A leader of the people who sealed the covenant after the Captivity (Neh. 10:19).

NEBAJOTH [neh BAY yoth]

Ishmael's firstborn son (1 Chr. 1:29; Nebaioth, KJV, NRSV, NIV, NASB) and ancestor of an Arabian tribe named after him (Is. 60:7).

NEBAT [NEE bat]

The father of Jeroboam I (1 Kin. 11:26), first king of the northern kingdom of Israel.

NEBO [NEE boe]

The ancestor of seven Israelites who divorced their pagan wives after the Captivity (Ezra 10:43).

NEBUCHADNEZZAR [neb you kad NEZ ur] (*O god Nabu, protect my son*)

The king of the Neo-Babylonian Empire (ruled 605–562 B.C.) who captured Jerusalem, destroyed the Temple, and carried the people of Judah into captivity in Babylonia. He plays a prominent role in the books of Jeremiah (21—52) and Daniel (1:1—5:18) and also appears in 2 Kings (24:1—25:22), Ezra (1:7—6:5), and Ezekiel (26:7—30:10).

Nebuchadnezzar II was the oldest son of NABOPOLASSAR, the founder of the Neo-Babylonian, or Chaldean, dynasty of Babylon. Nabopolassar apparently was a general appointed by the Assyrian king. But in the later years of Assyria he rebelled and established himself as king of Babylon in 626 B.C. Nebuchadnezzar succeeded his father as king in 605 B.C., continuing his policies of conquest of surrounding nations.

In about 602 B.C., after being Nebuchadnezzar's vassal for three years, King Jehoiakim of the nation of Judah rebelled against the Babylonians. Nebuchadnezzar then "came up against him and bound him in bronze fetters to carry him off to Babylon" (2 Chr. 36:6). Apparently, however, Nebuchadnezzar's intention of carrying him to Babylon was abandoned; according to Jeremiah, Jehoiakim was "dragged and cast out beyond the gates of Jerusalem" and "buried with the burial of a donkey" (Jer. 22:19). After reigning for 11 years, Jehoiakim was succeeded by his son Jehoiachin.

Jehoiachin was only eight years old when he became king, and he reigned in Jerusalem about three months (2 Chr. 36:9). At that time Nebuchadnezzar took Jehoiachin captive to Babylon along with the prophet Ezekiel and "costly articles from the house of the LORD" (2 Chr. 36:10). He made Mattaniah, Jehoiachin's uncle (2 Kin. 24:17), king over Judah and Jerusalem, changing his name to Zedekiah.

For about eight years Zedekiah endured the Babylonian yoke and paid tribute to Nebuchadnezzar. In 589 B.C.,

NEBUCHADNEZZAR

however, in the ninth year of his reign, Zedekiah rebelled against the king of Babylon, perhaps trusting in the Egyptian promises of military aid. Nebuchadnezzar and his army came against Jerusalem and besieged the city for about two years (2 Kin. 25:2). The siege may have been temporarily lifted with the approach of the Egyptian army (Jer. 37:5).

In 586 B.C. Jerusalem fell to the army of Nebuchadnezzar. Under cover of darkness, Zedekiah and many of his men fled through a break in the city wall. But they were overtaken by the Chaldeans in the plains of Jericho and brought captive to Riblah, a city in the land of Hamath where Nebuchadnezzar was camped. Nebuchadnezzar ordered that the sons of Zedekiah be killed before his eyes. Then Zedekiah was bound and taken captive to Babylon, along with the leading citizens of Jerusalem (2 Kin. 25:1–7).

Nebuchadnezzar's policy of resettling conquered peoples and transporting them to other provinces of his empire provided him with slave labor for conducting his extensive building projects. He rebuilt many sanctuaries, including the temple of Nebo at Borsippa and the great temple of Marduk at Babylon. He accomplished an immense fortification of Babylon, including the building of its great wall.

Although the famous "hanging gardens" cannot be identified among the impressive ruins of Babylon, this fabulous construction project—one of the "seven wonders of the ancient world"—was built by Nebuchadnezzar on the plains of Babylon to cheer his wife, who was homesick for her native Median hills. Nebuchadnezzar also built a huge reservoir near Sippar, providing interconnecting canals in an elaborate irrigation system.

Nebuchadnezzar made an arrogant boast about all that he achieved (Dan. 4:30). But he was stricken at the height of his power and pride by God's judgment. Nebuchadnezzar was temporarily driven out of office, living with the beasts of the field and eating grass like an ox (Dan. 4:32). Later, he was succeeded as king by his son, EVIL–MERODACH.

NEBUCHADREZZAR [neb you kad REZ ur]

A form of NEBUCHADNEZZAR.

NEBUSHASBAN [neb you SHAZ ban] (*the god Nabu delivers me*)

An officer of Nebuchadnezzar, king of Babylon, at the time of the siege of Jerusalem in 586 B.C. (Jer. 39:13; Nebushazban, NIV, REB, NASB, NRSV).

NEBUSHAZBAN [neb you SHAZ ban]

A form of NEBUSHASBAN.

NEBUZARADAN [neb you zar AY dan] (*the god Nabu has given offspring*)

The captain of Nebuchadnezzar's bodyguard who played an important part in the destruction of Jerusalem in 586 B.C. An important Babylonian official, Nebuzaradan may have been second in command to Nebuchadnezzar himself. When Jerusalem fell to the Babylonians, Nebuzaradan came to the city (2 Kin. 25:1, 8) and took charge of destroying it. He commanded the troops who burned the temple, the palace, and all the houses of Jerusalem and tore down the walls of the city. He also was in charge of deporting the Israelites to Babylonia (2 Kin. 25:9–11).

After the fall of Jerusalem, Nebuchadnezzar told Nebuzaradan to take good care of the prophet Jeremiah (Jer. 39:11). Nebuzaradan showed kindness to Jeremiah and gave him the choice of remaining in Jerusalem or going to Babylon (Jer. 40:1–4).

NECHO [NEE koe]

A Pharaoh of Egypt who defeated Josiah in the Valley of Megiddo (609 B.C.). Pharaoh Necho II was himself defeated by Nebuchadnezzar, king of Babylon, in the battle of Carchemish (605 B.C.; 2 Chr. 35:20, 22). Variant spellings of this name in different passages and translations of the Bible include Neco, Necoh, and Nechoh.

NECHOH, NECO, NECOH [NEE koe]

Forms of NECHO.

NEDABIAH [ned uh BUY uh]

A descendant of David through Solomon (1 Chr. 3:18).

NEHEMIAH [knee uh MY ah] (*the Lord is consolation*)

The name of three men:

1. A clan leader who returned with Zerubbabel from the Captivity (Ezra 2:2; Neh. 7:7).

2. The governor of Jerusalem who helped rebuild the wall of the city (Neh. 1:1; 8:9; 10:1; 12:26, 47). Nehemiah was a descendant of the Jewish population that had been taken captive to Babylon in 586 B.C. In 539 B.C. Cyrus the Persian gained control over all of Mesopotamia. He permitted the Jewish exiles to return to the city of Jerusalem. Nearly a century later, in Nehemiah's time, the Persian ruler was Artaxerxes I Longimanus (ruled 465–424 B.C.). Nehemiah was his personal cupbearer (Neh. 1:11).

NEHEMIAH

N

In 445 B.C. Nehemiah learned of the deplorable condition of the returned exiles in Jerusalem (Neh. 1:2–3). The wall of the city was broken down, the gates were burned, and the people were in distress. Upon hearing this, Nehemiah mourned for many days, fasting and praying to God. His prayer is one of the most moving in the Old Testament (Neh. 1:5–11).

Nehemiah then received permission from Artaxerxes to go to Judah to restore the fortunes of his people. He was appointed governor of the province with authority to rebuild the city walls.

Once in Jerusalem, Nehemiah surveyed the walls at night (Neh. 2:12–15). He gave his assessment of the city's condition to the leaders and officials and then organized a labor force to begin the work.

Nehemiah and his work crew were harassed by three enemies: Sanballat the Horonite (a Samaritan), Tobiah the Ammonite official, and Geshem the Arab (Neh. 2:10, 19; 6:1–14). But neither their ridicule (Neh. 4:3) nor their conspiracy to harm Nehemiah (Neh. 6:2) could stop the project. The builders worked with construction tools in one hand and weapons in the other (Neh. 4:17). To the taunts of his enemies, Nehemiah replied: "I am doing a great work, so that I cannot come down" (Neh. 6:3). Jerusalem's wall was finished in 52 days (Neh. 6:14)—a marvelous accomplishment for such a great task. Nehemiah's success stems from the fact that he kept praying, "O God, strengthen my hands" (Neh. 6:9).

Nehemiah's activities did not stop with the completion of the wall. He also led many social and political reforms among the people, including a return to pure worship and a renewed emphasis on true religion.

3. A son of Azbuk and leader of half the district of Beth Zur (Neh. 3:16). After his return from the Captivity, Nehemiah helped with the repair work on the wall of Jerusalem.

NEHUM [NEE hum] (*consoled* [by God])

A leader of the Jews who returned from the Captivity with Zerubbabel (Neh. 7:7), also called Rehum (Ezra 2:2).

NEHUSHTA [nih HUSH tuh] (*serpent*)

The wife of Jehoiakim, king of Judah, and the mother of Jehoiachin, king of Judah (2 Kin. 24:8).

NEKODA [nih KOE dah] (*speckled*)

The name of two men in the Old Testament:

1. The founder of a family of Nethinim, or Temple servants (Ezra 2:48), whose descendants returned from the Captivity.

2. The founder of a family that could not prove their Israelite descent after the Captivity (Neh. 7:62).

NEMUEL [NEM you el]

The name of two men in the Old Testament:

1. A son of Eliab, of the tribe of Reuben (Num. 26:9).

2. A son of Simeon, a grandson of Jacob and Leah, and the ancestor of the Nemuelites (Num. 26:12). Nemuel is also called Jemuel (Gen. 46:10).

NEPHEG [NEE feg]

The name of two men in the Old Testament:

1. A son of Izhar, of the tribe of Levi (Ex. 6:21).

2. A son born to David in Jerusalem (2 Sam. 5:15).

NER [nur] (*light*)

Father of Abner, Saul's commander-in-chief (1 Sam. 14:50–51).

NEREUS [NEE roose]

A Roman Christian to whom the apostle Paul sent greetings (Rom. 16:15). An early tradition holds that Nereus was beheaded at Terracina about A.D. 97, probably during the reign of Nerva, emperor of Rome.

NERGAL–SAREZER, NERGAL–SHAREZER [nur GAL shah REE zur] (*Nergal, protect the king*)

A Babylonian officer who released Jeremiah from prison (Jer. 39:3, 13). Nergal-Sarezer had the title of Rabmag (Jer. 39:3, NRSV, NASB), which means a high official with military authority—a commander or general. Nergal–Sarezer has often been equated with Nergal-shar-usur, who married a daughter of Nebuchadnezzar and reigned as king of Babylon from 560–556 B.C.

NERI [NEE rye]

An ancestor of Jesus Christ (Luke 3:27).

NERIAH [nih RYE uh] (*the Lord is my lamp*)

The father of Baruch, the prophet Jeremiah's scribe (Jer. 32:12; 51:59).

NERO [NEE row]

The fifth emperor of Rome (ruled A.D. 54–68), known for his persecution of Christians. Nero began his reign with the promise that he would return to the poli-

NERO

NERO! I SWEAR ONE OF THESE DAYS YOU'RE GOING TO BURN THIS WHOLE HOUSE DOWN!!

Huyes

cies of the great emperor Augustus. For several years he succeeded, thanks mainly to the guidance of Burrus and Seneca, two of his advisors. Under his reign Rome extended its borders, solidified certain territories of the Roman Empire, and incorporated some good qualities of Greek culture.

Nero had considerable artistic interests. He wanted to change the image of Rome from a violent society to one that was more humane. The Romans, however, despised his love for the Greek way of life. His extravagance, coupled with poor management, brought on heavy taxation, depreciation of the Roman currency, and the confiscation of large landholdings by the state.

Nero's personal life was filled with tragedy. His mother, Agrippina, and Octavia, his legal wife, were murdered. Many of his advisors and officials were either killed or exiled. Tension became so great that by A.D. 68, after several attempted conspiracies, the Praetorian guard revolted and Nero was forced to flee Rome. In that same year, at the age of 30, he took his own life.

Many of Nero's cruelties are linked to the time of the great fire in Rome (A.D. 64). Nero was accused of setting fire to the city in order to divert attention from himself, but this has never been proven with certainty. The Christians, however, were made the scapegoats for this arson. Many of them, possibly even Peter and Paul, lost their lives.

Nero became a kind of apocalyptic figure, a person associated with the end times. Rumors persisted that he was alive and would some day return and reign again. Some interpreters of Scripture believe that Nero is the beast from the sea whose "deadly wound was healed" (Rev. 13:3, 12). Some Bible students have found in the mysterious number 666 (Rev.

13:18), when decoded, the name Nero Caesar. Possible references to Nero in the New Testament include Acts 25:11–12; 26:32; and Philippians 4:22.

NETHANEAL [neh THAN e al] (*God has given*)

The name of two men in the Book of Nehemiah:

1. A priest in the days of the high priest Joiakim (Neh. 12:21; Nethaneel, KJV; Nethanel, NIV).

2. A musician who blew a trumpet when the walls of Jerusalem were dedicated after the Captivity (Neh. 12:35–36; Nethaneel, KJV; Nethanel, NIV).

NETHANEEL [neh THAN ih el] (*God has given*)

The name of six men in the Old Testament (Nethanel, NIV):

1. A chief of the tribe of Issachar and one of the ten spies sent to explore the land of Canaan (Num. 2:5).

2. A priest who blew the trumpet when the Ark of the Covenant was brought to Jerusalem from the house of Obed–Edom (1 Chr. 15:24).

3. The father of Shemaiah (1 Chr. 24:6).

4. A prince of Judah sent by Jehoshaphat to teach the people of Judah (2 Chr. 17:7).

5. A chief Levite during the reign of Josiah of Judah (2 Chr. 35:9).

6. A son of Pashhur who divorced his pagan wife after the Captivity (Ezra 10:19, 22). Also see NETHANEAL; NETHANEL.

NETHANEL [neh THAN el] (*God has given*)

The name of two men in the Old Testament:

1. The fourth son of Jesse (1 Chr. 2:14–15; Nethaneel, KJV).

2. A son of Obed–Edom (1 Chr. 26:1, 4; Nethaneel, KJV). David appointed Nethanel a gatekeeper of the tabernacle.

NETHANIAH [neth uh NUY uh] (*the Lord has given*)

The name of four men in the Old Testament:

1. A son of Elishama, of the royal family of David (2 Kin. 25:25).

2. A leader of the fifth division of musicians and singers in the sanctuary during David's reign (1 Chr. 25:2, 12).

3. A Levite sent by King Jehoshaphat to teach the Law in the cities of Judah (2 Chr. 17:8–9).

4. Father of Jehudi (Jer. 36:14).

NEZIAH [nih ZIE uh]

The founder of a family of Nethinim (Temple servants) whose descendants returned to Jerusalem after the Captivity (Ezra 2:54).

NICANOR [nie KAY nor] (*victorious*)

One of seven men in the church at Jerusalem chosen to serve tables (Acts 6:5). Apparently these seven servants (or Deacons) were responsible for looking after the needs of the Greek-speaking widows, who had been neglected in the daily distribution of food.

NICODEMUS [nick oh DEE mus] (*conqueror of the people*)

A Pharisee and a member of the Sanhedrin who probably became a disciple of Jesus (John 3:1, 4, 9; 7:50). He was described by Jesus as "the teacher of Israel," implying he was well trained in Old Testament law and tradition.

Nicodemus was a wealthy, educated, and powerful man—well respected by his people and a descendant of the patriarch Abraham. Yet Jesus said to him, "You must be born again" (John 3:7). The Greek adverb translated "again" can also mean "from the beginning" (suggesting a new creation) and "from above" (that is, from God). In other words, Jesus told Nicodemus that physical generation was not enough, nor could his descent from the line of Abraham enable him to be saved. Only as a person has a spiritual generation—a birth from above—will he be able to see the kingdom of God.

The next time Nicodemus appears in the Gospel of John, he shows a cautious, guarded sympathy with Jesus. When the Sanhedrin began to denounce Jesus as a false prophet, Nicodemus counseled the court by saying, "Does our law judge a man before it hears him and knows what he is doing?" (John 7:51).

Nicodemus appears a third and final time in the Gospel of John. Obviously a wealthy man, he purchased about a hundred pounds of spices to be placed between the folds of the cloth in which Jesus was buried (John 19:39). Nothing else is known of Nicodemus from the Bible. But there is reason to believe that he became a follower of Jesus.

Christian tradition has it that Nicodemus was baptized by Peter and John, suffered persecution from hostile Jews, lost his membership in the Sanhedrin, and was forced to leave Jerusalem because of his Christian faith. Further mention is made of him in The Gospel of Nicodemus, an apocryphal narrative of the crucifixion and resurrection of Christ.

NICOLAS [NICK oh lus] (*conqueror of the people*)

One of the seven men chosen as Deacons to serve tables in the church at Jerusalem. Nicolas is called "a proselyte from Antioch" (Acts 6:3, 5; Nicolaus,

NIMROD

NRSV). This means he was a Gentile who had converted to Judaism before becoming a Christian. The church fathers accused Nicolas of denying the true Christian faith and founding the heretical sect known as the Nicolaitans (Rev. 2:6, 15).

NICOLAUS [nick uh LAY us]

A form of NICOLAS.

NIGER [NIE jur] (*black*)

The Latin surname of Simeon, one of the Christian prophets and teachers in the church of Syrian Antioch when Barnabas and Paul were called to missionary service (Acts 13:1–3). Some scholars believe he is the same person as Simon of Cyrene, who carried the cross of Christ (Matt. 27:32); but there is no evidence for this theory.

NIMROD [NIM rahd]

A son of Cush and grandson of Ham, the youngest son of Noah (Gen. 10:8–12; 1 Chr. 1:10). Nimrod was a "mighty one on the earth"—a skilled hunter-warrior who became a powerful king. He is the first mighty hero mentioned in the Bible.

The principal cities of Nimrod's Mesopotamian kingdom were "Babel, Erech, Accad, and Calneh, in the land of Shinar" (Gen. 10:10). From the land of Babylon he went to Assyria, where he built Nineveh and other cities (Gen. 10:11). In Micah 5:6 Assyria is called "the land of Nimrod."

The origin and meaning of the name Nimrod is uncertain, but it is doubtful that it is Hebrew. It may be Mesopotamian, originating from the Akkadian (northern Babylonian) god of war and hunting, Ninurta, who was called "the Arrow, the mighty hero."

Some scholars believe Nimrod was Sargon the Great, a powerful ruler over Accad who lived about 2400 B.C. Others think he was the Assyrian king Tukulti–Ninurta I (about 1246–1206 B.C.), who conquered Babylonia. However, if Nimrod was indeed a Cushite, he may have been the Egyptian monarch Amenophis III (1411–1375 B.C.).

Nimrod was more likely Assyrian. His fierce aggressiveness, seen in the combination of warlike prowess and the passion for the chase, makes him a perfect example of the warrior-kings of Assyria.

NIMSHI [NIM shy]

The grandfather of JEHU (2 Kin. 9:2, 14, 20). Jehu killed Joram, son of Ahab, and reigned as king of Israel.

NOADIAH [no uh DIE uh]

The name of a man and a woman in the Old Testament:

1. A Levite, a son of Binnui (Ezra 8:33). Noadiah was responsible for "the silver and the gold and the articles" brought back to Jerusalem from Babylon after the Captivity.

2. A prophetess who tried to hinder Nehemiah's efforts to rebuild the walls of Jerusalem (Neh. 6:14).

NOAH [NOE uh] (rest, relief)

The name of a man and a woman in the Bible:

1. A son of Lamech and the father of Shem, Ham, and Japheth. He was a hero of faith who obeyed God by building an ark (a giant boat), thus becoming God's instrument in saving mankind from total destruction by the Flood (Gen. 5:28— 9:29). The line of descent from Adam to Noah was as follows: Adam, Seth, Enosh, Cainan, Mahalaleel, Jared, Enoch, Methuselah, Lamech, and Noah (Gen. 5:1– 32). If this Genealogy does not allow for any gaps, Noah was only nine generations removed from Adam; and his father, Lamech, was 56 years old at the time of Adam's death.

Noah lived at a time when the whole earth was filled with violence and corruption. Yet Noah did not allow the evil standards of his day to rob him of fellowship with God. He stood out as the only one who "walked with God" (Gen. 6:9), as was true of his great-grandfather Enoch (Gen. 5:22). Noah was a just or righteous man (Gen. 6:9). The Lord singled out Noah from among all his contemporaries and chose him as the man to accomplish a great work.

When God saw the wickedness that prevailed in the world (Gen. 6:5), He disclosed to Noah His intention to destroy the world by a flood. He instructed Noah to build an ark in which he and his family would survive the catastrophe. Noah believed God and obeyed Him and "according to all that God commanded him, so he did" (Gen. 6:22). He is therefore listed among the heroes of faith (Heb. 11:7).

With unswerving confidence in the word of God, Noah started building the ark. For 120 years the construction continued. During this time of grace, Noah continued to preach God's judgment and mercy, warning the ungodly of their approaching doom (2 Pet. 2:5). He preached for 120 years, however, without any converts (1 Pet. 3:20). People continued in their evil ways and turned deaf ears to his pleadings and warnings until they were overtaken by the Flood.

When the ark was ready, Noah entered in with all kinds of animals "and the LORD shut him in" (Gen. 7:16), cut off completely from the rest of mankind.

Noah was grateful to the Lord who had delivered him from the Flood. After the Flood he built an altar to God (Gen. 8:20) and made a sacrifice, which was accepted graciously (Gen. 8:21). The Lord promised Noah and his descendants that He would never destroy the world again with a flood (Gen. 9:15). The Lord made an everlasting covenant with Noah and his descendants, establishing the rainbow as the sign of His promise (Gen. 9:12–17). The Lord also blessed Noah and restored the creation command, "Be fruitful and multiply, and fill the earth" (Gen. 9:1). These were the same words He had spoken earlier to Adam (Gen. 1:28).

Noah became the first tiller of the soil and keeper of vineyards after the Flood. His drunkenness is a prelude to the curse that was soon to be invoked on Canaan and his descendants, the Canaanites (Gen. 9:18–27). The Bible is silent about the rest of Noah's life after the Flood, except to say that he died at the age of 950 years (Gen. 9:28–29).

In the gospels of the New Testament, the account of Noah and the Flood is used as a symbol of the end times. Warning His hearers about the suddenness of His return, Jesus referred to the sudden catastrophe that fell upon unbelievers at the time of the Flood: "As the days of Noah were, so also will the coming of the Son of Man be" (Matt. 24:37).

2. A daughter of Zelophehad (Josh. 17:3).

NOBAH [NOE buh]

A chieftain of the tribe of Manasseh (Num. 32:42).

NOGAH [NO guh] (*brilliance*)

A son of David born in Jerusalem (1 Chr. 3:7; 14:6).

NOHAH [NO hah] (*rest*)

The fourth son of Benjamin (1 Chr. 8:2). Nohah is not mentioned among those who went with Jacob into Egypt (Gen. 46:21). He may have been born after the migration into Egypt.

NUN (*fish*)

The father of Joshua (pronounced *none*) and an Ephraimite (Ex. 33:11; Num. 27:18).

NYMPHA [NIM fah]

A form of NYMPHAS.

NYMPHAS [NIM fuhs] (*gift of the nymphs*)

A Christian at Laodicea or Colossae in whose house the Christians had met and to whom the apostle Paul sent greetings (Col. 4:15; Nympha, NASB, REB, NIV, NRSV).

O

OBADIAH–OZNI

OBADIAH [oh bah DIE ah] (*servant of the Lord*)

The name of 13 men in the Old Testament:

1. The governor of Ahab's palace (1 Kin. 18:3–7, 16).

2. A descendant of David and the head of a family (1 Chr. 3:21).

3. A son of Izrahiah, of the tribe of Issachar (1 Chr. 7:3).

4. A descendant of King Saul (1 Chr. 8:38).

5. A Levite, a son of Shemaiah (1 Chr. 9:16).

6. A Gadite captain who joined David at Ziklag (1 Chr. 12:9).

7. A leader of the tribe of Zebulun during the reign of David (1 Chr. 27:19).

8. A leader of Jehoshaphat commissioned to teach the Book of the Law (2 Chr. 17:7).

9. A Levite who supervised workmen repairing the Temple (2 Chr. 34:12).

10. A son of Jehiel, a descendant of Joab (Ezra 8:9).

11. A priest who sealed the covenant after the Captivity (Neh. 10:5).

12. A gatekeeper in Judah after the return from Captivity (Neh. 12:25).

13. A prophet of Judah (Obadiah 1). The fourth of the "minor" prophets, Obadiah's message was directed against Edom. Some scholars believe Obadiah was a contemporary of Jehoram, during whose reign (about 844 B.C.) Jerusalem was invaded by Philistines and Arabians (2 Chr. 21:16–17). Other scholars suggest a date following 586 B.C., the time of the destruction of Jerusalem by the Babylonians. Still others suggest an earlier Babylonian assault on Jerusalem, in 605 B.C.

Whatever date is assigned to Obadiah, he lived during a time of trouble for Jerusalem. His prophecy against Edom condemned the Edomites for taking sides against Jerusalem in its distress (Obadiah 15). The strongest mountain fortresses would be no defense for the Edomites against the Day—the time when God would bring His final judgment upon the world.

OBAL [OH bahl]

A son of Joktan and a descendant of Shem (Gen. 10:28), also called Ebal (1 Chr. 1:22, 40).

OBED [OH behd] (*worshiper*)

The name of five men in the Old Testament:

1. A son of Boaz and Ruth (Ruth 4:17–22; 1 Chr. 2:12) and an ancestor of Jesus (Matt. 1:5).

2. A son of Ephlal (1 Chr. 2:37–38).

3. One of David's mighty men (1 Chr. 11:47).

4. A Levite gatekeeper in the time of David (1 Chr. 26:7).

5. The father of Azariah (2 Chr. 23:1).

OBED–EDOM [OH bed EE dum] (*servant of Edom*)

The name of three or four men in the Old Testament:

1. A Gittite, possibly a Levite from Gath Rimmon, a Levitical city in Dan (2 Sam. 6:10–12; 1 Chr. 13:13–14; 15:25). Some scholars believe, however, that the word Gittite indicates he was a native of the Philistine city of Gath. If so, Obed–Edom was probably a member of David's bodyguard. David stored the Ark of the Covenant in the house of Obed–Edom for three months before moving it on to Jerusalem. During this time, Obed–Edom and all his household were blessed.

2. A Levite gatekeeper who helped transport the ark to Jerusalem (1 Chr. 15:18–24; 26:4, 8, 15).

O

3. A Levite musician who ministered before the ark when it was placed in the tabernacle (1 Chr. 16:5, 38). He may be the same person as No. 2.

4. The guardian of the sacred vessels in the Temple (2 Chr. 25:24).

OBIL [OH bill]

An Ishmaelite camel driver appointed keeper of David's royal camels (1 Chr. 27:30).

OCHRAN [OCK ran]

A form of OCRAN.

OCRAN [OCK ran]

The father of Pagiel (Num. 1:13; Ochran, KJV).

ODED [OH dead]

The name of two men in the Old Testament:

1. The father of Azariah the prophet (2 Chr. 15:1).

2. A prophet of Samaria during the reign of Pekah, king of Israel (2 Chr. 28:9). Pekah invaded Judah and defeated the army of Ahaz. Pekah then carried 200,000 captives to Samaria, the capital of the northern kingdom of Israel. As the victorious army drew near the city, Oded the prophet met them, urging a policy of mercy and forgiveness toward the Judahite captives. His request had a transforming effect on the Israelites, who fed and clothed the captives, brought them to Jericho, and gave them their freedom.

OG [ahg]

A king of the Amorites of the land of Bashan, a territory east of the Jordan River and north of the River Jabbok (Num. 21:33; 32:33). Og was king over 60 fortified cities, including Ashtaroth and Edrei. He was defeated by Moses and the Israelites (Deut. 3:6). Then his kingdom was given to the tribes of Reuben, Gad, and the half-tribe of Manasseh.

Og was the last survivor of the race of giants (Deut. 3:11). His huge iron bedstead was kept on display in Rabbah long after his death (Deut. 3:11).

OHAD [OH had]

A son of Simeon (Gen. 46:10; Ex. 6:15).

OHEL [OWE hell] (*shelter*)

A son or descendant of Zerubbabel (1 Chr. 3:20).

OHOLIAB [o HOLE ih ab]

A form of AHOLIAB.

OHOLIBAMAH [oh HOLE ih bah mah]

A form of AHOLIBAMAH.

OLYMPAS [oh LIMP us]

A Christian in Rome to whom the apostle Paul sent greetings (Rom. 16:15).

OMAR [OH mer]

A son of Eliphaz and grandson of Esau (Gen. 36:11, 15; 1 Chr. 1:36).

OMRI [UM rih]

The name of four men in the Old Testament:

1. The sixth king of the northern kingdom of Israel (885–874 B.C.). Omri is first mentioned as the commander of the army of Israel under King Elah. While Omri besieged the Philistine city of Gibbethon, another military figure, Zimri, conspired against Elah, killed him, and established himself as king. Zimri, however, had little support in Israel, and the army promptly made Omri its king. Omri returned to the capital with his army, besieged the city, and Zimri committed suicide. Tibni, the son of Ginath, continued to challenge Omri's reign; but after

four years Tibni died and Omri became the sole ruler of Israel (1 Kin. 16:21–28).

Omri was a king of vision and wisdom. From Shemer he purchased a hill on which he built a new city, Samaria, making it the new capital of Israel. Samaria was more defensible than Tirzah had been. Because it was strategically located, Omri was able to control the north-south trade routes in the region. Archaeological excavations at Samaria revealed buildings of excellent workmanship—an indication of the prosperity the city enjoyed during his reign.

The Moabite Stone tells of Omri's success against King Mesha of Moab (2 Kin. 3:4). But Omri's conflict with Syria proved to be less successful, and he was forced to grant a number of cities to the Syrians (1 Kin. 20:34).

2. A member of the tribe of Benjamin and a son of Becher (1 Chr. 7:8).

3. A member of the tribe of Judah and a son of Imri (1 Chr. 9:4).

4. The son of Michael and a prince of the tribe of Issachar during the time of David (1 Chr. 27:18).

ON [own]

A son of Peleth, of the tribe of Reuben (Num. 16:1). On joined Korah, Dathan, and Abiram in a rebellion against Moses and Aaron.

ONAM [OH namm]

The name of two men in the Old Testament:

1. A son of Shobal (1 Chr. 1:40).

2. Founder of a clan in Judah (1 Chr. 2:26, 28).

ONAN [OH nan]

The second son of Judah by the daughter of Shua the Canaanite (Gen. 38:2, 4). He was a wicked man, and the Lord put him to death (Gen. 38:10).

ONESIMUS [oh NESS ih muss] (useful)

A slave of Philemon and an inhabitant of Colossae (Col. 4:9; Philem. 10). When Onesimus fled from his master to Rome, he met the apostle Paul. Paul witnessed to him, and Onesimus became a Christian. In his letter to Philemon, Paul spoke of Onesimus as "my own heart" (Philem. 12), indicating that Onesimus had become like a son to him.

Paul convinced Onesimus to return to his master, Philemon. He also sent a letter with Onesimus, encouraging Philemon to treat Onesimus as a brother rather than a slave. Paul implied that freeing Onesimus was Philemon's Christian duty, but he stopped short of commanding him to do so. Onesimus accompanied Tychicus, who delivered the Epistle to the Colossians as well as the Epistle to Philemon.

Some scholars believe this Onesimus is Onesimus the bishop, praised in a letter to the second-century church at Ephesus from Ignatius of Antioch.

ONESIPHORUS [on ee SIF oh rus] (profitable)

A Christian from Ephesus who befriended the apostle Paul (2 Tim. 1:16–18; 4:18). Not only did Onesiphorus minister to Paul while the apostle was in Ephesus; he also ministered to Paul during his imprisonment in Rome (2 Tim. 1:17). Onesiphorus overcame any fears he had for his own safety to visit and minister to Paul in prison. Unable to repay Onesiphorus for his "mercy," Paul prayed that he might "find mercy from the Lord in that Day" (2 Tim. 1:18), referring to the Judgment Day.

OPHIR [OH fur]

A son of Joktan (Gen. 10:29; 1 Chr. 1:23). The name may possibly refer to a tribe that inhabited modern Somaliland.

OPHRAH [AHF rah]

A son of Meonothai, of the tribe of Judah (1 Chr. 4:14).

OREB [OH reb] *(raven)*

1. One of two Midianite princes defeated by Gideon and beheaded by the Ephraimites near the Jordan River (Judg. 7:25; 8:3; Ps. 83:11). Also see Zeeb.

OREN [OH ren] *(cedar)*

A son of Jerahmeel, of the tribe of Judah (1 Chr. 2:25).

ORNAN [AWR nan]

A Jebusite prince who owned a threshing floor on Mount Moriah (1 Chron 21:15). David purchased the property, where he built an altar to the Lord. Ornan was also called Araunah.

ORPAH [AWR pah]

A Moabite woman who married Chilion, one of the two sons of Elimelech and Naomi (Ruth 1:4). When Elimelech and his sons died in Moab, Orpah accompanied Naomi, her mother-in-law, part of the way to Bethlehem and then returned "to her people and to her gods" (Ruth 1:14) in Moab.

OSEE [OH zee]

Greek form of Hosea.

OSHEA [oh SHAY ah]

A form of Hoshea.

OSNAPPER [oz NAP purr]

The name for Ashurbanipal, a king of Assyria (Ezra 4:10).

OTHNI [OATH nih]

A Levite gatekeeper of the tabernacle in the days of David (1 Chr. 26:7).

OTHNIEL [OATH nih el]

The name of two men in the Old Testament:

1. The first judge of Israel (Judg. 1:13; 3:9, 11). Othniel was a son of Kenaz and probably was a nephew of Caleb. When the Israelites forgot the Lord and served the pagan gods of Canaan, the king of Mesopotamia oppressed them for eight years. When the Israelites repented of their evil and cried out to the Lord for deliverance, Othniel was raised up by the Lord to deliver His people. Othniel was one of four judges (the other three were Gideon, Jephthah, and Samson) of whom the Scripture says, "The Spirit of the LORD came upon him" (Judg. 3:10).

2. An ancestor of Heldai (1 Chr. 27:15).

OZEM [OH zim]

The name of two men in 1 Chronicles:

1. The sixth son of Jesse and a brother of David (1 Chr. 2:15).

2. A son of Jerahmeel (1 Chr. 2:25).

OZIAS [oh ZIE us]

A form of Uzziah.

OZNI [AHZ nih] *(my hearing)*

A member of the tribe of Gad and the ancestor of a tribal family, the Oznites (Num. 26:16), also called Ezbon (Gen. 46:16).

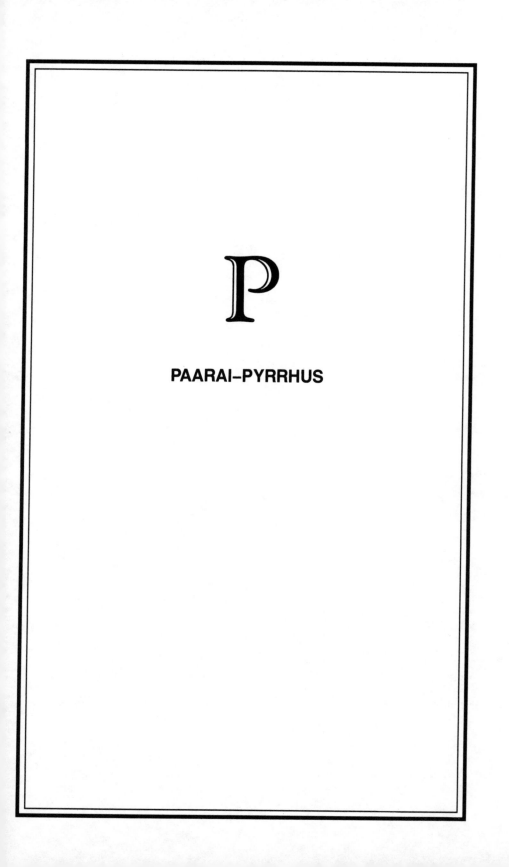

P

PAARAI–PYRRHUS

PAARAI [PAY uh righ]

One of David's mighty men (2 Sam. 23:35), also called Naarai the son of Ezbai (1 Chr. 11:37).

PAGIEL [PAY gih uhl]

Leader of the tribe of Asher during the wilderness wanderings (Num. 7:72; 10:26). Pagiel helped take the first census of Israel.

PAHATH–MOAB [PAY hath MOE ab] (governor of Moab)

The name of two men in the Old Testament:

1. The founder of a clan or family, members of which returned to Jerusalem after the Captivity. Under Zerubbabel's leadership, 2,812 members of the family returned (Ezra 2:6). Under Ezra's leadership, another company of 200 males of Pahath–Moab also returned from the Captivity (Ezra 8:4).

2. A man who sealed the covenant with Nehemiah (Neh. 10:14). Evidently he represented the entire clan of Pahath–Moab.

PALAL [PAY luhl]

A son of Uzai (Neh. 3:25). Palal helped Nehemiah repair the wall of Jerusalem after the Captivity.

PALLU [PAL oo]

Father of Eliab (Num. 26:8) and founder of the Palluites (Num. 26:5), also called Phallu (Gen. 46:9, KJV).

PALTI [PAL tigh] (my deliverance)

The name of two men in the Old Testament:

1. One of 12 men sent by Moses to spy out the land of Canaan (Num. 13:9).

2. A son of Laish, of the tribe of Benjamin (1 Sam. 25:44; Phalti, KJV; Paltiel,

NIV). Palti is the same person as PALTIEL No. 2 (2 Sam. 3:15).

PALTIEL [PAL tih uhl] (God is my deliverance)

The name of two men in the Old Testament:

1. A son of Azzan, of the tribe of Issachar (Num. 34:26). Paltiel helped Joshua divide the land west of the Jordan River.

2. A son of Laish, of the tribe of Benjamin (2 Sam. 3:15; Phaltiel, KJV).

PARMASHTA [par MASH tah]

A son of HAMAN, hanged like his father (Esth. 9:9).

PARMENAS [PAHR muh nuhs]

One of seven men chosen by the church in Jerusalem to assist the apostles in distributing food to the needy (Acts 6:5).

PARNACH [PAHR nak]

Father of Elizaphan (Num. 34:25).

PAROSH [PAHR ahsh] (flea)

The founder of a family, 2,172 of whom returned from the Captivity with Zerubbabel (Ezra 2:3; Pharosh, KJV; Neh. 7:8). Another group of this family returned from the Captivity with Ezra (Ezra 8:3).

PARSHANDATHA [pahr SHAN duh thuh]

The first of the ten sons of Haman, adviser to Ahasuerus (Xerxes), king of Persia (Esth. 9:7).

PARUAH [puh ROO uh] (blossoming)

The father of Jehoshaphat (1 Kin. 4:17).

PASACH [PAY sak]

A son of Japhlet, of the tribe of Asher (1 Chr. 7:33).

PASEAH [puh SEE uh]

The name of two or three men in the Old Testament:

1. A son of Eshton, of the tribe of Judah (1 Chr. 4:12).

2. The founder of a family of Temple servants who returned from the Captivity with Zerubbabel (Neh. 7:51; Phaseah, KJV).

3. The father of Jehoiada (Neh. 3:6). He may be the same person as No. 2.

PASHHUR [PASH ur]

The name of three or more men in the Old Testament:

1. The founder of a priestly family whose members returned from the Captivity (Ezra 2:38; Neh. 7:41). Members of this family divorced their pagan wives after the Captivity (Ezra 10:22). This Pashhur may be the Pashur of 1 Chronicles 9:12.

2. A priest who sealed the covenant after the Captivity (Neh. 10:3).

3. A son of Immer the priest (Jer. 20:1-6). Pashhur put Jeremiah in the stocks because Jeremiah's prophecies were so unfavorable.

4. A son of Melchiah and one of several officials who opposed Jeremiah because of his unpopular prophecies (Jer. 21:1; 38:1, 4).

5. The father of Gedaliah (Jer. 38:1) and a person who opposed Jeremiah. He may be the same person as No. 3 and/ or No. 4. The KJV consistently spells his name as Pashur.

PASHUR [PASH ur]

The founder of a priestly family whose descendants returned from the Captivity (1 Chr. 9:12). Pashur may be the Pashhur mentioned in Ezra 2:38 and Nehemiah 7:41.

PATHRUSIM [puh THROO zim]
(*southerners*)

The fifth son of Mizraim (1 Chr. 1:12). The term refers to the inhabitants of Pathros.

PATROBAS [PAT ruh buhs]

A Christian at Rome to whom Paul sent greetings (Rom. 16:14).

PAUL, THE APOSTLE

The earliest and most influential interpreter of Christ's message and teaching; an early Christian missionary; correspondent with several early Christian churches.

The Life of Paul.

Paul was born at Tarsus, the chief city of Cilicia (southeast Asia Minor). He was a citizen of Tarsus, "no mean city," as he called it (Acts 21:39). He was also born a Roman citizen (Acts 22:28), a privilege that worked to his advantage on several occasions during his apostolic ministry. Since Paul was born a Roman citizen, his father must have been a Roman citizen before him. "Paul" was part of his Roman name. In addition to his Roman name, he was given a Jewish name, "Saul," perhaps in memory of Israel's first king, a member of the tribe of Benjamin, to which Paul's family belonged.

His Jewish heritage meant much more to Paul than Roman citizenship. Unlike many Jews who had been scattered throughout the world, he and his family did not become assimilated to the Gentile way of life that surrounded them. This is suggested when Paul describes himself as "a Hebrew of the Hebrews" (Phil. 3:5), and confirmed by Paul's statement in Acts 22:3 that, while he was born in Tarsus, he was brought up in Jerusalem "at the feet of Gamaliel," the most illustrious rabbi of his day (Acts 5:34). Paul's parents wanted their son to be well-grounded in the best traditions of Jewish orthodoxy.

Paul proved an apt pupil. He outstripped many of his fellow students in his enthusiasm for ancestral traditions and in his zeal for the Jewish law. This zeal found a ready outlet in his assault on the infant church of Jerusalem. The church presented a threat to all that Paul held most dear. Its worst offense was its proclamation of one who had suffered a death cursed by the Jewish law as Lord and Messiah (Deut. 21:22–23). The survival of Israel demanded that the followers of Jesus be wiped out.

The first martyr of the Christian church was Stephen, one of the most outspoken leaders of the new movement. Luke told how Paul publicly associated himself with Stephen's executioners and then embarked on a campaign designed to suppress the church. Paul himself related how he "persecuted the church of God beyond measure and tried to destroy it" (Gal. 1:13).

Conversion and Apostolic Commission. At the height of Paul's campaign of repression, he was confronted on the road to Damascus by the risen Christ. In an instant his life was reoriented. The Jewish law was replaced as the central theme of Paul's life by Jesus Christ. He became the leading champion of the cause he had tried to overthrow.

The realization that Jesus, whom he had been persecuting, was alive and exalted as the Son of God exposed the weakness of the Jewish law. Paul's zeal for the law had made him an ardent persecutor. He now saw that his persecuting activity had been sinful; yet the law, instead of showing him the sinfulness of such a course, had really led him into sin.

The law had lost its validity. Paul learned that it was no longer by keeping the law that a person was justified in God's sight, but by faith in Christ. And if faith in Christ provided acceptance with God, then Gentiles might enjoy that acceptance as readily as Jews. This was one of the implications of the revelation of Jesus Christ that gripped Paul's mind. He was assured that he himself had received that revelation in order that he might proclaim Christ and His salvation to the Gentile world.

Paul began to carry out this commission not only in Damascus but also in the kingdom of the Nabatean Arabs, to the east and south. No details are given of his activity in "Arabia" (Gal. 1:17), but he did enough to attract the hostile attention of the authorities there, as the representative of the Nabatean king in Damascus tried to arrest him (2 Cor. 11:32–33).

After leaving Damascus, Paul paid a short visit to Jerusalem to make the acquaintance of Peter. During his two weeks' stay there, he also met James, the Lord's brother (Gal. 1:18–19). Paul could not stay in Jerusalem because the animosity of his former associates was too strong. He had to be taken down to Caesarea on the Mediterranean coast and put on a ship for Tarsus.

Paul spent the next ten years in and around Tarsus, actively engaged in the evangelizing of Gentiles. Very few details of those years have been preserved. At the end of that time BARNABAS came to Tarsus from Antioch and invited Paul to join him in caring for a young church there. A spontaneous campaign of Gentile evangelization had recently occurred at Antioch, resulting in the formation of a vigorous church. Barnabas himself had been commissioned by the apostles in Je-

P

rusalem to lead the Gentile evangelization in the city of Antioch.

About a year after Paul joined Barnabas in Antioch, the two men visited Jerusalem and conferred with the three "pillars" of the church there—the apostles Peter and John, and James the Lord's brother (Gal. 2:1–10). The result of this conference was an agreement that the Jerusalem leaders would concentrate on the evangelization of their fellow Jews, while Barnabas and Paul would continue to take the gospel to Gentiles.

The Jerusalem leaders reminded Barnabas and Paul, in conducting their Gentile mission, not to forget the material needs of the impoverished believers in Jerusalem. Barnabas and Paul (especially Paul) readily agreed to bear those needs in mind. This may have been the occasion when they carried a gift of money from the Christians in Antioch to Jerusalem for the relief of their fellow believers who were suffering hardship in a time of famine (Acts 11:30).

Apostle to the Gentiles. The way was now open for a wider Gentile mission. Barnabas and Paul were released by the church of Antioch to pursue a missionary campaign that took them to Barnabas' native island of Cyprus and then into the highlands of central Asia Minor (modern Turkey), to the province of Galatia. There they preached the gospel and planted churches in the cities of Pisidian Antioch, Iconium, Lystra, and Derbe. The missionaries then returned to Antioch in Syria.

The great increase of Gentile converts caused alarm among many of the Jewish Christians in Judea. They feared that too many Gentiles would hurt the character of the church. Militant Jewish nationalists were already attacking them. A movement began that required Gentile converts to become circumcised and fol-

low the Jewish law. The leaders of the Jerusalem church, with Paul and Barnabas in attendance, met in A.D. 48 to discuss the problem. It was finally decided that circumcision was not necessary, but that Gentile converts should conform to the Jewish code of laws in order to make fellowship between Jewish and Gentile Christians less strained (Acts 15:1–29).

After this meeting, Barnabas and Paul parted company. Paul chose SILAS, a leading member of the Jerusalem church and a Roman citizen like himself, to be his new colleague. Together they visited the young churches of Galatia. At Lystra they were joined by TIMOTHY, a young convert from Barnabas and Paul's visit some two years before. Paul in particular recognized qualities in Timothy that would make him a valuable helper in his missionary service. From that time to the end of Paul's life, Timothy was his most faithful attendant.

Paul and Silas probably planned to proceed west to Ephesus, but they felt the negative guidance of the Holy Spirit. They instead turned north and northwest, reaching the seaport of Troas. Here Paul was told in a vision to cross the north Aegean Sea and preach the gospel in Macedonia. This Paul and his companions did. By now their number had increased to four by the addition of Luke. The narrative reveals his presence at this point by using "we" instead of "they" (Acts 16:10).

Their first stop in Macedonia was the Roman colony of Philippi. Here, in spite of running into trouble with the magistrates and being imprisoned, Paul and his companions planted a strong church. They moved on to Thessalonica, the chief city of the province, and formed a church there, as well. But serious trouble broke out in Thessalonica. The missionaries were accused of rebelling against the Roman emperor by proclaiming Jesus as his rival. They were forced to leave the city quickly.

Paul moved south to Berea, where he was favorably received by the local synagogue, but his opponents from Thessalonica followed him, making it necessary for him to move on once more. Although churches of Macedonia would later give Paul much joy and satisfaction, he felt dejected at this time from being forced to flee city after city.

Paul, alone now, moved south into the province of Achaia. After a short stay in Athens, he came "in weakness, in fear, and in much trembling" (1 Cor. 2:3) to Corinth, the seat of provincial administration. Corinth had a reputation as a wicked city in the Greco–Roman world and it did not seem likely that the gospel would make much headway there. Surprisingly, however, Paul stayed there for 18 months and made many converts. While he was there, a new Roman proconsul, GALLIO, arrived to take up residence in Corinth. The beginning of his administration can be accurately dated as July 1, A.D. 51. Paul was prosecuted before Gallio on the charge of preaching an illegal religion, but Gallio dismissed the charge. This provided other Roman magistrates with a precedent that helped the progress of the gospel over the next ten years.

The church of Corinth was large, lively, and talented but deficient in spiritual and moral stability. This deficiency caused Paul much anxiety over the next few years, as his letters to the Corinthians reveal.

After his stay in Corinth, Paul paid a brief visit to Jerusalem and Antioch and then traveled to Ephesus, where he settled for the next three years. Paul's Ephesian ministry was perhaps the most active part of his apostolic career. A number of colleagues shared his activity and evangelized the city of Ephesus as well as the whole province of Asia (western Asia Minor).

Ten years earlier there had been no churches in the great provinces of Galatia, Asia, Macedonia, or Achaia. Now Christianity had become so strong in them that Paul realized his work in that part of the world was finished. He began to think of a new area where he might repeat the same kind of missionary program. He wanted to evangelize territories where the gospel had never been heard before, having no desire to "build on another man's foundation" (Rom. 15:20). He decided to journey to Spain, and to set out as soon as he could. This journey would also give him a long-awaited opportunity to visit Rome on the way.

Before he could set out, however, an important task had to be completed. Paul had previously organized a relief fund among the Gentile churches to help poorer members of the Jerusalem church. Not only had he promised the leaders in Jerusalem to do such a thing, but he hoped it would strengthen the bond of fellowship among all the churches involved.

Before leaving, Paul arranged for a member of each of the contributing churches to carry that church's donation. Paul himself would go to Jerusalem with them, giving the Jerusalem Christians an opportunity to see some of their Gentile brethren face to face in addition to receiving their gifts. Some of Paul's hopes and misgivings about the trip are expressed in Romans 15:25–32. His misgivings were well-founded.

A few days after his arrival in Jerusalem, Paul was attacked by a mob in the area of the Temple. He was rescued by a detachment of Roman soldiers and kept

P

in custody at the Roman governor's headquarters in Caesarea for the next two years. At the end of that period he exercised his privilege as a Roman citizen and appealed to Caesar in order to have his case transferred from the provincial governor's court in Judea to the emperor's tribunal in Rome. He was sent to Rome in the fall of A.D. 59. The great apostle spent a further two years in Rome under house arrest, waiting for his case to come up for hearing before the supreme tribunal.

Paul, the Prisoner of Jesus Christ.

The restrictions under which Paul lived in Rome should have held back his efforts to proclaim the gospel, but just the opposite actually happened. These restrictions, by his own testimony, "actually turned out for the furtherance of the gospel" (Phil. 1:12). Although he was confined to his lodgings, shackled to one of the soldiers who guarded him in four-hour shifts, he was free to receive visitors and talk to them about the gospel. The soldiers who guarded him and the officials in charge of presenting his case before the emperor were left in no doubt about the reason for his being in Rome. The gospel actually became a topic of discussion. This encouraged the Christians in Rome to bear more open witness to their faith, allowing the saving message to be proclaimed more fearlessly in Rome than ever before "and in this," said Paul, "I rejoice" (Phil. 1:18).

From Rome, Paul was able to correspond with friends in other parts of the Roman Empire. Visitors from those parts came to see him, bringing news of their churches. These visitors included EPAPHRODITUS from Philippi and EPAPHRAS from Colossae. From Colossae, too, Paul received an unexpected visitor, ONESI-MUS, the slave of his friend PHILEMON. He sent Onesimus back to his master with a letter commending him "no longer as a slave but . . . as a beloved brother" (Philem. 16).

The letters of Philippi and Colossae were sent in response to the news brought by Epaphroditus and Epaphras, respectively. At the same time as the letter to Colossae, Paul sent a letter to Laodicea and a more general letter that we now know as Ephesians. The Roman captivity became a very fruitful period for Paul and his ministry.

We have very little information about the rest of Paul's career. We do not know the outcome of his trial before Caesar. He was probably discharged and enjoyed a further period of liberty. It is not known whether he ever preached the gospel in Spain.

It is traditionally believed that Paul's condemnation and execution occurred during the persecution of Christians under the Roman Emperor NERO. The probable site of his execution may still be seen at Tre Fontane on the Ostian Road. There is no reason to doubt the place of his burial marked near the Basilica of St. Paul in Rome. There, beneath the high altar, is a stone inscription going back to at least the fourth century: "To Paul, Apostle and Martyr."

The Teaching of Paul.

Paul is the most influential teacher of Christianity. More than any other disciple or apostle, Paul was given the opportunity to set forth and explain the revelations of Jesus Christ. Because Paul was called to teach Gentiles rather than Jews, he was in the unique position of confronting and answering problems that could only be presented by those completely unfamiliar with Jewish tradi-

which the Messiah would revoke or replace the Law of Moses.

When Paul was confronted with the risen Christ on the Damascus Road, he realized that the Messiah had come and that in Him the Resurrection had begun to take place. Having been raised from the dead, Christ had now entered upon His reign. The age of the Spirit for His people on earth coincided with the reign of Christ in His place of exaltation in the presence of God. There "He must reign till He has put all enemies under His feet" (1 Cor. 15:25). The present age had not yet come to an end, because men and women, and especially the people of Christ, still lived on earth in mortal bodies. But the resurrection age had already begun, because Christ had been raised.

The people of Christ, while living temporarily in the present age, belong spiritually to the new age that has been inaugurated. The benefits of this new age are already made good to them by the Spirit. The last of the enemies that will be subdued by Christ is death. The destruction of death will coincide with the resurrection of the people of Christ. Paul wrote, "Each one in his own order: Christ the firstfruits, afterward those who are Christ's at His coming" (1 Cor. 15:23). The eternal kingdom of God will be consummated at that time.

The resurrection of the people of Christ, then, takes place at His coming again. In one of his earliest letters Paul said that, when Christ comes, "the dead in Christ will rise first. Then we who are alive and remain shall be caught up together with them in the clouds to meet the Lord in the air. And thus we shall always be with the Lord" (1 Thess. 4:16–17).

Further details are provided in 1 Corinthians 15:42–57. When the last trumpet announces the Second Coming of Christ, the dead will be raised in a "spiritual body," replacing the mortal body they wore on earth. Those believers who are still alive at the time will undergo a similar change to fit them for the new conditions. These new conditions, the eternal kingdom of God, are something that "flesh and blood cannot inherit"; they make up an imperishable realm that cannot accommodate the perishable bodies of this present life (1 Cor. 15:50).

The assurance that the faithful departed would be present at the Second Coming of Christ was a great comfort to Christians whose friends and relatives had died. But the question of their mode of existence between death and the Second Coming remained to be answered. Paul's clearest answer to this question was given shortly after a crisis in which he thought he faced certain death (2 Cor. 1:8–11).

Paul answered that to be "absent from the body" is to be "present with the Lord" (2 Cor. 5:8). Whatever provision is required for believers to enjoy the same communion with Christ after death as they enjoyed before death will certainly be supplied (2 Cor. 5:1–10). Or, as he put it when the outcome of his trial before Caesar was uncertain, "To live is Christ, and to die is gain," for to die would mean to "be with Christ, which is far better" (Phil. 1:21, 23).

The church as a whole and its members as individuals could look forward to a consummation of glory at the Second Coming of Christ. But the glory is not for them alone. In a vivid passage, Paul describes how "the creation eagerly waits for the revealing of the sons of God" (Rom. 8:19). This will liberate it from the change and decay to which it is subject at present and allow it to obtain "the glorious liberty of the children of God" (Rom. 8:21). In Genesis 3:17–19 man's first disobedience brought a curse on the earth. Paul looked forward to the removal of that curse and its replacement by the glory provided by the obedience of Christ, the "second Man" (1 Cor. 15:47).

This prospect is integrated into Paul's message, which is above all a message of reconciliation. It tells how God "reconciled us to Himself through Jesus Christ" (2 Cor. 5:18) and calls on people to "be reconciled to God" (2 Cor. 5:20). It proclaims God's purpose through Christ "to reconcile all things to Himself, . . . whether things on earth or things in heaven, having made peace through the blood of His cross" (Col. 1:20).

Paul and the Message of Jesus.

Some critics charge that Paul corrupted the original "simple" message of Jesus by transforming it into a theological structure. But the truth is completely otherwise. No one in the apostolic age had a surer insight into Jesus' message than Paul.

A shift in perspective between the ministry of Jesus and the ministry of Paul must be recognized. During His own ministry Jesus was the preacher; in the ministry of Paul He was the one being preached. The Gospels record the works and words of the earthly Jesus; in Paul's preaching Jesus, once crucified, has been exalted as the heavenly Lord. Jesus' earthly ministry was confined almost entirely to the Jewish people; Paul was preeminently the apostle to the Gentiles. Paul's Gentile hearers required that the message be presented in a different vocabulary from that which Jesus used in Galilee and Judea.

The gospel of Jesus and the gospel preached by Paul are not two gospels but one—a gospel specifically addressed to sinners. Paul, like Jesus, brought good news to outsiders. This was the assurance that in God's sight they were not outsiders, but men and women whom He lovingly accepted. In the ministry of Jesus, the outsiders were the social outcasts of Israel. In the ministry of Paul the outsiders were Gentiles. The principle was the same, although its application was different.

Paul's achievement was to communicate to the Greco–Roman world, in terms it could understand, the good news that Jesus announced in His teaching, action, and death. Paul did not have before him the gospels as we know them, but he knew the main lines of Jesus' teaching, especially parts of the Sermon on the Mount. This teaching was passed orally among the followers of Jesus before it circulated in written form. If Jesus summed up the law of God in the two great commandments of love toward God and love toward one's neighbor, Paul echoed Him: "All the law is fulfilled in one word, even in this: 'You shall love your neighbor as yourself'" (Gal. 5:14; also Rom. 13:9).

Paul's Legacy.

Paul was a controversial figure in his lifetime, even within the Christian movement. He had many opponents who disagreed with his interpretation of the message of Jesus. In the closing years of his life, when imprisonment prevented him from moving about freely, Paul's opponents were able to make headway with their rival interpretations. Even though Asia had been Paul's most fruitful mission field, at the end of his life he wrote, "All those in Asia have turned away from me" (2 Tim. 1:15).

In the following generation, however, there was a resurgence of feeling in

Paul's favor. His opponents were largely discredited and disabled by the dispersal of the church of that city shortly before the destruction of Jerusalem in A.D. 70. Throughout most of the church Paul became a venerated figure. His letters, together with the Gospels, became the foundation of the Christian movement.

Paul's liberating message has proved its vitality throughout the centuries. Repeatedly, when the Christian faith has been in danger of being shackled by legalism or tradition, Paul's message has allowed the gospel to set people free.

The relevance of Paul's teaching for human life today may be brought out in a summary of four of his leading themes:

1. True religion is not a matter of rules and regulations. God does not deal with men and women like an accountant, but He accepts them freely when they respond to His love. He implants the Spirit of Christ in their hearts so they may extend His love to others.

2. In Christ men and women have come of age. God does not keep His people on puppet strings but liberates them to live as His responsible sons and daughters.

3. People matter more than things, principles, and causes. The highest of principles and the best of causes exist only for the sake of people. Personal liberty itself is abused if it is exercised against the personal well-being of others.

4. Discrimination on the grounds of race, religion, class, or sex is an offense against God and humanity alike.

PAULUS, SERGIUS

(See SERGIUS PAULUS.)

PEDAHEL [PED uh hel] (*God delivers*)

A leader of the tribe of Naphtali who assisted Joshua in dividing the land of Canaan (Num. 34:28).

PEDAHZUR [pih DAH zur] (*the Rock delivers*)

The father of Gamaliel (Num. 1:10; 7:54).

PEDAIAH [pih DAY uh] (*the Lord delivers*)

The name of seven men in the Old Testament:

1. Father of Zebudah (2 Kin. 23:36).

2. A descendant of Jeconiah (1 Chr. 3:18–19) and the father of Zerubbabel (1 Chr. 3:19).

3. Father of Joel (1 Chr. 27:20).

4. A son of Parosh (Neh. 3:25). Pedaiah helped repair the wall of Jerusalem after the Captivity.

5. A Levite who stood with Ezra when the Book of the Law was read to the people (Neh. 8:4).

6. A son of Kolaiah, of the tribe of Benjamin (Neh. 11:7).

7. A treasurer of the Temple in Nehemiah's time (Neh. 13:13).

PEKAH [PEE kuh] ([God] *has opened the eyes*)

P

The son of Remaliah and 18th king of Israel (2 Kin. 15:25–31; 2 Chr. 28:5–15). Pekah became king after he assassinated King Pekahiah. Pekah continued to lead Israel in the idolatrous ways of Jeroboam I (2 Kin. 15:28).

Pekah took the throne at the time when Tiglath–Pileser III, king of Assyria, was advancing toward Israel. To resist this threat, Pekah formed an alliance with Rezin, king of Syria. He also hoped to enlist the sister Israelite nation of Judah in the alliance. Under the counsel of the prophet Isaiah, however, Judah's kings, Jotham and later Ahaz, refused. Pekah and Rezin attempted to enlist Judah by force, marching first against Jerusalem. They were unsuccessful, and so they divided their armies.

Rezin successfully captured Elath, and Pekah slew thousands in the districts near Jericho, taking many prisoners into Samaria. Later, these prisoners were returned to Jericho upon the advice of the prophet Oded. Pekah probably was unaware that he was God's instrument to punish Judah (2 Chr. 28:5–6).

As Tiglath–Pileser III of Assyria advanced, King Ahaz of Judah met him to pay tribute and ask his help against Syria and Israel (2 Kin. 16:10). Assyria planned to march against Syria, and so Damascus was taken and Rezin was killed. The Assyrians also invaded northern Israel, with city after city taken and their inhabitants deported to Assyria. Through the Assyrian army God brought His judgment on Israel and Syria, even as the prophet Isaiah had warned (Is. 7:8–9).

Pekah was left with a stricken nation, over half of which had been plundered and stripped of its inhabitants. Soon Hoshea, son of Elah, conspired against Pekah and assassinated him. However, in his own writings Tiglath–Pileser III claimed that he was the power that placed Hoshea on the throne of Israel, possibly indicating he was a force behind the conspiracy. Pekah's dates as king of Israel are usually given as 740–732 B.C.

PEKAHIAH [pek uh HIGH uh] (*the Lord has opened the eyes*)

A son of Menahem and the 17th king of Israel (2 Kin. 15:22–26). Pekahiah assumed the throne after his father's death. He was an evil king who continued the idolatrous worship first introduced by King Jeroboam I. After reigning only two years (about 742–740 B.C.), Pekahiah was killed by his military captain, PEKAH, and 50 Gileadites. Pekah then became king.

PELAIAH [peh LIE yuh] (*the Lord is wonderful*)

The name of two or three men in the Old Testament:

1. A son of Elioenai, descended from David through Shechaniah (1 Chr. 3:24).

2. A priest who explained the Law as Ezra read it to the people (Neh. 8:7).

3. A Levite who sealed the covenant after the Captivity (Neh. 10:10). He may be the same person as No. 2.

PELALIAH [pel uh LIGH uh] (*the Lord has intervened*)

A priest whose grandson returned from the Captivity (Neh. 11:12).

PELATIAH [pel uh TIE uh] (*the Lord has set free*)

The name of four men in the Old Testament:

1. A descendant of David (1 Chr. 3:21).

2. A captain of the Simeonites who destroyed the Amalekites who lived at Mount Seir during King Hezekiah's reign (1 Chr. 4:42).

3. A chief of the people who sealed the covenant after the Captivity (Neh. 10:22).

4. A son of Benaiah (Ezek. 11:1–13).

PELEG [PEE leg] (*division*)

A descendant of Noah through Shem and a son of Eber (Gen. 10:25). Peleg was an ancestor of Jesus (Luke 3:35; Phalec, KJV). He was named Peleg (meaning "division"), because "in his days the earth was divided" (Gen. 10:25; 1 Chr. 1:19), probably referring to the scattering of Noah's descendants as God's judgment following the attempt to build the tower of Babel (Gen. 11:8, 16–19).

PELET [PEE let] (*liberation*)

The name of two men in the Old Testament:

1. A son of Jahdai (1 Chr. 2:47).

2. A son of Azmaveth (1 Chr. 12:3).

PELETH [PEE leth]

The name of two men in the Old Testament:

1. Father of On (Num. 16:1).

2. A son of Jonathan (1 Chr. 2:33).

PENIEL [pih NIGH uhl]

A form of PENUEL.

PENINNAH [pih NIN uh] (ruby)

A wife of Elkanah (1 Sam. 1:2, 4). Peninnah taunted Hannah, Elkanah's other wife, because Peninnah had given birth to sons and daughters while Hannah had remained barren. When Hannah prayed for a child, the Lord answered her prayer by sending Samuel.

PENUEL [pih NOO uhl] (face of God)

The name of two men in the Old Testament:

1. A son of Hur and grandson of Judah (1 Chr. 4:4).

2. A son of Shashak, of the tribe of Benjamin (1 Chr. 8:25).

PERESH [PIR esh] (separate)

A son of Machir and Maachah (1 Chr. 7:16).

PEREZ [PIR ez] (breakthrough)

The firstborn of the twin sons of Judah by Tamar (Gen. 38:29; Pharez, KJV). Perez was an ancestor of David and Jesus (Ruth 4:12, 18; Matt. 1:3; Luke 3:33).

PERIDA [pih RIGH duh]

A form of PERUDA.

PERSIS [PUR sis]

A Christian at Rome who "labored much in the Lord" and to whom Paul sent greetings, calling her "beloved" (Rom. 16:12).

PERUDA [pih ROO duh]

One of Solomon's servants whose descendants returned with Zerubbabel from the Captivity (Ezra 2:55), also called Perida (Neh. 7:57).

PETER, SIMON

The most prominent of Jesus' twelve apostles. The New Testament gives a more complete picture of Peter than of any other disciple, with the exception of Paul. Peter is often considered to be a big, blundering fisherman. But this is a shallow portrayal. The picture of his personality portrayed in the New Testament is rich and many-sided. A more fitting appraisal of Peter is that he was a pioneer among the twelve apostles and the early church, breaking ground that the church would later follow.

The First Apostle to Be Called.

Peter's given name was Simeon or Simon. His father's name was Jonah (Matt. 16:17; John 1:42). Simon's brother, Andrew, also joined Jesus as a disciple (Mark 1:16). The family probably lived at Capernaum on the north shore of the Sea of Galilee (Mark 1:21, 29), although it is possible they lived in Bethsaida (John 1:44).

Peter was married, because the Gospels mention that Jesus healed his mother-in-law (Matt. 8:14–15). The apostle Paul later mentioned that Peter took his wife on his missionary travels (1 Cor. 9:5). Peter and Andrew were fishermen on the Sea of Galilee, and perhaps in partnership with James and John, the sons of Zebedee (Luke 5:10). In the midst of his labor as a fisherman, Peter received a call from Jesus that changed his life (Luke 5:8).

P

The Gospel of John reports that Andrew and Peter were disciples of John the Baptist before they joined Jesus. John also reports that Peter was introduced to Jesus by his brother Andrew, who had already recognized Jesus to be the Messiah (John 1:35–42). Whether Andrew and Peter knew Jesus because they were disciples of John is uncertain. But it is clear that they followed Jesus because of His distinctive authority.

The First Among the Apostles.

Jesus apparently gathered His followers in two stages: first as disciples (learners or apprentices), and later as apostles (commissioned representatives). Peter was the first disciple to be called (Mark 1:16–18) and the first to be named an apostle (Mark 3:14–16). His name heads every list of the Twelve in the New Testament. He was apparently the strongest individual in the band. He frequently served as a spokesman for the disciples, and he was their recognized leader (Mark 1:36; Luke 22:32). Typical of Peter's dominant personality was his readiness to walk to Jesus on the water (Matt. 14:28), and to ask Jesus the awkward question of how often he should forgive a sinning fellow believer (Matt. 18:21).

An inner circle of three apostles existed among the Twelve. Peter was also the leader of this small group. The trio—Peter, James, and John—was present with Jesus on a number of occasions. They witnessed the raising of a young girl from the dead (Mark 5:37; Luke 8:51); they were present at Jesus' transfiguration (Matt. 17:1–2); and they were present during Jesus' agony in Gethsemane (Matt. 26:37; Mark 14:33). During Jesus' final week in Jerusalem, two of the three, Peter and John, were sent to make preparations for their last meal together (Luke 22:8).

The First Apostle to Recognize Jesus as Messiah.

The purpose of Jesus' existence in the flesh was that people would come to a true picture of who God is and what He has done for our salvation. The first apostle to recognize that was Peter. He confessed Jesus as Lord in the region of Caesarea Philippi (Matt. 16:13–17).

Jesus began the process that would lead to Peter's awareness by asking a non-threatening question, "Who do men say that I, the Son of Man, am?" (Matt. 16:13). After the disciples voiced various rumors, Jesus put a more personal question to them, "But who do you say that I am?" (Matt. 16:15). Peter confessed Jesus to be the Messiah, the Son of God. According to Matthew, it was because of this confession that Jesus renamed Simon Cephas (in Aramaic) or Peter (in Greek), both meaning "rock."

Why Jesus called Simon a "rock" is not altogether clear. Peter's character was not always rock-like, as his denial of Jesus indicates. His new name probably referred to something that, by God's grace, he would become—Peter, a rock.

The First Apostle to Witness the Resurrection.

How ironic that the one who denied Jesus most vehemently in His hour of suffering should be the first person to witness His resurrection from the dead. Yet according to Luke (Luke 24:34) and Paul (1 Cor. 15:5), Peter was the first apostle to see the risen Lord. We can only marvel at the grace of God in granting such a blessing to one who did not seem to deserve it. Peter's witnessing of the resurrection was a sign of his personal restoration to fellowship with Christ. It also confirmed His appointment by God to serve as a leader in the emerging church.

The First Apostle to Proclaim Salvation to the Gentiles.

The earliest information about the early church comes from the Book of Acts. This shows clearly that Peter continued to exercise a key leadership role in the church for a number of years. Indeed, the first 11 chapters of Acts are built around the activity of the apostle Peter.

When the Holy Spirit visited the church in Samaria, the apostles sent Peter and John to verify its authenticity (Acts 8:14–25). But this event was only a prelude to the one event that concluded Peter's story in the New Testament: the preaching of the gospel to the Gentiles (Acts 10—11). The chain of events that happened before the bestowal of the Holy Spirit on Gentile believers—beginning with Peter's staying in the house of a man of "unclean" profession (Acts 9:43), continuing with his vision of "unclean" foods (Acts 10:9–16), and climaxing in his realization that no human being, Gentile included, ought to be considered "unclean" (Acts 10:34–48)—is a masterpiece of storytelling. It demonstrates the triumph of God's grace to bring about change in stubborn hearts and the hardened social customs of Jewish believers.

Following the death of James, the brother of John, and Peter's miraculous release from prison (Acts 12), Peter drops out of the narrative of Acts. Luke reports that he "went to another place" (Acts 12:17). We know, however, that Peter did not drop out of active service in the early church.

Peter probably broadened his ministry, once the mantle of leadership of the Jerusalem church fell from his shoulders to those of James. Peter played a key role at the Council of Jerusalem (Acts 15; Galatians 2), which decided in favor of granting church membership to Gentiles

PETER

NOW, THIS IS GOING ON MY RESUME!!

Hayes

P

without first requiring them to become Jews. Paul mentioned a visit of Peter to Antioch of Syria (Gal. 2:11), and he may refer to a mission of Peter to Corinth (1 Cor. 1:12). Peter dropped into the background in the Book of Acts not because his ministry ended. Luke simply began to trace the course of the gospel's spread to Gentile Rome through the ministry of Paul.

Peter in Rome: The First to Inspire the Writing of a Gospel.

According to early Christian tradition, Peter went to Rome, where he died. Only once in the New Testament do we hear of Peter's being in Rome. Even in this case, Rome is referred to as "Babylon" (1 Pet. 5:13). Little is known of Peter's activities in Rome, although Papias, writing about A.D. 125, stated that Peter's preaching inspired the writing of the first Gospel, drafted by Mark, who was Peter's interpreter in Rome. Peter was also the author of the two New Testament epistles that bear his name.

This early and generally reliable tradition supports the pioneer role played by Peter throughout his life and ministry. A number of other works—the Preaching of Peter, the Gospel of Peter, the Apocalypse of Peter, the Acts of Peter, and the Epistle of Peter to James—are apocryphal in nature. They cannot be accepted as trustworthy sources of information for the life and thought of the apostle.

Peter the First Pope?

Whether Peter was the first pope of Rome is a question that can only be answered by a study of church history. Jesus' statement to Peter in Matthew 16:18, "You are Peter, and on this rock I will build My church," does not mention papal succession. But it does emphasize Peter's prominent role in the founding of the church.

PETHAHIAH [peth ah HIGH ah] (*the Lord opens*)

The name of three or four men in the Old Testament:

1. A priest whose family was appointed by David as sanctuary priests (1 Chr. 24:16).

2. A Levite who divorced his pagan wife after the Captivity (Ezra 10:23).

3. A Levite who helped regulate the devotions of the people (Neh. 9:5). He may be the same person as No. 2.

4. An official of the Persian king for those who had returned from the Captivity (Neh. 11:24).

PETHUEL [pih THOO uhl]

Father of the prophet Joel (Joel 1:1).

PEULLETHAI [pee UHL uh thigh]

A form of PEULTHAI.

PEULTHAI [pee UHL thigh]

A gatekeeper of the tabernacle in the time of David (1 Chr. 26:5; Peullethai, NRSV, NIV, NASB).

PHALEC [FAY lek]

A form of PELEG.

PHALLU [FAL oo]

A form of PALLU.

PHALTI [FAL tigh]

A form of PALTI.

PHALTIEL [FAL tih uhl]

A form of PALTIEL.

PHANUEL [fuh NOO uhl] (*face of God*)

An Asherite and father of Anna (Luke 2:36). Anna gave thanks in the Temple for having lived long enough to see the Messiah.

PHARES, PHAREZ [FAR eez]

Forms of PEREZ.

PHAROSH [FAY rahsh]

A form of PAROSH.

PHASEAH [fuh SEE uh]

A form of PASEAH.

PHEBE [FEE bih]

A form of PHOEBE.

PHICHOL [FIGH kuhl]

The commander of the army of Abimelech who made covenants with Abraham (Gen. 21:22, 32) and Isaac (Gen. 26:26; Phicol, NASB, REB, NIV, NRSV).

PHICOL [FIGH kuhl]

A form of PHICHOL.

PHILEMON [fie LEE mun]

A wealthy Christian of Colossae who hosted a house church. Philemon was converted under the apostle Paul (Philem. 19), perhaps when Paul ministered in Ephesus (Acts 19:10). He is remembered because of his runaway slave, Onesimus, who, after damaging or stealing his master's property (Philem. 11, 18), made his way to Rome, where he was converted under Paul's ministry (Philem. 10).

Accompanied by Tychicus (Col. 4:7), Onesimus later returned to his master, Philemon. He carried with him the Epistle to the Colossians, plus the shorter Epistle to Philemon. In the latter, Paul asked Philemon to receive Onesimus, not as a slave but as a "beloved brother" (Philem. 16).

PHILETUS [fih LEE tuhs] (*beloved*)

A false teacher of the early church. Along with Hymenaeus, Philetus was condemned by the apostle Paul because he claimed the resurrection was already past (2 Tim. 2:17). Undoubtedly, Philetus advocated a Gnostic teaching that held that the body is evil and only the spirit will be saved. Because it upset the faith of some, such teaching is dangerous, Paul declared.

PHILIP [FILL ihp] (*lover of horses*)

The name of four men in the New Testament:

1. One of the twelve apostles of Christ (Matt. 10:3; Mark 3:18; Luke 6:14) and a native of Bethsaida in Galilee (John 1:44; 12:21). According to the Gospel of John, Philip met Jesus beyond the Jordan River during John the Baptist's ministry. Jesus called Philip to become His disciple. Philip responded and brought to Jesus another disciple, named Nathanael (John 1:43–51) or Bartholomew (Mark 3:18). Philip is usually mentioned with Nathanael.

Before Jesus fed the five thousand, He tested Philip by asking him how so many people could possibly be fed. Instead of responding in faith, Philip began to calculate the amount of food it would take to feed them and the cost (John 6:5–7).

When certain Greeks, who had come to Jerusalem to worship at the Feast of Passover, said to Philip, "Sir, we wish to see Jesus" (John 12:21), Philip seemed unsure of what he should do. He first told Andrew, and then they told Jesus of the request. Philip was one of the apostles who was present in the Upper Room following the resurrection of Jesus (Acts 1:13).

2. A son of Herod the Great and Mariamne; first husband of Herodias (Matt.

P

14:3; Luke 3:19). He was either the brother or half-brother of Herod Antipas. Since he is not called the tetrarch, scholars believe him to be a different Philip from Philip the tetrarch, a half-brother of Herod Antipas. Most scholars agree that this Philip was Herod Philip the first husband of Herodias. Herodias left him for Herod Antipas. He did not actually reign, but lived as a private citizen in Rome. According to the Jewish historian Josephus, although Philip was in the line of succession, he was passed over in the will of Herod the Great.

3. Philip the tetrarch, a son of Herod the Great by Cleopatra of Jerusalem. Luke 3:1 records that Philip was "tetrarch of Iturea and the region of Trachonitis" at the time when John the Baptist began his ministry. He married Salome, the daughter of Herod Philip and Herodias. According to Josephus, Philip's character was exceptional and his rule of 37 years (4 B.C.—A.D. 34) was just and fair. He improved the town of Paneas and renamed it Caesarea. It was later called Caesarea Philippi (Matt. 16:13) to avoid confusion with Caesarea on the Mediterranean Sea. He also turned the village of Bethsaida into a city and renamed it "Julias," in honor of Julia, the daughter of Augustus Caesar.

4. Philip the evangelist, one of the seven men chosen to serve the early church because they were reported to be "full of faith and the Holy Spirit" (Acts 6:5). Their task was to look after the Greek-speaking widows and probably all of the poor in the Jerusalem church. Following the stoning of Stephen, the first Christian martyr, many Christians scattered from Jerusalem (Acts 8:1). Philip became an evangelist and, in Samaria, preached the gospel, worked miracles, and brought many to faith in Christ (Acts 8:5–8).

Probably the most noted conversion as a result of Philip's ministry was the ETHIOPIAN EUNUCH, an official under Candace, the queen of the Ethiopians. Philip met the eunuch on the road from Jerusalem to Gaza. The eunuch was reading from Isaiah 53, the passage about the Suffering Servant. Philip used this great opportunity to preach Jesus to him. The eunuch said, "I believe that Jesus Christ is the Son of God" (Acts 8:37). Then Philip baptized him.

After this event, Philip preached in Azotus (the Old Testament Ashdod) and Caesarea (Acts 8:40). He was still in Caesarea many years later when the apostle Paul passed through the city on his last journey to Jerusalem (Acts 21:8). Luke adds that Philip had "four virgin daughters who prophesied" (Acts 21:9).

PHILIP HEROD

(See HEROD.)

PHILO JUDAEUS [FIE low joo DEE us]

A Jewish philosopher and teacher who is known for his allegorical interpretation of Scripture; also known as Philo of Alexandria. He was born into one of the most influential Jewish families in Alexandria, Egypt, around 20 B.C. and died in A.D. 50. Thus, he was teaching and writing during the time of Jesus. Philo was schooled in the Greek philosophers and dramatists as well as his own Jewish traditions. Most scholars agree that he was not familiar with the Hebrew Bible and did most of his work in the Greek translation known as the Septuagint.

Philo was very active in the synagogues of Alexandria and he learned from the numerous teachers and preachers who visited there. The stories and scholarly lectures he heard were incorporated into his writings. During the reign of the Roman Emperor, Gaius Caligula, Philo visited Rome to plead for the protection of the Jews of Alexandria. The persecution of Jews in Egypt made it impossible for Philo to isolate himself from diplomatic service.

Philo's writings were preserved by the Christian church. Many Jews thought his writings were suspect because they reflected Greek philosophy rather than Hebrew tradition, while the church viewed his works as close to the thoughts of the church fathers. Many Christian writers saw parallels between Philo and the Gospel of John, for example—especially in his idea of the Word, or Logos, of God being in the beginning with God (John 1:1).

Philo's writings dealt mainly with the Pentateuch and various themes within the writings of Moses. Among his many writings are *On the Creation*, which says that the creation (the laws of nature) is in harmony with the law as written in the first five books of Moses (the Pentateuch). *Allegorical Interpretation* is a comment on the first 17 chapters of Genesis. He does not deal with the text of Genesis itself so much as he uses it as a springboard to various themes from the rest of the Pentateuch. *On Dreams* is a series of sermons Philo gave in the synagogue; it is based on the dream stories in Genesis.

On the Ten Commandments is Philo's interpretation of the Ten Commandments; and *On the Special Laws* is a summary of the laws in the Pentateuch placed into the ten categories given in the Ten Commandments. Philo also wrote lives of the patriarchs, Abraham, Joseph, and Moses. These *Lives* deal with the patriarchs as models of righteous people.

PHILOLOGUS [fih LAHL uh guhs] (*talkative*)

A Christian to whom the apostle Paul sent greetings (Rom. 16:15).

PHINEHAS [FIN ih uhs] (*the Nubian*)

The name of three men in the Old Testament:

1. A son of Eleazar and grandson of Aaron (Ex. 6:25). During the wilderness wandering, Phinehas killed Zimri, a man of Israel, and Cozri, a Midianite woman whom Zimri had brought into the camp (Numbers 25). This action ended a plague by which God had judged Israel for allowing Midianite women to corrupt Israel with idolatry and harlotry. For such zeal Phinehas and his descendants were promised a permanent priesthood (Num. 25:11–13). Phinehas became the third high priest of Israel, serving for 19 years. His descendants held the high priesthood until the Romans destroyed the Temple in A.D. 70, except for a short period when the house of Eli served as high priests.

2. The younger of the two sons of Eli the priest (1 Sam. 1:3). Phinehas and his brother, Hophni, were priests also; but they disgraced their priestly office by greed, irreverence, and immorality (1 Sam. 2:12–17, 22–25). The Lord told Eli his two sons would die (1 Sam. 2:34). They were killed in a battle with the Philistines. When Phinehas' wife heard the news, she went into premature labor and died in childbirth. The child was named ICHABOD, which means "The glory has departed from Israel!" (1 Sam. 4:22). Because of the evil actions of Phinehas and Hophni, the high priesthood later passed from Eli's family.

3. The father of Eleazar (Ezra 8:33).

PHLEGON [FLEG ahn]

A Christian of Rome to whom the apostle Paul sent greetings (Rom. 16:14).

PHOEBE [FEE bih]

A servant of the church in Cenchrea, the eastern port of Corinth (Rom. 16:1; Phebe, KJV). The apostle Paul tells us little about Phoebe, other than "she has been a helper of many and of myself also" (Rom. 16:2). The Greek words he used to describe her suggest that Phoebe was a wealthy businesswoman. Many scholars believe she delivered Paul's letter to the Romans.

PHURAH [FYUR uh]

A form of PURAH.

PHUT [fuht]

A form of PUT.

PHUVAH [FOO vuh]

A form of PUVAH.

PHYGELLUS [FIGH juh luhs]

A Christian who deserted the apostle Paul in his hour of need (2 Tim. 1:15). He was probably afraid of being condemned by the Roman authorities.

PILATE, PONTIUS [PIE lat, PON chus]

The fifth Roman prefect of Judea (ruled A.D. 26–36), who issued the official order sentencing Jesus to death by crucifixion (Matthew 27; Mark 15; Luke 23; John 18—19).

Pilate's Personal Life.

The Jewish historian Josephus provides what little information is known about Pilate's life before A.D. 26, when Tiberius appointed him procurator of Judea. The sketchy data suggests that Pilate was probably an Italian-born Roman citizen whose family was wealthy enough for him to qualify for the middle class. Probably he held certain military posts before his appointment in Judea. He was married (Matt. 27:19), bringing his wife, Claudia Procula, to live with him at Caesarea, the headquarters of the province. Pilate governed the areas of Judea, Samaria, and the area south as far as the Dead Sea to Gaza. As prefect he had absolute authority over the non-Roman citizens of the province. He was responsible to the Roman governor who lived in Syria to the north (Luke 2:2).

Pilate never became popular with the Jews. He seemed to be insensitive to their religious convictions and stubborn in the pursuit of his policies. But when the Jews responded to his rule with enraged opposition, he often backed down, demonstrating his weakness. He greatly angered the Jews when he took funds from the Temple treasury to build an aqueduct to supply water to Jerusalem. Many Jews reacted violently to this act, and Pilate's soldiers killed many of them in this rebellion. It may be this or another incident to which Luke refers in Luke 13:1–2. In spite of this, Pilate continued in office for ten years, showing that Tiberius considered Pilate an effective administrator.

Pilate's later history is also shrouded in mystery. Josephus tells of a bloody encounter with the Samaritans, who filed a complaint with Pilate's superior, Vitellius, the governor of Syria. Vitellius deposed Pilate and ordered him to stand before the emperor in Rome and answer for his conduct. Legends are confused as to how Pilate died. Eusebius reports that he was exiled to the city of Vienne on the Rhone in Gaul (France) where he eventually committed suicide.

Pilate's Encounter with Jesus.

Since the Jews could not execute a person without approval from the Ro-

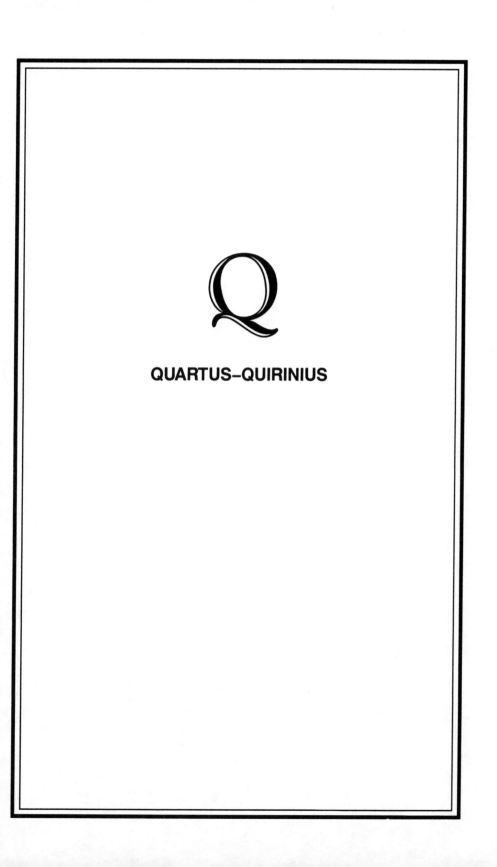

Q

QUARTUS–QUIRINIUS

QUARTUS [KWOR tus] (fourth)

A Christian who probably lived in Corinth and who sent greetings to the church in Rome (Rom. 16:23). According to early church tradition, Quartus was one of the 70 disciples whom Jesus sent out and who eventually became a bishop at Berytus.

QUEEN OF SHEBA

(See SHEBA.)

QUIRINIUS [kwy REN ih us]

Roman governor of Syria at the time of Jesus' birth (Luke 2:1–5; Cyrenius, KJV). Quirinius is mentioned in connection with a census taken for tax purposes. The census was not a local affair; the Roman emperor Augustus (ruled 31 B.C.–A.D. 14) had decreed that all the world, or the Roman Empire, should be taxed. For this purpose, Joseph and Mary made their pilgrimage to Bethlehem. While they were there, Jesus was born.

The Gospel of Luke reports that Quirinius was governor of Syria at a time when HEROD was still alive. According to historians, the governor of Syria at this time was Quintilius Varus. Quirinius may have been a military commander who shared civil duties with Varus.

Q

R

RAAMA–RUTH

RAAMA, RAAMAH [RAY uh muh]

A son of Cush (Gen. 10:7). Raama's sons were Sheba and Dedan.

RAAMIAH [ray uh MIGH uh]

A form of REELAIAH.

RABSARIS, THE [RAB suh ris] (*chief official*)

The title of two men in the Old Testament:

1. One of three officials sent from Lachish by Sennacherib, king of Assyria (2 Kin. 18:17).

2. An officer under Nebuchadnezzar, king of Babylon, and possibly the one who ordered the release of Jeremiah (Jer. 39:3, 13).

Rabsaris was a title of a high government official. The official in Nebuchadnezzar's court known as "the master of his eunuchs" (Dan. 1:3) probably held this office.

RABSHAKEH, THE [RAB shuh kuh] (*chief cupbearer*)

The title of an Assyrian military official under Sennacherib, king of Assyria (2 Kin. 18:17–37; Is. 36:2–22). The Rabshakeh accompanied the RABSARIS and the TARTAN from Lachish to Jerusalem. They presented Sennacherib's demand that Hezekiah, king of Judah, surrender the city of Jerusalem.

RACHAB [RAY kab]

A form of RAHAB.

RACHEL [RAY chuhl] (*lamb*)

The younger daughter of Laban; the second wife of Jacob; and the mother of Joseph and Benjamin.

Jacob met Rachel, the beautiful younger daughter of his uncle Laban, at a well near Haran in Mesopotamia as he fled from his brother Esau (Gen. 29:6, 11). Jacob soon asked Laban for Rachel as his wife (Gen. 29:15–18). However, it was customary in those days for the groom or his family to pay the bride's family a price for their daughter. Having no property of his own, Jacob served Laban seven years for Rachel, only to be tricked on the wedding day into marrying Rachel's older sister, Leah (Gen. 29:21–25). Jacob then had to serve another seven years for Rachel (Gen. 29:26–30).

Although Rachel was Jacob's favorite wife, she envied Leah, who had given birth to four sons—Reuben, Simeon, Levi, and Judah—while she herself had remained childless (Gen. 29:31–35). Her response was to give her handmaid Bilhah to Jacob. According to this ancient custom, the child of Bilhah and Jacob would have been regarded as Rachel's. Bilhah bore Dan and Naphtali (Gen. 30:1–8), but Rachel named them, indicating they were her children. Rachel's desperate desire to become fruitful is illustrated by her asking for Reuben's mandrakes, which she believed would bring fertility (Gen. 30:14–16). Mandrakes were considered love potions or magic charms by people of the ancient world.

Only after Zilpah, Leah's handmaid, produced two sons—Gad and Asher (Gen. 30:9–13)—and after Leah had borne two more sons and a daughter—Issachar, Zebulun, and Dinah (Gen. 30:17–21)—did Rachel finally conceive. She bore to Jacob a son named Joseph (Gen. 30:22–24), who became his father's favorite and who was sold into Egypt by his jealous brothers. Rachel died following the birth of her second son, whom she named Ben-Oni (son of my sorrow). But Jacob later renamed him Benjamin

R

(son of the right hand). Jacob buried Rachel near Ephrath (or Bethlehem) and set a pillar on her grave (Gen. 35:16–20). Jews still regard Rachel's tomb with great respect. The traditional site is about a mile north of Bethlehem and about four miles south of Jerusalem.

Although Rachel was Jacob's favorite wife, the line of David and ultimately the messianic line passed through Leah and her son Judah, not Rachel. "Rachel weeping for her children" (Jer. 31:15; Rahel, KJV; Matt. 2:18) became symbolic of the sorrow and tragedy suffered by the Israelites. Matthew points out that the murder of all the male children in Bethlehem, from two years old and under, by Herod the Great, was the fulfillment of Jeremiah's prophecy (Matt. 2:16–18).

RADDAI [RAD igh]

A son of Jesse (1 Chr. 2:14) and brother of David.

RAGAU [RAG oe]

A form of REU.

RAGUEL [RAG yoo uhl]

A form of REUEL.

RAHAB [RAY hab]

A harlot of Jericho who hid two Hebrew spies, helping them to escape, and who became an ancestor of David and Jesus (Josh. 2:1–21; 6:17–25; Matt. 1:5). Rahab's house was on the city wall of Jericho. Rahab, who manufactured and dyed linen, secretly housed the two spies whom Joshua sent to explore Jericho and helped them escape by hiding them in stalks of flax on her roof (Josh. 2:6).

Rahab sent the king's messengers on a false trail, and then let the two spies down the outside wall by a rope through the window of her house (Josh. 2:15).

When the Israelites captured Jericho, they spared the house with the scarlet cord in the window—a sign that a friend of God's people lived within. Rahab, therefore, along with her father, her mother, her brothers, and all her father's household, was spared. Apparently she and her family were later brought into the nation of Israel.

Matthew refers to Rahab as the wife of Salmon (Ruth 4:20–21; Matt. 1:4–5; Luke 3:32; Salma, 1 Chr. 2:11). Their son Boaz married Ruth and became the father of Obed, the grandfather of Jesse, and the great-grandfather of David. Thus, a Canaanite harlot became part of the lineage of King David out of which the Messiah came (Matt. 1:5; Rachab, KJV)—perhaps an early sign that God's grace and forgiveness is extended to all, that it is not limited by nationality or the nature of a person's sins.

The Scriptures do not tell us how Rahab, who came out of a culture where harlotry and idolatry were acceptable, recognized the Lord as the one true God. But her insights recorded in Joshua 2:9–11 leave no doubt that she did so. This Canaanite woman's declaration of faith led the writer of the Epistle to the Hebrews to cite Rahab as one of the heroes of faith (Heb. 11:31), while James commended her as an example of one who has been justified by works (James 2:25).

According to rabbinic tradition, Rahab was one of the four most beautiful women in the world and was the ancestor of eight prophets, including Jeremiah and the prophetess Huldah.

RAHAM [RAY ham] (*pity*)

A son of Shema, of the family of Caleb (1 Chr. 2:44).

RAHEL [RAY huhl]

A form of RACHEL.

RAKEM [RAY kem]

A descendant of Manasseh (1 Chr. 7:16).

RAM [ramm] (high, exalted)

The name of three men in the Bible:
1. The father of Amminadab of the tribe of Judah (Ruth 4:19; 1 Chr. 2:9–10). Ram was an ancestor of Jesus Christ through King David (Matt. 1:3–4; Luke 3:33; Aram, KJV).
2. The firstborn son of Jerahmeel of Judah (1 Chr. 2:25, 27). This Ram is apparently the nephew of No. 1.
3. The founder of a family or clan that included Elihu, one of the friends of Job (Job 32:2).

RAMIAH [ruh MIGH uh] (the Lord is exalted)

A son of Parosh who divorced his pagan wife after the Captivity (Ezra 10:25).

RAPHA [RAY fuh] ([God] has healed)

The name of two men in the Old Testament:
1. An ancestor of four Philistines from Gath who fell at the hands of David (2 Sam. 21:15–22).
2. The fifth son of Benjamin (1 Chr. 8:2).

RAPHAH [RAY fah] ([God] has healed)

A descendant of King Saul of the tribe of Benjamin (1 Chr. 8:37; Rapha, KJV), also called Rephaiah (1 Chr. 9:43).

RAPHU [RAY foo] (healed)

The father of Palti (Num. 13:9). Palti was one of 12 men sent by Moses into Canaan as spies.

REAIA [ree AY uh]

A form of REAIAH No. 2.

REAIAH [ree AY uh] (the Lord sees)

The name of three men in the Old Testament:
1. A son of Shobal (1 Chr. 4:2), also called Haroeh (1 Chr. 2:52).
2. A son of Micah (1 Chr. 5:5; Reaia, KJV).
3. The founder of a family of Temple servants whose descendants returned with Zerubbabel from the Captivity (Ezra 2:47; Neh. 7:50).

REBA [REE buh]

One of five Midianite kings killed by the Israelites in the plains of Moab (Num. 31:8).

REBECCA [ruh BEK uh]

A form of REBEKAH.

REBEKAH [ruh BEK uh]

The wife of Isaac and the mother of Esau and Jacob. The story of Rebekah (Genesis 24) begins when Abraham, advanced in age, instructs his chief servant to go to Mesopotamia and seek a bride for Isaac. Abraham insisted that Isaac marry a young woman from his own country and kindred, not a Canaanite.

When Abraham's servant arrived at Padan Aram, he brought his caravan to a well outside the city. At the well he asked the Lord for a sign that would let him know which young woman was to be Isaac's bride. When Rebekah came to the well carrying her water pitcher, she not only gave the servant a drink of water from her pitcher but she also offered to draw water for his camels. These actions were the signs for which the servant had prayed, and he knew that Rebekah was the young woman whom the Lord God had chosen for Isaac.

When the servant asked Rebekah her name and the name of her family, he

R

learned that she was the granddaughter of Nahor (Abraham's brother) and, therefore, was the grand-niece of Abraham. The servant then told Rebekah and her father the nature of his mission, and she chose to go to Canaan and become Isaac's wife.

When a famine struck the land of Canaan, Isaac took Rebekah to Gerar, a city of the Philistines (Gen. 26:1–11). Fearful that Rebekah's beauty would lead the Philistines to kill him and seize his wife, he told them she was his sister. Abimelech, king of the Philistines, criticized Isaac for this deception. A similar story is told of Abraham and Sarah, who were scolded for their deception by Abimelech, king of Gerar (Gen. 20:1–18).

Nor was Rebekah above deception. When the time came for Isaac to give his birthright to Esau, she conspired with Jacob and tricked Isaac into giving it to Jacob instead. Jacob was forced to flee to Padan Aram to escape Esau's wrath.

As a result of her scheming, Rebekah never again saw her son. Apparently she died while Jacob was in Mesopotamia. She was buried in the cave of Machpelah (Gen. 49:30–31), where Abraham, Isaac, Jacob, Sarah, and Leah were also buried.

Rebekah's name is spelled Rebecca in the New Testament (Rom. 9:10).

RECAB [REE kab], RECABITES [REE kab ights]

Form of RECHAB.

RECHAB [REE kab] (charioteer)

The name of three men in the Old Testament:

1. A son of Rimmon, a Benjamite from Beeroth (2 Sam. 4:2, 5, 9; Recab, NIV). Rechab and his brother Baanah were both captains in the army of Ishbosheth with whom David struggled for Israel's throne after Saul's death. While Ish-

bosheth was lying in his bed, Rechab and Baanah stabbed him and beheaded him. The next day they brought Ishbosheth's head to David, thinking he would be pleased and would reward them. Instead, "David commanded his young men, and they executed them, cut off their hands and feet, and hanged them by the pool in Hebron" (2 Sam. 4:12).

2. The father of JEHONADAB (2 Kin. 10:15, 23). Jehonadab assisted Jehu in his violent purge of the house of Ahab and zealous war against Baal worshipers. Jehonadab was the ancestor of the Rechabites (Jer. 35:1–19).

3. The father of Malchijah (Neh. 3:14). Malchijah may have been the head of the Rechabites after the Captivity. Malchijah helped Nehemiah rebuild the wall of Jerusalem.

REELAIAH [ree uh LIGH uh]

An Israelite chief who returned from the Captivity with Zerubbabel (Ezra 2:2), also called Raamiah (Neh. 7:7).

REGEM [REE guhm]

A son of Jahdai, of the tribe of Judah (1 Chr. 2:47).

REGEM-MELECH [ree guhm MEE lek]

One of a group of men sent to the Temple to ask about a day of national mourning (Zech. 7:2). They were instructed to ask the priests and prophets whether they should continue to observe fasts in remembrance of the destruction of the Temple.

REHABIAH [ree uh BIGH uh]

A son of Eliezer and grandson of Moses (1 Chr. 23:17; 26:25).

REHOB [REE hahb] (open space)

The name of two men in the Old Testament:

1. The father of Hadadezer (2 Sam. 8:3–12), king of Zobah.

2. A Levite who sealed Nehemiah's covenant (Neh. 10:11).

REHOBOAM [ree uh BOE uhm] (*the people is enlarged*)

The son and successor of Solomon and the last king of the united monarchy and first king of the southern kingdom, Judah (reigned about 931–913 B.C.). His mother was Naamah, a woman of Ammon (1 Kin. 14:31).

Rehoboam became king at age 41 (1 Kin. 14:21) at a time when the northern tribes were discontented with the monarchy. They were weary of Solomon's heavy taxation and labor conscription. To promote unity, Rehoboam went to Shechem—center of much of the discontent among the northern tribes—to be made king officially and to meet with their leaders. They in turn demanded relief from the taxes and conscription.

Rehoboam first sought advice from older men who were of mature judgment and who had lived through Solomon's harsh years. They assured him that if he would be the people's servant, he would enjoy popular support.

When he also sought the counsel of younger men, his arrogant contemporaries, he received foolish advice that he should rule by sternness rather than kindness. Misjudging the situation, he followed the foolish advice. The northern tribes immediately seceded from the kingdom and made JEROBOAM king.

When Rehoboam attempted to continue his control over the northern tribes by sending Adoram to collect a tax from the people (1 Kin. 12:18), Adoram was stoned to death. Rehoboam fled in his chariot to Jerusalem. The prophet Shemaiah prevented Rehoboam from retaliating and engaging in civil war (1 Kin. 12:22–24).

To strengthen Judah, Rehoboam fortified 15 cities (2 Chr. 11:5–12) to the west and south of Jerusalem, undoubtedly as a defensive measure against Egypt. The spiritual life of Judah was strengthened, too, by the immigration of northern priests and Levites to Judah and Jerusalem because of the idolatrous worship instituted at Bethel and Dan by Jeroboam (2 Chr. 11:13–17).

Rehoboam's military encounters were primarily with Jeroboam and Egypt. No specific battles with Jeroboam are described in the Bible, but "there was war between Rehoboam and Jeroboam all their days" (1 Kin. 14:30). This warring probably involved border disputes over the territory of Benjamin, the buffer zone between the two kingdoms.

In Rehoboam's fifth year Judah was invaded by Shishak (Sheshonk I), king of Egypt, who came against Jerusalem and carried away treasures from the Temple and from Solomon's house. When Shemaiah told him that this invasion was God's judgment for Judah's sin, Rehoboam humbled himself before God and was granted deliverance from further troubles (2 Chr. 12:1–12).

Rehoboam did not follow the pattern of David. Instead, he was an evil king (2 Chr. 12:14). During his 17-year reign, the people of Judah built "high places, sacred pillars, and wooden images" (1 Kin. 1:23) and permitted "perverted persons" to prosper in the land (1 Kin. 14:24). When he died, he was buried in the City of David (1 Kin. 14:31).

REHUM [REE huhm] (*compassion*)

The name of five men in the Old Testament:

1. A chief Israelite who returned from the Captivity with Zerubbabel (Ezra 2:2), also called Nehum (Neh. 7:7).

2. A Persian official in Samaria during the reign of Artaxerxes I (king of Persia, 465–425 B.C.). Rehum opposed the rebuilding of the walls and the Temple of Jerusalem (Ezra 4:8–9, 17, 23).

3. A leader of the Levites who helped repair the wall of Jerusalem (Neh. 3:17).

4. A leader of the people who sealed the covenant after the Captivity (Neh. 10:25).

5. A group of priests and Levites who returned with Zerubbabel from the Captivity (Neh. 12:3).

REI [ree] (*friendly*)

A man who supported Solomon when Adonijah, the son of David, tried to take over the throne (1 Kin. 1:8).

REKEM [REE kuhm]

The name of two men in the Old Testament:

1. A king of Midian killed by the Israelites during the time of Moses (Num. 31:8).

2. A son of Hebron, of the tribe of Judah (1 Chr. 2:43–44).

REMALIAH [rim uh LIE uh]

The father of King Pekah of Israel (2 Kin. 15:25–37; Is. 7:1–9).

REPHAEL [REF ay el] (*God heals*)

Gatekeeper of the sanctuary during the time of King David (1 Chr. 26:7).

REPHAH [REE fuh]

A descendant of Ephraim (1 Chr. 7:25) who became an ancestor of Joshua.

REPHAIAH [rih FAY uh] (*the Lord heals*)

The name of five men in the Old Testament:

1. The head of a family of the house of David (1 Chr. 3:21).

2. A son of Ishi, of the tribe of Simeon (1 Chr. 4:41–43).

3. A son of Tola, of the tribe of Issachar (1 Chr. 7:2).

4. A son of Binea (1 Chr. 9:43), also called Raphah (1 Chr. 8:37).

5. A son of Hur (Neh. 3:9) who helped Nehemiah rebuild the wall of Jerusalem.

RESHEPH [REE shef] (*a flame*)

A son of Beriah (1 Chr. 7:25).

REU [roo] (*friend*)

A son of Peleg and father of Serug (Gen. 11:18–21; 1 Chr. 1:25). Reu is listed in Luke's genealogy of Jesus (Luke 3:35; Ragau, KJV).

REUBEN [ROO ben] (*behold a son*)

The firstborn son of Jacob, born to Leah in Padan Aram (Gen. 29:31–32; 35:23). Leah named her first son Reuben because the Lord had looked upon her sorrow at being unloved by her husband. By presenting a son to Jacob, she hoped he would respond to her in love.

The only reference to Reuben's early childhood is his gathering of mandrakes for his mother (Gen. 30:14). Years later, as the hatred of Jacob's sons for Joseph grew, it was Reuben who advised his brothers not to kill their younger brother. He suggested that they merely bind him, which would have allowed him to return later to release Joseph to his father (Gen. 37:20–22). It also was Reuben who reminded his brothers that all their troubles and fears in Egypt were their just reward for mistreating Joseph (Gen. 42:22).

When Jacob's sons returned from Egypt, Reuben offered his own two sons as a guarantee that he would personally tend to the safety of Benjamin on the next trip to Egypt (Gen. 42:37). In view of these admirable qualities, it is tragic that he became involved in incest with Bilhah, his father's concubine (Gen. 35:22).

As the firstborn, Reuben should have been a leader to his brothers and should have received the birthright—the double portion of the inheritance (Deut. 21:17). His act of incest, however, cost him dearly. He never lost his legal standing as firstborn, but he forfeited his right to the birthright. When Reuben made his descent into Egypt with Israel, he was father of four sons who had been born to him in Canaan (Gen. 46:9).

REUEL [ROO uhl] *(friend of God)*

The name of four men in the Old Testament:

1. A son of Esau and Basemath, the daughter of Ishmael (Gen. 36:4, 10; 1 Chr. 1:35).

2. A priest of Midian who became Moses' father-in-law (Num. 10:29; Raguel, KJV). Reuel is also called Jethro (Ex. 3:1).

3. The father of Eliasaph (Num. 2:14), also called Deuel (Num. 10:20).

4. A son of Ibnijah (1 Chr. 9:8).

REUMAH [ROO muh]

A concubine of Nahor, Abraham's brother (Gen. 22:24).

REZIA [ree ZIGH uh]

A form of RIZIA.

REZIN [REE zin]

The name of two men in the Old Testament:

1. The last king of Syria. Rezin was killed by Tiglath–Pileser III, king of Assyria, in 732 B.C. Rezin allied himself with Pekah, king of Israel, to try to take away Judah's throne from Ahaz and the line of David (2 Kin. 15:37; 16:5–9). Together Rezin and Pekah besieged Jerusalem, but they were unable to capture Ahaz's stronghold. The prophet Isaiah counseled Ahaz not to fear Rezin and Pekah (Is. 7:4).

Instead of trusting the Lord, however, Ahaz panicked. He appealed for help to Tiglath–Pileser III, king of Assyria, by sending him silver and gold from the Temple and Ahaz's palace. The Assyrian king marched against Damascus and besieged it in 734 B.C. After a two-year siege, Damascus fell to the Assyrians, Rezin was killed by Tiglath–Pileser, and the Syrians were carried away as captives to Kir (2 Kin. 16:9).

2. The founder of a family of Nethinim, or Temple servants, whose descendants returned from the Captivity with Zerubbabel (Ezra 2:48).

REZON [REE zuhn]

A son of Eliadah (1 Kin. 11:23). Rezon was a subject of Hadadezer, king of Zobah; he fled from Hadadezer, perhaps at the time of his defeat by David (2 Sam. 8:3). Rezon then became captain over a band of raiders and went to Damascus, where he founded a dynasty. He opposed Israel in Solomon's time (1 Kin. 11:23–25).

RHESA [REE suh]

A son of Zerubbabel and an ancestor of Jesus (Luke 3:27).

RHODA [ROE duh] *(rose)*

A servant girl in the home of Mary, the mother of John Mark (Acts 12:13). According to tradition, this house in Jerusalem was the site of the Last Supper; it may also have been the headquarters of the early church in Jerusalem. Following his miraculous release from prison, the apostle Peter went to Mary's house.

R

Rhoda answered his knock and was filled with such surprise and joy that she forgot to let him in and ran back to tell the others. Peter had to continue knocking until someone let him in (Acts 12:16).

RIBAI [RIGH bigh]

The father of Ittai (2 Sam. 23:29) or Ithai (1 Chr. 11:31).

RIMMON [RIM uhn] (*pomegranate*)

A man from Beeroth in the territory of Benjamin. His two sons, BAANAH and RECHAB, murdered Saul's son Ishbosheth, beheaded him, and took his head to David—an act for which they were executed (2 Sam. 4:1–12).

RINNAH [RIN uh] (*a loud cry*)

A son of Shimon, of the tribe of Judah (1 Chr. 4:20).

RIPHATH [RYE fath]

A son of Gomer (Gen. 10:3). The same as Diphath (1 Chr. 1:6).

RIZIA [rih ZIGH uh]

A son of Ulla (1 Chr. 7:39; Rezia, KJV).

RIZPAH [RIZ puh]

A daughter of Aiah who became a concubine of King Saul (2 Sam. 3:7; 21:8, 10–11). She bore two sons, Armoni and Mephibosheth. After Saul's death, Abner had sexual relations with Rizpah (2 Sam. 3:7)—an act that amounted to claiming the throne of Israel. Ishbosheth (also called Esh–Baal), one of Saul's sons by another woman, accused Abner of immorality and, by implication, of disloyalty to Ishbosheth's authority. This accusation so enraged Abner that he transferred his loyalty from Saul to David.

Rizpah is a good example of the undying devotion of a mother. After the death

of her sons, she kept vigil over their bodies for several months. When David heard of this, he ordered that Saul and Jonathan's bones, still unburied, be mingled with those of Saul's sons and grandsons and that they be buried "in the country of Benjamin in Zelah, in the tomb of Kish his [Saul's] father" (2 Sam. 21:14).

ROHGAH [ROE guh]

A son of Shemer, of the tribe of Asher (1 Chr. 7:34).

ROMAMTI–EZER [roe MAM tigh EE zur] (*I have exalted help*)

A singer in the 24th division of sanctuary musicians during David's reign (1 Chr. 25:4, 31).

ROSH [rahsh] (*chief*)

A descendant of Benjamin (Gen. 46:21) and one of those who went to Egypt with Jacob and Jacob's sons.

RUFUS [ROO fuhs]

The name of two men in the New Testament:

1. A son of Simon of Cyrene (Mark 15:21). Simon was the man who was compelled by the Romans to carry the cross of Jesus (Matt. 27:32; Luke 23:26).

2. A Christian in Rome to whom Paul sent greetings (Rom. 16:13).

RUTH [rooth] (*friendship*)

The mother of Obed and great-grandmother of David. A woman of the country of Moab, Ruth married Mahlon, one of the two sons of Elimelech and Naomi. With his wife and sons, Elimelech had migrated to Moab to escape a famine in the land of Israel. When Elimelech and both of his sons died, they left three widows: Naomi, Ruth, and Orpah (Ruth's sister-in-law). When Naomi decided to re-

RUTH

turn home to Bethlehem, Ruth chose to accompany her, saying, "Wherever you go, I will go" (Ruth 1:16).

In Bethlehem, Ruth was permitted to glean in the field of Boaz, a wealthy kinsman of Elimelech (Ruth 2:1). At Naomi's urging, Ruth asked protection of Boaz as next of kin—a reflection of the Hebrew law of Levirate Marriage (Deut. 25:5–10). After a nearer kinsman waived his right

to buy the family property and provide Elimelech an heir, Boaz married Ruth. Their son, Obed, was considered one of Naomi's family, according to the custom of the day.

Ruth's firm decision—"Your people shall be my people, and your God, my God" (Ruth 1:16)—brought a rich reward. She became an ancestor of David and Jesus (Matt. 1:5).

R

S

SABTA–SYRO-PHOENICIAN

SABTA, SABTAH [SAB tuh]

The third son of Cush and grandson of Ham (Gen. 10:7, Sabtah; 1 Chr. 1:9, Sabta). Sabta's descendants lived in Arabia, perhaps along the southwestern coast of the Red Sea.

SABTECA [SAB tuh kuh]

A form of SABTECHA.

SABTECHA [SAB tuh kuh]

The youngest son of Cush and grandson of Ham (Gen. 10:7, Sabtechah; 1 Chr. 1:9, Sabteca, NIV, NASB, NRSV).

SACAR [SAY kahr] *(reward)*

The name of two men in the Old Testament:
1. The father of Ahiam (1 Chr. 11:35; Sachar, NRSV). Sacar is also called Sharar (2 Sam. 23:33).
2. A son of Obed–Edom (1 Chr. 26:4).

SACHAR [SAY kahr]

A form of SACAR.

SACHIA [suh KIGH uh]

A form of SACHIAH.

SACHIAH [suh KIGH uh]

A descendant of Benjamin (1 Chr. 8:10; Sachia, NRSV, NASB; Sakia, NIV; Shachia, KJV, REB).

SADOC [SAY dahk]

A form of ZADOK.

SAKIA [suh KIGH uh]

A form of SACHIAH.

SALA [SAY luh]

A form of SHELAH.

SALAH [SAY luh] *(a sprout)*

A son of Arphaxad (Gen. 10:24). A grandson of Shem, Salah was the father of Eber and an ancestor of Christ. He is also called Shelah (1 Chr. 1:18, 24; Luke 3:35) and Sala (Luke 3:35, KJV).

SALATHIEL [suh LAY thih uhl]

A form of SHEALTIEL.

SALLAI [SAL eye]

The name of two men in the Old Testament:
1. A leading Benjamite who lived in Jerusalem after the Captivity (Neh. 11:8).
2. A priest who returned to Jerusalem with Zerubbabel after the Captivity (Neh. 12:20). He is also called Sallu (Neh. 12:7).

SALLU [SAL oo]

The name of two men in the Old Testament:
1. A chief of a family living at Jerusalem after the Captivity (Neh. 11:7).
2. A chief priest who came to Jerusalem with Zerubbabel after the Captivity (Neh. 12:7). He is also called Sallai (Neh. 12:20).

SALMA [SAL muh]

The name of two men in the Old Testament:
1. The father of Boaz and an ancestor of Jesus (1 Chr. 2:11). Salma is also called Salmon (Ruth 4:20–21; Matt. 1:4–5) and Sala (Luke 3:32, NRSV).
2. A son of Hur, of the family of Caleb (1 Chr. 2:51).

SALMAI [SAL migh]

A Temple servant whose descendants returned to Jerusalem after the Captivity (Neh. 7:48). Salmai is also called Shalmai (Ezra 2:46) and Shamlai (Ezra 2:46, REB, NRSV).

SALMON [SAL muhn] (*peaceable*)

The father of Boaz and an ancestor of Jesus (Ruth 4:20–21; Matt. 1:4–5). He is also called Salma (1 Chr. 2:11) and Sala (Luke 3:32, NRSV).

SALOME [suh LOE mee] (*peace*)

The name of two women in the New Testament:

1. The daughter of HERODIAS by her first husband Herod Philip, a son of Herod the Great. The New Testament identifies her only as Herodias' daughter (Matt. 14:6–11; Mark 6:22–28). At the birthday celebration of Herod Antipas, who was now living with Herodias, Salome danced before the king and pleased him greatly. He offered to give her anything she wanted. At her mother's urging, Salome asked for John the Baptist's head on a platter. Salome later married her uncle Philip, tetrarch of Trachonitis (Luke 3:1), and then her cousin Aristobulus.

2. One of the women who witnessed the crucifixion of Jesus and who later brought spices to the tomb to anoint His body (Mark 15:40; 16:1). Salome apparently was the mother of James and John, two of the disciples of Jesus. She is pictured in the Gospel of Matthew as asking special favors for her sons (Matt. 20:20–24). Jesus replied that Salome did not understand what kind of sacrifice would be required of her sons.

SALU [SAY loo]

A Simeonite and the father of Zimri (Num. 25:14).

SAMGAR–NEBO [SAM gahr NEE boe]

A Babylonian prince, an officer of King Nebuchadnezzar, who participated in the siege (588–586 B.C.) and capture of Jerusalem (Jer. 39:3). He took his seat with other nobles in the Middle Gate of Jerusalem after the Chaldean army had taken the city.

SAMLAH [SAM luh]

The fifth of the ancient kings of Edom (Gen. 36:36–37).

SAMSON [SAM suhn] (*sunny*)

A hero of Israel known for his great physical strength as well as his moral weakness. The last of the "judges," or military leaders, mentioned in the Book of Judges, Samson led his country in this capacity for about 20 years.

Samson lived in a dark period of Israelite history. After the generation of Joshua died out, the people of Israel fell into a lawless and faithless life. The author of the Book of Judges summarized these times by declaring, "There was no king in Israel; everyone did what was right in his own eyes" (Judg. 17:6; 21:25). The standard of God's Word, His Law as handed down by Moses, was ignored.

Samson was a product of that age, but his parents gave evidence of faith in the Lord. During a time when the Philistines were oppressing the Israelites (Judg. 13:1), the Lord announced to Manoah and his wife that they would bear a son who would be raised as a Nazirite (Judg. 13:5, 7). This meant that Samson should serve as an example to Israel of commitment to God. Through most of his life, however, Samson fell far short of this mark.

Samson's mighty physical feats are well-known. With his bare hands he killed a young lion that attacked him (Judg. 14:5–6). He gathered 300 foxes (jackals; Judg. 15:4, REB) and tied them together, then sent them through the grain fields with torches in their tails to destroy the crops of the Philistines.

On one occasion, he broke the ropes with which the enemy had bound him (Judg. 15:14). He killed a thousand Philistine soldiers with the jawbone of a donkey (Judg. 15:15). And, finally, he carried away the massive gate of Gaza, a city of the Philistines, when they thought they had him trapped behind the city walls (Judg. 16:3).

But in spite of his great physical strength Samson was a foolish man. He took vengeance on those who used devious means to discover the answer to one of his riddles (Judg. 14). When deceived by his enemies, his only thought was for revenge, as when his father-in-law gave away his wife to another man (Judg. 15:6–7). He had not learned the word of the Lord, "Vengeance is mine" (Deut. 32:35).

Samson's life was marred by his weakness for pagan women. As soon as he became of age, he fell in love with one of the daughters of the Philistines. He insisted on marrying her, in spite of his parents' objection (Judg. 14:1–4).

This was against God's law, which forbade intermarriage of the Israelites among the women of Canaan. On another occasion he was almost captured by the Philistines while he was visiting a prostitute in the city of Gaza.

Samson eventually became involved with DELILAH, a woman from the Valley of Sorek (Judg. 16:4), who proved to be his undoing (Judges 16). The Philistines bribed her to find out the key to his strength. She teased him until he finally revealed that the secret was his uncut hair, allowed to grow long in accord with

SAMSON

S

the Nazirite law. While Samson slept, she called the Philistines to cut his hair and turned him over to his enemies. Samson became weak, not only because his hair had been cut but also because the Lord had departed from him (Judg. 16:20).

After his enslavement by the Philistines, Samson was blinded and forced to work at grinding grain. Eventually he came to his senses and realized that God had given him his great strength to serve the Lord and his people. After a prayer to God for strength, he killed thousands of the enemy by pulling down the pillars of the temple of Dagon (Judg. 16:28–31). That one great act of faith cost Samson his life, but it won for him a place among the heroes of faith (Heb. 11:32). Out of weakness he was made strong by the power of the Lord (Heb. 11:34).

Samson was a person with great potential who fell short because of his sin and disobedience. Mighty in physical strength, he was weak in resisting temptation. His life is a clear warning against the dangers of self-indulgence and lack of discipline.

SAMUEL [SAM yoo uhl] (name of God)

The earliest of the great Hebrew prophets (after Moses) and the last judge of Israel. Samuel led his people against their Philistine oppressors. When he was an old man, Samuel anointed Saul as the first king of Israel and later anointed David as Saul's successor. Samuel is recognized as one of the greatest leaders of Israel (Jer. 15:1; Heb. 11:32).

Samuel's birth reveals the great faith of his mother, HANNAH (1 Sam. 1:2–22; 2:1). Unable to bear children, she prayed earnestly for the Lord to give her a child. She vowed that if the Lord would give her a son she would raise him as a Nazirite (1 Sam. 1:11) and dedicate him to the

Lord's service. Eventually, Samuel was born as an answer to Hannah's prayer.

Hannah made good on her promise to dedicate her son to the Lord's service. At a very early age, Samuel went to live with Eli the priest, who taught the boy the various duties of the priesthood. Here Samuel heard the voice of God, calling him to special service as a priest and prophet in Israel (1 Sam. 3:1–20). After Eli's death, Samuel became the judge of Israel in a ceremony at Mizpah (1 Samuel 7). This event was almost turned to disaster by an attack from the Philistines, but the Lord intervened with a storm that routed the enemies and established Samuel as God's man. The godly Samuel erected a memorial stone, which he called "Ebenezer," meaning "Stone of Help." "Thus far the LORD has helped us," he declared (1 Sam. 7:12).

In the early part of his ministry, Samuel served as a traveling judge. With his home in Ramah, he made a yearly circuit to Bethel, Gilgal, and Mizpah. In the person of Samuel, judges became more than military leaders called upon for dramatic leadership in times of national crises. Samuel became a judge with a permanent leadership office, an office approaching that of a king.

When the people clamored for a king like those of the surrounding nations (1 Sam. 8:5), Samuel was reluctant to grant their request. He took this as a rejection of his long years of godly service on behalf of the people. He also was aware of the evils that went along with the establishment of a royal house. But the Lord helped Samuel to see the real issue: "Heed the voice of the people in all that they say to you; for they have not rejected you, but they have rejected Me, that I should not reign over them" (1 Sam. 8:7).

The person whom Samuel anointed as first king of Israel turned out to be a poor choice. Saul was handsome, likeable, and tall. But he had a tragic flaw that led ultimately to his own ruin. He disobeyed God by taking spoils in a battle rather than wiping out all living things, as God had commanded (1 Sam. 15:18–26). Saul's false pride and extreme jealousy toward David also led him into some serious errors of judgment.

When God rejected Saul as king, He used Samuel to announce the prophetic words (1 Sam. 15:10–35). Samuel was faithful in presenting the stern words of rejection. Although he had no further dealings with Saul, Samuel mourned for him and for the death of the dream (1 Sam. 15:35). Samuel was then sent by the Lord to Bethlehem, to the house of Jesse, where he anointed the young man David as the rightful king over His people (1 Sam. 16:1–13).

In addition to his work as judge, prophet, and priest, Samuel is also known as the traditional author of the Books of First and Second Samuel. He may have written much of the material contained in 1 Samuel during the early years of Saul's reign. After Samuel's death (1 Sam. 25:1), these books were completed by an unknown writer, perhaps Abiathar, the priest who served during David's administration.

When Samuel died, he was buried in his hometown of Ramah and was mourned by the nation (1 Sam. 25:1; 28:3). But he had one more message to give. After Samuel's death, Saul visited a fortune teller at En Dor (1 Samuel 28). This fortune teller gave Saul a message that came from the spirit of Samuel: "The LORD has departed from you and has become your enemy" (1 Sam. 28:16). Even from the grave Samuel still spoke the word of God!

In many ways Samuel points forward to the person of the Savior, the Lord Jesus Christ. In the story of Samuel's birth, the direct hand of the Lord can be seen. In his ministry as judge, prophet, and priest, Samuel anticipates the ministry of the Lord as well as the work of his forerunner, John the Baptist. As Samuel marked out David as God's man, so John the Baptist pointed out Jesus as the Savior.

SANBALLAT [san BAL uht] (*the god Sin has given life*)

A leading opponent of the Jews after their return from the Captivity; he tried to hinder Nehemiah in his work of rebuilding the walls of Jerusalem (Neh. 2:10, 19–20; 4:1–23; 6:1–19; 13:28).

Sanballat's designation as the Horonite probably indicates the town of his origin, possibly Horonaim of Moab (Is. 15:5; Jer. 48:3, 5, 34) or Beth Horon in Ephraim near Jerusalem (2 Chr. 8:5). In papyri found at the Jewish settlement in Elephantine, Egypt, Sanballat is called the governor of Samaria. His daughter married "one of the sons of Joiada, the son of Eliashib the high priest" (Neh. 13:28). Nehemiah viewed such a "mixed marriage" as a defilement of the priesthood, so he drove Joiada away.

Sanballat's opposition to Nehemiah's work may have stemmed from jealousy. He may have felt that his authority was threatened by the reawakening of the land of Judah. After mocking Nehemiah and his crew, he tried to slip through the broken wall of Jerusalem with people from other enemy nations to kill the Jews. Nehemiah thwarted this plot, setting up guards from half the people while the other half worked (Neh. 4:7–23). Neither did he fall for Sanballat's ploy to come outside the wall for a "friendly" discussion (Neh. 6:3).

S

In spite of Sanballat's open opposition and trickery, Nehemiah carried out the task he felt called by God to accomplish. After the wall was completed, he reported that even the enemies of the project realized "this work was done by our God" (Neh. 6:16).

SAPH [saf]

A Philistine giant killed by one of David's mighty men (2 Sam. 21:18), also called Sippai (1 Chr. 20:4).

SAPPHIRA [suh FIGH ruh]

A dishonest woman who, along with her husband Ananias, held back goods from the early Christian community after they had agreed to share everything. Because of their hypocrisy and deceit, they were struck dead by God (Acts 5:1–11). This may seem like a severe punishment for such an offense. But it points out the need for absolute honesty in all our dealings with God.

SARAH, SARAI [SAR uh, SAR eye]
(noble lady)

The name of two women in the Bible:
1. The wife of ABRAHAM, and the mother of ISAAC. Sarah's name was originally Sarai, but it was changed to Sarah by God, much as her husband's name was changed from Abram to Abraham. Ten years younger than Abraham, Sarah was his half-sister; they had the same father but different mothers (Gen. 20:12).

Sarah was about 65 years old when she and Abraham left Haran (Gen. 12:5; 17:7). Passing through Egypt, Abraham introduced Sarah as his sister, apparently to keep himself from being killed by those who would be attracted by Sarah's beauty (Gen. 12:10–20; also see 20:1–18).

In spite of God's promise to Abraham that he would become the father of a chosen nation, Sarah remained barren. When she was 75, she decided that the only way to realize God's promise was to present to Abraham her Egyptian maidservant, HAGAR, by whom he could father a child. Hagar bore a son named ISHMAEL (Gen. 16:1–16).

When Sarah was 90 years old, far beyond her childbearing years, she gave birth to a son, Isaac—the child of promise (Gen. 21:1–7). After Isaac was born, Sarah caught Ishmael mocking the young child and, with God's approval, sent both Ishmael and Hagar into the wilderness.

At the age of 127, Sarah died at Kirjath Arba (Hebron) and was buried by Abraham in the cave of Machpelah (Gen. 23:1–20). Sarah is the only woman in the Bible whose age was recorded at death—a sign of her great importance to the early Hebrews. The prophet Isaiah declared Abraham and Sarah as the father and mother of the Hebrew people: "Look to Abraham your father, and to Sarah who bore you" (Is. 51:2).

In the New Testament the apostle Paul pointed out that "the deadness of Sarah's womb" (Rom. 4:19) did not cause Abraham to waver in his faith; he believed the promise of God (Rom. 9:9). The apostle Peter cited Sarah as an example of the holy women who trusted in God, possessed inward spiritual beauty, and were submissive to their husbands (1 Pet. 3:5–6). The writer of the Epistle to the Hebrews also includes Sarah as one of the spiritual heroines in his roll call of the faithful (Heb. 11:11).

2. A daughter of Asher (Num. 26:46, KJV; Serah, NKJV, NIV).

SARAPH [SAR if]

A descendant of the tribe of Judah. At one time Saraph ruled in Moab (1 Chr. 4:22).

campaign of Sargon II in 711 B.C., King Hezekiah of Judah (reigned 716–687 B.C.) had been asked to join the rebellion against the Assyrians, but he refused. During the reign of Sennacherib, Hezekiah went against the wise counsel of the prophet Isaiah and joined a coalition against Assyria led by Tyre and Egypt.

Sennacherib began his western military campaign in 701 B.C., when Tyre and Sidon refused to pay tribute to Assyria. He marched down the Phoenician coast and captured Sidon and many other cities. The cities that refused to submit were destroyed. After the Assyrians defeated the Egyptians, they laid siege to Lachish, which, along with Jerusalem, was one of the best fortified cities in Judah. The account of his campaign in Judah is found in 2 Kings 18:13—19:37 and

Isaiah 36—37. After a cruel siege, Lachish fell. Sennacherib sacked 46 towns and villages in Judah, taking away thousands of prisoners and much spoil. Hezekiah refused Sennacherib's demand to surrender Jerusalem (2 Kin. 18:17; Is. 36:1–21), but he did agree to pay 300 talents of silver and 30 talents of gold in tribute.

The siege of Jerusalem proved unsuccessful for two reasons: (1) Hezekiah protected his water supplies (2 Kin. 20:20) and (2) Hezekiah steadfastly trusted in God rather than in material and military support from his allies (2 Kin. 19:32–34).

Although Sennacherib, in his description of the siege of Jerusalem, boasts of shutting up Hezekiah "like a bird in a cage," he makes no reference to the

S

outcome of the siege—evidence that his campaign failed. The Bible narrates what happened in dramatic words: "And it came to pass on a certain night that the angel of the LORD went out, and killed in the camp of the Assyrians one hundred and eighty-five thousand; and when people arose early in the morning, there were the corpses—all dead" (2 Kin. 19:35).

The ancient Greek historian Herodotus tells of a similar incident, although he sets the scene in Egypt: "Thousands of fieldmice swarmed over them during the night, and ate their quivers, their bowstrings, and the leather handles of their shields, so that on the following day, having no arms to fight with, they abandoned their position and suffered severe losses during their retreat."

The "fieldmice" mentioned by Herodotus may have been plague-carrying rodents, instruments of the Lord's judgment. An army of mice bearing the "Black Death" (the bubonic plague) would have been more than a match for the mighty Assyrian army.

After the destruction of his army, Sennacherib returned to Nineveh. While worshiping in the temple of his god Nisroch, he was assassinated by his sons Adrammelech and Sharezer. He was succeeded by Esarhaddon, another son (2 Kin. 19:36–37; Is. 37:37–38).

SENUAH [suh NOO uh]

A Benjamite whose son Judah was second in command in Jerusalem after the Captivity (Neh. 11:9; Hassenuah, NASB, REB, NIV, NRSV). Also see SENAAH.

SEORIM [see OHR im]

A priest in the fourth division of priests in the sanctuary at Jerusalem in David's time (1 Chr. 24:8).

SERAH [SEE ruh]

A granddaughter of Jacob by Zilpah, the handmaid of Jacob's wife Leah (Gen. 46:17; 1 Chr. 7:30). Serah was a daughter of Asher (Num. 26:46; Sarah, KJV). With her four brothers she went into Egypt with Jacob.

SERAIAH [sih RAY uh]

The name of several men in the Old Testament:

1. David's scribe, or secretary (2 Sam. 8:17). Also see SHEVA.

2. A son of Azariah and chief priest at Jerusalem when this city was captured by Nebuchadnezzar of Babylon (2 Kin. 25:18). Nebuchadnezzar executed Seraiah at Riblah. Seraiah was the father of Jehozadak, the grandfather of the high priest Jeshua; he was an ancestor of Ezra.

3. A son of Tanhumeth, from Netophah in southern Judah (Jer. 40:8).

4. A son of Kenaz, brother of Othniel, and father of Joab (1 Chr. 4:13–14).

5. A Simeonite, son of Asiel (1 Chr. 4:35).

6. A priest who returned with Zerubbabel from the Captivity (Ezra 2:2). In Nehemiah 7:7, he is called Azariah.

7. A priest and clan leader who signed the new covenant under Nehemiah (Neh. 10:2). He is probably the same as Seraiah No. 6.

8. A son of Hilkiah (Neh. 11:11). A priest, Seraiah was a ruler of the house of God after the Captivity.

9. A chief priest who returned from Babylon with Zerubbabel (Neh. 12:1). He may be the same person as No. 6.

10. A priest, son of Azriel. Seraiah was sent by Jehoiakim to capture Jeremiah and his secretary-scribe, Baruch (Jer. 36:26).

11. A son of Neriah. Seraiah was the "quartermaster" who accompanied Zedekiah, king of Judah, to Babylon (Jer. 51:59, 61; staff officer, NIV).

SERED [SIR ed]

The oldest son of Zebulun (Gen. 46:14) and founder of the Sardites (Num. 26:26; Seredites, NIV, NRSV).

SERGIUS PAULUS [SUR jee uhs PAW luhs]

The Roman proconsul, or governor, of Cyprus who was converted to Christianity when the apostle Paul visited that island on his first missionary journey, about A.D. 46 (Acts 13:7). Luke describes Sergius Paulus as an intelligent man. This Sergius Paulus may have been the same man as L. Sergius Paulus, a Roman official in charge of the Tiber during the reign of the emperor Claudius (ruled A.D. 41–54).

SERUG [SIR uhg]

A son of Reu and the father of Nahor (Gen. 11:20–23). Serug is listed as an ancestor of Jesus in Luke's genealogy (Luke 3:35; Saruch, KJV).

SETH [seth] (*appoint, compensate*)

The third son of Adam and Eve, born after Cain murdered Abel (Gen. 4:25–26; 5:3–8; Sheth, KJV). The father of Enosh (or Enos) and an ancestor of Jesus Christ (Luke 3:38), Seth died at the age of 912.

SETHUR [SEE thur]

A spy, representing the tribe of Asher, sent by Moses to spy out the land of Canaan (Num. 13:13).

SHAAPH [SHAY af]

The name of two men in the Old Testament:

1. A descendant of Caleb through Jahdai (1 Chr. 2:47).

2. A son of Caleb by his concubine Maachah (1 Chr. 2:49).

SHAASHGAZ [shay ASH gaz]

A servant (chamberlain, KJV; eunuch, NIV) in the household of Ahasuerus, king of Persia (Esth. 2:14).

SHABBETHAI [SHAB uh thigh] (*born on the Sabbath*)

A Levite mentioned in connection with Ezra's order to the people to divorce their foreign wives (Ezra 10:15). Shabbethai probably was the same man who helped the people understand the Law after Ezra read it to them (Neh. 8:7).

SHACHIA [shah KIGH uh]

A form of SACHIAH.

SHADRACH [SHAD rak] (*command of [the god] Aku*)

The name that Ashpenaz, the chief of Nebuchadnezzar's eunuchs, gave to Hananiah, one of the Jewish princes who were carried away to Babylon in 605 B.C. (Dan. 1:7; 3:12–30).

Shadrach was one of the three faithful Jews who refused to worship the golden image that King Nebuchadnezzar of Babylon set up (Dan. 3:1). Along with his two companions, MESHACH and ABED–NEGO, Shadrach was "cast into the midst of a burning fiery furnace" (Dan. 3:11, 21). But they were protected by a fourth "man" in the fire (Dan. 3:25), and they emerged without even the smell of fire upon them (Dan. 3:27).

SHAGE, SHAGEE [SHAY gih]

Forms of SHAGEH.

SHAGEH [SHAY gih]

The father of one of David's mighty men (1 Chr. 11:34; Shage, KJV, REB; Shagee, NASB, NIV, NRSV). Shageh may be the same person as Agee (2 Sam. 23:11).

SHAHARAIM [shay uh RAY uhm]
(*double dawn*)

A Benjamite whose nine sons became the heads of tribes (1 Chr. 8:8–11).

SHALLUM [SHAL uhm] (*the requited one*)

The name of 13 or 14 men in the Old Testament:

1. A son of Jabesh (2 Kin. 15:10). Shallum became the 16th king of Israel by assassinating Zechariah and claiming the throne.

2. The husband of Huldah the prophetess in the days of Josiah, king of Judah (2 Chr. 34:22).

3. A son of Sismai (1 Chr. 2:40–41).

4. A son of King Josiah of Judah (1 Chr. 3:15). Shallum is better known by the name JEHOAHAZ, given to him when he became king of Judah after his father's death. After reigning three months in Jerusalem, Jehoahaz was deposed by Pharaoh Necho and replaced by Eliakim (whose name was changed to Jehoiakim), another of the sons of Josiah. Pharaoh Necho took Jehoahaz to Egypt, where he died.

5. A son of Shaul (1 Chr. 4:24–25). Shallum was the father of Mibsam and a descendant of Simeon.

6. A son of Zadok (1 Chr. 6:12–13). Shallum was the father of Hilkiah and an ancestor of Ezra (Ezra 7:2).

7. A son of Naphtali (1 Chr. 7:13), also called Shillem (Gen. 46:24).

8. Chief of the gatekeepers of the sanctuary in David's time (1 Chr. 9:17).

9. The father of Jehizkiah (2 Chr. 28:12).

10. A Levite and gatekeeper of the sanctuary in Ezra's time (Ezra 10:24). During the Captivity, Shallum had married a pagan wife and was told to divorce her.

11. A son of Bani (Ezra 10:42). During the Captivity, Shallum had married a pagan wife and was told to divorce her.

12. A son of Hallohesh (Neh. 3:12). A leader in Jerusalem, Shallum helped Nehemiah repair the city wall.

13. The uncle of Jeremiah the prophet (Jer. 32:7). He may be the same person as No. 2.

14. The father of Maaseiah (Jer. 35:4).

SHALLUN [SHAL uhn] (*the requited one*)

A ruler of part of Mizpah who repaired the Fountain Gate at Jerusalem (Neh. 3:15; Shallum, NRSV, NASB).

SHALMAI [SHAL migh]

A Temple servant whose descendants returned to Jerusalem after the Captivity (Ezra 2:46). He is also called Salmai (Neh. 7:48) and Shamlai (Ezra 2:46, REB, NRSV).

SHALMAN [SHAL muhn]

An unidentified king or conqueror mentioned by the prophet Hosea (Hos. 10:14). This name may be an abbreviated form of Shalmaneser V, king of Assyria. But other scholars believe it refers to a ruler of Moab or even to Shallum, a king of Israel.

SHALMANESER [shal muh NEE zur]

The name of five Assyrian kings, only one of whom is mentioned in the Bible.

Shalmaneser V (727–722 B.C.), the son and successor of Tiglath–Pileser III (745–727 B.C.; called "Pul" in 2 Kin. 15:19). He is the only Assyrian king named Shalmaneser mentioned in the Bible (unless SHALMAN of Hosea 10:14 is a contraction of the name). Shalmaneser received tribute from Hoshea, king of Israel. Then he imprisoned Hoshea and besieged Samaria for three years (2 Kin. 17:3–6; 18:9–10), until it fell in 722 B.C. This marked the end of the northern kingdom of Israel.

SHAMA [SHAY muh] (hearer)

One of David's mighty men (1 Chr. 11:44).

SHAMARIAH [sham uh RIGH uh] (whom the Lord guards)

A son of Rehoboam (2 Chr. 11:19; Shemariah, NRSV, NIV, REB, NASB).

SHAMED [SHAH med]

A form of SHEMED.

SHAMER [SHAY mur] ([God is] preserver)

The name of two men in the Old Testament:

1. A son of Mahli (1 Chr. 6:46; Shemer, NIV, NASB, NRSV).
2. A son of Heber, of the tribe of Asher (1 Chr. 7:34, KJV; Shemer, NKJV, NRSV, NASB; Shomer, NIV). He is also called Shomer (1 Chr. 7:32).

SHAMGAR [SHAM gahr]

The third judge of Israel (Judg. 3:31) who delivered the nation from oppression by the Philistines. Using an ox goad as a weapon, Shamgar killed 600 Philistines who were terrorizing the main travel routes. Shamgar was a "son of Anath"—which may mean he was a resident of Beth Anath (Judg. 1:33), a fortified city in the territory of Naphtali.

SHAMHUTH [SHAM huhth]

A captain of David's army who commanded 24,000 men (1 Chr. 27:8). Shamhuth is probably the same person as Shammah the Harodite (2 Sam. 23:25) and Shammoth the Harorite (1 Chr. 11:27).

SHAMIR [SHAY mur]

A son of Michah (1 Chr. 24:24) and a Levite who lived in David's time.

SHAMLAI [SHAM ligh]

A form of SALMAI; SHALMAI.

SHAMMA [SHAM uh]

A son of Zophah, of the tribe of Asher (1 Chr. 7:37).

SHAMMAH [SHAM uh]

The name of four or five men in the Old Testament:

1. A son of Reuel and a descendant of Esau (1 Chr. 1:37).
2. The third son of Jesse and a brother, or half-brother, of David (1 Sam. 16:9; 17:13; Shimea, 1 Chr. 2:13).
3. A son of Agee the Hararite (2 Sam. 23:11). Shammah was one of David's mighty men.
4. Another Hararite and also one of David's mighty men (2 Sam. 23:33). He may be the same person as No. 3.
5. A Harodite and another of David's mighty men (2 Sam. 23:25). He is also called Shammoth the Harorite (1 Chr. 11:27).

SHAMMAI [SHAM eye]

The name of three men in the Old Testament:

1. A son of Onam and great-grandson of Judah (1 Chr. 2:28, 32).
2. A son of Rekem, of the tribe of Judah (1 Chr. 2:44–45).

S

3. A descendant of Judah (1 Chr. 4:17).

SHAMMOTH [SHAM ahth]

One of David's mighty men (1 Chr. 11:27). Shammoth is probably the same person as Shamhuth (1 Chr. 27:8) and Shammah the Harodite (2 Sam. 23:25).

SHAMMUA [sha MOO uh]

The name of four men in the Old Testament:

1. The representative of the tribe of Reuben among the 12 spies who explored the land of Canaan (Num. 13:4).

2. A son of David by Bathsheba (2 Sam. 5:14; Shammuah, KJV; 1 Chr. 14:4). Shammua is also called Shimea (1 Chr. 3:5).

3. The father of Abda (Neh. 11:17). Shammua is also called Shemaiah (1 Chr. 9:16).

4. A priest in the days of Nehemiah (Neh. 12:18).

SHAMMUAH [sha MOO uh]

A form of SHAMMUA No. 2.

SHAMSHERAI [SHAM shuh righ]

A son of Jeroham, of the tribe of Benjamin (1 Chr. 8:26).

SHAPHAM [SHAY fuhm]

A chief of the tribe of Dan (1 Chr. 5:12).

SHAPHAN [SHAY fuhn] (*rock badger*)

The name of several men in the Old Testament:

1. A scribe during the reign of King Josiah of Judah who helped Josiah carry out his religious reform (2 Kin. 22:3–14).

He is probably the same person as Shaphan No. 2, 3, or 4.

2. The father of Ahikam (2 Kin. 22:12). A chief officer in Josiah's court during the prophet Jeremiah's time, Ahikam protected Jeremiah from death (Jer. 26:24).

3. The father of Elasah, who carried a letter from Jeremiah to the Babylonian captives (Jer. 29:3).

4. The father of Gemariah (Jer. 36:10–12). It was in the house of Gemariah that Baruch the scribe read Jeremiah's scroll to the people during the reign of Jehoiakim.

5. The father of Jaazaniah (Ezek. 8:11).

SHAPHAT [SHAY fat] (*judge*)

The name of five men in the Old Testament:

1. A representative of the tribe of Simeon sent by Moses to spy out the land of Canaan (Num. 13:2, 5).

2. The father of Elisha the prophet (1 Kin. 19:16).

3. A son of Shemaiah of the family of Jeconiah and a descendant of David (1 Chr. 3:22).

4. A descendant of Gad in the days of Jotham of Judah (1 Chr. 5:12).

5. An overseer of David's herds (1 Chr. 27:29).

SHARAI [SHAR eye]

A Jew who divorced his pagan wife after the Captivity (Ezra 10:40).

SHARAR [SHAH rur]

The father of Ahiam the Hararite (2 Sam. 23:33). Sharar is also called Sacar (1 Chr. 11:35; Sachar, KJV, NRSV).

SHAREZER [shuh REE zur] (*protect the king*)

A son of the Assyrian king Sennacherib (2 Kin. 19:37). In 681 B.C. Sharezer killed his father and fled to the land of Ararat.

Also see SHEREZER.

SHASHAI [SHAY shigh]

A son of Bani who married a pagan wife during the Captivity (Ezra 10:40).

SHASHAK [SHAY shak]

An ancestor of King Saul (1 Chr. 8:14, 25).

SHAUL [shahl] (*asked* [of God])

The name of two men in the Old Testament:

1. The founder of a tribal family known as the Shaulites (Num. 26:13).

2. A Levite descended from Kohath (1 Chr. 6:24).

SHAVSHA [SHAV shuh]

The scribe, or state secretary, in David's administration (1 Chr. 18:16; secretary, NIV, NASB, NRSV).

Also see SHEVA.

SHEAL [SHEE uhl]

A Jew who divorced his foreign wife after the Captivity (Ezra 10:29).

SHEALTIEL [shee AL tih uhl] (*I asked from God*)

A son of Jehoiachin (Jeconiah), king of Judah (1 Chr. 3:17; Matt. 1:12; Salathiel, KJV). Shealtiel apparently was an ancestor of Zerubbabel, the Jewish governor of Jerusalem after the Captivity. Shealtiel may have been Zerubbabel's father (Ezra 3:2), or his uncle or grandfather (1 Chr. 3:17–19). In the New Testament, Shealtiel is listed in the genealogy of Jesus Christ (Luke 3:27; Salathiel, KJV). He was a descendant of David through his son Nathan (2 Sam. 5:14).

SHEAR–JASHUB [shee ur JAY shuhb] (*a remnant shall return*)

A symbolic name given to a son of the prophet Isaiah in the days of King Ahaz

of Judah (Is. 7:3). The name emphasized Isaiah's prophecy that a remnant of the nation would return to the land after their years of captivity in a foreign country (Is. 10:21–22).

SHEARIAH [shee uh RIGH uh]

A son of Azel, of the tribe of Benjamin (1 Chr. 8:38). Sheariah was a descendant of King Saul.

SHEBA [SHEE buh] (*oath*)

The name of five men in the Old Testament:

1. A descendant of Ham (Gen. 10:7). Sheba's descendants are believed to have settled on the shores of the Persian Gulf.

2. A son of Joktan of the family of Shem, whose descendants have been traced to southern Arabia (Gen. 10:28).

3. A grandson of Abraham (Gen. 25:3). Sheba was a son of Jokshan, who was a son of Abraham by Keturah. Sheba and his descendants probably lived in Edom or northern Arabia.

4. A son of Bichri, of the tribe of Benjamin (2 Sam. 20:1–22). After the death of Absalom, Sheba led a short-lived rebellion against King David and was forced to retreat inside the city of Abel of Beth Maachah. This city was then besieged by Joab, the captain of David's army. In order to save their city, the people of Abel cut off Sheba's head and threw it over the wall to Joab (2 Sam. 20:1–22).

5. A chief of the tribe of Gad who lived in Gilead in Bashan during the reign of Jeroboam II of Israel (1 Chr. 5:13).

SHEBA, QUEEN OF

A queen who came to visit King Solomon. She tested him with "hard questions" and found that Solomon's wisdom

S

and prosperity exceeded his fame (1 Kin. 10:1–13). Some scholars believe she represented the region of Ethiopia, south of Egypt. But others insist she ruled among the tribes of southwestern Arabia. In the New Testament, Jesus referred to her as "the queen of the South," who "came from the ends of the earth to hear the wisdom of Solomon" (Matt. 12:42).

Also see SHEBA.

SHEBANIAH [sheb uh NIGH uh]

The name of four men in the Old Testament:

1. A Levite trumpeter who helped transport the Ark of the Covenant to the Temple in Jerusalem (1 Chr. 15:24).

2. A Levite who helped at the Feast of Tabernacles after the Captivity (Neh. 9:4–5).

3. A priestly family that lived one generation after the Captivity (Neh. 12:14). A representative of this family sealed the covenant with Nehemiah (Neh. 10:4).

4. A priest who sealed the covenant with Nehemiah after the Captivity (Neh. 10:12).

SHEBER [SHEE bur]

A son of Caleb and a descendant of David (1 Chr. 2:48).

SHEBNA [SHEB nuh]

A high official in the court of Hezekiah, king of Judah (2 Kin. 18:18, 26; Shebnah, NRSV; 18:37; 19:2; Is. 36:3, 11, 22; 37:2). Shebna is described as a scribe (NKJV, NASB), a secretary (NIV, NRSV), and an adjutant-general (REB), probably indicating he held an office similar to secretary of state. As the administrator of Hezekiah's palace, Shebna was a man of great influence. But the prophet Isaiah predicted he would fall from power and die as an outcast because of his pride (Is. 22:15–25). An inscription bearing what

appears to be his name was found on the lintel of a tomb near Jerusalem.

SHEBUEL [shih BOO uhl]

The name of two men in the Old Testament:

1. A descendant of Gershon (1 Chr. 23:16). Shebuel was ruler of the tabernacle treasury in the time of David (Shubael, 1 Chr. 24:20).

2. A son of Heman the musician (1 Chr. 25:4; Shubael, 1 Chr. 25:20).

SHECANIAH [shek uh NIGH uh] (the Lord is a neighbor)

The name of three men in the Old Testament:

1. A priest whose descendants were organized for special service during David's reign (1 Chr. 24:11).

2. A priest during the reign of King Hezekiah of Judah (2 Chr. 31:15). Shecaniah helped distribute the Temple offering among the priests.

3. The descendant of a family, perhaps that of Shecaniah No. 1, that returned from the Captivity (Ezra 8:3; Shechaniah, KJV).

SHECHANIAH [shek uh NIGH uh] (the Lord is a neighbor)

The name of six men in the Old Testament:

1. The head of a family in the lineage of David (1 Chr. 3:21–22).

2. A person who returned with Ezra from the Captivity (Ezra 8:5).

3. A son of Jehiel (Ezra 10:2). Shechaniah divorced his foreign wife after the Captivity.

4. The father of Shemaiah (Neh. 3:29). Shemaiah was the keeper of the East Gate in Jerusalem in Nehemiah's time.

5. The father-in-law of Tobiah the Ammonite (Neh. 6:17).

SHEREZER [sheh REE zur]

A man sent by the people of Bethel to ask about the observance of the anniversary feast commemorating the destruction of Jerusalem (Zech. 7:2; Sharezer, NASB, NIV, NRSV).

SHESHAI [SHEE shigh]

A son of Anak. Sheshai and his tribe were defeated by Caleb during the conquest of the land of Canaan (Josh. 15:14).

SHESHAN [SHEE shan]

A son of Ishi, of the tribe of Judah (1 Chr. 2:31).

SHESHBAZZAR [shesh BAZ ur] (sin [the moon-god], protect the father)

A governor of Judah appointed by Cyrus, king of Persia. Sheshbazzar was given authority to return the gold and silver articles taken by the Babylonians to the Temple in Jerusalem (Ezra 1:8, 11). Sheshbazzar may have been the same person as Shenazzar (1 Chr. 3:18), the son of Jehoiachin.

SHETH [sheth] (appoint, compensate)

The name of two men in the Old Testament:

1. A Moabite chief (Num. 24:17).
2. The third son of Adam and Eve, born after the murder of Abel by Cain (1 Chr. 1:1, KJV; Seth, NKJV). Also see SETH.

SHETHAR [SHEE thahr]

A high Persian official, one of seven princes "who had access to the king's presence" (Esth. 1:14).

SHETHAR–BOZENAI [SHEE thahr BAHZ uh nigh]

A form of SHETHAR–BOZNAI.

SHETHAR–BOZNAI [SHEE thahr BAHZ nigh]

An official, perhaps a royal scribe, of the Persian Empire (Ezra 5:3; Shethar-Bozenai, NIV, NRSV). Shethar–Boznai attempted to hinder the returned Jewish exiles from rebuilding the Temple.

SHEVA [SHEE vuh]

The name of two men in the Old Testament:

1. A scribe in King David's administration (2 Sam. 20:25). Sheva is also called Seraiah (2 Sam. 8:17), Shavsha (1 Chr. 18:16), and Shisha (1 Kin. 4:3).
2. A son of Maachah (1 Chr. 2:49).

SHIBAH [SHIGH buh]

A form of SHEBAH.

SHILHI [SHIL high]

The maternal grandfather of Jehoshaphat, king of Judah (1 Kin. 22:42).

SHILLEM [SHIL uhm] (repayment)

The youngest son of Naphtali (Gen. 46:24) and the founder of a tribal family known as the Shil–Lemites (Num. 26:49). Shillem was also called Shallum (1 Chr. 7:13).

SHILONI [shih LOE nigh]

The father of Zechariah (Neh. 11:5; the Shilonite, NRSV, NASB; a descendant of Shelah, NIV). Zechariah was an ancestor of Maaseiah, one of the Jewish princes who lived in Jerusalem in Ezra's time.

SHILSHAH [SHIL shuh] (triad)

A son of Zophah, of the tribe of Asher (1 Chr. 7:37).

SHIMEA, SHIMEAH [SHIM ih uh]

The name of five men in the Old Testament:

S

1. The third son of Jesse and brother of David (2 Sam. 13:3). Shimeah was the father of Jonadab (2 Sam. 13:3, 32) as well as Jonathan, who slew a Philistine giant (2 Sam. 21:21). Shimeah is also called Shammah (1 Sam. 16:9) and Shimma (1 Chr. 2:13, KJV).

2. A son of David born in Jerusalem (1 Chr. 3:5). Shimea is also called Shammua (2 Sam. 5:14; 1 Chr. 14:4).

3. A Levite of the family of Merari (1 Chr. 6:30).

4. A Levite of the family of Gershon (1 Chr. 6:39).

5. A Benjamite, descendant of Jeiel (1 Chr. 8:32). He is also called Shimeam (1 Chr. 9:38).

SHIMEAM [SHIM ih uhm]

A son of Mikloth, of the tribe of Benjamin (1 Chr. 9:38), also called Shimeah (1 Chr. 8:32).

SHIMEATH [SHIM ih ath]

An Ammonitess, the mother of one of the assassins of King Joash. Her son's name is given as Jozachar (2 Kin. 12:21) or Zabad (2 Chr. 24:26).

SHIMEI [SHIM ih uh]

The name of 18 or 19 men in the Old Testament:

1. A son of Gershon and grandson of Levi (Num. 3:18; Zech. 12:13), also called Shimi (Ex. 6:17).

2. A son of Gera of Saul's family and the tribe of Benjamin (2 Sam. 16:5–13; 1 Kin. 2:8). Shimei grew bitter because David had taken the throne from the family of Saul. He insulted David when the king was fleeing from his own son, Absalom. When David finally won the struggle for the throne, Shimei repented. David accepted Shimei's apology and promised to let him live. After David's death, his son and successor, Solomon,

would not allow Shimei to go beyond Jerusalem's walls. Shimei obeyed Solomon's command at first, but eventually he left the city and was promptly executed at Solomon's command.

3. One of David's officers. Shimei remained loyal to David and Solomon when Adonijah attempted to seize the throne (1 Kin. 1:8).

4. One of Solomon's 12 supply officers who provided food for the king's household (1 Kin. 4:18).

5. A son of Pedaiah and brother of Zerubbabel (1 Chr. 3:19). A member of the royal house, Shimei was the great-grandson of King Jehoiakim of Judah (1 Chr. 3:16–19).

6. A son of Zacchur (1 Chr. 4:26–27).

7. The son of Gog (1 Chr. 5:4).

8. A Levite and the son of Libni (1 Chr. 6:29).

9. A Levite, the son of Jahath (1 Chr. 6:42).

10. A descendant of Benjamin and head of a family in Aijalon (1 Chr. 8:21; Shimhi, KJV, also called Shema (1 Chr. 8:13).

11. Head of a family of Levites in David's time (1 Chr. 23:9).

12. A Levite who headed the tenth course of sanctuary singers during David's reign (1 Chr. 25:3, 17).

13. A supervisor of David's vineyards (1 Chr. 27:27).

14. A descendant of Heman who helped cleanse the Temple in King Hezekiah's time (2 Chr. 29:14).

15. A Levite with responsibility for the tithes and offerings in Hezekiah's time (2 Chr. 31:12–13). He may be the same person as No. 14.

16. A Levite who divorced his foreign wife (Ezra 10:23).

17. A member of the family of Hashum who divorced his foreign wife (Ezra 10:33).

18. A son of Bani who divorced his foreign wife (Ezra 10:38).

19. A son of Kish and grandfather of Mordecai (Esth. 2:5).

SHIMEON [SHIM ih uhn] (hearing)

A son of Harim who divorced his foreign wife after the Captivity (Ezra 10:31).

SHIMHI [SHIM high]

A form of SHIMEI No. 10.

SHIMI

A form of SHIMEI No. 1.

SHIMMA [SHIM muh]

A form of SHIMEA No. 1.

SHIMON [SHIGH muhn]

A Judahite, father of four sons (1 Chr. 4:20).

SHIMRATH [SHIM rath] (guard)

The ninth son of Shimei, of the tribe of Benjamin (1 Chr. 8:21).

SHIMRI [SHIM righ] (the Lord watches)

The name of four men in the Old Testament:

1. A son of Shemaiah, of the tribe of Simeon (1 Chr. 4:37).

2. The father of Jediael (1 Chr. 11:45).

3. A tabernacle gatekeeper during David's time (1 Chr. 26:10; Simri, KJV).

4. A Levite who assisted in the cleansing of the Temple during Hezekiah's religious reformation (2 Chr. 29:13).

SHIMRITH [SHIM rith]

A Moabitess, the mother of Jehozabad (2 Chr. 24:26), also called Shomer (2 Kin. 12:21).

SHIMROM [SHIM rahm]

A form of SHIMRON No. 1.

SHIMRON [SHIM rahn] (guard)

A son of Issachar (Gen. 46:13; Shimrom, KJV) and founder of the Shimronites (Num. 26:24).

SHIMSHAI [SHIM shigh]

The scribe or secretary of Rehum, a Samaritan official in the Persian Empire. Rehum and Shimshai opposed the rebuilding of the Temple and the wall of Jerusalem (Ezra 4:8–9, 17, 23).

SHINAB [SHIGH nab] ([the god] Sin is my father)

The king of Admah defeated by Chedorlaomer and his allies in the time of Abraham (Gen. 14:2).

SHIPHI [SHIGH figh]

A Simeonite who lived in the time of Hezekiah, king of Judah (1 Chr. 4:37).

SHIPHRAH [SHIF ruh]

One of two Hebrew midwives (also see PUAH) in Egypt at the time of the birth of Moses. These women defied Pharaoh's command to kill all the male babies of the Hebrew people (Ex. 1:15).

SHIPHTAN [SHIF tuhn] (judging)

The father of Kemuel (Num. 34:24). Kemuel assisted Moses in dividing the land west of the Jordan River among the tribes of Israel.

SHISHA [SHIGH shuh]

The father of Elihoreth and Ahijah, scribes in Solomon's administration (1 Kin. 4:3). Also see SHEVA.

SHISHAK [SHIGH shak]

A Libyan war chieftain who became pharaoh of Egypt (reigned from about 940 B.C. to about 915 B.C.). Shishak (Sheshonk in Egyptian) is known for his expedition against the southern kingdom of Judah after the United Kingdom split into two nations following Solomon's death about 920 B.C.

In about 926 B.C., in the fifth year of the reign of King Rehoboam (reigned about 931–913 B.C.), Shishak invaded Judah and captured many of its fortified cities (1 Kin. 14:25). He then marched against Jerusalem, Rehoboam's capital city, forcing Rehoboam to pay tribute and plundering the treasures of the Temple and Rehoboam's palace (1 Kin. 14:25–26).

The Egyptian account of Shishak's invasion of Judah was recorded on the wall of the temple of the Egyptian god Amon at Karnak (ancient Thebes), in southern Egypt. More than 100 cities captured or destroyed by Shishak are listed, including Adoraim, Aijalon, and Socoh. Cities from the northern kingdom of Israel, such as Shechem, Beth Shean, and Megiddo, are also listed on this monument as being captured by Shishak.

SHITRAI [SHIT righ]

The chief shepherd over the royal herds in Sharon during David's administration (1 Chr. 27:29).

SHIZA [SHIGH zuh]

Father of Adina (1 Chr. 11:42).

SHOBAB [SHOE bab]

The name of two men in the Old Testament:

1. A son born to David by Bathsheba after he became king (2 Sam. 5:14).

2. A member of the family of Hezron, of the house of Caleb (1 Chr. 2:18).

SHOBACH [SHOE bak]

Commander of the army of HADADEZER, king of Zobah in David's time (2 Sam. 10:16, 18). Israel was victorious in battle,

and Shobach was killed. Shobach is also called Shophach (1 Chr. 19:16, 18).

SHOBAI [SHOE bigh]

A Levite who founded a family of tabernacle gatekeepers. Shobai's descendants returned from the Captivity with Zerubbabel (Neh. 7:45).

SHOBAL [SHOE buhl]

The name of two or three men in the Old Testament:

1. A son of Seir the Horite (Gen. 36:20).

2. A son of Hur (1 Chr. 2:50, 52). Shobal was the founder of Kirjath Jearim.

3. A descendant of Judah (1 Chr. 4:1–2). He may be the same person as No. 2.

SHOBEK [SHOE bek]

A Jewish chief who sealed the covenant under Nehemiah after the Captivity (Neh. 10:24).

SHOBI [SHOE bigh]

A son of Nahash from Rabbah of the Ammonites (2 Sam. 17:27). Shobi provided supplies for David's army in their campaign against Absalom.

SHOHAM [SHOW ham] (*a precious stone*)

A Levite who served in the tabernacle sanctuary during David's reign (1 Chr. 24:27).

SHOMER [SHOW mur] ([God is] *preserver*)

The name of a man and a woman in the Old Testament:

1. The mother of Jehozabad (2 Kin. 12:21), also called Shimrith (2 Chr. 24:26).

2. A son of Heber (1 Chr. 7:32), also called Shamer and Shemer (1 Chr. 7:34, KJV, NRSV, NASB).

SHOPHACH [SHOW fack]

A form of SHOBACH.

SHUA [SHOO uh]

The name of one man and one woman in the Old Testament:

1. The father of one of Judah's wives (Gen. 38:2, 12; Shuah, KJV; 1 Chr. 2:3, Bathshua, REB).

2. A daughter of Heber (1 Chr. 7:32).

SHUAH [SHOO a]

The name of two men in the Old Testament:

1. A son of Abraham and Keturah, Abraham's concubine (1 Chr. 1:32).

2. A brother of Chelub, of the tribe of Judah (1 Chr. 4:11, KJV, REB; Shuhah, NRSV, NIV, NASB).

SHUAL [SHOO al] *(fox)*

A son of Zophah, of the tribe of Asher (1 Chr. 7:36).

SHUBAEL [SHOO bale]

The name of two men in the Old Testament:

1. A descendant of Amram (1 Chr. 24:20). Shubael had charge of the Temple treasures in David's time. He is also called Shebuel (1 Chr. 23:16; 26:24).

2. One of the sons of Heman, of the tribe of Levi (1 Chr. 25:20). Shubael served as a sanctuary musician in David's time. He is also called Shebuel (1 Chr. 25:4).

SHUHAH [SHOO ha]

A form of SHUAH.

SHUHAM [SHOO ham]

A son of Dan and founder of the Shuhamites (Num. 26:42), also called Hushim (Gen. 46:23).

SHULAMITE [SHOO lum ite]

A young woman mentioned in Song of Solomon 6:13 (Shulammite, NRSV, NIV, REB, NASB). Many scholars interpret Shulamite as Shunammite—a woman from the city of Shunem (1 Sam. 28:4).

Others believe this woman was ABISHAG, the lovely young Shunammite brought to David in his old age (1 Kin. 1:1–4, 15) and who later apparently was a part of Solomon's harem (1 Kin. 2:17–22).

SHULAMMITE [SHOO lum ite]

A form of SHULAMITE.

SHUNAMMITE [SHOO nam ite]

A female native or inhabitant of Shunem. Two different Shunammites are mentioned in the Bible:

1. ABISHAG, a lovely young woman who ministered to King David in his old age (1 Kin. 1:3, 15).

2. A woman who befriended the prophet Elisha (2 Kin. 4:8–36).

SHUNI [SHOO nih]

A son of Gad (Gen. 46:16) and founder and chief of a tribal family, the Shunites (Num. 26:15).

SHUPHAM [SHOO fam]

A son of Benjamin (Num. 26:39; Shephupham, NRSV) and founder of a tribal family, the Shuphamites (Num. 26:39). His name is also spelled Shephuphan (1 Chr. 8:5), Shuppim (1 Chr. 7:12, 15), and Muppim (Gen. 46:21).

SHUPPIM [SHUP em]

The name of two men in the Old Testament:

1. A descendant of Benjamin (1 Chr. 7:12, 15), also called Shupham (Num.

S

26:39), Shephuphan (1 Chr. 8:5), and Muppim (Gen. 46:21).

2. A Levite gatekeeper of the tabernacle in David's time (1 Chr. 26:16).

SHUTHELAH [SHOO thuh lah]

The name of two men in the Old Testament:

1. A son of Ephraim and founder of a tribal family, the Shuthalhites (Num. 26:35–36).

2. A descendant of Ephraim (1 Chr. 7:21).

SIBBECAI [SIB uh kie]

A form of SIBBECHAI.

SIBBECHAI [SIB uh kie]

One of David's mighty men (1 Chr. 11:29; Sibbecai, NRSV). Sibbechai killed the giant Saph during a battle with the Philistines. Sibbechai is also called Mebunnai (2 Sam. 23:27).

SIHON [SIGH hun]

A king of the Amorites defeated by the Israelites during their journey toward the land of Canaan. Moses asked Sihon to let the Israelites pass peacefully through his kingdom, located east of the Jordan River. Sihon refused and later attacked the Israelites at Jahaz. In the battle that followed Sihon and his army were killed (Num. 21:21–32), and his territory was given to the tribes of Gad and Reuben (Num. 32:33). Sihon's defeat is mentioned often in the Old Testament (Deut. 1:4; Josh. 2:10; Ps. 135:11; Jer. 48:45).

SILAS [SIGH lus] (person of the woods)

A prominent member of the early church at Jerusalem and companion of the apostle Paul. Silas accompanied Paul to Antioch of Syria to report the decision of the Jerusalem Council to accept Gen-

tile Christians into the church (Acts 15:22, 27, 32).

Paul chose Silas as his companion on his second missionary journey. During their travels, Paul and Silas were imprisoned at Philippi (Acts 16:19, 25, 29). Silas and Paul were also together during the riot at Thessalonica (Acts 17:4). Later they were sent to Berea, where Silas remained with Timothy; both Silas and Timothy soon followed Paul to Athens (Acts 17:14–15), although they may not have caught up with him until reaching Corinth (Acts 18:5). Silas played an important role in the early Christian work in Corinth.

In his letters, Paul referred to Silas as Silvanus (1 Thess. 1:1; 2 Thess. 1:1). The time, place, and manner of his death are unknown.

SILVANUS [sill VAIN us]

A form of SILAS.

SIMEON [SIM ih un] ([God] hears)

The name of four men in the Bible:

1. The second son of Jacob and Leah (Gen. 29:33). Simeon's descendants became one of the twelve tribes of Israel. He and his brother Levi tricked the Hivites of Shechem and massacred all the males because one of them had raped Dinah, their sister (Gen. 34:2, 25, 30). Simeon was the brother whom Joseph kept as security when he allowed his brothers to leave Egypt and return to their father Jacob in the land of Canaan (Gen. 42:24).

2. A devout Jew who blessed the infant Jesus in the Temple (Luke 2:25, 34). The Holy Spirit had promised Simeon that he would not die until he had seen the long-awaited Messiah. Simeon recognized the child as the Messiah when Mary and Joseph brought him to the Temple to present Him to the Lord.

3. An ancestor of Joseph listed in the genealogy of Jesus Christ (Luke 3:30).

4. A Christian prophet or teacher in the church at Antioch of Syria (Acts 13:1). Some scholars believe Simeon was the same person as Simon of Cyrene, who bore Jesus' cross (Luke 23:26).

SIMON [SIME un] ([God] *hears*)

The name of nine men in the New Testament:

1. Simon Peter, the Galilean fisherman who became an apostle of Christ (Matt. 4:18; 10:2). Simon was the son of Jonah (Matt. 16:17; John 21:15) and a brother of the apostle ANDREW (John 1:40). Also see PETER, SIMON.

2. Another of the Twelve, called the Canaanite to distinguish him from Simon Peter. The name may also indicate he was a member of a fanatical Jewish sect, the Zealots (Matt. 10:4; Mark 3:18; Luke 6:15; Acts 1:13). Members of this group were fanatical opponents of Roman rule in Palestine. As a Zealot, Simon would have hated any foreign domination or interference.

3. One of Jesus' brothers (Matt. 13:55).

4. A former leper in whose house Mary, the sister of Lazarus, anointed Jesus' feet with a precious ointment (Matt. 26:6–13; Mark 14:3–9; John 12:1–8). Mary, Martha, and Lazarus were present when this happened, and Martha took an active part in serving the dinner. This has led to speculation that Simon was a member of the family or at least was a very close friend.

5. A man of Cyrene who was forced to carry Jesus' cross (Matt. 27:32; Mark 15:21; Luke 23:26). Simon was the father

SIMON

OK.. WHERE'D YA WANT THIS THING?

Hayes

S

of Alexander and Rufus, men who were known to the early Christians in Rome (Rom. 16:13).

6. A Pharisee in whose house Jesus ate (Luke 7:36–50). On that occasion a woman who was a sinner anointed Jesus' feet. Simon felt that Jesus should not have allowed her to come near Him. But Jesus explained that sinners like her were the very ones who needed forgiveness.

7. The father of Judas Iscariot (John 13:2). Both father and son are called Iscariot. The NRSV has "Judas the son of Simon Iscariot" (John 6:71; 13:26).

8. A sorcerer known as Simon Magus, or Simon the magician, who tried to buy spiritual powers from the apostle Peter (Acts 8:9–24). Simon's feats were so impressive that the people of Samaria declared, "This man is the great power of God" (Acts 8:10), and followed him. But when Philip the evangelist preached, the Samaritans believed and were baptized. Simon also believed and was baptized.

Later the apostles Peter and John visited Samaria to make sure these believers received the power of the Holy Spirit. When Simon saw that the Holy Spirit was bestowed by the laying on of hands, he attempted to buy this power. Peter rebuked him, "Your money perish with you, because you thought that the gift of God could be purchased with money! You have neither part nor portion in this matter, for your heart is not right in the sight of God" (Acts 8:20–21).

9. A tanner of Joppa and friend of the apostle Peter (Acts 9:43; 10:6, 17, 32).

SIMON MACCABAEUS [mack kuh BEE us]

A son of Mattathias, and father of John Hyrcanus or Hyrcanus I.

SIMON PETER

(See PETER, SIMON.)

SIMRI [SIM rih]

A form of SHIMRI.

SIPPAI [SIP pih eye]

A form of SAPH.

SISAMAI [SIS ah my]

A form of SISMAI.

SISERA [SIS uh rah]

The name of two men in the Old Testament:

1. The commander of the army of Jabin, king of Canaan. Deborah and Barak defeated Jabin's army under Sisera's command at the River Kishon. Sisera was later killed by a Kenite woman who drove a tent peg into his temple (Judg. 4:1–22).

2. One of the Nethinim who returned from the Captivity with Zerubbabel (Neh. 7:55).

SISMAI [SIS my]

A son of Eleasah and father of Shallum (1 Chr. 2:40; Sisamai, KJV).

SITHRI [SITH rih]

A form of ZITHRI.

SO [soh]

A king of Egypt whom Hoshea, the last king of Israel (ruled about 732–723 B.C.), tried to enlist as an ally against Assyria (2 Kin. 17:4). Some scholars identify So with Sib'e. In 720 B.C. this Egyptian king allied himself with Hanunu, the king of Gaza, against Sargon of Assyria. Sargon soundly defeated this coalition at the Battle of Raphia, about 32 kilometers (20 miles) south of Gaza. Other scholars regard So as the name of a city, Sais, in the western delta of Egypt. This was the residence of Tefnakhte, an Egyptian ruler during the days of King Hoshea. If this theory is correct, then 2 Kings 17:4 would read: "He had sent messengers to So [Sais], to the king of Egypt."

SOCHOH, SOCO, SOCOH [SOW koe]

A son of Heber listed in the genealogy of Judah (1 Chr. 4:18; Shocho, KJV).

SODI [SOW dih] ([God is] my secret counsel)

The father of Gaddiel (Num. 13:10).

SOLOMON [SAHL uh mun] (peaceful)

The builder of the Temple in Jerusalem and the first king of Israel to trade commercial goods profitably to other nations; author of much of the Book of Proverbs and perhaps also the author of the Song of Solomon and Ecclesiastes.

Solomon succeeded David his father as king of Israel. Solomon's rise met with widespread approval from the people, but David's officials were slow to accept the new king. They did warm up considerably, however, when they realized David was determined to anoint Solomon as his heir. Solomon became Israel's king because God had told David that Saul's heirs would not follow him to the throne. Thus, Solomon became king although there was no clear precedent for his succession.

According to the chronology in 1 Kings 11:42, Solomon was about 20 years old when he was crowned. He assumed leadership of Israel at a time of great material and spiritual prosperity. During his 40-year reign (970–931 B.C.), he expanded his kingdom until it covered about 50,000 square miles—from Egypt in the south to Syria in the north to the borders of Mesopotamia in the east.

Great Beginnings.

One of the first things Solomon did as king was to go to Gibeon to offer sacrifices to the Lord. God appeared to the new king at night and asked him, "What shall I give thee?" Solomon asked for an understanding heart to judge the people of Israel and the ability to tell good from evil. God not only granted Solomon's request, but He also promised him riches and honor if he would walk in the steps of his father (1 Kin. 3:4–15).

Solomon organized Israel much as David had done, but he enlarged and expanded its government. He divided the country into 12 districts, each of which was responsible for providing the court with regular supplies one month out of the year, with a supply officer in charge of each district. As the years passed, Solomon's court reached a standard of luxury that had never existed in Israel's history.

Wisdom.

Solomon is usually remembered as a wise man. His Proverbs and his "Song of Songs" demonstrate his deep knowledge of the natural world (plants, animals, etc.). He also had a profound knowledge of human nature, as demonstrated by the two women who claimed the same child. His suggestion that the child be physically divided between the two was a masterful strategy for finding out who was the real mother (1 Kin. 3:16–28). Solomon's concern with the ethics of everyday life is evident in his Proverbs. They show that Solomon loved wisdom and was always trying to teach it to others. They also indicate he was a keen observer who could learn from the mistakes of others.

Solomon's sayings in these Proverbs are so true that they sound almost trite today. Their clarity sometimes hides

S

their depth. During his lifetime, Solomon's fame as a man of wisdom spread to surrounding lands, and leaders came from afar to hear him speak. When the Queen of Sheba came to test his wisdom, he answered all her questions with ease. After she saw the extent of his empire and the vastness of his knowledge, she confessed that she had underestimated him (2 Chr. 9:1–12).

Solomon's Temple.

One of Solomon's first major feats was the construction of the Temple in Jerusalem as a place for worship of the God of Israel. The task was enormous, involving much planning and many workers. A work force of 30,000 was employed in cutting timber from the cedars of Lebanon. Also working on this massive project were 80,000 cutters of stone in the quarries of Jerusalem, 70,000 ordinary workers, and many superintendents. Gold, silver, and other precious metals were imported from other lands. Hiram, king of Tyre, sent architects and other craftsmen to assist with the project. The building was completed after seven years. The Temple was famous not for its size—since it was relatively small—but for the quality of its elaborate workmanship (1 Kings 6–7).

After the Temple was completed, Solomon planned an elaborate program of dedication. He invited the leaders of all twelve tribes to attend as he presided over the ceremony. The Ark of the Covenant was brought into the most sacred place in the Temple as a cloud filled the room to hide God's presence. King Solomon then blessed the crowd, recounted the history of the building of the Temple, and offered long prayers of dedication while standing at the altar. This reveals the admirable spirit of devotion in Sol-

omon's heart. The dedication ceremony lasting seven days was followed by observance of the Feast of Tabernacles (1 Kings 8—9).

Immediately after the dedication, the Lord appeared to Solomon once again. He assured the king that his prayers had been heard and that the Temple had been blessed. He also warned Solomon that the divine favor and protection which had been bestowed upon Israel would continue only if their faith remained uncorrupted by other beliefs. If idolatry should be introduced, Israel would be punished and the Temple would be destroyed (1 Kin. 9:1–9).

Other Buildings.

After completing the Temple, Solomon built the palace complex, a series of five structures that took 13 years to complete. He also built many cities to assist the development of his trade empire. Among these were Tadmor (also called Palmyra) and Baalath (also called Baalbek) in Syria. To protect his kingdom, he built fortresses and lodgings for his army. These fortifications, especially the ones at Jerusalem, Gezer, Megiddo, and Hazor, had strong double walls and massive gateways.

Commercial Enterprises.

Trade with other nations was another of Solomon's contributions to the nation of Israel. The international situation was favorable for a strong leader to emerge in Israel; traditional centers of strength in Egypt and Syria were at an all-time low. Solomon entered into trade agreements with a number of nations, increasing Israel's wealth and prestige.

Although Solomon had a strong army, he relied upon a system of treaties with his neighbors to keep the peace. Egypt was allied with Israel through the marriage of Solomon to the daughter of the Pharaoh. The seafaring cities of Tyre and Sidon were also united to Israel by trade agreements.

Some of Israel's trade was conducted overland by way of camel caravans. But the most significant trade was by sea across the Mediterranean Sea through an alliance with Tyre. Solomon's ships apparently went as far west as Spain to bring back silver.

Soon Solomon became the ruler of a huge commercial empire. Archaeologists believe that Solomon's trading may have brought him into conflict with the Queen of Sheba. One purpose of her famous visit to Solomon may have been to establish trade agreements between Solomon's kingdom and her own nation (1 Kin. 10:1–13).

Solomon's Sins.

Solomon's reign brought changes not only to Israel but also to his own life. Near the end of his life, the king lost the ideals of his youth, becoming restless and unsatisfied. The Book of Ecclesiastes, proclaiming that "all is vanity" ("meaningless," NIV), supports the view that the world's wisest man had become a pathetic figure in his old age.

Solomon's greatest sin was his loss of devotion to the God of the Hebrew people. In this, he fell victim to his own trade agreements. By custom, beautiful women were awarded to the most powerful member of a treaty to seal the covenant. The constant influx of wives and concubines in Solomon's court led eventually to his downfall.

Thus, Solomon broke the Mosaic Law and violated the warning not to stray from the path of his father David.

The large number of foreign women in Solomon's court made many demands upon the king. He allowed these "outsiders" to practice their pagan religions. The result was that Jerusalem, and even its holy Temple, was the scene of pagan practices and idol worship (1 Kin. 11:1–13).

Solomon's own faith was weakened. Eventually he approved of, and even participated in, these idolatrous acts. The example he set for the rest of the nation must have been demoralizing. This unfortunate error was a severe blow to the security of Solomon's throne and to the nation he had built.

The End of Solomon's Throne.

Years before Solomon's death, his heavy taxation of the people brought unrest and rebellion. Surrounding nations began to marshal their forces to free themselves of Israel's tyranny, but the most serious uprising came from within the nation itself. When Solomon's son Rehoboam ascended the throne after his father, Jeroboam, a young leader who had been exiled to Egypt, returned to lead a successful civil war against him. The result was a division of Solomon's United Kingdom into two separate nations—the southern kingdom of Judah and the northern kingdom of Israel.

Solomon's Character.

In many ways, Solomon's 40-year reign as king of the Hebrew people is a puzzle. In his early years he was both noble and humble—undoubtedly one of the best rulers of his day. Although he was surrounded by wealth and luxury as a young man, he seemed to be a person of honor and integrity. He was the first king in Israel who was the son of a king. The glory of his empire was a reflection of his own royal tastes, which he satisfied through a shrewd and successful foreign policy.

Unfortunately, Solomon was not strong enough to withstand the temptations that go along with a long life of luxury. His contribution to the nation of Israel is figured largely in material terms. He made Jerusalem one of the most beautiful cities of the ancient world, and he will always be remembered as a great builder. The tragedy is that after the building of the Temple, Solomon did very little to promote the religious life of his people.

SOPATER [SOW pa tur]

A Christian from Berea who accompanied the apostle Paul from Greece to the province of Asia (Acts 20:4; son of Pyrrhus, NRSV). Sopater may be the Sosipater who joined Paul in sending greetings to fellow Christians (Rom. 16:21).

SOPHERETH [so FEH reth] (scribe)

A servant of Solomon whose descendants returned from the Captivity with Zerubbabel (Ezra 2:55; Hassophereth, NRSV; Neh. 7:57).

SOSIPATER [soh SIP ah tur]

A believer who joined the apostle Paul in sending greetings to the Roman Christians (Rom. 16:21). Sosipater may be the same person as SOPATER (Acts 20:4).

SOSTHENES [SOS thuh knees]

The ruler of the synagogue at Corinth during the apostle Paul's first visit to this city (Acts 18:17). When the Roman ruler of the area refused to deal with the angry mob's charges against Paul, they beat Sosthenes. This may be the same Sosthenes as the one greeted by Paul in one of his Corinthian letters (1 Cor. 1:1). If so, he must have become a Christian

some time after the mob scene in his city.

SOTAI [SOW tih]

A servant of Solomon (Ezra 2:55) whose descendants returned from the Captivity with Zerubbabel.

STACHYS [STAY kis]

A Christian at Rome to whom the apostle Paul sent greetings (Rom. 16:9).

STEPHANAS [STEFF ah nus] (crown-bearer)

A Christian in the church at Corinth who was baptized by the apostle Paul (1 Cor. 1:16). The church at Corinth sent Stephanas, Fortunatus, and Achaicus to Paul while he was at Ephesus, informing him of the situation in Corinth. Paul apparently was encouraged by the good news they brought (1 Cor. 16:17).

STEPHEN

One of the first seven deacons of the early church and the first Christian martyr. The story of Stephen is found in Acts 6:7—7:60.

In the period following Pentecost, the number of Christians in the New Testament church grew steadily. Followers were eventually recruited not only from among the Jews in Palestine but also from among the Jews in Greek settlements. The church had to appoint several men to handle the work of providing aid to these needy Christians.

Stephen was one of the first seven "good and worthy men" chosen to provide relief to these needy Christians from Greek backgrounds. Since Stephen is mentioned first in the list of the seven administrators, he was probably the most important leader in this group. Although they are not specifically named as deacons, these seven men are considered to be the forerunners of the office of deacon that developed later in the early church. Stephen assumed a place of prominence among these seven leaders as the church grew (Acts 6:7).

Stephen was probably critical of the system of Old Testament laws, claiming they had already lost their effectiveness because they had reached fulfillment in Christ. This viewpoint, which Stephen argued very skillfully, brought him into conflict with powerful leaders among the Jewish people. Stephen became well-known as a preacher and a miracle-worker (Acts 6:8). His work was so effective that renewed persecution of the Christians broke out.

Members of certain Jewish synagogues felt that Stephen had blasphemed Moses and God. They accused him of being disloyal to the Temple and rejecting Moses. He was also accused of hostility toward Judaism—a charge that had never been made before against other disciples. In debates the Jews were no match for Stephen; even Saul was outwitted by him. Thus, they resorted to force.

Stephen was arrested and brought before the Sanhedrin, the Jewish council, where charges were placed against him. False witnesses testified against him. The high priest then asked Stephen if these things were true. Stephen was not dismayed. When he stood before them his face was "as the face of an angel" (Acts 6:15).

The lengthy speech Stephen made in his own defense is reported in detail in Acts 7:2–53. Stephen summarized Old Testament teachings, showing how God had guided Israel toward a specific goal. He reviewed Israel's history in such a way that he replied to all the charges made against him without actually denying anything. This amounted to a criticism of the Sanhedrin itself. Stephen denounced the council as "stiff-necked and uncircumcised in heart and ears" and accused them of resisting the Holy Spirit. Then he charged that they had killed Christ, just as their ancestors had killed the prophets. He accused them of failing to keep their own law (Acts 7:51–53).

Stephen's speech enraged the Sanhedrin so that they were "cut to the heart, and they gnashed at him with their teeth" (Acts 7:54). At this moment Stephen had a vision of God in heaven, with Jesus on His right hand. Stephen's fate was sealed when he reported this vision to his enemies. The crowd rushed upon him, dragged him out of the city, and stoned him to death (Acts 7:55–58).

Among the people consenting to Stephen's death that day was Saul, who later became the apostle Paul—great Christian missionary to the Gentiles. As he was being stoned, Stephen asked God not to charge his executioners with the sin of his death (Acts 7:59–60).

Stephen's martyrdom was followed by a general persecution that forced the disciples to flee from Jerusalem into the outlying areas. This scattering led to the preaching of the gospel first to the Samaritans and then to the Gentiles in the nations surrounding Palestine.

SUAH [SUE ah]

A son of Zophah, of the tribe of Asher (1 Chr. 7:36).

SUSANNA [SUE zan nah] (a lily)

A woman who provided food for Jesus and His disciples during His early ministry in Galilee (Luke 8:3). No further details of her life are known.

SUSI [SOO sih]

The father of Gaddi, of the tribe of Manasseh (Num. 13:11).

SYNTYCHE [SIN tih keh]

A woman in the church at Philippi who apparently was in conflict with another church member. The apostle Paul called upon them to settle their differences (Phil. 4:2).

SYRO-PHOENICIAN [sigh row feh KNEE shun]

A Gentile woman whose daughter was healed by Jesus (Mark 7:26). She was from Phoenicia, a nation northeast of Palestine that had been incorporated into the Roman province of Syria—thus the term, Syro-Phoenician. Although she was not a citizen of the Jewish nation, she believed Jesus could heal her daughter. Jesus commended her because of her great faith.

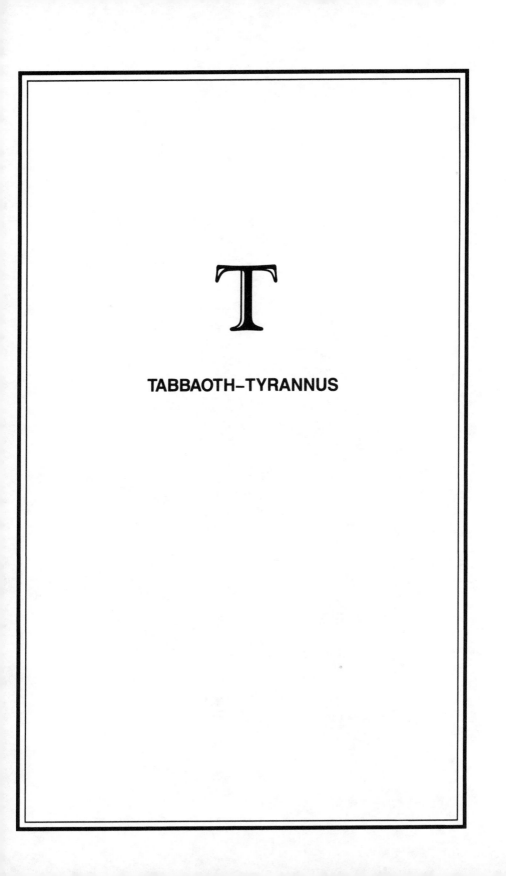

T

TABBAOTH–TYRANNUS

TABBAOTH [TAB ih ahth] *(signets)*

The head of a family of Temple servants who returned from the Captivity (Neh. 7:46).

TABEEL [TAB ih uhl] *(God is good)*

The name of two men in the Old Testament:

1. An Aramean in Samaria who protested the rebuilding of the walls of Jerusalem (Ezra 4:7).

2. The father of the man proposed by Rezin (king of Syria) and Pekah (king of Israel) to be the puppet king of Judah (Is. 7:6).

TABITHA [TAB ih thuh]

A form of DORCAS.

TABRIMMON [tab RIM uhn] *([the god] Rimmon is good)*

Father of Ben–Hadad I, king of Syria (1 Kin. 15:18; Tabrimon, KJV).

TAHAN [TAY han] *(graciousness)*

The name of two men in the Old Testament:

1. A descendant of Ephraim (Num. 26:35).

2. An ancestor of Joshua (1 Chr. 7:25–27).

TAHASH [TAY hash]

A form of THAHASH.

TAHATH [TAY hath] *(that which is beneath)*

The name of three men in the Old Testament:

1. A Kohathite Levite, a son of Assir (1 Chr. 6:24, 37).

2. A descendant of Ephraim (1 Chr. 7:20).

3. Another descendant of Ephraim (1 Chr. 7:20). He apparently was a grandson of Tahath No. 2.

TAHPENES [TAH puh neez]

A queen of Egypt who lived during the time of David and Solomon (1 Kin. 11:19–20). The Pharaoh gave Tahpenes' sister in marriage to HADAD the Edomite. But she died shortly after giving birth to her son, Genubath. Tahpenes raised the child in Pharaoh's house.

TAHREA [tuh REE uh]

A form of TAREA.

TALMAI [TAL migh]

The name of two men in the Old Testament:

1. One of the three sons of Anak (Num. 13:22; Josh. 15:14; Judg. 1:10). They were known as Anakim, a race of giants who were driven out of Hebron by Caleb's army and were finally killed by the tribe of Judah.

2. A king of Geshur whose daughter Maacah was one of David's wives and the mother of Absalom (2 Sam. 3:3).

TALMON [TAL muhn]

A Levite gatekeeper whose descendants returned from the Captivity with Zerubbabel (1 Chr. 9:17; Neh. 7:45).

TAMAH [TAH muh]

One of the Nethinim (Temple servants) whose descendants returned from the Captivity with Ezra (Ezra 2:53; Thamah, KJV; Neh. 7:55).

TAMAR [TAY mur] *(palm)*

The name of three women in the Bible:

1. The widow of Er and Onan, sons of Judah (Gen. 38:6–30; Matt. 1:3; Thamar, KJV). According to the law of Levi-

rate Marriage, Judah's third son, Shelah, should have married Tamar; their first child would have been regarded as his brother's and would have carried on his name. However, Judah withheld his third son from marrying Tamar. Undaunted, Tamar disguised herself as a harlot and offered herself to Judah. Twin sons, Perez and Zerah, were born of their union. Judah and Tamar became ancestors of Jesus through Perez (Matt. 1:3).

2. The lovely daughter of David by Maacah and sister of Absalom (2 Sam. 13:1–22, 32; 1 Chr. 3:9). Tamar was raped by her half-brother Amnon. She fled to Absalom, who plotted revenge. Two years later Absalom got his revenge for Tamar by arranging Amnon's murder.

3. Absalom's only surviving daughter, possibly named after his sister Tamar (2 Sam. 14:27).

TANHUMETH [tan HOO mith] (*comfort*)

A Netophathite whose son Seraiah remained with Gedaliah after the Captivity (2 Kin. 25:23).

TAPHATH [TAY fath]

One of Solomon's daughters (1 Kin. 4:11). She married the son of Abinadab, Solomon's supply officer in the district of Naphath–Dor.

TAPPUAH [TAP yoo uh] (*apple*)

A son of Hebron, of the tribe of Judah (1 Chr. 2:43).

TARAH [TAY ruh]

A form of TERAH.

TAREA [tuh REE uh]

A son of Micah and a descendant of Saul (1 Chr. 8:35; Tahrea, 1 Chr. 9:41).

TARSHISH [TAR shish] (*jasper*)

A high official at Shushan (Susa). He was one of seven princes of Persia and Media "who had access to the king's presence" (Esth. 1:14). Tarshish was one of those present at the royal banquet of King Ahasuerus that Vashti, the queen, refused to attend.

TARSHISHAH [TAR shish uh]

A son of Javan and great-grandson of Noah (Gen. 10:4; Tarshish, KJV, NIV).

TARTAN [TAR tan]

The title of the commander-in-chief (supreme commander, NIV) of the Assyrian army. The Assyrian word turdennu (Tartan) means "first in rank." Two Tartans are mentioned in Scripture:

1. A messenger sent by Sennacherib to the surrender of Jerusalem (2 Kin. 18:17).

2. A general of Sargon sent to besiege and capture Ashdod (Is. 20:1).

TATTENAI [TAT uh nigh]

The Persian governor of Samaria during the reign of Darius the Great (ruled 521–486 B.C.). When Tattenai sent a letter to Darius (Ezra 5:7–17), asking whether the work of restoring the Temple was authorized, the decree of King Cyrus ordering that it should be rebuilt was found.

TEBAH [TEE buh]

A son of Nahor and Reumah (Gen. 22:24).

TEBALIAH [tee buh LIE uh] (*the Lord has dipped*)

A Temple gatekeeper after the Captivity (1 Chr. 26:11).

TEHAPHNEHES [teh HAF nuh hez]

A form of TAHPANHES.

TEHINNAH [tih HIN uh] (*supplication*)

A son of Eshton, of the tribe of Judah (1 Chr. 4:12).

TELAH [TEE luh]

A son of Resheph and the father of Tahan (1 Chr. 7:25).

TELEM [TEE lem] (*a lamb*)

A gatekeeper who divorced his pagan wife after the Captivity (Ezra 10:24).

TEMA [TEE muh]

The 9th of the 12 sons of Ishmael (Gen. 25:15; 1 Chr. 1:30).

TEMAN [TEE muhn] (*on the right hand*)

A son of Eliphaz and a grandson of Esau (Gen. 36:11). Teman was an Edomite chief (Gen. 36:15; 1 Chr. 1:36) who gave his name to the region where his descendants settled (Gen. 36:34).

TEMENI [TEM uh nie]

A son of Ashhur and Naarah (1 Chr. 4:6).

TERAH [TEE ruh]

The father of Abraham and an ancestor of Christ (Gen. 11:26–27; Luke 3:34; Thara, KJV). Descended from Shem, Terah also was the father of Nahor and Haran. He lived at Ur of the Chaldeans most of his life; at Ur he worshiped the moon-god (Josh. 24:2). From Ur, Terah migrated with his son Abraham, his grandson Lot (Haran's son), and his daughter-in-law Sarah (Abraham's wife) to Haran, a city about 800 kilometers (500 miles) north of Ur and about 445 kilometers (275 miles) northeast of Damascus. Terah died in Haran, another city where the moon-god was worshiped, at the age of 205 (Gen. 11:24–32).

TERESH [TEE resh]

One of the two eunuchs who conspired against King Ahasuerus (Xerxes) of Persia. When Mordecai discovered their plot, they were hanged (Esth. 2:21).

TERTIUS [TUR shee uhs] (*third*)

The scribe or secretary to whom the apostle Paul dictated his letter to the Romans (Rom. 16:22).

TERTULLUS [tur TUHL uhs] (*third*)

A professional orator hired to prosecute the Jews' case against the apostle Paul (Acts 24:1–2). Tertullus accompanied Ananias the high priest and the elders from Jerusalem to Caesarea to accuse Paul before Felix, the Roman governor of Judea.

Tertullus' speech followed the common Roman pattern of his day. He began by flattering the judge, the "most noble Felix," for the peace and prosperity he had brought to the nation. He then charged Paul with crimes the apostle had not committed (Acts 21:26–40; 23:26–30; 24:10–21).

THADDAEUS [tha DEE uhs]

One of the twelve apostles of Jesus (Matt. 10:3; Mark 3:18; Thaddeus, KJV), also called Lebbaeus (Matt. 10:3) and Judas the son of James (Luke 6:16; Acts 1:13). He is carefully distinguished from Judas Iscariot (John 14:22). Nothing else is known about this most obscure of the apostles, but some scholars attribute the Epistle of Jude to him.

THAHASH [THAY hash]

The third son of Reumah, the concubine of Nahor (Gen. 22:24; Tahash, NASB, NIV, NRSV). Nahor was the brother of Abraham.

THAMAH [THAY muh]

A form of TAMAH.

THAMAR [THAY mahr]

A form of TAMAR.

THARA [THAR uh]

A form of TERAH.

THARSHISH [THAHR shish]

A son of Bilhan, of the tribe of Benjamin (1 Chr. 7:10).

THEOPHILUS [thih AHF uh luhs] (*lover of God*)

A Christian to whom Luke dedicated the Gospel of Luke and the Book of Acts (Luke 1:3; Acts 1:1). The fact that Luke spoke of Theophilus as "most excellent" indicates that he was a prominent man of high rank and possibly a Roman. He may have chosen the name when he was converted to Christianity. According to tradition, both Luke and Theophilus were natives of Antioch in Syria. Much speculation surrounds Theophilus, but little is known for certain about him.

THEUDAS [THOO duhs]

A false leader of whom Gamaliel spoke before the Sanhedrin, about A.D. 32. According to Gamaliel's account, about 400 men joined Theudas, but "he was slain, and all who obeyed him were scattered and came to nothing" (Acts 5:36).

Scholars are uncertain of the identity of Theudas. Luke records that Judas the Galilean rose up in the days of the census. It is certain that this Judas was Judas the Gaulanite who, according to the Jewish historian Josephus, incited a riot over the census in the time of Quirinius, about A.D. 6. Then Josephus mentions a magician named Theudas who, acting as a false prophet, persuaded many people to cross the Jordan River and was beheaded for his efforts by the Romans. But this Theudas lived about 4 B.C., after Judas.

Josephus has rarely been found in error, but Luke has also been established as a reliable historian. It is not unlikely then that there were two insurrectionists named Theudas who lived many years apart. Perhaps Luke's Theudas was one of the revolutionaries who arose during the turbulent last year of Herod the Great's rule. Or Theudas may have been the Greek name for one of the three revolutionaries named by Josephus: Judas, Simon, or Matthias.

THIMNATHAH [THIM nuh thuh]

A form of TIMNAH.

THOMAS [TAHM uhs] (*twin*)

One of the twelve apostles of Jesus; also called *Didymus*, the Greek word for "twin" (Matt. 10:3; Mark 3:18; Luke 6:15). Thomas is probably best known for his inability to believe that Jesus had indeed risen from the dead. For that inability to believe, he forever earned the name "doubting Thomas."

Thomas was not present when Jesus first appeared to His disciples after His resurrection. Upon hearing of the appearance, Thomas said, "Unless I see in His hands the print of the nails, and put my finger into the print of the nails, and put my hand into His side, I will not believe" (John 20:25). Eight days later, Jesus appeared again to the disciples, including Thomas. When Jesus invited him to touch the nail prints and put his hand into His side, Thomas' response was, "My Lord and my God!" (John 20:28). Of that incident the great church father Augustine remarked, "He doubted so that we might believe."

Thomas appears three other times in the Gospel of John. (Except for the listing

THOMAS

of the disciples, Thomas does not appear in the other three gospels.) When Jesus made known his intention to go into Judea, Thomas urged his fellow disciples, "Let us also go, that we may die with Him" (John 11:16). Knowing that His earthly life would soon end, Jesus said He was going to prepare a place for His followers and that they knew the way. Thomas asked, "Lord, we do not know where You are going, and how can we know the way?" (John 14:5). To that Jesus gave his well-known answer: "I am the way, the truth, and the life" (John 14:6).

After the resurrection, Thomas was on the Sea of Galilee with six other disciples when Jesus signaled to them from the shore and told them where to cast their net (John 21:2). Thomas was also with the other disciples in the Jerusalem upper room after the Ascension of Jesus.

According to tradition, Thomas spread the gospel in Parthia and Persia, where he died. Later tradition places Thomas in India, where he was martyred. The Mar Thoma church in India traces its origins to Thomas.

T

TIBERIUS [tie BEER ih us] (*son of the Tiber*)

Tiberius Claudius Nero Caesar (42 B.C.–A.D. 37), the second emperor of Rome (A.D. 14–37). The adopted son and son-in-law of Octavian (Augustus Caesar), Tiberius succeeded Augustus as emperor.

Tiberius is mentioned by name only once in the Bible. Luke 3:1 states that John the Baptist began his ministry "in the fifteenth year of the reign of Tiberius Caesar," or A.D. 28. Luke 3:1 is very important in helping to establish the chronology of the life and ministry of Jesus. Tiberius is also frequently referred to simply as "Caesar" (Luke 23:2; John 19:12, 15). The Pharisees and Herodians sought to entrap Jesus by asking him a question concerning tribute to Caesar: "Tell us . . . is it lawful to pay taxes to Caesar, or not?" The "Caesar" in question is Tiberius, and the coin they brought to Jesus bore Tiberius' image (Matt. 22:15–22; Mark 12:13–17; Luke 20:20–26). Jesus began his ministry and was crucified during the reign of Tiberius.

Born in Rome on November 16, 42 B.C., Tiberius became emperor in his fifty-fifth year and reigned for twenty-three years, until his death in March, A.D. 37, at the age of seventy-eight. Some historians believe that Caligula, the mad successor to Tiberius, hastened Tiberius' death.

TIBNI [TIBB nie]

A man who is sometimes listed as the sixth king of Israel (884–880 B.C.). He and Omri were rival kings for three years, but Omri eventually emerged as victorious (1 Kin. 16:21–22).

TIDAL [TIE duhl]

The "king of nations" (king of Goiim, NASB, NIV, NRSV) who joined an alliance with three other kings—Chedorlaomer, Amraphel, and Arioch—and attacked the cities of the plain (Gen. 14:1, 9).

TIGLATH–PILESER [TIG lath puh LEE zur] (*the firstborn of* [the god] *Esharra is my confidence*)

A king of Assyria (ruled 745–727 B.C.) and, under the name Pul (2 Kin. 15:19), king of Babylonia (729–727 B.C.). He is also called Tilgath–Pilneser (1 Chr. 5:6, 26; 2 Chr. 28:20).

The accession of Tiglath–Pileser to the throne ended a period of political and military weakness in Assyrian history. He moved first to reestablish Assyrian dominance in Babylon and also attacked his powerful opponent to the north, Urartu. In 740 B.C. he conquered Arpad in northern Syria. The effect of this victory was far-reaching (2 Kin. 19:13; Is. 37:13). Tribute came in from Tyre, Damascus, Cilicia, and Carchemish. During this period, Tiglath–Pileser penetrated all the way to Israel, where he received tribute from Menahem. The fabulous sum of 1,000 talents of silver "from all the very wealthy" probably resulted in the unpopularity of Menahem (2 Kin. 15:17–22). When Pekahiah, Menahem's son, succeeded to the throne, he ruled for only two years before he was assassinated. In all likelihood, the murder was a result of his father's unpopular policy of submission to Assyria (2 Kin. 15:23–26).

While serving as king of Israel, Pekah adopted a strong anti-Assyrian policy by aligning himself with Rezin, king of Syria. Both Pekah and Rezin sought to force Ahaz, king of Judah, to join the revolt. But Ahaz appealed to Tiglath–Pileser for help. In 734 B.C. Tiglath–Pileser moved south along the coast to cut off possible Egyptian aid to the revolt. In 733 B.C. he marched into Israel, devastating much of Galilee and deporting many Israelites (2 Kin. 15:29). Finally, he moved against the real power of the region, Damascus, which fell in 732 B.C.

After devastating the countryside, Tiglath–Pileser captured the city of Damascus, executed Rezin, and sent much of the Syrian population into exile. Meanwhile, Hoshea had assassinated Pekah to become the new king of Israel (2 Kin. 15:30). Hoshea paid tribute to Tiglath–Pileser, as did the kings of Ashkelon and Tyre. When Tiglath–Pileser died in 727 B.C., the borders of his country had been dramatically enlarged and every enemy of Assyria had been severely weakened.

TIKVAH [TICK vah] (expectation)

The name of two men in the Old Testament:

1. The father-in-law of Huldah the prophetess, wife of Shallum (2 Kin. 22:14; Tokhath, NASB, NIV; Tikvath, KJV). Tikvah is also spelled as Tokhath in the NKJV (2 Chr. 34:22).

2. The father of Jahaziah (Ezra 10:15).

TIKVATH [TIK vath]

A form of TIKVAH.

TILGATH–PILNESER [TIL gath pil NEE zur]

A form of TIGLATH–PILESER.

TILON [TIE luhn]

A son of Shimon, of the tribe of Judah (1 Chr. 4:20).

TIMAEUS [tih MEE uhs]

The father of the blind beggar Bartimaeus (Mark 10:46; Timeus, KJV).

TIMEUS [tih MEE us]

A form of TIMAEUS.

TIMNA [TIM nuh]

The name of a woman and a man in the Old Testament:

1. A daughter of Seir the Horite and sister of Lotan (Gen. 36:22; 1 Chr. 1:39).

2. A son of Eliphaz and grandson of Esau (1 Chr. 1:36), also Timnah (Gen. 36:40; 1 Chr. 1:51).

TIMNAH [TIM nuh]

A chief of Edom (Gen. 36:40; 1 Chr. 1:51), also spelled Timna (1 Chr. 1:36).

TIMON [TIE muhn]

One of the seven original "deacons" appointed to serve tables in the early church in Jerusalem (Acts 6:5).

TIMOTHY [TIM uh thih] (honored by God)

Paul's friend and chief associate, who is mentioned as joint sender in six of Paul's epistles (2 Cor. 1:1; Phil. 1:1; Col. 1:1; 1 Thess. 1:1; 2 Thess. 1:1; Philem. 1).

Timothy first appears in the second missionary journey when Paul revisited Lystra (Acts 16:1–3). Timothy was the son of a Gentile father and a Jewish–Christian mother named Eunice, and the grandson of Lois (Acts 16:1; 2 Tim. 1:5). Timothy may have been converted under Paul's ministry, because the apostle refers to him as his "beloved and faithful son in the Lord" (1 Cor. 4:17) and as his "true son in the faith" (1 Tim. 1:2). Timothy was held in high regard in Lystra and Iconium, and Paul desired to take him along as a traveling companion (Acts 16:3).

Timothy played a prominent role in the remainder of the second missionary journey. When Paul was forced to leave Berea because of an uproar started by Jews from Thessalonica, Silas and Timothy were left behind to strengthen the work in Macedonia (Acts 17:14). After they rejoined Paul in Athens (Acts 18:5), Paul sent Timothy back to the believers in Thessalonica to establish them and to encourage them to maintain the faith (1 Thess. 3:1–9). Timothy's report of the faith and love of the Thessalonians greatly encouraged Paul.

During Paul's third missionary journey, Timothy was active in the evangelizing of Corinth, although he had little success. When news of disturbances at Corinth reached Paul at Ephesus, he sent Timothy, perhaps along with Erastus (Acts 19:22), to resolve the difficulties. The mission failed, perhaps because of fear on Timothy's part (1 Cor. 16:10–11). Paul then sent the more forceful Titus, who was able to calm the situation at Corinth (2 Cor. 7). Later in the third journey, Timothy is listed as one of the group that accompanied Paul along the coast of Asia Minor on his way to Jerusalem (Acts 20:4–5).

Timothy also appears as a companion of Paul during his imprisonment in Rome (Col. 1:1; Phil. 1:1; Philem. 1). From Rome, Paul sent Timothy to Philippi to bring back word of the congregation that had supported the apostle so faithfully over the years.

Timothy's strongest traits were his sensitivity, affection, and loyalty. Paul commends him to the Philippians, for example, as one of proven character, faithful to Paul like a son to a father, and without rival in his concern for the Philippians (Phil. 2:19–23; also 2 Tim. 1:4; 3:10). Paul's warnings, however, to "be strong" (2 Tim. 2:1) suggest that Timothy suffered from fearfulness (1 Cor. 16:10–11; 2 Tim. 1:7) and perhaps youthful lusts (2 Tim. 2:22). But in spite of his weaknesses, Paul was closer to Timothy than to any other associate.

Writing about A.D. 325, Eusebius reported that Timothy was the first bishop of Ephesus. In 356 Constantius transferred what was thought to be Timothy's remains from Ephesus to Constantinople (modern Istanbul) and buried them in the Church of the Apostles, which had been built by his father Constantine.

TIRAS [TIRE us]

A son of Japheth (Gen. 10:2; 1 Chr. 1:5). Nothing else is known about Tiras. Some scholars believe Tiras' descendants were also an ancient people known by this name, but they are not mentioned in the Bible.

TIRHAKAH [tur HAY kuh]

The third king of the 25th dynasty of Egypt (reigned 689–664 B.C.). During his reign he opposed three Assyrian kings—Sennacherib, Esarhaddon, and Ashurbanipal (the biblical Osnapper)—in a struggle for control of Israel. Tirhakah is mentioned twice in the Bible (2 Kin. 19:9; Is. 37:9). Tirhakah gave military aid to Hezekiah, king of Judah (reigned 715–686 B.C.) to aid his resistance against Sennacherib.

TIRHANAH [tur HAY nuh]

A son of Caleb and his concubine Maachah (1 Chr. 2:48).

TIRIA [TIR igh uh]

A son of Jahaleleel, of the tribe of Judah (1 Chr. 4:16).

TIRZAH [TUR zuh]

The youngest of the five daughters of Zelophehad (Num. 26:33; Josh. 17:3).

TITIUS [TISH ee uhs]

A man of Corinth who worshiped God. His house was next door to the synagogue (Acts 18:7; Titius Justus, NRSV,

NIV, REB, NASB; Justus, KJV, NKJV). Also see JUSTUS.

TITUS [TIGH tuhs]

A "partner and fellow worker" (2 Cor. 8:23) of the apostle Paul. Although Titus is not mentioned in the Book of Acts, Paul's letters reveal that he was the man of the hour at a number of key points in Paul's life.

Paul first mentions Titus in Galatians 2:1–3. As an uncircumcised Gentile, Titus accompanied Paul and Barnabas to Jerusalem as a living example of a great theological truth: Gentiles need not be circumcised in order to be saved.

Titus next appears in connection with Paul's mission to Corinth. While Paul was in Ephesus during his third missionary journey, he received disturbing news from the church at Corinth. After writing two letters and paying one visit to Corinth, Paul sent Titus to Corinth with a third letter (2 Cor. 7:6–9). When Titus failed to return with news of the situation, Paul left Ephesus and, with a troubled spirit (2 Cor. 7:5), traveled north to Troas (2 Cor. 2:12–13).

Finally, in Macedonia, Titus met the anxious apostle with the good news that the church at Corinth had repented. In relief and joy, Paul wrote yet another letter to Corinth (2 Corinthians), perhaps from Philippi, sending it again through Titus (2 Cor. 7:5–16). In addition, Titus was given responsibility for completing the collection for the poor of Jerusalem (2 Cor. 8:6, 16–24; 12:18).

Titus appears in another important role on the island of Crete (Titus 1:4). Beset by a rise in false teaching and declining morality, Titus was told by Paul to strengthen the churches by teaching sound doctrine and good works, and by appointing elders in every city (Titus 1:5). Paul then urged Titus to join him in Ni-

copolis (on the west coast of Greece) for winter (Titus 3:12). Not surprisingly, Titus was remembered in church tradition as the first bishop of Crete.

A final reference to Titus comes from 2 Timothy 4:10, where Paul remarks in passing that Titus has departed for mission work in Dalmatia (modern Yugoslavia).

Titus was a man for the tough tasks. According to Paul, he was dependable (2 Cor. 8:17), reliable (2 Cor. 7:6), and diligent (2 Cor. 8:17); and he had a great capacity for human affection (2 Cor. 7:13–15). Possessing both strength and tact, Titus calmed a desperate situation on more than one occasion. He is a good model for Christians who are called to live out their witness in trying circumstances.

TIZITE [TIGH zight]

A name of Joha, one of David's mighty men (1 Chr. 11:45).

TOAH [TOE uh]

The great-great-grandfather of Samuel the prophet (1 Chr. 6:34), also called Tohu (1 Sam. 1:1).

TOBADONIJAH [tahb ad uh NIGH juh] (*good is the Lord, my Master*)

A Levite sent by King Jehoshaphat to teach the law of Moses in the cities of Judah (2 Chr. 17:8).

TOBIAH [toe BIGH uh] (*the Lord is good*)

The name of two men in the Old Testament:

1. The founder of a tribal family whose descendants returned from the Captivity but could not trace their genealogy (Ezra 2:60).

2. An Ammonite official who tried to prevent the Jews from rebuilding the wall of Jerusalem (Neh. 2:10; 4:3; 6:1–19).

TOBIJAH [toe BIGH juh] (*the Lord is good*)

The name of two men in the Old Testament:

1. A Levite sent by Jehoshaphat to teach the law of Moses in the cities of Judah (2 Chr. 17:8).

2. A Jewish captive from whom the prophet Zechariah received a gift of silver and gold to make an elaborate crown for Joshua the high priest (Zech. 6:10, 14).

TOGARMAH [toe GAHR muh]

A son of Gomer (Gen. 10:3; 1 Chr. 1:6).

TOHU [TOE hoo]

A form of TOAH.

TOI [TOE eye]

A king of Hamath who sent his son as a friendly ambassador to King David (2 Sam. 8:9–10). He is also called Tou (1 Chr. 18:9–10).

TOKHATH [TOE kath]

A form of TIKVAH.

TOLA [TOE luh] (*worm*)

The name of two men in the Old Testament:

1. A son of Issachar (Gen. 46:13; 1 Chr. 7:1–2) and the ancestor of the Tolaites (Num. 26:23).

2. A man of the tribe of Issachar who judged Israel 23 years (Judg. 10:1–2).

TOU [TOE oo]

A form of TOI.

TROPHIMUS [TROF ih muss]

A Gentile Christian who lived in Ephesus and who accompanied Paul to Jerusalem at the end of Paul's third missionary journey (Acts 20:4). When certain Jews from Asia saw Trophimus the Ephesian with Paul in Jerusalem, they supposed that Paul had brought "Greeks" (uncircumcised Gentiles) into the Court of Israel (an inner court beyond the Court of the Gentiles), defiling the Temple (Acts 21:28–29).

The people seized Paul, dragged him out of the Temple, and tried to kill him. But Paul was rescued by the commander of the Roman garrison and sent to Rome for trial.

Apparently Trophimus accompanied Paul on the trip toward Rome. In his Second Epistle to Timothy, Paul revealed, "Trophimus I have left in Miletus sick" (2 Tim. 4:20).

TRYPHAENA [trigh FEE nuh]

A form of TRYPHENA.

TRYPHENA [trigh FEE nuh]

A woman at Rome to whom the apostle Paul sent greetings (Rom. 16:12; Tryphaena, NRSV, REB, NASB). Tryphena is mentioned with another woman, Tryphosa. They may have been sisters, twins, or perhaps fellow deaconesses. Paul described them as women "who have labored in the Lord."

Also see TRYPHOSA.

TRYPHOSA [trigh FOE suh]

A woman in Rome to whom the apostle Paul sent greetings (Rom. 16:12), along with another woman, TRYPHENA.

TUBAL [TOO buhl]

The fifth son of Japheth and grandson of Noah (Gen. 10:2; 1 Chr. 1:5).

TUBAL-CAIN [too buhl KANE] (*Tubal the smith*)

A son of Lamech and Zillah. Tubal-Cain was the "father" of all metalworkers (Gen. 4:22).

TYCHICUS [TIKE ih kuhs]

A Christian of the province of Asia (Acts 20:4). Tychicus was a faithful friend, fellow worker, and messenger of the apostle Paul (Eph. 6:21–22; Col. 4:7–8). Along with other disciples, Tychicus traveled ahead of Paul from Macedonia to Troas, where he waited for the apostle's arrival (Acts 20:4).

Paul also sent Tychicus to Ephesus to deliver and perhaps to read his epistle to the Christians in that city (Eph. 6:21). He did the same with the Epistle to the Colossians (Col. 4:7). Paul sent him as a messenger to Titus in Crete (Titus 3:12) and afterward to Ephesus (2 Tim. 4:12).

TYRANNUS [tigh RAN uhs] (*tyrant*)

A man of Ephesus who owned a school or lecture hall at which the apostle Paul reasoned daily for two years (Acts 19:9–10). Tyrannus was either a teacher of rhetoric and philosophy or a Jewish rabbi who taught the law in his private synagogue. He allowed Paul to speak of Jesus so that people from throughout the province of Asia heard of Him.

T

U

UCAL–UZZIEL

UCAL [YOU cal]

An unknown person to whom Agur addressed his proverbs along with Ithiel (Prov. 30:1). Some scholars, however, do not believe Ithiel and Ucal are proper names. Therefore, "to Ithiel—to Ithiel and Ucal" (Prov. 30:1, NKJV) becomes "I am weary, O God, I am weary and worn out" (REB).

UEL [YOU ehl]

A son of Bani who married a pagan wife and then divorced her after the Captivity (Ezra 10:34).

UKNAZ [UHK naz]

The marginal reading of 1 Chronicles 4:15 (KJV; Kenaz, NKJV). Also see KENAZ.

ULAM [YOU lamm]

The name of two men in the Old Testament:

1. A son of Sheresh, of the tribe of Manasseh (1 Chr. 7:16–17).

2. A son of Eshek, of the tribe of Benjamin (1 Chr. 8:39). The sons of Ulam were "mighty men of valor—archers" (1 Chr. 8:40).

ULLA [UHL uh] (burden, yoke)

A descendant of Asher who became the father of three tribal leaders: Arah, Haniel, and Rizia (1 Chr. 7:39).

UNNI [UHN eye]

The name of two men in the Old Testament:

1. A Levite musician who accompanied the Ark of the Covenant brought by David to Jerusalem (1 Chr. 15:18, 20).

2. A Levite who returned from the Captivity with Zerubbabel (Neh. 12:9; Unno, NRSV).

UNNO [UHN oh]

A form of UNNI.

URBANUS [uhr BAIN us] (refined, polite)

A Christian in Rome to whom the apostle Paul sent greetings as "a fellow worker in Christ" (Rom. 16:9; Urbane, KJV).

URI [YOU rye] ([God is] my light)

The name of three men in the Old Testament:

1. A son of Hur and father of Bezaleel (Ex. 31:2). Bezaleel was the chief artisan of the tabernacle.

2. The father of Geber (1 Kin. 4:19). Geber was one of 12 governors in charge of providing food for Solomon and his household.

3. A gatekeeper who, at Ezra's urging, divorced the wife whom he had married during the Captivity (Ezra 10:24).

URIAH [you RYE uh] (the Lord is my light)

The name of three men in the Old Testament:

1. A Hittite married to Bathsheba. Uriah was one of David's mighty men (2 Sam. 11:3–26; 12:9–10, 15; 1 Kin. 15:5; Matt. 1:6; Urias, KJV).

Judging from the usual interpretation of his name and good conduct, Uriah was a worshiper of God. David's adultery with Uriah's wife, Bathsheba, occurred while Uriah was engaged in war at Rabbah, the Ammonite capital. Uriah was immediately recalled to Jerusalem to hide what had happened, but his sense of duty and loyalty only frustrated the king. Failing to use Uriah as a shield to cover his sin with Bathsheba, David ordered this valiant soldier to the front line of battle, where he was killed.

2. A priest, the son of Koz and father of Meremoth. Uriah helped rebuild the wall of Jerusalem under Nehemiah. He stood with Ezra the scribe as Ezra read

U

the law and addressed the people (Ezra 8:33). The NKJV spells his name Urijah in Nehemiah 3:4, 21; 8:4.

3. A priest, one of two faithful witnesses to a scroll written by the prophet Isaiah (Is. 8:2).

URIEL [YOU rih ehl] (God is my light)

The name of two or three men in the Old Testament:

1. A Levite of the family of Kohath (1 Chr. 6:24).

2. A chief of the Kohathites (1 Chr. 15:5, 11). Uriel was one of many priests employed by David when the Ark of the Covenant was brought to Jerusalem from the house of Obed–Edom. He may be the same as No. 1.

3. A man of Gibeah and father of a daughter named Michaiah (2 Chr. 13:2).

URIJAH [you RYE jah] (the Lord is my light)

The name of three men in the Old Testament:

1. A priest in Jerusalem who built an altar according to the pattern provided by King Ahaz (2 Kin. 16:10–16). When the wicked Ahaz sought help from the Assyrian King Tiglath–Pileser, he embraced pagan worship at an Assyrian altar and instructed Urijah to build a replica for his worship in Jerusalem. The priest fashioned the heathen altar, placing it in the court of the Temple in the place of the bronze altar of God. Without protest, he complied with Ahaz's instructions, offering all sacrifices and offering on the new altar.

2. A prophet, the son of Shemaiah of Kirjath Jearim and a contemporary of Jeremiah (Jer. 26:20–23). Like Jeremiah, this prophet of God was faithful to the Word of God, prophesying against Jerusalem and Judah. When King Jehoiakim tried to kill him, he sought asylum in Egypt. The king, however, had Urijah returned to Jerusalem, where he was killed.

3. Another form of URIAH No. 2.

UTHAI [YOU thigh]

The name of two men in the Old Testament:

1. A son of Ammihud of the tribe of Judah (1 Chr. 9:4). Uthai lived in Jerusalem after the Captivity.

2. A son of Bigvai (Ezra 8:14). With his brother Zabbud and 70 males, Uthai returned to Jerusalem with Ezra.

UZ [uhz]

The name of four men in the Old Testament:

1. A son of Aram and grandson of Shem (Gen. 10:23). The name may refer to an Aramean tribe or people.

2. A son of Nahor and Milcah (Gen. 22:21, NASB, NIV, NRSV; Huz, KJV, NKJV).

3. A son of Dishan, a Horite in the land of Edom (Gen. 36:28).

4. One of the sons (or descendants) of Shem (1 Chr. 1:17).

UZAI [YOU zie]

The father of Palal. Palal helped rebuild the walls of Jerusalem. "Palal the son of Uzai made repairs opposite the buttress, and on the tower" (Neh. 3:25).

UZAL [YOU zal]

A son of Joktan (Gen. 10:27). The name Uzal may refer to an Arabian tribe or settlement (Ezek. 27:19, NRSV). Recent scholarship identifies Uzal with a town named Azalla, in the neighborhood of Medina.

UZZA, UZZAH [UHZ uh] (strength)

The name of five men in the Old Testament:

URIAH

1. A man who was struck dead by God because he touched the Ark of the Covenant (2 Sam. 6:3–8; 1 Chr. 13:7–11).

2. A person in whose garden Manasseh, king of Judah, and Amon (Manasseh's son), also king of Judah, were buried (2 Kin. 21:18, 26).

3. A Levite of the family of Merari (1 Chr. 6:29).

4. A descendant of Ehud mentioned in the family tree of King Saul (1 Chr. 8:7).

5. An ancestor of a family of Nethinim (Temple servants) who returned with Zerubbabel from the Captivity (Ezra 2:49; Neh. 7:51).

UZZI [UHZ eye] ([God is] *my strength*)

The name of several men in the Old Testament:

1. A high priest descended from Aaron, Eleazar, and Phinehas (1 Chr. 6:5–6, 51). Uzzi was an ancestor of Ezra (Ezra 7:4).

2. A grandson of Issachar and father of Izrahiah (1 Chr. 7:2–3).

3. A son of Bela (1 Chr. 7:7).

4. The father of Elah, a Benjamite (1 Chr. 9:8). He may be the same person as No. 3.

5. An overseer of the Levites in Jerusalem after the Captivity (Neh. 11:22).

6. A priest, head of the house of Jedaiah in the days of the high priest Joiakim (Neh. 12:19).

7. A priest who helped dedicate the rebuilt walls of Jerusalem (Neh. 12:42). He may be the same person as No. 6.

UZZIA [you ZIE ah] (*the Lord is my strength*)

A native of Ashtaroth, an ancient city of Bashan, and one of David's mighty men (1 Chr. 11:44).

UZZIAH [you ZIE uh] (*the Lord is my strength*)

The name of five men in the Old Testament:

1. The son of Amaziah and Jecholiah; ninth king of Judah and father of Jotham (2 Kin. 15:1–7; 2 Chr. 26). Uzziah is also called Azariah (2 Kin. 14:21; 15:1–7).

U

Uzziah ascended the throne at age 16 and reigned longer than any previous king of Judah or Israel—52 years. He probably co-reigned with his father and had his son Jotham as his co-regent during his final years as a leper. A wise, pious, and powerful king, he extended Judah's territory and brought the nation to a time of great prosperity. In the south he maintained control over Edom and rebuilt port facilities at Elath on the Gulf of Aqaba. To the west he warred against the Philistines, seizing several cities. He also apparently defeated and subdued the Ammonites.

The foolishness of Uzziah's father Amaziah in fighting Joash, the king of Israel, had left the city of Jerusalem in a vulnerable position (2 Chr. 25:23). So Uzziah focused his attention on securing the defenses of both his capital and his country. He reinforced the towers of the city gates. On these towers and walls he placed huge catapults capable of shooting arrows and hurling stones at the enemy (2 Chr. 26:15). He also maintained a well-equipped army and fortified strategic places in the desert. His successes were directly related to his spiritual sensitivity, because he sought the Lord through a prophet who encouraged him to honor and obey God (2 Chr. 26:5).

However, Uzziah's heart was lifted up in pride. No longer satisfied to be a mortal king, he desired to be like some of his contemporaries—a divine king. He entered the Temple to burn incense. When Azariah the high priest and 80 associates confronted him, he responded in anger instead of repentance. God judged him by striking him with leprosy. Uzziah was forced to live the rest of his life in a separate place, with his son Jotham probably acting as king. At Uzziah's death the prophet Isaiah had a transforming vision of the Lord, high and lifted up on a throne (Is. 1:1; 6:1–13; 7:1).

2. A Levite of the family of Kohath, Uzziah was the son of Uriel and the father of Shaul (1 Chr. 6:24).

3. The father of Jehonathan (1 Chr. 27:25). Jehonathan was an officer of David over the storehouses.

4. A priest commanded by Ezra to divorce his pagan wife (Ezra 10:21).

5. The father of Athaiah (Neh. 11:4).

UZZIEL [uh ZEYE el] (*God is my strength*)

The name of six men in the Old Testament:

1. A Levite, son of Kohath, and founder of a tribal family (Ex. 6:18; Lev. 10:4). Uzziel was the ancestor of the Uzzielites (Num. 3:27; 1 Chr. 26:23).

2. One of four sons of Ishi, of the tribe of Simeon (1 Chr. 4:42).

3. A son of Bela and grandson of Benjamin (1 Chr. 7:7).

4. One of the sons of Heman (1 Chr. 25:4).

5. A Levite, son of Jeduthun (2 Chr. 29:14). Uzziel helped cleanse the Temple during King Hezekiah's religious reformation.

6. The son of Harhaiah (Neh. 3:8). Uzziel was a goldsmith who helped repair a part of the damaged wall of Jerusalem.

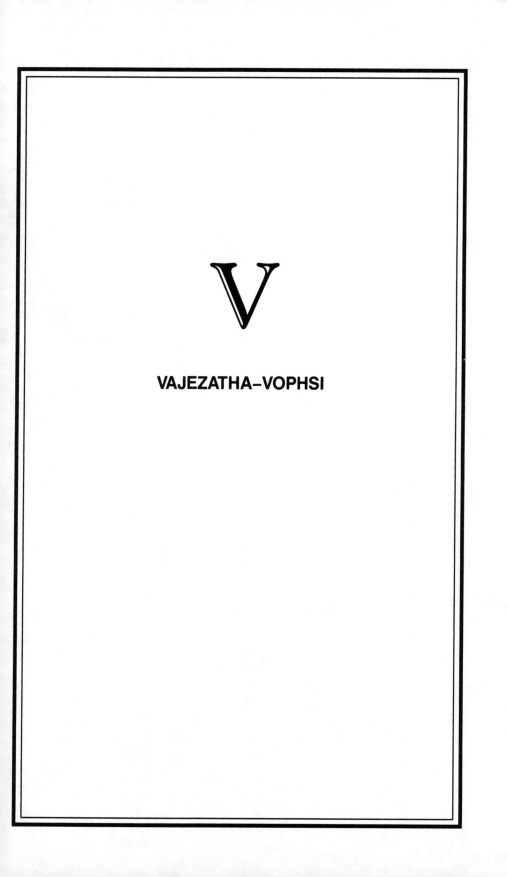

V

VAJEZATHA–VOPHSI

VAJEZATHA [vah JEZ ah thah]

One of the ten sons of Haman, all of whom were hanged like their father after he tried to destroy all the Jews in the Persian Empire (Esth. 9:9–10, 13).

VANIAH [vah NIE ah]

One of the sons of Bani who divorced his pagan wife after returning from the Captivity (Ezra 10:36).

VASHNI [VASH nie]

KJV word for the firstborn son of Samuel the prophet (1 Chr. 6:28). Most modern versions, however, have Joel instead of Vashni.

VASHTI [VASH tie]

The beautiful queen of King Ahasuerus (Xerxes I, reigned 486–465 B.C.) who was banished from court for refusing the king's command to exhibit herself during a period of drunken feasting (Esth. 1:11). Her departure allowed Esther to become Ahasuerus' new queen and to be used as God's instrument in saving the Jewish people from destruction.

VOPHSI [VAHF sigh]

The father of Nahbi, of the tribe of Naphtali (Num. 13:14).

V

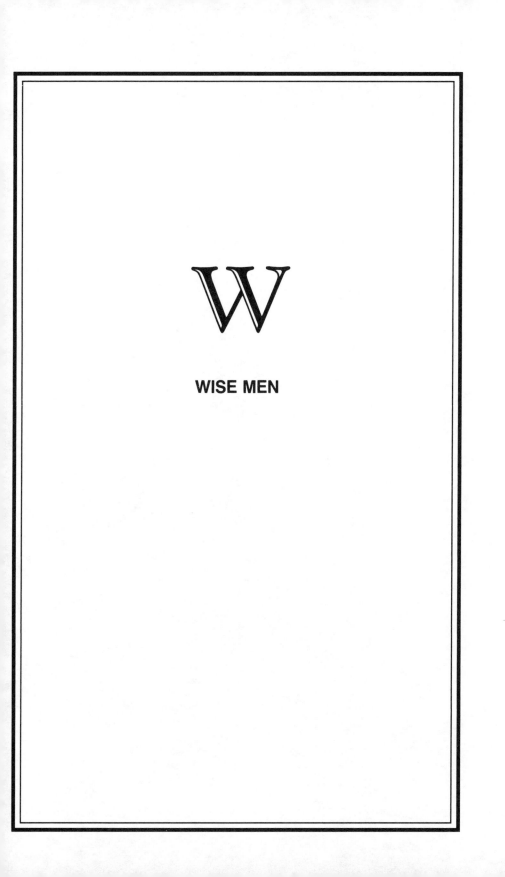

W

WISE MEN

WISE MEN

The men from the East who were led by a star to come to Palestine to worship the infant Christ (Matt. 2:1, 7, 16). The Greek word for wise men in this account (*magoi*) is rendered as "astrologers" where it occurs in the Septuagint, the Greek translation of the Old Testament (Dan. 1:20; 2:2) and as "sorcerer" in its other occurrences in the New Testament (Acts 13:6, 8).

The Greek historian Herodotus, writing in the fifth century B.C., identified the Magi as a caste of Medes who had a priestly function in the Persian Empire. In the Book of Daniel the "astrologers"

(*magoi*) are grouped with magicians, sorcerers, and Chaldeans as advisers to the court of Babylon with responsibility for interpreting dreams.

The role of the star in Matthew 2 suggests a connection with astrology. These astrologers, pursuing their observations of the stars in the heavens, encountered a sign of God (Matt. 24:29–30). God broke through their misguided system to make the great event known.

The joy, rejoicing, worship, and gifts that mark the response of these wise men to the birth of Jesus is quite a contrast to the troubled state and murderous intent of Herod and his advisers in Jerusalem (Matt. 2:1–12).

W

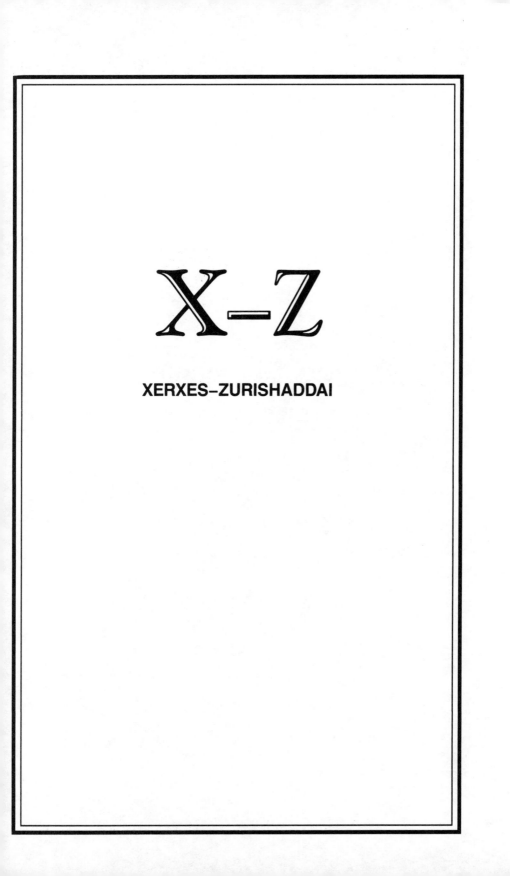

X–Z

XERXES–ZURISHADDAI

XERXES [ZURK sees]

The Greek name of AHASUERUS, the king mentioned in the Book of Esther (Esth. 1:1; 2:1; 3:1, NIV). Known as Xerxes the Great, he was the king of Persia from 486–465 B.C.

ZAAVAN [ZAY ah van]

A son of Ezer the Horite (Gen. 36:27).

ZABAD [ZAY bad] (*gift, endowment*)

The name of seven men in the Old Testament:

1. A Judahite of the family of Hezron, of the house of Jerahmeel (1 Chr. 2:36–37). Zabad was a son of Nathan and the father of Ephlal.

2. An Ephraimite of the family of Shuthelah (1 Chr. 7:21). Zabad was a son of Tahath and the father of Shuthelah.

3. One of David's mighty men (1 Chr. 11:41) and a son of Ahlai.

4. One of two servants of King Joash of Judah who conspired against their king and murdered him (2 Chr. 24:26). Zabad was the son of Shimeath the Ammonitess. He is also called Jozachar (2 Kin. 12:21).

5, 6, 7. Three Jews who were persuaded by Ezra to divorce their pagan wives (Ezra 10:27, 33, 43).

ZABBAI [ZAB ay eye]

The name of one or two men in the Old Testament:

1. One of the sons, or descendants, of Bebai (Ezra 10:28). Zabbai divorced his pagan wife after the Captivity.

2. The father of a certain Baruch (Neh. 3:20). Baruch helped repair the wall of Jerusalem after the Captivity. Zabbai may be the same person as Zaccai (Ezra 2:9; Neh. 7:14) or the same person as Zabbai No. 1.

ZABBUD [ZAB uhd]

One of the sons, or descendants, of Bigvai (Ezra 8:14; Zaccur, NIV). Zabbud returned from the Captivity with Ezra.

ZABDI [ZAB die] (*gift* [of the Lord])

The name of four men in the Old Testament:

1. The grandfather of Achan (Josh. 7:1, 17–18). Achan took spoils of battle from Jericho and was responsible for Israel's defeat at Ai in the days of Joshua. Zabdi is also called Zimri (1 Chr. 2:6).

2. A Benjamite mentioned in the family tree of King Saul (1 Chr. 8:19).

3. A state official in David's administration. Zabdi was custodian of the royal wine-cellars (1 Chr. 27:27).

4. The grandfather of Mattaniah (Neh. 11:17). Mattaniah led a prayer of thanksgiving after the return from the Captivity. Zabdi is also called Zichri (1 Chr. 9:15).

ZABDIEL [ZAB dih ehl] (*my gift is God*)

The name of two men in the Old Testament:

1. The father of Jashobeam, a descendant of Perez of the tribe of Judah (1 Chr. 27:2).

2. An overseer of the priests in Jerusalem in the days of Nehemiah (Neh. 11:14).

ZABUD [ZAY bud] (*bestowed* or *endowed*)

An official in Solomon's administration (1 Kin. 4:5). He was a "principal officer" (KJV) and "a personal advisor to the king" (NIV).

ZABULON [ZAB you lon]

Greek form of ZEBULUN (Rev. 7:8, KJV).

Z

ZACCAI [ZACK cay eye]

A person whose descendants returned from the Captivity with Zerubbabel (Ezra 2:9; Neh. 7:14). Also see ZABBAI No. 2.

ZACCHAEUS [zack KEY us] (*pure*)

A chief tax collector of Jericho who had grown rich by overtaxing the people. When Jesus visited Jericho, Zacchaeus climbed a tree in order to see Jesus (Luke 19:3). Jesus asked him to come down and then went to visit Zacchaeus as a guest. As a result of Jesus' visit, Zacchaeus became a follower of the Lord, repented of his sins, and made restitution for his wrongdoing. He gave half of his goods to the poor and restored fourfold those whom he had cheated. In associating with people like Zacchaeus, Jesus showed that He came to call sinners to repentance.

ZACCHUR [ZACK coor] (*well remembered*)

A Simeonite, descended through Mishma (1 Chr. 4:26; Zaccur, NIV, NRSV).

ZACCUR [ZACK cure] (*well remembered*)

The name of six men in the Old Testament:
1. The father of Shammua (Num. 13:4).
2. A Merarite Levite, a son of Jaaziah (1 Chr. 24:27).
3. A Gershonite Levite, head of a course of musicians set up by King David (1 Chr. 25:2; Neh. 12:35).
4. A son of Imri (Neh. 3:2). Zaccur helped rebuild the wall of Jerusalem after the Captivity.
5. A Levite who sealed the covenant after the Captivity (Neh. 10:12).

6. An administrator who helped Nehemiah in his reforms (Neh. 13:13).
Also see ZABBUD; ZACCHUR.

ZACHARIAH [zack ah RYE uh]

A form of ZECHARIAH.

ZACHARIAS [zack ah RYE us] (*the Lord has remembered*)

The name of two men in the New Testament:
1. The prophet whom the Jews "murdered between the temple and the altar" (Matt. 23:35, KJV) because he rebuked them for breaking God's commandments (Luke 11:51, KJV). This may be a reference to Zechariah, who was stoned to death in the court of the house of the Lord (2 Chr. 24:20–22).
2. The father of John the Baptist (Luke 1:13; 3:2). Zacharias was a priest of the division of Abijah. His wife, Elizabeth, was one "of the daughters of Aaron" (Luke 1:5), meaning she also was of priestly descent.
Also see ZECHARIAH.

ZADOK [ZAY dock] (*just, righteous*)

The name of several men in the Bible:
1. A high priest in the time of David. Zadok was a son of Ahitub (2 Sam. 8:17) and a descendant of Aaron through Eleazar (1 Chr. 24:3). During David's reign he served jointly as high priest with Abiathar (2 Sam. 8:17).

Both Zadok and Abiathar fled from Jerusalem with David when the King's son Absalom attempted to take over the throne. They brought the Ark of the Covenant out with them. After Absalom had been killed, David asked Zadok and Abiathar to urge the people to recall David to the throne (2 Sam. 19:11).

When David was dying, another of his sons, Adonijah, tried to take the throne.

This time only Zadok remained faithful to the king. When David heard of the plot, he ordered Zadok and the prophet Nathan to anoint Solomon king (1 Kin. 1:7–8, 32–45).

Consequently, Abiathar was deposed and Zadok held the high priesthood alone (1 Kin. 2:26–27). In this way the high priesthood was restored to the line of Eleazar, son of Aaron.

2. The grandfather of Jotham, king of Judah (2 Kin. 15:33; 2 Chr. 27:1).

3. A high priest in Solomon's Temple (1 Chr. 6:12; 9:11).

4. A valiant warrior who joined David's army at Hebron (1 Chr. 12:28).

5. A son of Baana who helped repair part of the Jerusalem wall after the Captivity (Neh. 3:4). He may be the same person as No. 7.

6. A son of Immer who helped repair Jerusalem's wall (Neh. 3:29). He may be the same person as No. 9.

7. An Israelite who sealed the covenant with Nehemiah (Neh. 10:21). He may be the same person as No. 5.

8. A son of Meraioth (Neh. 11:11).

9. A scribe in the time of Nehemiah (Neh. 13:13). Zadok was appointed a treasurer over the storehouse.

10. An ancestor of Jesus (Matt. 1:14; Sadoc, KJV).

ZAHAM [ZAY ham]

A son of King Rehoboam of Judah (2 Chr. 11:19).

ZALAPH [ZAY lahf]

The father of Hanun (Neh. 3:30). Hanun helped repair a section of the wall of Jerusalem in the time of Nehemiah.

ZACCHAEUS

ZALMON [ZAL muhn]

One of David's mighty men (2 Sam. 23:28). He is also called Ilai (1 Chr. 11:29).

ZALMUNNA [zal MUN nah]

(See ZEBAH, ZALMUNNA.)

ZAPHNATH-PAANEAH [ZAF nath pay ah NEE ah]

The Hebrew form of the Egyptian name given to Joseph by Pharaoh when the king of Egypt raised Joseph to the rank of "prime minister" of the kingdom (Gen. 41:45; Zaphenath-paneah, NASB, REB, NIV, NRSV).

ZARA, ZARAH [ZAY rah]

Forms of ZERAH.

ZATTU [ZAT two]

The founder of a family of Israelites who returned from the Captivity with Zerubbabel (Ezra 2:8; Neh. 7:13). Some men of this family had married pagan wives, but Ezra convinced them to divorce these women (Ezra 10:27). The leader of this family signed the pledge of reform in Nehemiah's time (Neh. 10:14).

ZAZA [ZAY zah]

A son of Jonathan and descendant of Jerahmeel, of the tribe of Judah (1 Chr. 2:33).

ZEBADIAH [zebb ah DIE ah] (*the Lord has given*)

The name of nine men in the Old Testament:

1. A Benjamite, one of the sons of Beriah (1 Chr. 8:15).

2. A Benjamite, one of the sons of Elpaal (1 Chr. 8:17).

3. A son of Jeroham of Gedor (1 Chr. 12:7). With his brother, Zebadiah joined David at Ziklag.

4. A gatekeeper of the sanctuary in David's time (1 Chr. 26:2).

5. A captain of the fourth division of David's army (1 Chr. 27:7). Zebadiah took command of this division after Asahel was killed by Abner.

6. A leader sent by King Jehoshaphat to teach the Law in the cities of Judah (2 Chr. 17:7–8).

7. A son of Ishmael in the time of King Jehoshaphat (2 Chr. 19:11).

8. A son of Michael who returned with Ezra from the Captivity (Ezra 8:8).

9. A priest of the house of Immer (Ezra 10:20) who divorced his foreign wife.

ZEBAH, ZALMUNNA [ZEE bah, zal MUN nah]

Two Midianite kings who were killed by the army of GIDEON (Judg. 8:5–21; Ps. 83:11). The execution of Zebah and Zalmunna was a blood revenge, because these Midianite kings had previously killed Gideon's brothers at Tabor (Judg. 8:18–19). Gideon's victory over Zebah and Zalmunna was a turning point for the Israelites in their struggle against the Midianites. It was long remembered in Israel (Ps. 83:11; Is. 9:4; 10:26).

ZEBEDEE [ZEBB uh dee] (*gift* [of the Lord])

The father of James and John, (Matt. 4:21–22; Mark 1:19–20). Apparently Zebedee's wife was named Salome (Matt. 20:20; Mark 15:40). He was a fisherman on the Sea of Galilee, perhaps living in Capernaum or Bethsaida. Zebedee was probably wealthy since he had "hired servants" (Mark 1:20). In later references to Zebedee, he appears in the phrase "sons [or son] of Zebedee" (Matt. 10:2; Mark 10:35; Luke 5:10; John 21:2).

ZEBIDAH [zeh BUY dah]

A form of ZEBUDAH.

ZEBINA [zeh BUY nah]

A descendant of Nebo who divorced his foreign wife after the Captivity (Ezra 10:43).

ZEBUDAH [zeh BOO dah] (*gift*)

The mother of Jehoiakim, king of Judah (2 Kin. 23:36; Zebidah, NASB, REB, NIV, NRSV). Zebudah was a daughter of Pedaiah of Rumah and the wife of Josiah, king of Judah.

ZEBUL [ZEE buhl]

The ruler of the city of Shechem under Abimelech (Judg. 9:28–41). When Zebul warned Abimelech of a plot to seize control of the city, Abimelech destroyed Shechem and killed its entire population. He then sowed the city's ruins with salt.

ZEBULUN [ZEBB you lun]

The tenth of Jacob's 12 sons; the sixth and last son of Leah (Gen. 30:19–20; 35:23; 1 Chr. 2:1). Zebulun had three sons: Sered, Elon, and Jahleel (Gen. 46:14; Num. 26:26–27). These are the only details about Zebulun that appear in the Bible.

ZECHARIAH [zeck ah RIE a] (*the Lord remembers*)

The name of about 30 men in the Bible:

1. The 15th king of Israel (2 Kin. 14:29; 15:8, 11; Zachariah, KJV), the last of the house of Jehu. The son of Jeroboam II, Zechariah became king when his father died. He reigned only six months (about 753/52 B.C.) before being assassinated by Shallum.

2. The father of Abi or Abijah, mother of Hezekiah (2 Kin. 18:2; Zachariah, KJV; 2 Chr. 29:1).

3. A chief of the tribe of Reuben (1 Chr. 5:7).

4. A son of Meshelemiah (1 Chr. 9:21; 26:2, 14) and a Levite doorkeeper in the days of David.

5. A son of Jeiel, of the tribe of Benjamin (1 Chr. 9:37), also called Zecher (1 Chr. 8:31).

6. A Levite musician in the days of David (1 Chr. 15:18).

7. A priest and musician in the days of David (1 Chr. 15:24).

8. A descendant of Levi through Kohath (1 Chr. 24:25).

9. A descendant of Levi through Merari (1 Chr. 26:11).

10. A Manassite of Gilead and the father of Iddo (1 Chr. 27:21).

11. A leader sent by King Jehoshaphat to teach the people of Judah (2 Chr. 17:7).

12. The father of Jahaziel, a Levite who encouraged Jehoshaphat against Moab (2 Chr. 20:14).

13. A son of King Jehoshaphat (2 Chr. 21:2).

14. A son of Jehoiada (2 Chr. 24:20). This Zechariah was stoned to death at the command of Joash, king of Judah (v. 21).

15. A prophet in the days of Uzziah, king of Judah (2 Chr. 26:5).

16. A Levite who helped cleanse the Temple during the reign of King Hezekiah of Judah (2 Chr. 29:13).

17. A Levite who supervised Temple repairs during Josiah's reign (2 Chr. 34:12).

18. A prince of Judah in the days of Josiah (2 Chr. 35:8).

19. A prophet in the days of Ezra (Ezra 5:1; 6:14; Zech. 1:1, 7; 7:1, 8) and author of the Book of Zechariah. A leader in the restoration of the nation of Israel following the Captivity, Zechariah was a contemporary of the prophet Hag-

Z

gai, the governor Zerubbabel, and the high priest Joshua. Zechariah himself was an important person during the period of the restoration of the community of Israel in the land of Palestine after the Captivity.

The Book of Zechariah begins with a note concerning the prophet. He is named as a grandson of Iddo, one of the heads of the priestly families who returned with Zerubbabel from Babylon (Zech. 1:1, 7; also Ezra 5:1; 6:14). This means that Zechariah himself was probably a priest and that his prophetic activity was in close association with the religious center of the nation. His vision of Joshua the high priest (Zech. 3:1–5) takes on added importance, since he served as a priest in association with Joshua. Zechariah began his ministry while still a young man (Zech. 2:4) in 520 B.C., two months after Haggai completed the prophecies that are recorded in the Book of Haggai.

20. A leader of the Jews who returned to Palestine with Ezra after the Captivity (Ezra 8:3).

21. A son of Bebai who returned with Ezra from the Captivity (Ezra 8:11).

22. A leader of Israel after the Captivity (Ezra 8:16). He may be the same person as No. 20 or No. 21.

23. An Israelite who divorced his pagan wife after the return from the Captivity (Ezra 10:26).

24. A man who stood with Ezra at the public reading of the law (Neh. 8:4).

25. A descendant of Perez, of the tribe of Judah (Neh. 11:4).

26. A person whose descendants lived in Jerusalem after the Captivity (Neh. 11:5).

27. A priest descended from Pashhur (Neh. 11:12).

28. A Levite who led a group of musicians at the dedication of the rebuilt wall of Jerusalem (Neh. 12:35–36).

29. A priest who took part in the dedication ceremony for the rebuilt wall of Jerusalem (Neh. 12:41).

30. A son of Jeberechiah (Is. 8:2) and a witness who recorded a prophecy given to Isaiah.

31. A prophet whom the Jews stoned (Matt. 23:35; Luke 11:51). He may be the same as No. 14.

ZECHER [ZEE ker]

A form of ZECHARIAH.

ZEDEKIAH [zedd eh KIE ah] (*the Lord my righteousness*)

The name of five men in the Old Testament:

1. A false prophet, son of Chenaanah, who advised King Ahab of Israel to attack the Syrian army at Ramoth Gilead (1 Kin. 22:11). Zedekiah's flattery and unfounded optimism proved to be lies; the king was mortally wounded in the battle.

2. The last king of Judah (597–586 B.C.). The son of Josiah, Zedekiah was successor to Jehoiachin as king (2 Kin. 24:17–20; 25:1–7; 2 Chr. 36:10–13). After Jehoiachin had reigned only three months, he was deposed and carried off to Babylonia. Nebuchadnezzar installed Zedekiah on the throne as a puppet king and made him swear an oath that he would remain loyal (2 Chr. 36:13; Ezek. 17:13). Zedekiah's original name was Mattaniah, but Nebuchadnezzar renamed him to demonstrate his authority over him and his ownership of him (2 Kin. 24:17). Although Zedekiah reigned in Jerusalem for 11 years, he was never fully accepted as their king by the people of Judah.

Because Zedekiah was a weak and indecisive ruler, he faced constant political unrest. Almost from the first he appeared restless about his oath of loyalty to Babylon, although he reaffirmed that commitment in the fourth year of his reign (Jer. 51:59). However, he was under constant pressure from his advisors to revolt and look to Egypt for help. A new coalition composed of Edom, Moab, Ammon, and Phoenicia was forming against Babylonia and they urged Judah to join (Jer. 27:3). Adding to the general unrest was the message of false prophets who declared that the yoke of Babylon had been broken (Jeremiah 28).

In his ninth year Zedekiah revolted against Babylonia. King Nebuchadnezzar invaded Judah and besieged Jerusalem. While Jerusalem was under siege, other Judean cities were falling to the Babylonians (Jer. 34:7).

The final months of the siege were desperate times for Zedekiah and the inhabitants of Jerusalem. The king made frequent calls on the prophet Jeremiah, seeking an encouraging word from the Lord. Jeremiah's message consistently offered only one alternative: Surrender to Nebuchadnezzar in order to live in peace and save Jerusalem. To his credit, Zedekiah was not arrogant and heartless (Jer. 36:22–23). But he regarded God's prophetic word superstitiously and "did not humble himself before Jeremiah the prophet, who spoke from the mouth of the LORD" (2 Chr. 36:12).

In 586 B.C. the wall of Jerusalem was breached, and Zedekiah fled the city. The army of the Babylonians pursued the king, overtaking him in the plains of Jericho. He was brought before Nebuchadnezzar and forced to watch the slaying of his sons. Then his own eyes were put out and he was led away to Babylonia (2 Kin. 25:6–7). Zedekiah died during the years of the Captivity of the Jewish people in Babylon. His reign marked the end

of the nation of Judah as an independent, self-governing country.

3. A prominent Jewish official who sealed the covenant with Nehemiah after returning from the Captivity (Neh. 10:1; Zidkijah, KJV).

4. A false prophet denounced by the prophet Jeremiah (Jer. 29:21).

5. A prince of Judah, son of Hananiah, in the days of the prophet Jeremiah and Jehoiakim, king of Judah (Jer. 36:12).

ZEEB [ZEE ebb] (a wolf)

One of two princes of the Midianites defeated by the army of Gideon. The men of Ephraim beheaded Oreb and Zeeb and brought their heads to Gideon on the other side of the Jordan River (Judg. 7:25; 8:3).

ZELEK [ZEE lehk]

An Ammonite, one of David's mighty men (2 Sam. 23:37; 1 Chr. 11:39).

ZELOPHEHAD [zeh LOW fee had]

A man of the tribe of Manasseh who died during the wilderness wandering, leaving five daughters. Because Zelophehad had no male heirs, his daughters— Mahlah, Noah, Hoglah, Milcah, and Tirzah—went to Moses and requested that they inherit their father's property. Moses allowed this, with one stipulation; they were to marry within their father's tribe (Num. 26:33; 27:1–11; 36:2–11).

ZELOTES [zeh LOW tees] (full of zeal)

A nickname of Simon, one of the twelve apostles of Jesus (Luke 6:15; Acts 1:13, KJV), to distinguish him from Simon Peter. Modern versions translate as the Zealot.

ZEMIRAH [zeh MY rah]

A Benjamite of the family of Becher (1 Chr. 7:8; Zemira, KJV, REB).

Z

ZENAS [ZEE nahs]

A Christian missionary who worked with Titus on the island of Crete (Titus 3:13). The apostle Paul called Zenas a lawyer, or a man skilled in the Jewish law, an expert in the Torah.

According to church tradition, Zenas was the first bishop of Diospolis (Lydda) in Palestine and the author of the apocryphal Acts of Titus.

ZEPHANIAH [zeff ah NIE ah] (the Lord has hidden)

The name of four men in the Old Testament:

1. A son of Maaseiah (2 Kin. 25:18; Jer. 21:1; 29:25, 29; 37:3).

2. A Levite of the family of Kohath (1 Chr. 6:36).

3. An Old Testament prophet and the author of the Book of Zephaniah (Zeph. 1:1). As God's spokesman to the southern kingdom of Judah, Zephaniah began his ministry about 627 B.C., the same year as the great prophet JEREMIAH. Zephaniah was a member of the royal house of Judah, since he traced his ancestry back to King Hezekiah. He prophesied during the reign of King Josiah (ruled 640–609 B.C.). One theme of his message was that through His judgment God would preserve a remnant, a small group of people who would continue to serve as His faithful servants in the world (Zeph. 3:8–13).

4. Father of Josiah (Zech. 6:10).

ZEPHI, ZEPHO [ZEE fie, ZEE foe] (watchtower)

The third son of Eliphaz the Edomite, descended from Esau (Zepho, Gen. 36:11; Zephi, 1 Chr. 1:36).

ZEPHON [ZEE fun]

One of the seven sons of Gad and founder of a tribal family, the Zephonites (Num. 26:15). He is also called Ziphion (Gen. 46:16).

ZERAH [ZEE ruh] (sprout)

The name of seven men in the Old Testament:

1. An Edomite chief descended from Esau and also from Ishmael (Gen. 36:13, 17; 1 Chr. 1:37).

2. The father of Jobab (Gen. 36:33; 1 Chr. 1:44). Jobab was one of the early kings of Edom.

3. One of the twins born to Judah by Tamar, his daughter-in-law (Gen. 38:30; 46:12, Zarah, KJV; Matt. 1:3, Zara, KJV). He founded a tribal family of Judah, the Zarhites (Num. 26:20).

4. A son of Simeon, second son of Jacob and Leah (Num. 26:13; 1 Chr. 4:24), also called Zohar (Gen. 46:10; Ex. 6:15). He was the founder of a tribal family, the Zarhites (Num. 26:13).

5. A Gershonite Levite (1 Chr. 6:21).

6. The father of Ethni, a Levite (1 Chr. 6:41).

7. A Cushite (2 Chr. 14:9, NIV, REB), or Ethiopian (KJV, NKJV, NRSV, NASB), who led a large army against King Asa of Judah. Zerah's warriors were defeated by Asa's smaller army.

ZERAHIAH [zehr ah HIGH ah] (the Lord shines forth)

The name of two men in the Old Testament:

1. A son of Uzzi and father of Meraioth (1 Chr. 6:6, 51–52; Ezra 7:3–4). A priest, Zerahiah was a descendant of Phinehas and an ancestor of Ezra.

2. The father of Elihoenai (Ezra 8:4).

ZERESH [ZEE resh]

The wife of HAMAN the Agagite (Esth. 5:10, 14; 6:13). Zeresh advised Haman to satisfy his hatred for the Jews by building a gallows for Mordecai (Esth. 5:14). Later, however, when she learned that Mordecai was of Jewish descent, she warned Haman that Mordecai would prevail. She predicted Haman's downfall.

ZERETH [ZEE reth]

The first son of Helah, the wife of Asshur (1 Chr. 4:5, 7).

ZERI [ZEE rye]

One of the "sons of Jeduthun," a group of Levitical singers established during the reign of David. Apparently Zeri was the head of this family after the return from the Captivity (1 Chr. 25:3).

ZEROR [ZEE rohr]

An ancestor of King Saul (1 Sam. 9:1).

ZERUAH [zeh ROO ah]

The mother of Jeroboam, the first king of the northern kingdom of Israel, and wife of Nebat (1 Kin. 11:26).

ZERUBBABEL [zeh RUB uh buhl]
(offspring of Babylon)

Head of the tribe of Judah at the time of the return from the Babylonian Captivity; prime builder of the Second Temple.

Zerubbabel is a shadowy figure who emerges as the political and spiritual head of the tribe of Judah at the time of the Babylonian captivity. Zerubbabel led the first group of captives back to Jerusalem and set about rebuilding the Temple on the old site. For some 20 years he was closely associated with prophets, priests, and kings until the new Temple was dedicated and the Jewish sacrificial system was reestablished.

As a child of the Captivity, Zerubbabel's name literally means "offspring of Babylon." He was the son of Shealtiel or Salathiel (Ezra 3:2, 8; Hag. 1:1; Matt. 1:12) and the grandson of Jehoiachin, the captive king of Judah (1 Chr. 3:17). Zerubbabel was probably Shealtiel's adopted or levirate son (1 Chr. 3:19). Whatever his blood relationship to king Jehoiachin, Zerubbabel was Jehoiachin's legal successor and heir.

A descendant of David, Zerubbabel was in the direct line of the ancestry of Jesus (Luke 3:27; Matt. 1:12). Zerubbabel apparently attained considerable status with his captors while living in Babylon. During the early reign of Darius, he was recognized as a "prince of Judah" (Ezra 1:8). Zerubbabel was probably in the king's service since he had been appointed by the Persians as governor of Judah (Hag. 1:1).

With the blessings of Cyrus (Ezra 1:1–2), Zerubbabel and Jeshua the high priest led the first band of captives back to Jerusalem (Ezra 2:2). They also returned the gold and silver vessels that NEBUCHADNEZZAR had removed from the ill-fated Temple (Ezra 1:11). Almost immediately they set up an altar for burnt offerings, kept the Feast of Tabernacles, and took steps to rebuild the Temple (Ezra 3:2–3, 8).

After rebuilding the Temple foundation the first two years, construction came to a standstill for 17 years. This delay came principally because of opposition from settlers in Samaria who wanted to help with the building (Ezra 4:1–2). When the offer was refused because of the Samaritans' association with heathen worship, the Samaritans disrupted the building project (Ezra 4:4). Counselors were hired who misrepresented the captives in court (Ezra 4:5), causing the Persian king to withdraw his support (Ezra 4:21). The delay in build-

Z

ing also was due to the preoccupation of Zerubbabel and other captives with building houses for themselves (Hag. 1:2–4).

Urged by the prophets Haggai and Zechariah (Ezra 5:1–2), Zerubbabel diligently resumed work on the Temple in the second year of the reign of Darius Hystaspes of Persia (Hag. 1:14). This renewed effort to build the Temple was a model of cooperation involving the captives, the prophets, and Persian kings (Ezra 6:14). Zerubbabel received considerable grants of money and materials from Persia (Ezra 6:5) and continuing encouragement from the prophets HAGGAI and ZECHARIAH (Ezra 5:2).

The Temple was finished in four years (516/515 B.C.) and dedicated with great pomp and rejoicing (Ezra 6:16). The celebration was climaxed with the observance of the Passover (Ezra 6:19). If there was a discordant note, it likely came from older Jews who had earlier wept because the new Temple lacked the splendor of Solomon's Temple (Ezra 3:12).

For some mysterious reason, Zerubbabel is not mentioned in connection with the Temple dedication. Neither is he mentioned after this time. Perhaps he died or retired from public life upon completion of the Temple. His influence was so great, however, that historians designate the Second Temple as "Zerubbabel's Temple."

God was apparently pleased with Zerubbabel's role in bringing the captives home and reestablishing Temple worship (Ezra 3:10). On God's instructions, Haggai promised Zerubbabel a special blessing: "I will take you, Zerubbabel My servant, the son of Shealtiel, says the LORD, and will make you as a signet ring; for I have chosen you" (Hag. 2:23).

ZERUIAH [zeh roo EYE ah]

A sister, or perhaps half sister, of David (1 Chr. 2:16). Her three sons—Abishai, Joab, and Asahel—were commanders in David's army. One of her sons, ASAHEL, was killed by Abner (2 Sam. 2:17–23). Most of the references to Zeruiah, therefore, are as the mother of JOAB (2 Sam. 2:13, 8:16) and ABISHAI (1 Sam. 26:6; 2 Sam. 16:9).

ZETHAM [ZEE tham] (olive tree)

A Gershonite Levite, a descendant of Laadan (1 Chr. 23:8; 26:22).

ZETHAN [ZEE than] (olive tree)

A descendant of Bilthan, of the tribe of Benjamin (1 Chr. 7:10).

ZETHAR [ZEE thar]

One of the seven eunuchs, or household servants, who had charge of the harem of King Ahasuerus (Xerxes) of Persia (Esth. 1:10).

ZIA [ZIE ah]

A Gadite who lived in Bashan (1 Chr. 5:13).

ZIBA [ZIE bah]

A servant of King Saul (2 Sam. 9:2–4, 9–12; 16:1–4; 19:17, 29). When Saul and Jonathan were killed by the Philistines at Mount Gilboa, David wished to remember his promise to Jonathan and asked if any descendants of Saul still lived. Ziba answered that a son of Jonathan, Mephibosheth, lived in the house of Machir in Lo Debar (2 Sam. 9:3–6). David brought Mephibosheth to Jerusalem and decreed that he should eat bread at the king's table (vv. 10–11). He also commanded Ziba to work the land for Mephibosheth.

Years later, when Absalom revolted against David, Ziba met David with much-needed provisions. David rewarded Ziba for his faithfulness by giving him part of Mephibosheth's land (2 Sam. 19:24–30).

ZIBEON [ZIHB eh uhn]

The name of one or two men in the Old Testament:

1. A Hivite, grandfather of Aholibamah, one of Esau's wives (Gen. 36:2).

2. One of the sons of Seir the Horite (Gen. 36:20, 24, 29; 1 Chr. 1:38, 40). Zibeon was the father of two sons: Ajah and Anah (Gen. 36:24; 1 Chr. 1:40). This Zibeon may be the same person as No. 1.

ZIBIA [ZIB ih ah] (gazelle)

One of the seven sons of Shaharaim and his wife Hodesh (1 Chr. 8:9).

ZIBIAH [ZIB ih ah] (gazelle)

A woman of Beersheba who became the wife of AHAZIAH and the mother of JEHOASH or Joash—both kings of Judah (2 Kin. 12:1; 2 Chr. 24:1).

ZICHRI [ZICK rih] ([God] has remembered me)

The name of 12 men in the Old Testament:

1. One of the three sons of Izhar (Ex. 6:21).

2. The son of Shimei (1 Chr. 8:19).

3. The son of Shashak (1 Chr. 8:23).

4. The son of Jeroham (1 Chr. 8:27).

5. A Levite who lived in Jerusalem after the Captivity (1 Chr. 9:15). Zichri is believed to be the same person as Zabdi (Neh. 11:17).

6. A Levite descended from Moses' son, Eliezer (1 Chr. 26:25). Zichri and his kinsmen were responsible for the treasuries in David's time (v. 26).

7. The father of Eliezer (1 Chr. 27:16). Eliezer was the officer over the Reubenites during the days of David.

8. A man of the tribe of Judah and father of Amasiah (2 Chr. 17:16). Amasiah was a captain in the army of King Jehoshaphat.

9. The father of Elishaphat (2 Chr. 23:1).

10. A "mighty man of Ephraim" who killed Maaseiah the king's son during the reign of Ahaz, king of Judah (2 Chr. 28:7).

11. The father of Joel (Neh. 11:9). Joel was overseer of the Benjamites after the Captivity.

12. A priest in the family of Abijah in the days of Nehemiah (Neh. 12:17).

ZIDKIJAH [zid KIE jah]

A form of ZEDEKIAH.

ZIHA [ZIE hah]

The name of two men in the Old Testament:

1. The founder or head of a family of Nethinim (Temple servants) who returned with Zerubbabel from Babylon to Palestine (Ezra 2:43; Neh. 7:46).

2. An overseer of the Nethinim in Jerusalem (Neh. 11:21).

ZILLAH [ZIHL lah] (shadow)

The second wife of Lamech (Gen. 4:19, 22–23). She bore a son, Tubal–Cain, who was the originator of metal-working. Zillah also bore a daughter, Naamah.

ZILLETHAI [ZIHL eh thigh]

The name of two men in the Old Testament:

1. A son of Shimei listed in the family tree of King Saul (1 Chr. 8:20; Zilthai, KJV).

2. A captain of the tribe of Manasseh who defected to David at Ziklag (1 Chr. 12:20; Zilthai, KJV).

Z

ZILPAH [ZILL pah]

The mother of Gad and Asher (Gen. 30:9–13; 35:26). Zilpah was one of the female slaves of Laban, the father of Leah and Rachel. When Leah married Jacob, Laban gave her Zilpah to serve as her maid (Gen. 29:24; 46:18). Later, Leah gave Zilpah to Jacob as a concubine (Gen. 30:9).

ZILTHAI [ZILL thigh]

A form of ZILLETHAI.

ZIMMAH [ZIMM ah]

The name of two men in the Old Testament:

1. A descendant of Jahath (1 Chr. 6:20) and a tabernacle musician in David's time.

2. A Gershonite Levite, the father of Joah (2 Chr. 29:12).

ZIMRAN [ZIMM ran]

The first son of Abraham by Keturah (Gen. 25:2; 1 Chr. 1:32), his female slave, or concubine.

ZIMRI [ZIMM rye] ([God is] *my protection*)

The name of four men in the Old Testament:

1. A son of Salu, a Simeonite prince (Num. 25:14). In an outrageous move, Zimri brought a Midianite woman, COZBI, into the camp while Israel was repenting for having worshiped Baal. When PHINEHAS, the son of Eleazar, saw Zimri take her to his tent, he was enraged, took a javelin in his hand, went into Zimri's tent, and thrust both of them through.

2. The fifth king of Israel (1 Kin. 16:8–20). Before he became king, Zimri was a servant of King Elah and commander of half of his chariots. One day, Zimri killed the drunken Elah and proclaimed himself king. When Omri, the commander of Elah's army, heard about the assassination, he abandoned the siege of Gibbethon and besieged Tirzah, the capital city. When Zimri saw that the city was taken, he "burned the king's house down upon himself" (1 Kin. 16:18). Zimri's reign lasted only seven days (1 Kin. 16:15).

3. The oldest of the five sons of Zerah (1 Chr. 2:6).

Also see ZABDI No. 1.

4. A Benjamite, son of Jehoaddah (1 Chr. 8:36) or Jarah (1 Chr. 9:42). Zimri was a descendant of King Saul and of King Saul's son, Jonathan.

ZINA [ZIE nah]

The second son of Shimei, a Gershonite Levite (1 Chr. 23:10; Ziza, REB, NIV). He is also called Zizah (1 Chr. 23:11).

ZIPH [ziff]

The name of two men in the Old Testament:

1. A son of Mesha of the family of Caleb, tribe of Judah (1 Chr. 2:42).

2. The oldest of the four sons of Jahaleleel (1 Chr. 4:16).

ZIPHAH [ZIE fah]

A son of Jahaleleel, of the tribe of Judah (1 Chr. 4:16).

ZIPHION [ZIFF ih on]

A son of Gad (Gen. 46:16), also called Zephon (Num. 26:15).

ZIPPOR [ZIP or] (*bird, sparrow*)

The father of Balak (Num. 22:2; Josh. 24:9). Balak was the king of Moab who hired BALAAM the soothsayer (Josh. 13:22) to curse Israel.

ZIPPORAH

ZIPPORAH [zip POE rah] (female bird)

A daughter of Jethro, priest of Midian, and wife of Moses (Ex. 2:21–22; 4:25; 18:2–4). Their sons were Gershom and Eliezer. When the Lord sought to kill Moses because Eliezer had not been circumcised, Zipporah grabbed a sharp stone and immediately circumcised the child. She and the two sons must have returned to Jethro rather than continuing on to Egypt with Moses, because she is not mentioned again until after the Exodus. Along with Jethro, she and her two sons visited Moses in the wilderness after the Hebrew people left Egypt (Ex. 18:1–5).

ZITHRI [ZITH rye]

A son of Uzziel, a descendant of Levi through Kohath (Ex. 6:22; Sithri, NRSV, NIV, REB, NASB). Zithri was a cousin of Moses.

ZIZA [ZIE zah]

The name of three men in the Old Testament:

1. A son of Shiphi (1 Chr. 4:37). Ziza was one of the leaders who participated in the expansion of the tribe of Simeon toward Gedor during the reign of Hezekiah, king of Judah.

2. A son of Rehoboam, king of Judah (2 Chr. 11:20).

3. A Gershonite Levite, second son of Shimei (1 Chr. 23:10–11, REB, NIV).

Also see ZINA.

ZIZAH [ZIE zah]

A Gershonite Levite, the second son of Shimei (1 Chr. 23:11; Ziza, REB, NIV). He is also called Zina (1 Chr. 23:10).

Z

ZOBEBAH [zoe BEE bah]

A son of Koz, of the tribe of Judah (1 Chr. 4:8).

ZOHAR [ZOE har]

The name of three men in the Old Testament:

1. The father of Ephron (Gen. 23:8; 25:9), a Hittite prince from whom Abraham purchased the cave of Machpelah.

2. A son of Simeon and grandson of Jacob (Gen. 46:10). He is also called Zerah (Num. 26:13).

3. A son of Helah, of the tribe of Judah (1 Chr. 4:7; Jezoar, KJV, REB; Izhar, NRSV, NASB).

ZOHETH [ZOE heth]

A son of Ishi (1 Chr. 4:20) and head of a family in the tribe of Judah.

ZOPHAH [ZOE fah]

A son of Helem, of the tribe of Asher (1 Chr. 7:35–36).

ZOPHAI [ZOE fie]

A son of Elkanah, a Kohathite Levite (1 Chr. 6:26). Zophai is called Zuph in 1 Samuel 1:1 and 1 Chronicles 6:35.

ZOPHAR [ZOE fer]

The third of the "friends" of Job to speak. He is called a Naamathite (Job 2:11; 11:1; 20:1; 42:9), indicating he was from Naamah, in northern Arabia. Zophar's two discourses are found in Job 11:1–20 and 20:1–29. He accused Job of wickedness and hypocrisy, urged Job to turn from his rebellion, and charged that God was punishing Job far less than his sins deserved (Job 11:6).

Also see BILDAD; ELIHU; ELIPHAZ.

ZUAR [ZOU er]

The father of Nethaneel (Num. 1:8). Nethaneel was leader of the tribe of Issachar at the time of the Exodus.

ZUPH [zuff]

An Ephraimite, an ancestor of the prophet Samuel (1 Sam. 1:1).

Also see ZOPHAI.

ZUR [zuhr] (rock)

The name of two men in the Old Testament:

1. A Midianite leader, the father of Cozbi (Num. 25:15). Zur was one of the five kings of Midian killed in a battle against the Hebrew people under Moses (Num. 31:8; Josh. 13:21).

2. A Benjamite, the brother of Kish, King Saul's father (1 Chr. 8:30; 9:36).

ZURIEL [ZOU rih ehl] (my rock is God)

A son of Abihail (Num. 3:35). A Levite, Zuriel was chief of the house of Merari at the time of the Exodus.

ZURISHADDAI [zou rih SHAD die] (the Almighty is my rock)

The father of Shelumiel (Num. 1:6; 2:12; 7:36, 41; 10:19). Shelumiel was the leader of the tribe of Simeon at the time of the Exodus.

ON THE SEVENTH DAY, GOD RESTED.

CROSS-REFERENCED TO MAJOR TRANSLATIONS

KJV	King James Version
NASB	New American Standard Bible
NIV	New International Version
NKJV	New King James Version
NRSV	New Revised Standard Version
RSV	Revised Standard Version
REB	The Revised English Bible